1776-1830 THE CULTURAL LIFE OF THE NEW NATION

*the text of this book is printed
on 100% recycled paper*

THE NEW AMERICAN NATION SERIES

Edited by HENRY STEELE COMMAGER *and*

RICHARD B. MORRIS

* In preparation

1776-1830 # THE
CULTURAL
LIFE OF THE
NEW NATION

BY RUSSEL BLAINE NYE

HARPER TORCHBOOKS
The University Library
HARPER & ROW, Publishers
New York

Contents

Illustrations

Editors' Introduction

THE American nation was fittingly born at a time when science and rationalism were challenging the validity of traditional beliefs and the established order. Conceived in a revolution which spelled severance of the ties of empire and European dependency, the new nation was in turn affected by, if it did not itself initiate, an era of revolutions which overturned monarchy, aristocracy, and entrenched conservatism. The Revolutionary War powerfully activated the spirit of nationalism, and that burgeoning nationalism left its imprint on all our political and cultural institutions. It spawned a native, indigenous literature and art, a group of American churches independent of control from abroad, a special educational approach and system, new and original concepts of constitutional law and government, and a search for a usable past, for memorials, annals, and heroes so central to any national tradition.

This account of intellectual and cultural ferment in an era of slowly maturing nationalism is skillfully set forth in this volume by Professor Russel B. Nye. He shows how Locke, and Newton, and Rousseau were embedded in the matrix of our national culture, how they shaped our thinking, and how their ideas were in turn adapted and modified. He traces the special rôle of the American scientist, examines the impact of science on theology, and demonstrates how it contributed to the decline of the older Calvinism, how science encouraged independence in theological speculation, and sparked new religious trends. His synthesis explains, too, the resurgence of religiosity in the early nineteenth century, points to a clear connection between revivalism on the frontier and the moral crusading ardor which accompanied it, and argues persuasively that the victory of evangelical religion in the West helped to prepare the way for the triumph of Andrew Jackson.

If the spirit of revolution, independency, and nationalism in America signalized in one sense what has been called "the slaying of the European father," its rapid development sprang from special if not unique conditions. No other Western nation, as Mr. Nye shows, began its modern history with the advantage of operating from a nonfeudal framework and without having to overthrow an entrenched nobility. Even though church establishments survived for a time in some states, the multiplicity of Protestant sects prevented any one denomination from exercising the degree of control that established churches had exerted upon European cultural life.

Unshackled by tradition, American nationalism was spurred by the sense of limitless space and free opportunity which the great continental domain held forth. Whether or not Woodrow Wilson overstated the Turner thesis when he suggested that "the full freedom of a virgin world has ruled our course and formed our policies like a Fate," there can be no gainsaying the fact that the process of building countless new settlements created opportunities for thousands of ambitious men seeking careers. It forced new settlers to make political decisions, and, allowing for regional variations, set an egalitarian tone and marked the extension of what we may call the democratic style. Without the expanding frontier and the great European immigration the new American nation, politically and culturally, would have lacked that unusual vigor and dynamism and that emphasis on practicality which especially characterized its growth in this period under review.

One of the numerous virtues of this book is that it gives us a balanced account of cultural development in what was in many respects the most dynamic period of American history. Setting these developments in the framework of the American Enlightenment, Professor Nye shows how a developing American point of view patterned the new society, explains how it determined the educational standards of free men, and considers its impact upon theology, literature, architecture, and art. In this new synthesis the author prudently avoids an omnibus survey of all aspects of our cultural growth. But what he has stressed and interpreted is essential to our understanding of the intellectual and cultural foundations of the new nation.

This volume is one of The New American Nation Series, a comprehensive and co-operative survey of the history of the area now embraced in the United States from the days of discovery to our own time. Each volume of this series is part of a carefully planned whole, and fitted as well as possible to other volumes in the series; each is designed to be complete in itself. For the most part the series follows a chronological organization, but separate volumes or groups of volumes will be devoted to such subjects as constitutional history, foreign affairs, and westward expansion. Professor Nye's is the second of a group of volumes treating the cultural life of America from the founding of Jamestown to our own times.

HENRY STEELE COMMAGER
RICHARD BRANDON MORRIS

Preface

MY AIM in writing this book has been to present, as comprehensively and concisely as possible within the brief limits of a single volume, a study of the cultural development of the United States from the Revolutionary War to 1830. I have interpreted cultural history to mean chiefly the development of key American ideas and institutions. There is, naturally, a great deal left undone within it; the complex, fugitive thing we call American culture cannot be captured within one volume, and in the last analysis much of it simply defies exposition. A good deal more remains to be said, therefore, about the development of American culture during this period. For example, I have not been able to consider properly the development of American business (certainly an important facet of American life) or of American law, to study in any detail the impact of technology on American ideas, or to gauge properly the great contributions of immigration to the American point of view. Some of these things, perhaps, have been done better elsewhere, and others may be done soon.

The major part of the research and writing of this book was done at Michigan State University. I owe a debt to the Library staff for its assistance, and especially to persons in the Social Science and Literature Division and the Division of Inter-library Loan, who found books when they were needed most. To my colleagues Branford Millar and Herbert Weisinger, who asked the right questions and expressed the right doubts at the right times, I am especially grateful. Most of all, I acknowledge with gratitude the editorial guidance of Henry Steele Commager, whose marginal comments saved the manuscript from many errors and whose provocative suggestions had much to do with giving this book whatever usefulness it may have.

East Lansing, Michigan   RUSSEL B. NYE

PART ONE

The Frame of the American Enlightenment

This great pressure of a people always moving to new frontiers, in search of new lands, new power, the full freedom of a virgin world, has ruled our course and formed our policies like a Fate.

WOODROW WILSON, "The Ideals of America," *Atlantic Monthly*, C (1902), 726.

CHAPTER 1

The Foundations of American Thought

THE period of American history that began with the American Revolution and closed with the ascent of Andrew Jackson to the Presidency presents something of an intellectual and cultural puzzle. The Revolution, while it disturbed the continuity of American life perhaps less than its participants supposed, nevertheless provides a convenient bench mark in the development of American civilization. America at the beginning of the period, in 1776, was much different from the America of 1676 or even 1756, and not solely because of a lapse in time. Revolution and independence crystallized latent trends of thought, energized others, and brought still others to fruition.

Independence meant much more than political sovereignty. It meant a severance of ties with Europe and its conservative influences, as well as conversion from a colonial to a national psychology. American nationalism, powerfully activated by the prewar argument and by the war itself, became a primary factor in the development of ideas and institutions coexistent with the Declaration of Independence.[1] As inheritors of the Age of Reason, the eighteenth-century Americans held strong beliefs in the efficacy of rationalism and science, with strong doubts about the validity of traditional beliefs and the established order—though as inheritors too of a Calvinistic tradition they at least tempered their enthusiasm for swift changes.

In 1776 the molds of seventeenth- and early eighteenth-century

[1] For general discussions of American nationalism, see Hans Kohn, *American Nationalism* (New York, 1957), and Benjamin T. Spencer, *The Quest for Nationality* (Syracuse, 1957).

thought were gradually breaking; the keynote of the revolutionary and post-revolutionary periods is change, fluidity, development. The social patterns of British colonial life, though they by no means disappeared, became more flexible in the new nation. Theological authoritarianism lost its hold on the American mind. Mercantile statism moved toward laissez faire. The Revolutionary War itself, in many ways, was a manifestation and not a cause of this diffused, gradual, yet pervasive change from a colonial to an independent America. The real American revolution came about as the result of the assimilation and rationalization of one hundred and fifty years of the American experience, combined with the ideas of the Enlightenment.[2] The men who chose the course of national independence, and who after the war to attain it accepted the challenge of creating a new nation, were children of the Enlightenment, optimistic, confident, with few doubts of their ability to succeed.

The eighteenth century took the ideas of the seventeenth and clarified, explained, and codified them in a spirit quite different from that of their fathers. Eighteenth-century Europe produced very few significant ideas that it could honestly call its own. Drawing on the stock bequeathed to them, the men of the first half of the eighteenth century adapted, formalized, synthesized, and expressed the germinal principles of seventeenth-century thinking in a way that in effect created out of it a new learning. What the seventeenth century began, the Enlightenment of the eighteenth believed it had finished. Unanswered questions appeared to be answered; paradoxes resolved themselves; the patterns fell into place. This sense of achievement of order and synthesis gave the Enlightenment a sense of well-being, a feeling of self-satisfaction. As Macaulay remarked later in his *History of England* (1849–55), the era of neoclassicism displayed "a strong persuasion that the whole world was full of secrets of high moment to the happiness of man, and that man had, by his Maker, been entrusted with the key which, rightly used, would give them success." There were, until the latter decades of the eighteenth century at least, probably fewer disagreements about the

[2] For general studies of colonial America, see Clinton Rossiter, *Seedtime of the Republic* (New York, 1953), and Max Savelle, *Seeds of Liberty* (New York, 1948). Daniel Boorstin, *The Colonial Experience* (New York, 1958), and Marcus Cunliffe, *The Nation Takes Shape* (Chicago, 1958), are also excellent cultural-social-political studies of colonial and republican America. The best single volume on the development of colonial culture is probably Louis B. Wright, *The Cultural Life of the American Colonies* (New York, 1957), in The New American Nation Series.

nature of man, Deity, the universe, and society than at any other time since the Middle Ages.[3]

There was an Enlightenment in America, but it was late, eclectic, and American. It is misleading to assume that eighteenth-century America was merely a reflection of eighteenth-century Britain, or Europe. In the first place, the relative isolation of the colonies (and later of the early Republic) was always a complicating factor in the development of their patterns of thinking. The cultural lag in the transmission of ideas from one shore of the Atlantic to the other meant that European ideas, conceived in the late seventeenth or early eighteenth century to meet one set of conditions, had their greatest impact in America in the late eighteenth century and after—under wholly different circumstances and to meet different necessities. Thus Hamilton, Adams, Paine, Barlow, Jefferson, and others were working with ideas and principles fifty to a hundred years old, in another time and place, for new purposes, and occasionally with different meanings—all mixed with the latest arrivals from England and Europe and with American adaptations of old and new.[4] It should not be forgotten that Goethe, Rousseau, Wordsworth, Coleridge, and Schiller all were writing while Americans still cited Locke, Newton, Grotius, Pufendorf, and Voltaire. And, of course, American thinkers chose from Britain and Europe only what ideas they needed, and only those which had particular appeal to them. They could (and did) blandly use Locke's justification of a seventeenth-century revolution to support their own; they could use French radicalism, aimed at "tyrants," with no tyranny of their own to overthrow; they could adapt and develop a whole battery of Enlightenment ideas and theories in a fashion which the British could never have accepted, or the French tolerated.

The Enlightenment in England, for example, was a relatively conservative compromise of new and old ideas with British conditions—except for such Britishers as Joseph Priestley, Horne Tooke, Thomas Paine, and William Godwin, who belonged to a minority of left-wing

[3] Ernst Cassirer, *The Philosophy of the Enlightenment* (Princeton, 1951), and Basil Willey, *The Eighteenth Century Background* (London, 1939), are excellent studies of eighteenth-century thought. See also the articles by Gay and Lovejoy, cited in the Bibliography, and, for specifically American ideas, those by Howard and Heiser.

[4] An interesting discussion is Frank J. Klingberg, "Ideas That Did Not Migrate from England to America," *Pennsylvania Magazine of History*, LXIII (1939), 380–389, and Robert R. Gardner, "Ideas That Did Not Migrate from America to Europe," *ibid.*, 369–379.

radicals. The French Encyclopedists and revolutionaries, on the other hand, transformed their versions of these compromises of the Age of Reason into hardened, definite principles, sometimes carrying them to extremes. Both British and French philosophers of the Enlightenment, for example, accepted the fact of a mechanistic universe and the fact of man's ability to reason.[5] The next step was to apply the rationalistic test to specific institutions—government, education, science, systems of morality and ethics, religion, and so on—in terms of the mechanistic scheme. The manner in which Frenchmen such as Volney, Voltaire, Diderot, Holbach, Helvetius, and others did this appealed particularly to the Americans, who were in the process of creating a state and a society, and who needed hard-and-fast rules.[6] The British thinkers of the eighteenth century, by and large, could never go quite so far or be so definite in accepting the rationalistic, mechanistic scheme. Edmund Burke, representing England's Age of Reason, was but one of several who protested against what he conceived to be the extremes of French radical thought. Paine, Barlow, Jefferson, and other Americans read both the British and the French radicals, praised them, and hoped to adapt much of their thinking to American uses. The Enlightenment in America, therefore, represented an extension of only certain aspects of the Age of Reason in England and Europe, tending to accept as settled what were in England really still unsettled issues, and what were in France settled only in *avant-garde* circles.

The rise of Romanticism in literature and philosophy introduced another disturbing factor in the development of late eighteenth-century American thought. In the latter portion of the eighteenth century, European and British philosophers and critics revived interest in a body of ideas which had been relatively neglected in the seventeenth and earlier eighteenth centuries. These ideas were developed, extended, ramified, and diffused throughout Europe, Britain, and America. In the process men on both sides of the Atlantic questioned and revised many of their conceptions and altered the framework of their thinking. These Ro-

---

[5] See C. B. R. Kent, *The English Radicals* (London, 1899); Daniel Mornet, *French Thought in the Eighteenth Century* (New York, 1929); and John Morley, *Diderot and the Enclyclopaedists* (London, 1880).

[6] For example, see M. M. Barr, *Voltaire in America, 1744–1800* (New York, 1941); Paul M. Spurlin, *Montesquieu in America 1760–1801* (New York, 1940); Howard Mumford Jones, *America and French Culture* (Chapel Hill, 1927); Bernard Fäy, *The Revolutionary Spirit in France and America* (New York, 1927).

mantic ideas were not "new" in the narrow sense of the word; but they *were* new in the sense that they represented a sharp break with the dominant ideas of the preceding century. Romanticism was never wholly assimilated into a unified system. Sometimes Romantic concepts existed side by side with much older ideas, and sometimes they contradicted themselves. Still, the body of ideas, or climate of opinion, which characterized the thinking of the closing decades of the eighteenth century and the opening decades of the nineteenth, displayed sufficient unity and consistency to warrant calling the period the Age of Romanticism.

Romantic thought rested on three general concepts. First, on the idea of organism. Things were conceived as wholes, or units, with their own internal laws of governance and development. This held true of men as individuals, or of the state as an aggregation of persons, or of nature as an organism, or of a work of art as a unit. Second, on the idea of dynamism, that is, of motion and growth. Beliefs and institutions were assumed to be fluid, changing, capable of adaptation. The age had, as the philosopher A. O. Lovejoy has pointed out, "a dislike of finality." Third, on the idea of diversity, the value of differences of opinions, cultures, tastes, societies, characters—as opposed to the uniformitarian norm of the Enlightenment. To the earlier eighteenth century, rationality meant uniformity; diversity meant irrationality, and therefore error. To the late eighteenth century the *consensus gentium* seemed less important than private, individual judgment, and diversity seemed both "natural" and right.[7]

The eighteenth century studied nature and man in order to establish their relationships, either by analogy or as parts of an intricate machine in which they were locked in mutual interdependency. It studied the external world to find evidences of God, laws of morality and development, and even hints about man's own nature. It studied man, as Alexander Pope said in his *Essay on Man* (1732–34), that men must, to find what kind of being he was and where he fitted into the great, universal, mechanistic scheme. The eighteenth century looked at nature with an intellectual and aesthetic appreciation of its order, perfection, and harmony. Looking at man, it found him to be a creature of both reason and passion, yet it recognized too that his emotional nature was compatible with his reason and could be controlled by it.

[7] A. O. Lovejoy, "The Meaning of Romanticism for the Historian of Ideas," *Journal of the History of Ideas,* II (1941), 257–278.

The nineteenth century's response to nature and man was different in both degree and kind. The thinkers of the nineteenth century studied the inner side of humanity and found there, as others had before, both reason and passion. But the Romantic Age stressed the emotional aspects of man's nature until they became a higher source of truth than reason—until emotion, passion, and intuition blended into a human power called (among other names) the Imagination, or "reason in its highest form." In this spirit Wordsworth defined the Imagination as

> . . . but another name for absolute power,
> And clearest insight, amplitude of mind,
> And Reason in its most exalted mood.

Romanticism stressed the study of man. Nature to the nineteenth century became less important for itself and more so for the impact it had on man, important chiefly insofar as men perceived and used it with their inner senses. The Enlightenment, viewing nature rationally, had seen man and nature as a unified entirety, as complementary parts of a total design. The Romantics, depending for their comprehension upon flashes of intuitive insight and moments of emotional revelation, neither tried to understand nor succeeded in understanding man and nature as a whole. The earlier age associated man and nature with reason; the later, with "feeling," "sensibility," or Imagination. Both saw what Newton had sketched out in his great picture of nature. The difference lay in the eye and mind of the beholder.[8]

There were, however, certain aspects of Romanticism which Americans, by reason of their frontier, transatlantic, colonial position, tended to accept and others in which they showed little interest. Romanticism in America turned out to be a much more constructive, individualistic, and democratically based movement than in Britain or Europe, a trend reinforced by the frontier tradition, which provided excellent conditions for its growth. In Europe, Romantic individualism frequently took the form of an attack on established institutions, mores, social and political and economic codes; the Romantic rebelled, sometimes spectacularly, against the *status quo*. In America, where feudalism, traditionalism, and political privilege had been under attack successfully for at least

---

[8] For a general consideration of American Romanticism, see G. H. Orians, "The Rise of Romanticism," in H. H. Clark (ed.), *Transitions in American Literary History* (Durham, N.C., 1954); and the relevant chapters of R. E. Spiller *et al., Literary History of the United States* (New York, 1948), I.

two generations before the Romantic movement was well under way, the Romantic needed to be much less the rebel or iconoclast in the European sense. The American Romantic tended to be more constructive than destructive; he had fewer entrenched enemies, a much more open and fluid society in which to operate, and much less to destroy. He also had much more opportunity to create. He did not need to expend his energy in tearing down eighteenth-century codes, inhibitions, and stratifications; for the process was well advanced before 1776 and nearly completed by the early decades of the nineteenth century, when the young rebellious European and British Romantics were in full cry. American Romanticism thus produced not Byron but Longfellow, not Marx but Thoreau. Its nature was democratic, not aristocratic; and instead of attacking the *status quo* with Byron's *Manfred,* it did it with Emerson's *Self-Reliance.* Despite their admiration for the European and British Romantics, the Americans were of a different temper and temperament. They simply could not accept the utter rebelliousness of Schiller, the seemingly irresponsible anti-institutionalism of Byron, the outlaw morality of the young Goethe, the moody sentimental return to original sin that marked much of contemporary French and German poetry and philosophy. They had too much faith in and respect for the individual, too much left of their hereditary intensity of moral feeling. They put their own distinctive stamp on the Romantic movement as they imported it.

The period 1776–1830 in America is therefore a period of contradictions, a period in which there were two (or more) sides to every intellectual argument, a period of transition and change in which old and new answers to major questions might exist side by side. It was, intellectually speaking, more or less in balance—the afterglow of the Enlightenment still shining, the dawn of Romanticism just breaking. Eighteenth-century patterns of belief still persisted, yet at the same time those patterns were being challenged, changed, and eventually broken. Ideas once firmly nailed down were working loose.

The structure of American thought in the period 1776–1830 derived ultimately from the prevailing concepts of man and nature. "Man," wrote the French philosopher Diderot, who was much admired in certain American circles, "is the single term from which we ought to set out and to which we ought to trace back." As a guide for man, God provided nature, whose patterns men might copy in their daily lives to attain the perfect society.[9] Nature, according to Volney, another French philosopher who enjoyed American popularity, consisted of "The regular and constant order of facts by which God rules the universe; the order which his wisdom presents to the sense and reason of men, to serve them as an equal and common rule of conduct, and to guide them, without distinction of race or sect, towards perfection and happiness."

The term possessed a variety of meanings to the American eighteenth century, but dominant among them was the concept of nature as a static, perfect framework of divinely, rationally conceived structures—a "frame of Nature," as the poet Philip Freneau described it in his poem "On the Constitution . . . of Nature," in which one might

> . . . see, with most exact design
> The world revolve, the planets shine,
> The nicest order, all things meet,
> A structure in itself complete.
> Here beauty, order, power behold
> Exact, all perfect, uncontrolled,
> All in its proper place arranged,
> Immortal, endless, and unchanged.

This "frame of Nature" reflected the mind of the Divine Architect who had constructed it and who ruled it by His natural law. "God Almighty is himself a Mechanic," wrote Thomas Cooper of South Carolina later, whose world machine illustrated the "variety, ingenuity, and utility of his handiworks."

The chief attributes of nature, as the eighteenth century saw it, were permanence, stability, balance, beneficence, law, and order. Change was one aspect of nature, true (no one could fail to observe the infinite variety of things he saw about him), but variety in the natural world was merely a surface aspect. Nature's fundamental structure remained always fixed; the details might vary, the basic laws never. There might be cyclical movement to maintain the *status quo,* or variations about a norm, but never real change in nature. Quite literally, the French philosopher Abbé Pluche remarked in his *Spectacle de la nature* (1732), there could be "nothing new under the sun, no new production, no species which has not been from the beginning"; and John Taylor of

---

[9] For a concise general discussion of the concept of nature in the seventeenth and eighteenth centuries, see "The Uniformity of Nature" and "Through Nature to Nature's God," in Charles C. Gillespie, *Genesis and Geology* (New York, 1951).

Caroline wrote later that man found a permanent base for action and thought only in "the constancy of nature, in her moral as well as her physical operations." Nature, to Americans of the late eighteenth century, meant "things as they are or have become," the "natural order of things," the original state of things as created, the final state of things as they had become by realizing their own inner principles of development within their original limits. The English scientist John Ray had defined nature as consisting of "the works created by God at first, and by Him conserved to this Day in the State and Creation in which they were first made." All of this the eighteenth-century American knew; most of all he learned it from Newton, "high-soul'd Newton" (as President Timothy Dwight of Yale called him in his poem *The Triumph of Infidelity*) who "wing'd by heaven abroad, explained alike the works, and word, of God."[10]

The "frame of Nature" displayed certain general inherent characteristics.[11] The world was an eminently rational place. "It can't be nature, for it is not sense," the British satirist Charles Churchill wrote in 1764 in *The Farewell,* and Edmund Burke, in his *Regicide Peace* (1797), repeated that "Never, no never, did nature say one thing and wisdom say another." Nature's first quality was order, the perfection of symmetry and the symmetry of perfection. This concept the philosophers of the period expressed in the metaphor of a Great Chain of Being, in which everything in the universe served as links in a chain stretching from stones to men, everything in its place, everything with its function.[12] "How wondrous is this scene!" wrote the American painter Charles Willson Peale:

[10] Carl Becker's *Declaration of Independence* (New York, 1942), and his *Heavenly City of the Eighteenth Century Philosophers* (New York, 1932), treat Newton's impact on eighteenth-century thought. However, see also Henry Guerlac, "Newton's Changing Reputation in the Eighteenth Century," in Raymond O. Rockwood, *Carl Becker's Heavenly City Revisited* (Ithaca, 1958), for a revised estimate.

[11] The concept of nature in eighteenth-century America is well summarized in Daniel Boorstin, *The Lost World of Thomas Jefferson* (New York, 1948). See also Gilbert Chinard, "Eighteenth Century Theories on America as a Human Habitat," *Proceedings of the American Philosophical Society,* XCI (1947), 27–57; Basil Willey, *The Eighteenth Century Background* (London, 1939); and Isaiah Berlin, *The Age of Enlightenment* (Boston, 1956), Introduction.

[12] A. O. Lovejoy, *The Great Chain of Being* (Cambridge, 1933), is the classic exposition of this concept in eighteenth-century thought. See also A. M. Sibley, *Alexander Pope's Popularity in America, 1725–1835* (New York, 1949).

> Each shell, each crawling insect, holds a rank
> Important in the plan of him who form'd
> This scale of beings; holds a rank, which lost
> Would break the chain and leave behind a gap
> Which nature's self would rue.

The function of science, obviously, was to study that chain, noting relationships, supplying missing parts, categorizing phenomena, identifying functions. To William Bartram, the Pennsylvania naturalist, the world was "a glorious apartment of the boundless place of the sovereign creator" where one might search endlessly and joyfully among His furnishings.

A second quality of nature was its variety. Everywhere one looked, one was impressed by what Jefferson once called the "unbounded liberality" of the universe. Improved microscopes showed the smallest particles of nature teeming with life. Probing space with telescopes, men found in the heavens the same "endless variety which," the astronomer David Rittenhouse concluded, "obtains through the works of Nature." The staggering variety of the universe, and its apparently inexhaustible differentiations, helped Romantic poets and philosophers later to understand its dynamism, growth, and adaptability.

A third quality of nature was its benevolence. It was hard to find real evil or untruth in the universe, nothing that might indicate that it had not been planned by God for man's good. In nature, Benjamin Silliman said in his Yale lectures in the 1820's, "there is no falsehood. Nature is straightforward and consistent. There are no polluting influences; all the associations . . . are elevated and virtuous." Everything had a purpose, and that purpose was beneficent—as the Deity who planned it was benevolent—and the more that men discovered about the world, the more they were convinced. Scientist John Mitchell, while writing a zoological essay on the opossum's pouch, paused to exclaim, "And how often then are we obliged, in discovering and prying into the works of nature, to acknowledge that the *Almighty* had not only given being to, but has likewise provided for the well-being of this, as well as of other creatures!" For this reason scientists postulated that God placed the highest mountains in Africa so that they might gather rains for the driest continent. It was true, they admitted, that men sometimes failed to recognize the benevolent potential of nature (Paine thought that gunpowder must surely have a better purpose than killing), so that one of the valid aims of science was to discover the *proper* uses and functions of the natural world.

Nature existed to be put to use. It served as a source of knowledge of truth and of God, and as an exposition to man of divine law. "The Creation," wrote Thomas Paine in *The Age of Reason* (1794–95), "speaketh an universal language. . . . In fine, do we want to know what God is? Search not the book called the Scriptures, which any human hand might make, but the Scripture called the Creation." "Order, proportion, and fitness pervade the universe," wrote James Wilson, the Pennsylvania lawyer. "Around us we see; within us we feel; above us we admire a rule, from which a deviation cannot, or should not, or will not be made." Everything in nature, thought Benjamin Silliman, "points toward the infinite Creator." The celestial bodies which "roll round their axes, dance their orbits, and perform their revolutions in that beautiful order and concept" of nature, James Otis believed, illustrated the existence of an "omniscient, omnipotent, infinitely good, and gracious Creator." Nature and nature's laws, the men of the late eighteenth century agreed, provided a pattern by which men might order their own society and their lives until, as the poet Freneau hoped, "Paradise anew shall flourish," and men "shall live in a constant summer." And eventually, the poet-philosopher Joel Barlow believed, man could attain "a perfect state of society in a perfect state of nature," if he would but

> Look through earth and meditate the skies,
> And find some general laws in every breast,
> Where ethics, faith, and politics may rest.

The prevailing eighteenth-century European concept of nature underwent modifications, of course, in an American environment. To European or British philosophers who lived in a world where physical nature had been long since subdued, it was easy to think of nature as a friendly power, manifesting a generous deity. In the New World, where nature was much less domesticated, one very practical, urgent problem was to find out about it, tame it, and use it—for food, shelter, wealth, security—on a quite unphilosophical basis. Nature, as the settler well knew, could be disorderly, cruel, and downright dangerous, capable of killing a man in an unguarded moment. Americans could observe and enjoy the beauty and order of nature and thrill to its profusion and perfection, yet they could never accept so completely (as some Europeans had done) the idea of it simply as a generalized abstraction.[13]

With all their convictions, however, Americans of the later decades of the eighteenth century could not quite secure an unclouded vision of the great Newtonian design of nature that they were supposed to see. The great unified pattern of eighteenth-century thought began to lose coherence after 1750; and the Enlightenment's great synthesis and formalization of knowledge became less clear and certain, as increased knowledge, greater ranges of observation, and plain experience seemed to modify accepted generalizations. Some things simply did not fit into the Age of Reason's framework. Others seemed to deny the conclusions (and occasionally the fundamental principles) of the harmonious, smoothly moving universe that the Age of Reason took for granted. Men saw flashes, now and then, of something else—of inexplicable confusions and contradictions in their tidy universe—dark glimpses, as Franklin once said uneasily, of a world "constructed of defective materials." It was not so easy in 1790, or in 1810, as it had been a half-century earlier to be serenely confident of how things were. The farther men pushed out along the lines of thought opened by their fathers and grandfathers, the less certain they became that they held all the answers to the riddles of nature, the less certain they were that they were asking the right questions.

Philosophers and scientists after 1750, for example, had a great deal of trouble making nature conform to the accepted pattern. Newtonian physics, in addition to its stress on fixity and permanence in the natural world, also recognized that motion was a basic natural fact. While Newton recognized the atom or some similar particle as the permanent, indivisible foundation of matter, he also recognized that visible creation was "a law-bound system of matter *in motion.*" Even if the basic mate-

---

[13] Americans puzzled over the place of the Indian in the picture of nature, since in actual fact he failed to live up to the philosophers' expectations. See Roy Harvey Pearce, *The Savages of America* (Baltimore, 1953), and Albert Keiser, *The Indian in American Literature* (New York, 1933). Senator King of Georgia indicated a solution to the puzzle by explaining later that "he had seen sufficient to convince him that the wild Indian of the woods had more nobleness of character than the half-civilized Indians, who . . . were as unfit for the duties appertaining to civilized life as they were for that courage and enterprise which distinguished the true Indian." *Register of Debates,* Twentieth Congress, First Session, p. 663. The literary convention of the "noble savage" in his "natural state" was never so popular in America as it should have been by all the prevailing theories of nature.

rial of nature moved within a fixed framework of physical law, it *did* move. If what men called nature was produced by permutations and shifting combinations of particles of matter in motion, it was logical to assume that mutability or change was also a fundamental natural law, and that nothing men saw about them in nature was either beginning or end. The theme of mutability, so popular in British and American literature toward the close of the eighteenth century, reflected an awareness of this changeable quality of nature—of "the vicissitudes of things," in Freneau's phrase, or in another of his poems, *The House of Night:*

> Hills sink to plains, and man returns to dust,
> That dust supports a reptile or a flower;
> Each changeful atom by some other nurs'd,
> Takes some new form, to perish in an hour.

There was, then, running parallel to the principle of stability in nature, the principle of change—nature could be organic as well as static, developmental as well as fixed. Nature might not mean simply "things as they are" but also "things as they may become." The thinkers of the later eighteenth century, working from Newtonian physics, thus held two complementary but contradictory views of nature at the same time. Much of their speculation consisted in an attempt to reconcile these views, particularly as they applied to society, politics, art, theology, and morals. In this they could never quite succeed.

Other blemishes appeared in the picture of nature drawn by the earlier Newtonians. Intoxicated as they were with the beautiful symmetry of axiom and pattern in the natural world, scientists and philosophers nevertheless found it hard to make all the data they collected fit into the great mechanistic scheme. With the advances of science and improved methods of observation, the variety and multiplicity of natural phenomena simply overwhelmed them. As Archbishop King of Dublin had pointed out in the seventeenth century, the Creator had evidently been so "insatiably generative" that finding out where everything fitted was sometimes very hard indeed. For example, what did one do with fossilized mammoth bones? If a species had disappeared, it meant that the Great Architect must have made some error in constructing the Chain of Being. This was unthinkable, so Jefferson in his *Notes on Virginia* decided to include the mammoth in his catalogue of living animals; since logically it must exist, it must exist at some place where men had not been able to observe it.[14]

If nature and nature's God were benevolent, how did one explain disease and death, as well as such things as fetid swamps, deserts, volcanoes, earthquakes, and other natural catastrophes?[15] Hume, Berkeley, Kant, and others had already noted some of the defects of the mechanistic scheme; but with Newton dominating the times, men lost themselves in admiration of the intricate order of nature. Once having agreed that Nature was supremely orderly and benevolent, the scientist and philosopher were often forced into devious and sometimes unconvincing explanations of her actions. Occasionally they had to admit that what they could not explain they could only accept in the hope that that which was natural was best, or, as Alexander Pope had concluded in his *Essay on Man,* "Whatever is, is right."

There were doubts too about the absolute perfection of nature as a model for man, or for a guide for his actions. Dr. Benjamin Rush, the great Philadelphia physician, was not so sure. "In religion and morals as well as in medicine," he wrote, "nature leads to error and destruction. When we worship the sun, a cat, a crocodile, or the devil, we follow nature. When we lie, steal, commit murder or adultery, we follow nature," for Rush knew from his own experience that nature had its cruel and irrational aspects. So long as one dealt only with Nature in the abstract, one could find in it assurances of order and divinity. But with the swift expansion of science in the eighteenth century, men found that nature constantly presented them with new problems. One might, like Rush, reluctantly conclude that the over-all design of nature was disciplined and benevolent, but, also like Rush, one might have doubts about the details. Not all believed, as Joel Barlow wrote so exuberantly in his *Vision of Judgment* (1787), that "following Nature is the march of man."

Still, with all their doubts, the American of the late eighteenth century by and large believed that nature could be trusted. It was humanly

[14] See "From Vulcanism to Paleontology," in Gillespie, *Genesis and Geology,* pp. 73–98.

[15] There was much speculation over the Lisbon earthquake of 1755, which killed 50,000 Portuguese in eight minutes, ravaged portions of Spain and North Africa, and whose shock was felt in Scotland, 5,000 miles away. For a study of its impact on contemporary thought, see T. D. Kendrick, *The Lisbon Earthquake* (London, 1956).

possible, American philosophers agreed with the French, to find a rational system of living in agreement with nature's laws, to discover "natural" rules for thought and action which, when combined, produced lives of happiness and perfection. To do this, they believed that men first had to control and develop themselves in harmony with divine, natural forces. They found it necessary to study themselves, as well as nature, to find a "science of human nature."

The problem seemed at first disarmingly simple. The earlier eighteenth century assumed that humanity had always existed since its creation exactly as it existed then. When Pope wrote in his famous couplet that "the proper study of mankind is man," he implied that such a study was not extraordinarily difficult and that men everywhere were much like himself—an eighteenth-century Englishman. The "innate ideas" of Descartes were assumed to be the normal modes of thought common to minds everywhere and always; the human "understanding" of Locke presumably existed in all men.

There was no good reason, then, why the eighteenth century should not discover a science of human nature as successfully as it had discovered a science of nature. Assuming that nature and human nature were parallel, Enlightenment thinkers believed that an analysis of man would reveal in him the same kinds of laws of thought and behavior that they had observed in the natural world. They even called it "human nature" in order to emphasize its resemblances to nature, and based their study of it on the analogy of the established natural sciences. When, like Benjamin Rush, they studied what he called "the anatomy of the human mind," some of them found what they expected to find—that man, like nature, was inherently good, rational, and orderly.

However, there were two sides and a middle to this argument. Only the most enthusiastic optimist could fully accept the implications of the parallel thus perceived to exist between man and nature. The study of history, the lessons of practical experience in human relations, and the strong heritage of colonial Calvinism all served to temper American optimism concerning man's innate goodness. Neither the seventeenth-century Calvinists nor the philosophers of the eighteenth-century British Enlightenment had ever placed great reliance on human virtue and reason. There were plenty of American political philosophers, theologians, and businessmen who placed little store in broad generalizations about the purity of human nature. "The fundamental folly" of a belief in man's natural goodness, in Timothy Dwight's opinion, had already "deluged Republican France in misery and ruin" and would likely do the same in the United States if allowed to run to its logical conclusions.

Some Americans simply did not believe that men were good. Alexander Hamilton spoke of "the ordinary depravity of human nature" and warned his countrymen against the "deceitful dream of a Golden Age" dreamed by those who refused to admit "the imperfections, weaknesses, and evils" incident to human nature. Fisher Ames of Massachusetts considered man to be "the most ferocious of all animals." John Adams said bluntly, "All men are men, and not angels," adding that "whoever would found a state . . . must presume that all men are bad by nature." Calvinist Timothy Dwight took the same view: "You will find all men substantially alike, and all naturally ignorant and wicked." Those "visionary philosophers," continued Dwight, who teach that men are "naturally wise and good . . . have drawn consequences from these principles in defiance of every fact, repugnant to every reason, and fraught with folly, danger, and mischief."

Others were more hopeful. James Madison, though well aware of "the infirmities and depravities of the human character," spoke encouragingly in his *Federalist* paper No. 55 of "other qualities which justify a certain portion of esteem and self-confidence." Thomas Paine, after some doubts, concluded that men were naturally altruistic, for if God were beneficent and his Creation harmonious, how could man, the crown of creation, be bad? Philip Freneau, the poet, believed men were more likely to be good than bad, for nature, "born with ourselves . . . inclines the tender mind to take the path of right, fair virtue's way"—though Freneau also saw the "tiger in the mind" of man that only reason could chain. James Wilson of Pennsylvania, who was unable to believe men fundamentally good and who refused to consider them wholly depraved, decided that God had implanted in them an intuitive sense of decency and conscience that they did not always observe. Believer in human dignity and worth that he was, Benjamin Franklin still wondered when "men would cease to be wolves to one another." Men, he told Joseph Priestley in 1792, were a "sort of Beings very badly constructed." Jefferson, much more sanguine in his view of human nature than others in politics, believed man "a rational animal, endowed by nature with rights, and with an innate sense of justice, and that he could be restrained from wrong and protected in right." "Although I do not, with some enthusiasts," he wrote du Pont de Nemours in 1816, "believe that the human condition will advance to such a state of perfection that there shall no longer be pain or vice in the world, yet I believe men susceptible of much improvement . . . and that the diffusion of knowledge among the people is to be the instrument by which it is to be effected."

The leaders of American thought in the later eighteenth century, then, held varying shades of opinion concerning the qualities of human nature. Some believed men were not to be trusted, and if they were to improve themselves at all it must be within a rigid pattern of checks and balances imposed on them by society and government. Others believed that men were by inclination rational and good; that if they were freed from the bonds of corrupt institutions and given freedom to think and act, they might achieve progress toward a millennium. And many others, of course, took positions between these extremes. These two traditions, and the variations rung upon them, were clearly reflected in the political divisions of the United States in the years 1783–1820.[16]

Those who (like Fisher Ames and perhaps John Adams) believed men not inherently trustworthy, emphasized the need for a political system in the United States which would restrain and control them. Men's rights, they felt, must be guarded by the state against their own inbred tendencies to violate them. The keys to a just government, therefore, lay in *order, balance, control.* Others (like Freneau, Barlow, Tom Paine) believed that man's natural goodness, freed from the shackles of corrupt institutions and false precedents, could create a society of *freedom, liberation, fulfillment*—key words to the political philosophers of this tradition. The majority of Americans of the period, however, probably shared with Jefferson his balanced view of human nature. Unable to accept an unqualified belief in man's natural goodness, they were confident nevertheless that, under proper conditions, men could be relied on to think and do the right thing—if they were free, secure, educated, "habituated to think for themselves and to follow reason as their guides" (as Jefferson phrased it)—or, as Paine wrote, free to listen to "the simple voice of nature and reason." Bad institutions and bad ideas made bad men; there might be, Joel Barlow thought, some vices "chargeable to the permanent qualities of man," but "men well in-

---

[16] See Leon Howard, "The Late Eighteenth Century: An Age of Contradictions," in Clark (ed.), *Transitions,* pp. 60–61, and Clinton Rossiter, *Seedtime of the Republic* (New York, 1953), pp. 370–375.

structed," he repeated, "are always just." "Leave the mind unchained and free," wrote Freneau in his poem *On the Abuse of Human Power* (1815),

> And what they ought, mankind will be . . .
> But good and great, benign and just,
> As God and Nature made them first.

The most important factor in the general acceptance by eighteenth-century Americans of a qualified belief in the goodness of human nature was their conviction that the dominant quality of the human mind was reason. "Fix Reason firmly in her seat," Jefferson wrote young Peter Carr in 1787, "and call to her tribunal every fact, every opinion." The men of the American Enlightenment learned early from John Locke that they possessed a quality of mind that "sets Man above the rest of sensible beings, and gives him all the Advantage and Dominion that he has over them." They agreed also with the contemporary British philosopher William Godwin that "sound reasoning and truth, when adequately communicated, must always be victorious over error." "God has given us reason," remarked Benjamin Franklin, "whereby we are capable of observing his wisdom in the Creation." David Rittenhouse, the great Philadelphia scientist, thought that men were most certainly "wise enough to govern themselves according to the dictates of that reason their creator has given them."

But it would be an overstatement to call the eighteenth century simply the Age of Reason without qualification; its philosophers and poets and its politicians and artists—who were neither naïve nor dogmatic—never placed a blind or an uncritical faith in the power of man's rational intellect. They knew perfectly well that men's thoughts and actions were powerfully influenced by their emotions and passions. They did not believe that the conflict between reason and emotion that went on in men's minds was always a victory for reason. Men were not perfect thinking machines. Like Franklin, they knew that a sadly large proportion of mankind, as he wrote his sister, were simply "weak and ignorant men and women."

The eighteenth century, in its later decades, was rationalistic, true, but it was also shrewdly realistic. It believed that reason was better than irrationality, that logic was better than superstition or prejudice, that knowledge was better than ignorance. It was convinced that men could do much to solve their problems by thinking logically and clearly—but it did not expect too much of them. The thinkers of the period did believe that man possessed reason (though he did not always use it well) and they were confident that he could find a balance between the emotion and the intellect which would enable him to overcome error and to improve his moral, political, and social condition. Though the eighteenth century was, in a general sense, most certainly an Age of Reason, it qualified its trust in that power by some realistic reservations at the same time that it affirmed its faith in reason's functions.

Science (the rational approach to nature) became the handmaiden of reason in man's search for truth. The impact of Newton's ideas on the Enlightenment (which could almost be called the Age of Newton) spread far beyond scientific thinking itself. Newton's discoveries provided the eighteenth century with useful justification for its generalizations.[17] Since Newton found a law of gravity that operated through all nature, it was logical to assume that there existed other such pervasive natural laws, equally discoverable by the same methods of scientific investigation. The concept of a mechanistic universe of natural laws suggested that it was possible to discover parallel "natural laws" governing human nature, society, political and economic life, religion, and other fields of human action and endeavor. As the eighteenth-century scientist reached out for generalizations about nature, based on observation, experiment, and induction, so did the philosopher, the theologian, the political economist, the lawyer, even the artist.

In this spirit, Franklin wrote in his proposal to found the American Philosophical Society, men might make discoveries "to benefit mankind in general." The American Enlightenment, following out the implications of Newtonianism, thus placed great confidence in the scientific method as a tool for discovering and interpreting knowledge in any field. According to Joel Barlow, "Fair science, of celestial birth . . . leads mankind to Reason and to God." William Smith, who taught chemistry at the University of Pennsylvania, apostrophized science as the hope of a new Golden Age:

> It comes! at last the promised Aera comes.
> For lo! her azure wing bright Science spreads.
> Oh Science! onward thy reign extend,
> O'er realm yet unexplored till Time shall end!

[17] Herbert Drennon, "Newtonianism: Its Methods, Theology, and Metaphysics," *Englische Studien*, LXVIII (1933–34), 297–409, is a useful study.

However, such confident acceptance of Newtonian science brought some eighteenth-century Americans, when they carried Newton's methods into other fields, into sharp conflict with traditional beliefs. For example, a great deal of intellectual effort was expended during the period 1776–1830 in an attempt merely to harmonize the implications of the new science with the older theology. Reason and science together did not give men all the answers they needed, particularly those to questions of moral action.

In addition to reason, the seventeenth-century philosophers had suggested, man possessed a moral sense implanted in him by the Creator for his guidance. Lord Kames's *Elements of Criticism* (first edition, 1762), a standard college textbook in the eighteenth century, assured ten generations of American students that "a sense common to the species" provided men with the ability of "ascertaining what actions are right and what wrong, what proper and what improper."[18] Dr. Benjamin Rush, clinically dissecting the human mind, discovered in it three faculties: reason, or the power of identifying facts; the moral faculty, or the power of distinguishing good from evil; and conscience, or the power of translating the findings of the reason and the moral faculty into action.[19] Reason could be nullified by ignorance or clouded by improper training, but the moral sense was, Jefferson said, "a sense of right and wrong . . . as much a part of his [man's] nature as the sense of hearing, seeing, feeling."

The Reverend Samuel West assured his Dartmouth parishioners in 1776 that the Deity had invested them "with moral powers and faculties by which we are enabled to discern the difference between right and wrong, truth and falsehood, good and evil." "Without this controlling faculty," said James Wilson, the Pennsylvania lawyer, "we should appear a fabric destitute of order, but possessed of it, all our powers may combine in one uniform and regular direction."[20] This moral sense might be weak in some men, as both Rush and Jefferson

[18] Shaftesbury's *Inquiry Concerning Virtue and Merit* (1699), also widely studied in philosophy courses, also affirmed the existence of a moral sense in all men.

[19] *The Influence of Physical Causes on the Moral Faculty* (1786). Rush also listed seventeen environmental or physical causes which might blunt or pervert the moral faculty, and even invented medical names for a weakened moral sense (*micronomia*) and its absence (*anomia*).

[20] Wingate Thornton, *The Pulpit and the American Revolution* (Boston, 1860), p. 259, and J. D. Andrews (ed.), *Works of James Wilson* (2 vols., 1896), I, 110.

were willing to admit, but it existed in all men and could, by proper exercise, be strengthened—just as Franklin explained, in his *Autobiography*, he had exercised and strengthened his with his list of daily rules. Possessed of the reason to perceive divine law in nature, and of a moral sense to act in accordance with it, men were doubly armed for the business of living.

The philosophers, theologians, and moralists of the period believed that they knew a great deal about the depths and contours of the human mind, what it was made of, and how it worked. By studying and analyzing man, they believed that they might discover those basic laws of human nature which governed his thoughts and actions, thus establishing that "science of human nature" by which men might discover themselves as they had discovered outward nature. "Let the intellectual, as well as the material philosopher," John Taylor of Caroline wrote confidently, "reason from facts, and the phenomena of mind will become as well understood for temporal purposes as those of the body."

The attempt to find a science of human nature was not wholly successful. Chiefly, it broke down because the analogy of the physical sciences distorted its method; since mathematicians, physicists, chemists, and astronomers seemed to have found correct methods of investigation suited to their particular objectives, too many American (and British and European) philosophers assumed that the same methods could be successfully applied to human problems. The scientific scheme simply failed to provide places for all the elements that composed the psychological experiences of mankind. Despite their confidence that man was a rational, moral animal and that he was (at least under certain conditions) inclined to be good, the philosophers of the time could never explain convincingly why this was so. And as the concept of a fixed, invariable machine of nature began to break down, piece by piece, so did the concept of invariable, immutable human nature. The plain fact was that there seemed to be deep, irrational drives in men that could not be accounted for. There were differences among men that could not be categorized. There were forces of custom, prejudice, habit, mores, and tradition which refused to disappear under the clear light of reason. Nature would stay put, whether or not men understood it fully. Human nature would not.

Starting out with the hopeful belief that the better men understood human nature, the more of its problems could be solved, Americans of the late eighteenth century discovered that the more they found out about the human mind, the more it seemed to operate in new and surprising ways. New knowledge of one's self caused new ways of thinking and acting and created new difficulties for the searcher. The great new problem of the era after 1750 became *self*-understanding, *self*-knowledge. The drift from the Age of Reason to the Romantic Age involved a shift from the idea that human nature was fixed and uniform (and that it could be studied scientifically) to the idea that human nature was variable. Man became not a datum, but a problem—not an aggregate, but an individual. The self became the center of life and thought, subjectivity (not science) the mode of approaching human problems. "It is by self-inspection . . ." wrote James Marsh, the Vermont educator and philosopher, in 1832, "that we can alone arrive at any rational knowledge of the central and absolute ground of all being." And in the same way Ralph Waldo Emerson saw in 1836 "The ancient precept, Know Thyself," and the modern axiom, "Study nature," become one and the same.

Deep into the nineteenth century, of course, American writers continued to use the older terms *reason, human nature,* and *moral sense,* but with vague and elusive meanings. The difficulty was that these men kept thinking, trying to work new facts, speculations, and experiences into an eighteenth-century framework that did not always fit, and that they continued to do so even when they realized that this new knowledge would not fit. The men of the later eighteenth century, as they probed deeper into man's mind and nature, found humanity tremendously puzzling, more so than the Enlightenment had ever dreamed. They could not avoid drifting into arguments over theology and psychology (what *was* human nature, and what *was* the mind like?) that eventually robbed them of the blithe assurance that by reason and the scientific method they might discover that science of human nature which the earlier Enlightenment thought so easily done.

So the discussion by 1830 came full circle, returning to the same central issue that had occupied the seventeenth century—the nature of man—to which neither the eighteenth nor the nineteenth centuries ever found a really satisfactory answer. In this process, which stretched over the half-century from 1770 to 1830 and beyond, the Age of Reason lost much of its gloss and self-assurance, and finally disappeared into the Romantic Age.[21]

[21] A brilliant discussion of the attempt to find a "science of human nature"

First, philosophers called into question the infallibility of the human reason. Even those who expressed great faith in man's reason could not wholly agree that there was no other source of knowledge and truth open to him. There was strong suspicion, in the latter decades of the eighteenth century, that reason was perhaps not the deified, primary power that Locke and others had presumed it to be. Franklin, though confident that men were rational, was at the same time cautious about overoptimism. Reason, he once told his sister Jane Mecom, "so often misleads us, that I have sometimes been almost tempted to wish we had been furnished with a good sensible Instinct instead of it." And was reason the "head," the sole source and guide of man? Was there such a thing as *intuitive* truth, and what part did the "heart" or "affections" play in the search for truth? If by reason one meant the ability to observe facts and generalize from them to a broad, demonstrable conclusion, one might find general agreement that rationalism worked. But what were *facts*—in theology, morals, society, and politics—and could men reason in these areas as purely and precisely as they did in science?

There seemed to be certain principles which defied logical proof or scientific validation, principles which one accepted as "self-evident" or *a priori* truths, simply because one knew that they *must* be true and because they had always been accepted as true. Hamilton, Jefferson, Adams—indeed the whole array of American revolutionary philosophers—accepted such self-evident truths as grounds for revolution, and few if any of the postwar generation ever thought otherwise. Paine once defined a "natural right" as "a right founded in right," providing an excellent illustration of circular a priori reasoning.[22] Samuel Dickinson, while giving a Fourth of July oration at Bleckerstown, Massachusetts, in 1797, felt that he needed to spend no time proving to his listeners the existence of the "unalienable rights of humanity." "You, my countrymen," he concluded, *"feel the reality.* They are a sacred deposit in the bosom of every American." So even as eighteenth-century Americans proclaimed the deity of reason, they searched for self-evident truths not found in Locke and for truths not subject to reason. Reason alone was not enough to provide all they needed to know.

---

and its fate is that of R. G. Collingwood, *The Idea of History* (Oxford, 1946), pp. 83–86.

[22] Moncure Conway (ed.), *Writings* (New York, 1894), II, 35, "The Public Good."

While the American Enlightenment figuratively worshiped Mr. Locke, whose empirical doctrines pervaded the eighteenth century, it also tempered its idolatry. It was not enough to say with Locke that the sum total of primary ideas came from experience alone; while saying it (and Locke was required reading for all educated men), the men of the Republican period realized that other sources of knowledge might well exist. James Wilson put his sharp legal mind to work on the problem, and discovered two different kinds of truth—"truths given in evidence by the external senses" by which men gained knowledge of the material world, and those other truths "given in evidence by our moral faculty," by which men gained moral, spiritual, and ethical knowledge. But Wilson then hesitantly suggested the existence of still a third class of principles, "which we are required and determined by the constitution of our nature and faculties to believe"—or in other words, self-evident, unprovable truths.[23]

Joel Barlow, wrestling with this same problem, concluded that there were actually three kinds of truths: rational, scientific, and self-evident.[24] It was impossible to validate this last kind by empirical proof or experimental demonstration, yet such truths were "as perceptible when first presented to the mind as our age or world of experience could make them." John Harris, trying to define the term for his *Dictionary of Arts and Sciences* (1708–10), had written that a "self-evident" axiom was "a generally received ground principle or rule in any art or science," which cannot be demonstrated "because 'tis its self much better known than anything can be brought to prove it." All experience, all observable data, he continued, supported such self-evident axioms.

The Revolutionary Age in America therefore accepted certain self-evident truths almost as acts of faith. Such truths undeniably existed, not drawn from thin air, but built on experience—on data gained from reading about, observing, and living life. Furthermore, if Americans were to conduct a revolution and build a state on a foundation constructed from principles that could not be scientifically proved or demonstrated, they were forced to assume that these principles were both self-evident and true, and to act upon that assumption. In this spirit John Adams could write of the Declaration of Independence that it

[23] Andrews (ed.), *Works,* I, 219, 492–494, 506.
[24] See the discussion of Barlow's thought in Howard, "Late Eighteenth Century," pp. 68, 70.

was "the will of Heaven that the two countries should be sundered," just as Jefferson could write in its preamble that "Nature's God" had given Americans the authority to sunder them.[25] So paradoxically, while Americans read Locke, and hopefully tested truth by reason and experiment in the laboratory, they did so with reservations, recognizing that the unprovable might also be valid.

The American eighteenth century never clearly defined reason, though perfectly certain of its existence. Its philosophers were well aware that the passions and emotions had powerful effects on men's minds, and that the "feelings" might be a source of ideas as well as of reactions to them. As the early decades of the nineteenth century passed, the term expanded to include the intuition, the emotions, the "sentiments" or "affections," the "fancy." The vogue in America of the sentimental novel and poem, and the popularity of such figures as Byron, Scott, Goethe, and Sterne, all testified to the decline of eighteenth-century rationalism and the rise of emotionalism. The wave of religious revivalism—in part an emotional reaction against the stubborn rationalism of an earlier Calvinism—was in itself evidence of a growing respect for the inner feelings over hard-headed reason. By the second and third decades of the nineteenth century the term was subject to a confusing number of interpretations. Even the deist poet Philip Freneau, for all his worship of reason, could write (twenty-eight years before Wordsworth and Coleridge published the *Lyrical Ballads*) a glowing ode to Fancy, that "wakeful, vagrant, restless thing . . . the regent of the mind."

By degrees intuitive knowledge, during the period 1770–1830, took on validity equal to, or superior to, rational knowledge. Men became *feeling* beings, rather than creatures of reason alone. James Marsh of the University of Vermont, for example, thought in 1828 that one might find truth "by those immutable laws of the understanding which belong in common to all men" (like Locke), but nevertheless one must "try the conclusions by one's own consciousness" as a final test. Sylvester Judd, at Harvard Divinity School in the eighteen-thirties (and who later wrote a long and uninspired epic poem about this theme), concluded that man found truth only in "the impersonal, boundless, authoritative depths of *his own nature.*" Philosopher Caleb Sprague Henry, at about the same time, found that "the instantaneous but real fact

---

[25] Albert Weinberg, *Manifest Destiny* (Baltimore, 1935), Chap. I, contains an interesting discussion of this point.

of spontaneous apperception of truth" took place only "in the intimacy of consciousness." George Bancroft, writing in 1835, a bare half-century after the high tide of rationalism, defined reason as "an internal sense . . . not that faculty which deduces inferences from the experience of the senses, but that higher faculty which from the infinite treasures of its own consciousness, originates truth, and assents to it by the force of intuitive evidence."

By Bancroft's time, then, the self-evident truth was an accomplished fact—meaning that truth which is evident to the individual, inward self-consciousness, a truth derived from intuitional sources. In this way Joel Barlow's problem (and that of his era) of how to establish the validity of that which *must* be true, but which cannot be proved rationally or scientifically, found its solution. In this fashion Coleridge, Carlyle, Kant, and Cousin displaced the great Mr. Locke, and the world of Jefferson and Paine gave way to the world of Emerson.[26]

[26] Compare here the painter Washington Allston's concept of aesthetic truth, evolved in the eighteen-twenties: "How are we to distinguish an idea from a mere notion? We answer, by its self-affirmation. For an ideal truth, having its own evidence in itself, can neither be proved nor disproved, by anything out of itself; whatever, then, impresses the mind *as* truth, *is* truth until it can be shown to be false." R. H. Dana, Jr. (ed.), *Lectures on Art and Poems*, Cambridge, Mass., 1850, p. 253.

CHAPTER 2

The Roots of an American Faith

IF A majority of eighteenth-century Americans agreed on one idea, it was probably the perfectibility of man and the prospect of his future progress.[1] In this they resembled their French contemporaries rather than those philosophers of the main stream of the British Enlightenment. To most British thinkers of the times, the terms progress and perfectibility had much more tentative and limited meanings than they had in France or America. Excellence, in the English view, consisted for the most part in conforming to a universal norm of thought and conduct which was much the same for all rational beings. Human progress—if it could be called such—was possible only in the sense that erring men and corrupt institutions might be restored to agreement with that norm. The vision of a steady, universal, inexorable upward march of man and society toward ever-higher perfection occurred only to Frenchmen (such as Turgot, Helvetius, and Condorcet) and to a very few Englishmen such as William Godwin, who wrote with supreme confidence in his *Political Justice* (1793): "The vices and moral weaknesses of men are not invincible; man is perfectible, or in other words, susceptible of per-

---

[1] See Arthur A. Ekirch, *The Idea of Progress in America, 1815–1860* (New York, 1944); and R. E. Delmage, "American Ideas of Progress, 1750–1860," *American Philosophical Society Proceedings,* XCI (1947), 309–318. Macklin Thomas, "The Idea of Progress in Franklin, Freneau, Barlow, and Rush" (unpublished dissertation, University of Wisconsin, 1938), is an excellent study. See also Merle Curti, "The Great Mr. Locke, America's Philosopher, 1783–1861," *Huntington Library Bulletin,* II (1937), 107–151. Another interesting discussion of Locke's ideas in America is that of Louis Hartz, "American Political Thought and the American Revolution," *American Political Science Review,* XLVI (1952), 321–342.

petual improvement. . . . There is no characteristic of man which seems at present at least so eminently to distinguish him . . . as his improveability."

Americans tended to agree with Godwin and the French. Jefferson thought that "no definite limits could be assigned to the improveability of the human race." Joel Barlow, whose long poem *The Columbiad* (1809) was hardly more than a rhymed paean to the law of progress, believed that "all things in the physical world, as well as in the moral and intellectual world, are progressive in nature." "Where," he asked rhetorically in his *Advice to the Privileged Orders* (1791), "shall we limit the progress of human wisdom, and the force of its institutions?" Franklin, impressed by "the growing felicity of mankind, the improvement in philosophy, morals, politics, and even the conveniences of common living," wished it had been his destiny "to be born two or three centuries hence." Washington wrote Lafayette that he too indulged a "fond, perhaps an enthusiastic idea, that as the world is much less barbarous than it has been, its melioration must still be progressive." John Adams, though well aware of the "infirmities and deprivation of human nature," still believed man "capable of great things," and James Wilson of Pennsylvania concluded that "we have more and better things before us, than all that we have yet acquired or enjoyed." Dr. Benjamin Rush, throwing caution to the winds, proclaimed himself "fully persuaded that it is possible to produce such a change in the moral character of man, as shall raise him to a resemblance of angels—nay more, to the likeness of God himself."[2]

Surveying the past, observing man's steady advance from savagery to civilization, the men of the later eighteenth century found ample (though sometimes qualified) proof that there existed in man and the universe an inherent drive toward perfection—though they agreed that

[2] For statements about progress and perfectibility, see P. L. Ford (ed.), *Writings of Jefferson* (10 vols., New York, 1892–1899), V, 358; VI, 249; VII, 22, 347; IX, 269, 396; X, 249, 280; Albert H. Smyth (ed.), *The Writings of Benjamin Franklin* (10 vols., New York, 1905–1907), I, 298; IX, 12, 102, 657; X, 66–68; John C. Fitzpatrick (ed.), *The Writings of George Washington* (39 vols., Washington, D.C., 1931–1944), V, 211, 245; XXVII, 224, XXX, 214–218; Charles Francis Adams (ed.), *The Works of John Adams* . . . (10 vols., Boston, 1856), I, 23, 66; III, 452; Henry Cabot Lodge (ed.), *Works of Alexander Hamilton* (11 vols., New York, 1904), I, 18, 108; IX, 280–281, 460; J. D. Andrews (ed.), *Works of James Wilson* (Philadelphia, 1896), I, 325. Rush is quoted in Thomas, "Idea of Progress," p. 246.

if men were to improve they needed education, self-discipline, experience, rational thinking, and the help of science and democracy. The concept of progress was not itself new, of course, but Americans of the eighteenth century combined with it a body of doctrine and the beginnings of a method by which they hoped to improve humanity through a "science" of human development. The Enlightenment believed that it knew a great deal about nature and man; its American philosophers hoped to discover an orderly, workable way of directing man's progress, and of making use of the forces of nature and human nature to do it. To this great and noble problem the age addressed itself with confidence.

At this point, however, the philosophers stumbled into a contradiction. If human nature was a fixed, unvarying constant, how then was it improvable? If it were by definition unchangeable, how could it be changed for the better? Acceptance of the Chain of Being concept carried with it the corollary of staticism, for if, as Pope said,

> Order is Heav'ns first law, and this confest,
> Some are and must be greater than the rest,

all beings had stations within the hierarchy or order and presumably should remain in them. The principle of stability, inherent in the Newtonian scheme of things, pointed in one direction. The principle of progress and change, inspired by the conviction that man by use of his reason could make himself and his world better, pointed in another.

Here the American experience itself helped to provide an answer. It was not easy to persuade Americans, who had wrested a civilization out of the wilderness and who were at the moment building a nation where none had existed, that progress was impossible—at least in the United States. They had accomplished a great deal toward improving their world, and they had the evidence around them to prove it, for they had no doubts whatever but that the United States was better than anything that had ever gone before, quite possibly the best that would ever be as it continued to improve. Jefferson, in his later years, saw the great march of progress "passing over us like a cloud of light," and so did many others of his generation. If it were possible to create better institutions (as Americans had) it must be equally possible to make better men. The majority of Americans could simply not agree with

Pope's "Whatever is, is right," since they were busily and successfully making "what is" better—nor did they feel that Pope and the Enlightenment had ever properly considered the potential of American society.

Timothy Dwight of Yale, who was certainly no radical and who hated French philosophy like poison, illustrated this basic contradiction in American thought. Dwight considered human nature thoroughly untrustworthy; yet a deep faith in progress, *American* progress, threaded through his whole intellectual life. In the first flush of enthusiasm over Cornwallis' surrender he expressed a firm belief in "the tendency of human affairs, unless interrupted by extraordinary events, to be constantly progressive towards what may be termed natural perfection." Thirty years of American history may have tempered his enthusiasm but did not change his mind. Late in life he wrote, "The melioration of our character will undoubtedly make a slow progress, yet I believe it is really progressive." Certainly Dwight, like many others, was aware of the difficulty of holding two contradictory views at the same time, but like the others he was little bothered by it. Belief in progress ran through the early years of the United States as a consistent theme. William Ellery Channing, who belonged to the next generation, echoed it in 1824 in words that might as easily have been written in 1774 or 1794: "If there be one striking feature in human nature, it is the susceptibleness of improvement."[3]

The United States took shape at a particular moment in history when Americans shared in and accepted certain portions of the common heritage of British and European culture and ideas. It derived from that heritage, but the fact that American culture and thought developed within an *American* environment influenced that heritage even as the new nation derived from it. American conditions were different, sometimes in kind, sometimes in degree. What happened in America happened in a new, comparatively isolated, frontier nation with a brief history and shallow roots. The new country had no hereditary monarchy or aristocracy, no feudal past, no deeply entrenched state church, no absolute caste system, no fixed aesthetic, and after 1776 not even a "tyrant." The country began with an achieved liberation and a firm belief in progress.

---

[3] See also Salmon Chase, writing in the *North American Review*, XXXIV (1832), 228: "The law of man's nature, impressed on him by his God, is onward progress."

The Revolution by which this liberation was made real was unquestionably part and parcel of the eighteenth-century Enlightenment; the arguments that accompanied the Declaration and the Constitution derived directly from patterns of thinking already rather firmly fixed. Those "natural rights" and "self-evident truths" which the revolutionaries submitted to a candid world were all already explicit or implicit in the prevailing Enlightenment philosophy. How much these and other ideas provided an impulse to rebellion and independence, and how much they were used instead to vindicate them, will probably always remain an open question. But in either case, the principles of the Enlightenment, adjusted to American necessities and developed in an American setting, provided the underpinnings of thought in the Revolutionary and Republican eras. The theory of progress was one of these important principles.

The major strain of formal philosophical thought in eighteenth-century America was Lockean empiricism; but out of the welter of theological and political argument that characterized the latter decades of the century, there arose a number of dissatisfactions with Locke. His philosophy of knowledge, some theologians thought, led straight to religious skepticism; there was suspicion that perhaps Berkeley's did too. The free-wheeling eighteenth-century appeal to "self-evident principles" was not wholly acceptable to philosophers who searched for some way to establish those principles on some basis other than mere faith. The idealism of Berkeley (which said that men cannot fully perceive reality), the skepticism of Hume (which doubted it), and the *tabula rasa* theory of Locke (which treated the mind as an empty receptacle) all seemed to lead away from positive belief in such necessary ideas as the reality of the soul, the existence of God, and the verity of standards of morality and truth. Orthodox Calvinist theology, especially after 1750, needed the assistance of a positive philosophical system to help it shore up its crumbling defenses.

In their search for an epistemology, American thinkers of the eighteenth century found conveniently at hand the Scots philosophy of "common sense," which did not conflict with science and rationalism on the one side, nor with orthodox Protestantism on the other. The common-sense philosophy, developed in Scottish academic circles by men such as Francis Hutcheson, Thomas Reid, Dugald Stewart, James Beattie,

Adam Ferguson, and others, provided a much more acceptable theory of knowledge than did Locke, Hume, or Berkeley.[4]

There are, wrote Reid in his *Inquiry into the Human Mind* (1764), certain "original and natural judgments" which do not come from sensation or reflection, and which "serve to direct us in the common affairs of life, when our reasoning faculty would leave us in the dark. They are part of our constitutions, and all the discourses of our reason are grounded upon them. They make up what is called the *common sense of mankind;* and what is manifestly contrary to any of these first principles, is what we call absurd." In this fashion Reid and others reaffirmed the existence of "self-evident principles"—of "primary truths," Stewart called them, "fundamental laws of human belief." These principles, truths, or laws, were never listed or classified, but the Scots thinkers were certain they existed. "It is impossible to doubt them," wrote the philosopher Thomas Brown, "because to disbelieve them would be to deny what our very constitution was formed to admit."

Scottish "common sense" also had particular appeal to the period in that it fitted contemporary American ideas concerning human nature. Speculations in the early part of the eighteenth century had led to the conclusion that the mind was distinct from the body, with a pattern and functions of its own. Generally, it was assumed that the mind possessed three sets of powers: first, the understanding, reason, or "perception," an intellectual faculty by which men reasoned, reflected, remembered, and created ideas from experience; second, the "sensibilities," "passions," "propensities," or "affections," by which men comprehended pleasure, pain, love, hate, anger, and other emotions; and third, the will or "volition" which enabled men to act on the motivations provided by the reason and the emotions. "The scripture teaches us," Asa Burton wrote in his *Essays on Some of the First Principles of Metaphysics* (1824), "that the mind is created with three distinct faculties, whose operations are very different from each other. *Perceptions* of objects are the operation of the understanding. The *affections* are the operations of the heart. The *volitions* are the operations of the will." Scottish philosophy, allowing for differences of terminology, either supported or easily adapted itself to this generally accepted traditional view of the human mind, reaffirming the rational, moral nature of man.[5]

[4] For the most authoritative analysis of the Scottish system, see James Mc-Cosh, *The Scottish Philosophy* (New York, 1875).

[5] S. E. Ahlstrom, "The Scottish Philosophy and American Theology," *Church History*, XXIV (1955), 257–272.

The first important emissary of the "common sense" school to arrive in the colonies was John Witherspoon, who left Scotland to become president of the College of New Jersey in 1768, where he found Berkeleian idealism already solidly entrenched. Witherspoon soon made Presbyterian New Jersey (Princeton) a Scottish stronghold, aided by another emigrant, Archibald Alexander, who lectured in Princeton's theological school. At Harvard, Scottish texts were introduced in 1792 by Professor David Tappan, and by 1810 the common-sense philosophy was taught at least equally with Locke in a majority of American colleges and universities. Samuel Stanhope Smith, one of Witherspoon's students who later succeeded him as Princeton's president, clearly explained the American variety of the Scottish school in his *Lectures on Moral and Political Philosophy* (1812). Men possess, said Smith, two sets of senses, external and internal. External senses provide knowledge of the outside world, which passes through the nerves and becomes ideas in the mind. These ideas group by association, and are made into new ideas by rational organization and synthesis. Internal sensations are of three kinds: first, those of the mind itself, which originates first principles such as the idea of God, the existence of the soul, or the certainty of will; second, those of beauty and taste; third, those of morality, or ideas of good and bad. These senses are common to all men.

Scottish philosophy thus provided a means by which men could establish workable standards of religious, aesthetic, and moral truth. It was, surely, "common sense," avoiding the "pedantry and jargon" and the "running to and fro," as the Reverend Samuel Miller complained, of fine-spun metaphysics. It was an extremely useful weapon against the skepticism of Hume and the rationalism of the deists, as well as an affirmation of the older belief in the moral sense. It supported the integrity of the individual and of his mind, for as Reid pointed out, "a being and an individual being mean the same thing." Most convenient of all, it was a unified, compact system which destroyed nothing and gave more or less satisfactory answers to bothersome theological questions.[6]

The expansion of education after 1740 in the American colonies, particularly on the collegiate level, meant that philosophy became a

[6] The place of Scottish philosophy in the development of the American philosophical tradition is treated in Joseph L. Blau, *Men and Movements in American Philosophy* (New York, 1952); H. W. Schneider, *A History of American Philosophy* (New York, 1946); and I. Woodbridge Riley, *American Thought from Puritanism to Pragmatism* (rev. ed., New York, 1925).

"taught" subject, requiring a philosophical system that could be reduced to axiomatic textbook or lecture form. Here too the Scottish system filled the need. The most important subject required of a college student in the eighteenth century (and well into the nineteenth) was one called variously Moral Philosophy, Moral Science, Metaphysics, or Natural Philosophy, usually taken during the fourth year of study. Almost always taught by the college president or reigning scholar, this course served as the capstone of the student's academic career, containing in it elements of science, political science, economics, psychology, history, theology, and logic.

The heavy preponderance of Princeton and Yale theologians on college faculties meant that a course in Moral Philosophy very likely was Scottish philosophy. Though Locke was standard fare, Hutcheson, Reid, Beattie, and Stewart consistently appeared in lists of college texts, with Bishop Paley and Bishop Butler added to support religious orthodoxy. The aim of the course in Moral Philosophy was to create informed, virtuous leaders of society. It was intended, as the Reverend John Gros of Columbia College said, to furnish "rules for the direction of the will of man in his moral state, such rules to serve for the guidance of the individual, community, and nation." The impact of such a course, taught by a succession of brilliant men to a hundred years of college students and emphasizing the "common sense" approach to problems of knowledge and virtue, undoubtedly was a major influence in the development of American thought during the period from the Revolution to the Civil War. The Scots philosophers' insistence on the reality of innate ideas, and their acceptance of the validity of intuitional knowledge, prepared the ground for the seeds of German philosophy, Platonism, Neoplatonism, and Oriental thought that later bloomed into the New England transcendental movement.[7]

[7] For a discussion of this point, see E. W. Todd, "Philosophical Ideas at Harvard, 1817–1837," *New England Quarterly*, XVI (1943), 63–90. A thorough discussion of the course in Moral or Natural Philosophy is that of George P. Schmidt, *The Old Time College President* (New York, 1930), Chap. V. With the rapid expansion of knowledge in the sciences and social science, however, it soon became clear that a single course could no longer suffice. Natural Philosophy came to mean the study of science, eventually breaking up into specialized subject-matter areas of chemistry, mathematics, physics, and so on. Moral Philosophy gradually divided into the study of politics, economics, ethics, and theology, with Mental Philosophy or Intellectual Philosophy emphasizing psychology.

It is manifestly impossible to point to a particular year in American history and say, "Here American nationalism began." Whatever the exact date, it is nevertheless agreed that the seventeenth-century colonists apparently possessed a sense of separation from Europe, a perception of their colonial status, that they bequeathed undiminished to the eighteenth century. This feeling of nationality, dim yet perceptible, prompted people such as President Dawes of the College of New Jersey to speak without self-consciousness long before the Revolution of "my country," or William Smith of Philadelphia to allude to the colonies as "our nation," with no idea of disloyalty to their King. By mid-century the term "American" had a meaning distinct from "British" or "English" as the term "West Indian"—for example—most assuredly did not.[8] It was quite normal for Franklin's Poor Richard, who was certainly no revolutionary, to refer to his countrymen as "American patriots" as early as 1752. The eighteenth-century colonists, by the time of the French and Indian Wars, had developed a common outlook and a common sense of relationship that, perhaps, could be accurately described only as *American*.

There were several reasons for this. First, it was not always possible to continue to do, or to believe, the same things in the same way in the New World as in the Old. Placed in a new environment more than a thousand miles from the mother country, the American colonists were bound in time to reveal certain differences with the home population. By 1750, English customs, law, church, politics, manners, and even language in the Americas had been separated from the homeland for more than a hundred years. The colonies were English, of course; British life and institutions always provided a common central point for colonial culture. Yet their habits of thought and patterns of action were not merely imitations of the originals.[9]

During this same period other unifying forces were at work within the colonies. The first half of the eighteenth century brought improve-

[8] Hans Kohn, *American Nationalism* (New York, 1957).

[9] James Kirke Paulding, in his essay on "National Literature," *Salamagundi* (second series, August 19, 1820), argued that the development of a distinctively American way of life arose from "the peculiarities of their [the settlers'] character; in the motives which produced the resolution to emigrate to the wilderness, in the courage and perseverance with which they consummated this gallant enterprise, and in the wild and terrible peculiarities of their intercourse, their adventures, and their contests with the savages."

ments in intercolonial communications and great increases in intercolonial trade. New England ships sailed to southern ports, New York and Pennsylvania merchants traded with Boston, southern produce sold in New York and New Jersey. Northern boys married southern girls and vice versa; Northerners traveled South and Southerners North. Newspapers carrying news of happenings in other colonies circulated freely— especially after Franklin, who was made Deputy Postmaster General in 1753, reorganized the mail services. By mid-century travelers in the colonies remarked that there seemed to be more similarities among the colonies than differences, and correspondingly greater contrasts between the colonies and England. America was no longer a microcosm of Britain.

The struggle between France and England during the first fifty years of the eighteenth century did much to encourage the nascent nationalism of the American colonies. During the French and Indian wars the colonies for the first time co-operated in a massive common effort against a common enemy. Whatever their provincial differences, many colonists could unite in fear of the "Gallic peril" of Louis XV and France. The colonists acquitted themselves well (or so they at least claimed, with some British doubts) in a grueling and bitter contest— so well, in fact, that they were convinced at its close that they had tipped the scales for the British cause. Americans in 1763 believed they were not only Britons, but a very special and important kind of Briton, responsible for having saved England itself from French conquest.[10]

The aggressive patriotism of the war years swiftly gave way to disillusion as England, apparently unaware of the colonies' importance within the Empire, showed few signs of recognizing it. Franklin spoke for many colonists when in 1767, after having helped to win victory for England, he found that every Englishman "seems to consider himself a piece of a sovereign over America; seems to jostle himself into the throne with the King and talks of *our subjects* in the colonies." The French and Indian Wars exposed deep-seated conflicts between the colonies and the mother country. With the French gone from North Amer-

---

[10] An excellent discussion of the development of American national feeling during the French and Indian Wars and after is that of Max Savelle, *Seeds of Liberty* (New York, 1948), Chap. X. See also the relevant portions of Merrill Jensen, *The New Nation* (New York, 1950), on nationalism during the Confederation period.

ica, England no longer needed to make concessions to the colonies to gain their co-operation against the French; the British policy of "salutary neglect" and leniency was finished. American colonists were thereafter caught in a conflict of divided loyalties—between their genuinely patriotic allegiance to England and the Crown and their own growing sense of nationality (to use Franklin's expressive phrase) as "American Subjects of the King." When the time came for final decisions, many colonists, such as the Reverend Jonathan Boucher, found themselves tragically torn between home and King, between a budding Americanism and older British loyalty. Boucher, who finally stayed with his King, tried to explain that he was American, yet also English: "It is folly to imagine that, as an Englishman, interested in the welfare of England, I am not equally interested in the welfare of America. . . . With respect to America, it has been the country of my choice. I am married in America; and settled in it, if I may leave, most probably for life. . . . My connexions and friends, whom I love as I do my own soul, are all of this country."

What Americans wanted and needed after 1765 was recognition by England of their right to exist as separate, special kinds of Englishmen, and the right of the American colonies to exist as a self-conscious unit within the imperial system. Franklin spent years in London vainly attempting to explain this to the British. No American in his right mind considered leaving the Empire; few, indeed, would have received the suggestion with anything but horror. But the need for recognition pervaded American thinking, colored American emotions, and influenced American political decisions after 1765. When infant American nationalism collided with British nationalism, neither the British imperial system nor its leadership was flexible enough to allow it expression. The course of events led inevitably to Patrick Henry's cry of 1774, "The distinctions between Virginians . . . and New Englanders are no more. All America is thrown into one˙ mass. I am not a Virginian, but an American."

The Revolutionary conflict brought the final phase of colonial unification. In 1776, the term "British Americans," formerly used by the colonists in their communications with Britain to describe themselves, disappeared with the Declaration of Independence, and along with it the term "United Colonies." "Our great title is Americans," wrote Paine. Noah Webster, twenty years later, reminded his countrymen that "we ought not to consider ourselves as inhabitants of a particular state only, but as *Americans*." By the time James Kirke Paulding wrote his *Letters from the South* in 1817, there were no doubts about it. "The people of the United States constitute one great nation," said Paulding, "and that whether a man be born east, west, north, or south, provided he is born within the limits of the country, he is still an American."[11]

The nationalism of the postwar years was of course in large part a natural psychological consequence of wartime emotions. However, as memories of the military conflict receded, other factors emerged to keep alive the fervent patriotism of 1776. Consistent (and sometimes savage) attacks on the new United States by British and Continental critics forced Americans to defend themselves, their right to exist as a nation, and their future way of life. They found it necessary to answer the question "What is an American?" time and time again. In their attempts to fashion answers, they were forced to study, analyze, and explain—to themselves as well as to their critics—exactly what the American nation was and hoped to be.

During the war, of course, the prevailing British attitude to Americans was often openly contemptuous. Franklin remarked bitterly in 1775 that an American "was understood to be a sort of Yahoo," and noted "the base reflections on American courage, religion, understanding, etc. in which we were treated with utmost contempt." Few Americans were willing to forgive or forget the British general's arrogant sneer that with "a few British regulars" he could "geld all the American males, some by force and the rest with a little coaxing." The British tradition of conde- scension and rudeness to colonials, well illustrated by Dr. Samuel John- son's remark that he could "love all mankind, *except an American*," continued after the war in the remarks of dozens of travelers, reviewers, and commentators, ranging from the ill-tempered poet Tom Moore (who in 1814 found America "one dull chaos, one unfertile strife") to Sidney Smith's famous gibe of 1818 that "prairies, steamboats, and grist- mills" should be the "natural objects for centuries to come" of Ameri-

[11] See the discussion of the evolution of the term "American" in Merle Curti, *The Roots of American Loyalty* (New York, 1946), Chap. 1. See also Fulmer Mood, "The Origin, Evolution, and Application of the Sectional Con- cept 1750–1900," in Merrill Jensen (ed.), *Regionalism in America* (Madison, Wis., 1951), and Earl Bradsher, "The Rise of Nationalism in American Liter- ature," in N. M. Caffee and Thomas Kirby (eds.), *Studies for William A. Reed* (Baton Rouge, 1940), for additional discussions of nationalistic feeling.

can culture. James Fenimore Cooper, while traveling on the Continent a few years later, found twenty-three instances in which Englishmen had written insulting remarks after American names on hotel registers.[12]

Most Englishmen and Europeans, one American writer wistfully concluded, considered Americans "infantile in our acquisitions and savage in our manners; because we are inhabitants of a new world." Americans replied, naturally, by pointing out the inaccuracies, prejudices, and plain ignorance of their harsher critics—as Jefferson, Barton, Morse, Franklin, and many others did so successfully. The replies themselves, however, were less meaningful in the development of an American sense of nationality than the fact that Americans, in order to reply, were compelled to study exactly what they were, and why they were so.

No one in 1790 would deny that the United States was new, nor that it was different from Europe. But Americans were not willing to concede that its newness, or its difference, spelled America's doom. Nations, like human beings, James K. Paulding pointed out in 1817 in his *Letters from the South,* "progress from infancy to maturity, from maturity to age." The fact that the United States was young meant only that glorious maturity would follow. Gradually, it also occurred to Americans that it was not necessarily shameful to be different from British or Europeans. For at least a half-century Americans had considered themselves to be a particular kind of Englishman; during the Revolution, they discovered that they were no longer British at all—and that England and Europe were really alien lands. As Jefferson remarked later, "The European nations constitute a separate division of the globe . . . they have a set of interests of their own in which it is our business never to engage ourselves. America has a hemisphere to itself."[13] When the line of settlement moved westward within the United States and when larger numbers of non-English immigrants flooded the hinterlands and cities, the sense of separateness, so well expressed by Jefferson, Paine, and others, swiftly increased. Americans agreed that the United States was new, and that it was different—or as Crèvecoeur had summed it up in 1782, "The American is a new man, who acts upon new principles." They were willing to concede that the American en-

---

[12] Van Wyck Brooks, *The World of Washington Irving* (New York, 1944), p. 331. Brooks has an interesting discussion (pp. 330 ff.) of anti-American feeling in England in the early nineteenth century.

[13] To Von Humboldt, *Works,* Ford ed., IX, 431.

vironment and the American experiment created Americans, who were different from Englishmen and Europeans and who quite possibly were superior because they *were* different.[14]

This sense of difference, which developed apparently quite swiftly in post-Revolutionary America, is aptly illustrated by the contrasting views of American history taken before and after Yorktown. Historians of the early eighteenth century wrote from the assumption that the history of the American colonies was English history; American events, it was assumed, were to be viewed as things happening to Englishmen in another part of the world. Mather, Archdale, Callender, Price, Beverley, Douglass, and other early chroniclers and annalists wrote with little or no concept of American history as a new or different thing. Postwar historians, looking back at exactly the same events, saw the colonial period as a dynamic series of acts moving straight to a goal—the creation of the United States—and studied it as an era of genesis and prophecy. This was the major difference between Thomas Hutchinson's *History of Massachusetts Bay* (first volume, 1764) and Jeremy Belknap's *History of New Hampshire* (first volume, 1784). The history of Massachusetts meant nothing more to Hutchinson than an account of some Englishmen in a transatlantic colony. To Belknap the history of New Hampshire was the record of the emergence of a new way of life that had developed different social and political institutions and a new kind of people.[15]

At the conclusion of the Revolution, American chroniclers turned furiously to the task of setting down and interpreting the history of this way of life—for the study of the history of one's own nation, as Voltaire had pointed out, made one a better citizen and a more loyal one.[16]

[14] Kohn, *American Nationalism*, pp. 137–140. Discussions of the feeling of separation and difference in foreign policy are in Felix Gilbert, "The English Backgrounds of American Isolationism in the Eighteenth Century," *William and Mary Quarterly*, I (1944), 138–161, and Max Savelle, "The Appearance of an American Attitude Toward External Affairs," *American Historical Review*, LII (1947), 655–667.

[15] See Ralph N. Miller, "The Historians Discover America" (unpublished dissertation, Northwestern University, 1946), for additional information.

[16] David Ramsay's history of the war in South Carolina appeared in 1785, Ramsay's and William Gordon's general histories in 1789, and Mercy Otis Warren's in 1805. A number of state histories appeared between 1795 and 1805. State historical societies, beginning with Massachusetts' in 1791, were organized in nearly every state before 1830, while the great editors and collectors of historical materials, such as Jedidiah Morse, Abiel Holmes, and Peter

An American, wrote Noah Webster, "as soon as he opens his lips, should rehearse the history of his own country; he should lisp the praise of Liberty and of those illustrious heroes and statesmen who have wrought a revolution in her favor." The belief that the American Revolution was a turning point in the history of the world drew men to write its history as soon as it was ended, in order that the states might "praise their Great Deliverer," in Benjamin Trumbull's phrase, "awaken their mutual sympathies, and promote their union and general welfare."

Americans of the late eighteenth and early nineteenth centuries wrote their history out of the prevailing belief that since by studying the past they might find in it certain axioms of national and human development, they might find out in their own past how their American society and nation came to be. Beneath historical phenomena, it was assumed, there lay general natural laws governing not merely "the history of government and politics," as the directors of the American Antiquarian Society wrote, but "the history of man in all his relations and interests, the history of science, of art, of religion, of social and domestic life." History, men believed, was the working out of nature's law, as to the seventeenth century it had been the workings of God's law. American philosophers and historians were quite familiar with the contemporary cyclical theory of history, which taught that societies and nations rose and fell in sequence, dependent upon their obedience to universal moral and natural law. They were uniformly convinced that the United States was on the rising curve of this cycle, that its upward path was divinely ordained to be permanent, and that the entire past of the human race was only preparation for the appearance of American society. As Paine wrote in *Common Sense*, "the birthday of a new world is at hand." The Revolution confirmed it.[17]

Appraising their past, their present, their resources and potentialities, Americans decided that the United States was blessed beyond all meas-

---

Force, began work after 1790. For a more complete account of early historical writing and collecting, see Michael Kraus, *The Writing of American History* (Norman, Okla., 1953), and L. W. Dunlap, *American Historical Societies* (Madison, Wis., 1944).

[17] Studies of contemporary historical theory are R. N. Stromberg, "History in the Eighteenth Century," *Journal of the History of Ideas,* XII (1951), 295–304, and Stow Persons, "The Cyclical Theory of History in Eighteenth Century America," *American Quarterly,* VI (1954), 147–164.

ure. The more historians, scientists, philosophers, and political theorists studied and speculated about their country, the more they were convinced that it was superior to Europe on almost every count, and that its future greatness was divinely assured. Benjamin Smith Barton, the scientist, believed that an American should "glow with emotions of a virtuous pride, when he reflects on the blessings his country enjoys." A fresh look at the land alone gave the American confidence in his future. London could be lost in an American forest without a trace; beside the Mississippi "the Nile is but a rivulet, and the Danube a mere ditch." The fertility of the American soil, the enormous variety and fecundity of its plant and animal life, the vast reaches and unlimited resources of its waters and woods, the salubrity and balance of its climate, all made the United States a mighty stage for new, great developments in human history. Lying close to an unspoiled, fresh, energetic nature, itself a new and fresh design on "Nature's simple plan," the United States, in Jonathan Trumbull's view, was "a land of health and plenty, formed for independency, and happily adapted to the genius of the people to whom it was to be given for possession." How could the American experiment fail in such a setting?

Few Americans were willing to claim superiority for the United States over Europe or Britain, however, solely because it was big and new. Jefferson, Rush, Barlow, and others concurred with the prevailing belief that human nature was much the same everywhere. What gave Americans the advantage over all other peoples—indeed, what made them Americans—was the fact that they possessed certain advantages denied to other men. The United States, for the first time in history, gave men the opportunity to put into practice basic principles of society and government impossible to test elsewhere. Americans had no monopoly on love of freedom, or respect for human values, of course—but only in America did men have the chance to work out such ideals, a chance to realize without hindrance the full potentials of the human character. Only the United States, they believed, seemed to have the human and material resources needed to maintain a society in which these ideals were fundamental. Americans were special—in the sense that they had a God-given opportunity to build a society on the virtues common to all men. For this reason what happened in and to the United States was of unparalleled importance to the human race. "Our experiment," Jefferson wrote a friend in the crucial months of 1787 as the delegates in Philadelphia hammered out a Constitution, "will be that men may be trusted to govern themselves without a master. Could the contrary of this be proved, I should conclude, either that there is no God, or that he is a malevolent being."

The United States was superior to England and Europe, therefore, because it was *not* like them; because it had left behind the Old World's ignorance, prejudice, and injustice; and because it had developed a new kind of social and political organization in a fresh new world. America was free, prosperous, enlightened, and *sui generis*. The old societies of England and Europe were doomed, so Noah Webster thought, for "a durable and stately edifice can never be erected on the moldering pillars of antiquity." The *American Patriotic Songbook*[18] in 1813 informed its singers that

> The fruits of our country, our flocks and our fleeces,
> The treasures immersed in our mountains that lie,
> While discord is tearing old Europe to pieces,
> Shall amply the wants of our people supply.

Intellectually, Timothy Dwight believed, the environment of the United States provided for "a depth of research, a candor of debate, and a friendliness to truth" impossible to find in Europe or England. "Look not to Europe, for examples just," he wrote in *Greenfield Hill* (1794),

> Of order, manners, customs, doctrines, laws
> Of happiness and virtue. Cast around
> The eye of searching reason, and declare
> What Europe offers but a patchwork sway.

A generation later the historian George Bancroft believed that "the absence of the prejudices of the Old World leaves us here the opportunity of consulting independent truth, and man is left to apply the instruction of freedom to every social relation and public interest." In government, religion, economy, wealth, intellect, and social improvement, Samuel Williams concluded in his *History of Vermont* (1809), the United States had already outstripped Europe (though he admitted to a slight lag in the arts). Benjamin Trumbull agreed that God had so ordained it. "Very conspicuous have been the exertions of Providence," he re-

---

[18] See Curti, *Roots of Loyalty*, Chap. I, for these and additional quotations.

marked in 1810, "in the discovery of the new world, in the settlement, growth, and perfection of the [American] states."

In considering their future, Americans projected several different images of themselves into the world scene. First, they visualized the United States as an asylum, as William Penn once expressed it, from "the anxious and troublesome solicitations, hurries, and perplexities of woeful Europe." Growing out of the "Come to America" theme of the promotional literature of early settlement, the belief took shape in the eighteenth century that the United States, with its wealth of resources and its open society, offered every man an equal chance for a fresh start. As Poor Richard viewed America somewhat overenthusiastically in 1752 as a place

> Where the sick Stranger joys to find a Home,
> Where casual Ill, maim'd Labor, freely come,
> Those worn with Age, Infirmity, and Care,
> Find Rest, Relief, and Health's returning fair,

so too did Thomas Paine in *Common Sense* offer America to the world as an "asylum for the persecuted lovers of civil and religious liberty from every part of Europe."

The successful conclusion of the Revolution gave a new and deeper dimension to the image of the United States as freedom's haven. Schubart in Germany saw the new states as "thirteen golden gates . . . open to the victims of intolerance and despotism." "Everything here turns to rottenness," the Abbé Gagliani wrote of Italy in 1776, "and everything hastens to renew itself in America." The *Pennsylvania Gazette*, shortly after the war, proudly described the new nation as "the asylum whither the indigent and oppressed, whom the lawless hand of European despotism would crush to earth, can find succour and protection, and join common fellowship in a country

> Where happy millions their own fields possess,
> No tyrant awes them, and no lords oppress."

John Filson, traveling in Kentucky, that "fertile region abounding with all the luxuries of nature," found it an "asylum in the wilderness for the distressed of mankind." Gilbert Imlay, another traveler, believed that the United States "seem calculated to become at once the emporium and protectors of the world" from the "corrupt principles" of

Europe. This tradition was a powerful one before the Revolution, and long after.[19]

Simply to serve as a haven for the world's oppressed was not enough. The larger mission of the United States, American leaders claimed, was to exemplify to the world the ability of men to govern themselves, to create and to spread new concepts of society and culture, to lead the way to a brighter and better future for mankind. "America's purpose," David Ramsay said flatly in 1794, "is to prove the virtues of republicanism, to assert the Rights of Man, and to make society better." The Abbé de Pradt, in Europe, believed that the United States was "destined to exert its influence all over the world," and that "no human power can stop its march." Chancellor James Kent, who was by no means a visionary liberal, believed that since Americans were "distinguished from all other people upon the face of the globe" in their devotion to liberty, they were therefore destined "to change the conditions of humanity" all over that globe. Many Americans considered the Revolution which established the United States to be a landmark in the history of a new kind of world; Dr. Richard Price of London, in fact, agreed that as "a step in the progressive course of human improvement," the American Revolution ranked "next to the introduction of Christianity among mankind." A Charleston editor of 1783 could thus without self-consciousness call the late conflict "the *greatest revolution* that ever took place—the expulsion of tyranny and slavery and the introduction of freedom, happiness, and independence" into a troubled world. "Its effects and consequences have already been awful over a great part of the earth," John Adams wrote, "and when and where are they to cease?"[20] All history pointed toward the American Revolution

---

[19] "O ye oppressed! Who groan in foreign lands/ No more submit to Tyrant's vile commands/ While here a calm retreat, from all your woes/ Invites to freedom, joy, and just repose." *The Universal Asylum and Columbian Magazine*, Philadelphia, January, 1791. See also M. Kraus, "America and the Utopian Ideal in the Eighteenth Century," *Mississippi Valley Historical Review*, XXII (1936), 487–505, and especially Edward M. Burns, *The American Sense of Mission* (New Brunswick, 1957).

[20] Voltaire's *Lettres Anglaises* (1734) mentioned that Penn had actually brought into existence the Golden Age of the philosophers in America, while the editor of the official court journal, *Gazette de France*, in 1774 concluded that in North America there was "an unborn love of liberty inherent in the soil, the sky, forests, and lakes" which affected "any European transplanted under this climate." R. E. Spiller *et al.*, *Literary History of the United States* (New York, 1948), I, 195–207.

and was hardly more than preparation for it. The historian George Bancroft in 1835 found its origins "deep in the intelligence that had been slowly ripening in the mind of cultural humanity" since the beginnings of human thought.

If the mission of American civilization was to exemplify and spread concepts of liberty, equality, and justice throughout the world, it seemed imperative to Americans that they cultivate their native Americanness, avoid emulation of Europe, and strive to develop their own life and culture in terms of their own experience.[21] To fulfill its divinely ordained purpose, America must continue always to be American. Mercy Otis Warren, in her *History of the American Revolution* (1805), pointed out that if the United States copied foreign ways or aped decadent Europe, its fate would soon be sealed. David Ramsay warned in 1785 that though the United States in a few years "had made more progress than Europe in two thousand years," unless it cherished "the whole lovely train of American virtues," it could easily lose its momentum and fall behind. Since "Nature and society have joined to produce and establish freedom in America," Samuel Williams of Vermont explained in his history of the state, the duty of Americans is to keep their traditions and ideals inviolate, free of any foreign taint.

After 1776 there were increased demands for the development of a distinctive "American way of life" related directly to American social and political ideals. The United States must have, its philosophers believed, native patterns of living and thinking to serve as instruments by which those ideals might better be realized. Americans needed, Benjamin Rush thought in 1792, "to study our own character, to examine the age of our country, and to adopt manners in everything, that shall be accommodated to our state of society, and to the forms of our government." "It is now full time," wrote James Sullivan, one of the founders of the Massachusetts Historical Society, "that we should assume a national character and opinions of our own." "Every engine should be employed to render the people of the country national," echoed Noah Webster, "to call their attachment home to their own country; and to inspire them with the pride of national character." The flamboyant jingoism of the postwar decades in the United States, self-puffery though

[21] Jefferson, in fact, once proposed that the Great Seal of the United States show the Israelites following a pillar of light, to emphasize that Americans were a chosen people, divinely selected to lead the world. Gilbert Chinard, *Thomas Jefferson* (Boston, 1928), p. 428.

much of it might have been, nevertheless had serious cultural purposes within it.

Europeans often found this fervid American nationalism crude and bumptious. The Duc de Liancourt, touring in the 1790's, thought there were too many Americans who were "sure nothing good is done, and that no one has any brains, except in America," while a British traveler in 1810 believed that "the national vanity of the United States surpasses that of any other country, not excepting France." Some Americans, such as Noah Webster, were no doubt aware of the dangers of over-zealous patriotism, but like him concluded that "national prejudices are probably necessary, in the present state of the world, to strengthen our government." Patriotism, Nathaniel Chipman explained in his *Sketches of the Principles of Government* (1793), was a God-inspired passion which must be tended, encouraged, and strengthened if the United States were to succeed in teaching men to govern themselves. Careful and conscious cultivation of the patriotic impulse, it was widely acknowledged, was essential to the creation of a national character and a national spirit. American holidays were given over to skyrocketing oratory, parades, and other evidences of national pride, especially on the Fourth of July, Washington's Birthday, and (for many years) the anniversary of the ratification of the Constitution.[22] Constant watering of the tree of patriotism sometimes led to enthusiastic nonsense, spread-eagle speeches, narrow prejudices, and flag-waving provincialism. And it could also inspire, as it did in Thomas Jefferson, a deep, dignified, and dedicated love of one's land: "The first object of my heart is my own country. In that is embarked my family, my fortune, and my own existence. I have not one farthing of interest, nor one fibre of attachment out of it."[23]

The men who shaped America were faced with the immediate and practical problem of achieving independence and of creating a new political, social, and cultural system out of thirteen disparate colonies. They inherited an ideological blueprint from Europe, of course, and they had the total experience of the western world on which to draw. When they found that the eighteenth-century theory of how to construct a new society had certain inadequacies in practice, they simply used common sense, even if the solutions they found did not always

[22] Curti, *Roots of American Loyalty,* pp. 122–135.
[23] To Elbridge Gerry, January 26, 1799.

square with the theory. Jefferson, an authentic child of the Enlightenment, always adjusted his ideas to the necessities of time and place, nor was he alone in so doing. Americans ranged eclectically among the ideas of the Enlightenment, choosing what they wished, modifying and adapting as experience, expediency, and necessity demanded.

While they did not accept all of the answers provided by the Enlightenment to the puzzling problems of man, nature, society, and Deity, Americans of the years 1776–1820 still believed that they had a firm foundation of ideas on which to build their state and society. Their Age of Reason aimed to produce a publicly announced standard of truth which worked. It provided an understandable view of man in relation to God and the universe, emphasizing the human traits of man and the common bonds of humanity. In his view of man, the eighteenth-century American stressed mind and intellect, showing decent respect for the individual and endowing him with dignity. The American Enlightenment failed to develop an adequate theory of human nature, and may have thought man better than he is; but from its ideas of tolerance, freedom of thought, and respect for man and his ability to improve, there grew basic American beliefs.

The American belief that human nature was essentially trustworthy, or at least capable of improvement within limits, reinforced the idea of progress and added depth to America's vision of its future. The United States, if it built its society on this concept of human nature, faced a magnificent future, or so many of its citizens believed. James Wilson of Pennsylvania, speaking at the Constitutional Convention, saw in the creation of the United States evidences of "a great design of Providence with regard to this globe," and Benjamin Rush thought the American Revolution "big with important consequences" to the entire world. Europe, wrote Robert Coram in 1791, never succeeded in producing a happy, enlightened civilization because "Europeans have been taught to believe that mankind have something of the Devil ingrafted in their nature . . . and are so void of reason as brutes." In America, wrote Freneau, far from Europe's "all-aspiring pride,"

> Reason shall new laws devise,
> And order from confusion rise,

bringing to the world "the happier day when Reason's sun shall light us on our way."

The United States seemed to many Americans (and to many Europeans) the logical place to begin the creation of the millennium. As an anonymous contributor to a Connecticut magazine wrote in 1786, "This country is reserved to be the last and greatest theater for the improvement of mankind." "All the doors and windows of the temple of nature," wrote Benjamin Rush in 1789, "have been thrown open by the convulsions of the late Revolution. This is the time therefore to press in upon her altars." "Let us keep nature in view," Coram advised his fellow citizens, "and frame our policy rather by the fitness of things, than by a blind adherence to contemptible precedents." As nature gradually exposed her secrets to men, and as an increasing knowledge of man's nature relieved him of his problems, life in the United States would become better and better and men ever more happy and wise. When the fundamental laws of human nature had been discovered (as science was even then discovering those of the physical world), then the Golden Age might arrive; men could then realize the full potentials of their own and divine nature and live in harmony with each other, the universe, and God. So Philip Freneau, welcoming the "Rising Glory of America" in 1771, hoped to see the day when

> A New Jerusalem, sent down from Heaven,
> Shall grace our happy land.

To speed the millennium was America's mission. "The future situation of America," thought Joel Barlow, "fills the mind with a peculiar dignity and opens an unbounded field of thought." "To anticipate the future glory of America," the Reverend Phillips Payson of Massachusetts wrote in 1773, "is ravishing and transporting to the mind." Five years later John Rodgers of New York City, another clergyman, told his congregation that since God had "put all the blessings of liberty, civil and religious, within our reach, perhaps there was never a nation that had the fair opportunity of becoming the happiest people on earth, that we have now."

If the men of the American Enlightenment seemed overoptimistic about the future, they did at least glimpse the tremendous potential resources of humankind, and recognize that freedom was something more than merely a better opportunity for ignorance and error. They were men of confidence and good will, civilized, rational, possessed of honest ideals. Their achievements were not small, and the legacy they left for posterity was large. Crusty John Adams, who did not always agree with the easy optimism of his times, looked back at the eighteenth century from the vantage point of his old age and found it good. "Nevertheless," he wrote Jefferson, "according to all the lights that remain to us, we may say that the eighteenth century, notwithstanding all its errors and vices, has been, of all that are past, the most honorable to human nature."

The beginnings of an American culture came, then, in a time of comparative confidence and certainty. After long and bitter contention with the world's greatest imperial power, the American colonists fought a successful war for what they believed to be fundamental and valid principles. They did not feel that the Revolution marked a sharp break between the colonies and their own past; the shift of political sovereignty from one side of the ocean to the other disturbed the continuity of American life no more than expected. What the Revolution did mean to the majority of Americans was a clean break with Europe and the European past.

After the peace, Americans speculated on the meaning of the war in terms of the future. They had committed themselves in their major documents (and by the war itself) to a certain kind of nation based on familiar eighteenth-century principles—progress, natural rights, self-government, the rationality and benevolence of man, nature, and God. They believed that they owed very little to custom, precedent, tradition, or authority. They thought of themselves as free individuals, capable of wise choice and of self-improvement. They possessed already, as David Humphreys of Connecticut said, "superior advantages for happiness over the rest of mankind," and their mission was, as Barlow wrote, "to excite emulation through the kingdoms of the earth, and meliorate the condition of the human race."

The Peace of Paris gave Americans the opportunity to wipe the slate clean, to create on their side of the Atlantic a model of that free, rational, orderly, dignified society toward which the eighteenth century believed men were destined to move. In other words, they believed that their mission was to found a new, *American* civilization, where, Joel Barlow prophesied in *The Columbiad,* "social man a second birth shall find, and a new range of reason lift his mind." There was little hope for Europe, where for centuries, Barlow pointed out, "the faculties of human reason and the rights of human nature have been the sport of chance and the prey of ambition." This new America would be different. The full intellectual strength of two generations of Americans was focused on this problem—to discover the identity, the destiny, and the responsibility of the United States—a nation whose goal, as Jefferson phrased it, was nothing less than "the happiness of associated man."

The intellectual and cultural history of the United States in the period 1776–1820 may therefore be best understood in terms of an orderly, controlled development of thought-patterns and institutions, motivated by nationalism and a belief in progress, assisted by science, within the framework of certain selected ideas of the Enlightenment and of the early phases of Romanticism.

CHAPTER 3

The New World of American Science

S CIENCE was so fundamental to the thought of the American Enlightenment, and the belief in its utility and promise so strong, that
a realization of its importance is central to a consideration of the cultural and intellectual patterns of the period. The American colonies, of
course, sprang into being at the inception of the wave of scientific discovery that marked the opening decades of the seventeenth century, and
grew to maturity during the great scientific developments of the eighteenth. New England and Virginia were settled by men of the same generation as Bacon, Kepler, Boyle, and Galileo; their sons and grandsons
were contemporaries of Newton and Leibnitz. During the century and
a half of American colonial growth, the great body of scientific knowledge was more widely known in America and Europe, and its application to the improvement of life more earnestly attempted, than ever
before.[1]

---

[1] For the backgrounds of eighteenth-century science, see A. N. Whitehead,
Science and the Modern World (New York, 1929); Allan H. Ferguson, *Natural
Philosophy Through the Eighteenth Century* (London, 1948); Abraham Wolf,
A History of Science, Technology, and Philosophy in the Eighteenth Century
(London, 1952); and J. D. Bernal, *Science in History* (London, 1954). Good
studies of American science in the colonial, Revolutionary, and early national
decades include the appropriate chapters of Daniel Boorstin, *The Lost World
of Thomas Jefferson* (New York, 1948); Brooke Hindle, *The Pursuit of
Science in Revolutionary America* (Chapel Hill, 1956); and John Krout and
Dixon R. Fox, *The Completion of Independence* (New York, 1944). Additional
material is found in R. S. Bates, *Scientific Societies in the United States* (New
York, 1945), and Theodore Hornberger, *Scientific Thought in American Colleges* (Austin, Tex., 1945). A key study is Harry Hayden Clark, "The Influence
of Science on American Ideas 1775–1809," *Transactions of the Wisconsin
Academy,* XXXV (1944), 305–349.

American colonists were intensely aware of the importance of science in determining the solution of social, religious, and political questions. American Calvinists, while not content to place their confidence in science alone, nevertheless absorbed contemporary scientific thought into their intellectual patterns, and accepted science both as illustration and reinforcement of the doctrine of divine revelation. Cotton Mather and John Winthrop, Jr., both better-than-average scientists and admirers of Newton, were good representatives of the colonial attitude. The eighteenth century continued and expanded this interest; men such as Harvard's John Winthrop, and of course Benjamin Franklin, were scientists of far more than merely American repute. This American heritage of science was transmitted from colonial leaders of thought to the Revolutionary and Republican generation without loss of force. "After the Revolution," wrote Dr. Amos Eaton, "a thirst for natural science seemed already to pervade the United States like the progress of an epidemic."[2]

In addition to the colonial heritage of scientific interest, there were strong nationalistic reasons for the postwar enthusiasm for science in the United States. Many American thinkers were convinced that science was destined to flourish in America—and that it was the instrument by which the United States might achieve moral, political, spiritual, and material leadership. Only in America, where liberty "unfetters and expands the human mind," wrote Samuel Cooper, "can science flourish." For that matter, they believed also that the United States had an obligation to advance scientific knowledge for the common good of all men. "The world," wrote Francis Hopkinson in 1792, "looks toward us as a country that may become a great nursery of arts and science." That this native scientific tradition developed slowly irritated some patriots. James de Kay of New York hoped that the War of 1812 might give American science "a proper feeling of nationality" with "beneficial consequences," while Benjamin Silliman, in founding the *American Journal of Science* in 1818, scolded Americans for leaning too heavily on Europe, warning American scientists that they must forge ahead for themselves.

A popular conception in European science during the eighteenth century was that everything American was necessarily inferior—its flora and fauna, its land, its institutions. Buffon, in his *Natural History* (1749–83), concluded that since America was literally a *new* world, like other things new it was likely to be savage, unformed, and undisci-

[2] Bernard Jaffe, *American Men of Science* (New York, 1948), p. 129.

plined. The Abbé Raynal, following Buffon, argued that since everything American was in an earlier and lesser stage of development than everything in Europe, America could therefore never catch up. All things in America, he wrote, "shrink and diminish under a niggardly sky and in an unprolific land, peopled with wandering savages." In a raw, new continent, it was assumed that nothing was likely to exist above a primary level, a view given wide popular currency by de Pauw's *Recherches Philosophiques sur les Américains* (1768) and one which continued to dominate European impressions of America throughout the latter years of the century.[3] According to the science of the day, since climate had a powerful influence on the development of culture, America's wild, untamed, "improperly balanced" climate presumably produced lesser breeds of plants, animals, and men, inhibited vigor, and encouraged disease. To refute this view, of course, required Americans to give close attention to American nature through scientific research. As a result, native science received great impetus to improvement by reason of the need Americans felt to counteract its British and European critics.[4]

A faith in science, specifically in American science, permeated the thinking of all ranks and classes of Americans during the years 1776–

[3] Henry W. Church, "Corneille de Pauw and the Controversy over his *Recherches Philosophiques sur les Américains,*" *PMLA,* LI (1936), 178–207, and Gilbert Chinard, "Eighteenth Century Theories of America as a Human Habitat," *Proceedings of the American Philosophical Society,* XCI (1947), 25–57. De Pauw, for example, said that American animals were "often ugly and deformed," that "poisonous trees grew" in American swamps, and that syphilis might be contracted by breathing "the pestilential air" of the country. Indians were "weak and devoid of finer sensibilities," their life characterized by "stupid insensibility." Buffon claimed that the Indian was "timid and cowardly," with "no vivacity, no activity of mind . . . no ardor for women . . . a weak automaton." It seems a pity that de Pauw and Buffon could not have suddenly met a Comanche, Sioux, or Iroquois brave in full war regalia, under proper frontier conditions.

[4] A brief summary of the Raynal-Buffon-de Pauw controversy is in Boorstin, *Lost World of Jefferson,* pp. 100–104. For a more comprehensive treatment, see Edwin T. Martin, *Thomas Jefferson: Scientist* (New York, 1952), Chaps. VI–VIII, and D. Boehm and E. Schwartz, "Jefferson and the Theory of Degeneracy," *American Quarterly,* IX (1957), 454–459. Americans now and then exacted a little revenge in exchange for European misinformation about their country. Franklin was not above pulling an English leg; he once blandly told his English friends about the delights of watching the whales leap like salmon up Niagara Falls. Marcus Cunliffe, *The Literature of the United States* (London, 1954), p. 47.

1820.[5] There were some doubters, of course, who feared that the findings of science might be misused, or misinterpreted, or applied to problems to which science had little or no relevance. President Charles Nisbet of the newly founded Dickinson College suspected that the more science discovered about nature, the less mindful men might be of the divinity of its Great Author; the Reverend John Mellen warned in his Dudleian lecture at Harvard in 1799 that overconfidence in science led to "an impious and atheistical philosophy." John Adams, by 1798, also had his doubts—learned societies, he thought, have "disorganized the world, and are incompatible with the social order." Hugh Henry Brackenridge's novel, *Modern Chivalry* (1792–1815), sharply satirized the American Philosophical Society, and Thomas Green Fessenden of Connecticut poked ridicule at scientific pretensions in his poem *Terrible Tractorations* in 1803. Even Philip Freneau, who enthusiastically agreed that science exposed "Nature's hidden stores" to man, thought it a "vain wish, to fathom all we see, for nature is all mystery." But it was not science that these men doubted—rather it was the misuse of its results, or an unwise overemphasis on its efficacy.

Science to the American eighteenth century meant British science, and that Newtonian science. Sir Isaac Newton, working in the atmosphere of Cartesianism and Baconian empiricism, had provided his descendants with a scientific method that satisfied both scientists and philosophers. He made it possible, by means of a relatively few fundamental laws, to determine in principle the properties and behavior, at least in principle, of all material bodies in the universe with a degree of precision and simplicity not possible before.[6] The scientist moved, he said, "from the phenomena of motions to investigate the forces of nature, and then from these forces to demonstrate the other phenomena"; he proceeded from a starting point of facts or effects to causes or laws, and employed these laws in investigations of other facts and laws. The Newtonian method, as the eighteenth century received and developed it, included three basic factors—experimentation, induction, empiricism —all of which provided the pattern for American scientific thinking from the early eighteenth century to the opening decades of the nineteenth.[7]

[5] See George N. Clark, *Science and Social Welfare in The Age of Newton* (Oxford, 1949).

[6] Isaiah Berlin, *The Age of Enlightenment* (Boston, 1956), p. 15.

[7] See F. E. Brasch, *Sir Isaac Newton, 1727–1927* (Baltimore, 1928), for a

Newton's *Principia* appeared in all good American libraries, and abridgments and popularizations of Newtonian writings (such as Peale's *Discourse . . . on the Science of Nature*) sold widely in the United States up to the middle of the nineteenth century. Forty books about Newton were published in English before 1789; Parson Weems sold a thousand copies of one of these (Goldsmith's *History of the Earth and Animated Nature*) to his Virginia clientele in one year. Voltaire's *Elements de la philosophie de Newton,* in an English translation, had great popularity in America; Pope, Young, Thomson, Addison, and other popular British poets and writers explained Newtonianism to the literate American.[8] Almanacs, the most widely circulated form of American writing, provided scientific instruction (along with much superstition and pseudo-science) to the common man. Newtonian principles pervaded the thinking of the era, and Americans, like Europeans, worshiped Newton's memory. "Placed alongside Newton," Jefferson once wrote, "every human character must appear diminutive."[9]

Implicit in the eighteenth century's acceptance of Newtonianism was the principle of the unity or solidarity of science—that is, the assumption that the physical and "moral" sciences (or nature and human nature) were based on and subject to the same laws. If truth could be found in science by the use of reason and the inductive method, it seemed logical to assume that it could be discovered in the same manner and by the same methods in any field of knowledge. The discovery of certain natural laws in the universe might thus be paralleled by the discovery of similar bodies of law in morality, ethics, and social action—because, as philosophers assumed, all kinds of human experience were equally susceptible to improvement by the organization and application of knowledge. Advances in physical science increased man's control over

---

discussion of Newtonian influences, and Brasch's "Newtonian Epoch in the American Colonies," *American Antiquarian Society Proceedings,* XLIX (n.s., October, 1939), 314–332. For a more specialized discussion, see I. Bernard Cohen, *Franklin and Newton* (Philadelphia, 1956), Chaps. I, "Eighteenth Century Newtonian Science," and II, "Physical Theory in the Age of Newton and Franklin."

[8] James D. Hart, *The Popular Book* (New York, 1950), pp. 322–333. An especially popular explanation of Newtonianism was W. B. Martin, *Philosophica Britannica, or a New and Comprehensive System of the Newtonian Philosophy* (London, 1747).

[9] Benjamin Franklin, however, in France almost equaled Newton as a symbol of scientific genius in the latter half of the eighteenth century. See Gilbert Chinard, *L'Apothese de Benjamin Franklin* (Paris, 1955).

nature; in the same way the scientific method might help him to achieve mastery of troublesome social, political, and economic problems with equally successful results.

Not long before this, men had learned from Locke that they were not necessarily evil; that the human mind was at birth a *tabula rasa*, or blank tablet, on which good or evil might be written. They also agreed with Locke that it was quite possible that men would find out "Those Measures, whereby a Rational Creature, put into the state which man is in this World, may and ought to govern his Opinions and Actions." The French encyclopedists—Helvetius, La Mettrie, and Holbach—and the English environmentalists, such as Godwin and Mary Wollstone-craft, developed this theory more fully and emphasized its practical application to human improvement. Evil, they agreed, was at least par-tially the result of environment; correcting the faults of institutions which constituted that environment offered mankind an escape from evil. As an analogy to Newtonian science, the creation of a "science of society" and the discovery of its basic laws therefore became as impor-tant to eighteenth-century men as the science of nature.

As Samuel Miller summarized it in his *Retrospect of the 18th Cen-tury* (1803), the prevailing Old World belief was that "man is the child of circumstances; and by ameliorating these, without the aid of religion, his true and highest salvation is to be obtained."[10] However, leaders of American thought were divided on this issue. Conservatives of the order of Hamilton and John Adams felt that errors of human nature were not solely the product of environment. Franklin, who suspected that the study of human society was more complex than that of physical science, warned that its results did not lend themselves to really scientific verifi-cation. Others, like Jefferson and Rush, had much more confidence in the success of the scientific method as applied to human affairs.

The attitude toward science in the late eighteenth and early nine-teenth centuries in America was thus characterized by a general accept-ance of four central principles: a belief in the inductive method as opposed to simple authority; a belief in the Newtonian doctrine of a mechanistic universe governed by immutable, discoverable laws; a be-lief (tempered, but nevertheless pervasive) in the efficacy of scientific method as applied to the study of human relations and human prob-lems; and a belief in the unity of science, implying a mechanistic rela-

[10] Miller's survey of science over the preceding century is still an informative account.

tionship among all branches of knowledge. An approach to the problem of nature and of human nature, based on these principles, in Jefferson's opinion "liberated the ideas of those who read and reflect." No other set of beliefs was quite so important in shaping American thought during the period.[11]

Faith in science, first of all, provided an underpinning for the contemporary belief in progress.[12] Nearly every leader of American thought agreed that science provided the best possible tool with which man might discover those fundamental laws and truths—in nature and human nature—on which progress depended. Each generation, wrote Jefferson, was a little wiser than the last because of "the progressive march of science." Franklin, in his old age, lamented that he had been born too soon, for with "the Academies of science, with nice Instruments and the Spirit of Enlightenment, the progress of human knowledge will be rapid, and Discoveries made, of which we have at present no Conception." Barlow, in his epic poem, *The Columbiad*, hailed the day when

> Science bright,
> Through shadowy nature leads with surer light . . .
> Gives each effect its own indubious cause,
> Divides her moral from her physic laws,
> Shows where the virtues find their nurturing food,
> And men their motives to be just and good.

Elihu Palmer, writing his *Political Happiness of Nations* (1800), believed that science had "already reviv'd the hopes of one-third of the human race, and its character bears a most indubitable relation to the emancipation of the whole. . . . To this source of improvement no limits can be assigned—it is indefinite and incalculable."

The impact of science on orthodox theology was particularly great.[13] The conflict between the "new science" and orthodoxy was, of course, not confined to the eighteenth century, nor to America, for its roots lay far deeper in the past. In the seventeenth century, dissatisfied with

[11] An excellent brief discussion of the importance of science in American thought is John C. Greene, "Science and the Public in the Age of Jefferson," *Isis*, XXXIX (March, 1958), 13–26.

[12] For a fuller discussion, see Macklin Thomas, "The Idea of Progress in Franklin, Freneau, Barlow, and Rush" (unpublished dissertation, Wisconsin, 1938), and H. H. Clark, "Influence of Science," pp. 324–326.

[13] See H. H. Clark, "Influence of Science," pp. 310–326, and Boorstin, *Lost World of Jefferson*, Chap. IV.

Descartes' cosmology, which seemed to eliminate God from the world order, British thinkers adopted the belief that a "spirit of nature," or God, was present in the universe in a specific, direct way. Newton gave this belief foundation and popularity. Mechanical laws alone, he decided, were incapable of explaining the origin and continuation of the universe; tracing the chain of causes and effects led the scientist to a belief in a First Cause or Intelligent Agent, of which the universe was an expression. Locke agreed that "the works of Nature everywhere sufficiently evidence a Deity." Sir Richard Blackmore, physician to Queen Anne and author of *Creation* (1712), logically deduced the existence of God "from the marks of wisdom, design, contrivance, and choice of ends and means which appear in the universe."[14]

The American colonists, conditioned by Newton and Locke, followed where the British led. The Puritan, contrary to later opinion, was neither fearful of nor uninterested in science. He believed sincerely that God revealed Himself in His creation, and that the study of goodness, design, and beauty in nature (as Cotton Mather said in *The Christian Philosopher*) reinforced the teachings of Scripture. The so-called "argument from design" received wide acceptance throughout the eighteenth century and well into the nineteenth, nor did many thinkers find in it any deep-seated conflict between science and religion. Dr. Benjamin Rush, eminent scientist that he was, saw no reason why science and theology might not advance together, each assisting the other; along with the study of science, he believed, the study of the Bible ought to be required in all schools. Charles C. Reich in 1793 published *Fifteen Discourses on the Marvelous Works of Nature* to show young people how God was implicit in a scientific study of the world. Benjamin Silliman believed that religious truth was not fully revealed in nature, but was "contained in the Scriptures alone." "With this double view," he continued, "I feel that Science and Religion may walk hand in hand." When Silliman edited a textbook in geology, he included a chapter on the geological action of the Flood. Paley's *Natural Theology* (1802), one of the most widely used of all college texts of the time, assured students that "there cannot be a design without a designer," and John Quincy Adams, who had studied Paley, agreed with him that "the indissoluble connection between earth and heaven is palpable and unquestionable." As late as 1885 the Reverend Thomas Gallaudet's

---

[14] A good discussion is Herbert Drennon, "Newtonianism: Its Methods, Theology, and Metaphysics," *Englische Studien,* LXVIII (1933–34), 297–409.

Youth's Book of Natural Theology (1832), a children's adaptation of Paley, was still popular.[15]

In one sense, then, eighteenth-century science served to buttress traditional Christian beliefs. However, some commentators turned Newtonian science (which had seemed even to Newton to reinforce orthodox theology) against itself. The problem was a matter of emphasis. Whereas to a seventeenth-century Calvinist, such as Richard Mather, the scientific study of nature had a certain religious value, it was "not sufficient for salvation nor for saving faith." To the late eighteenth-century thinker, who worshiped nature by the light of reason, science seemed the only trustworthy way of finding religious truth—a better, much more accurate way than by studying Scripture. Samuel Keimer's remark, in his *Universal Instructor* (1729), that "God is to be known *only* in his works" left no place for the Bible in religion. To those who studied the universe with the scientist's eye, nature might reveal a Deity, but a Deity who bore little resemblance to the Calvinist or Anglican God. The God of nature, it seemed to some, was really a Great Engineer or Sublime Architect, "a Fabricator," as Jefferson said, "of all things from matter and motion."

How could one align the findings of science with the myth, history, and occasionally obvious contradictions of the Bible? Some could not. Franklin trusted only "the sacred book of Nature." Jefferson quietly drew up his own Bible, made up only of passages which stood the test of rational proof and did not "contradict the laws of Nature." If, as the interpreters of Newton supposed, the Deity was a Great Fabricator who had designed and started the world machine, possibly His presence was unnecessary to its continuance. Whereas earlier thinkers found that the scientific study of Creation revealed God, those of the later eighteenth century found that the Creation revealed a quite different kind of Creator, in a quite different kind of way that made orthodox, Scriptural revelation not only unnecessary but perhaps impossible.

The Newtonian concept of the universe as an infinitely rational mechanism had certain implications which appeared to deny traditional, orthodox Christianity. American Calvinism itself, of course, had a strong rationalistic bent (emphasized by theologians such as John Wise and Jonathan Mayhew) which, when added to the weight of contemporary British and French philosophy, pointed toward a "religion of reason"

---

[15] See Wilson Smith, *Professors and Public Ethics: Studies of Northern Moral Philosophers before the Civil War* (Ithaca, 1956).

based on science. If reason were the prevailing principle of nature and of the human mind, religion must be inevitably brought to the bar of reason for judgment, just as science dealt with the facts of nature. Having produced a rational science, the later eighteenth century needed to evolve a rational religion, based on fundamental theological laws as immutable, pervasive, and rational as those natural laws revealed in science. The result was deism.

Deism, stemming from the contemporary trust in reason and science, colored the religious ideas of many leading thinkers of the late eighteenth and early nineteenth centuries in America. "Scientific deists" such as Paine and Elihu Palmer emphasized the parallels between the rational methods of discovering truth in science and those of discovering truth in religion. Those orthodox doctrines which, as Paine expressed it, "currently passed for Christianity" did not seem to stand up under rational scrutiny. Paine, for his own part, could not see how a belief in science and a belief in traditional Christianity could even be "held together in the same mind," and his *Age of Reason* (1794–96) was a carefully reasoned, critical attack on orthodox religious beliefs and on the Bible. Palmer's *Principles of Nature* (1802) and Ethan Allen's *Oracles of Reason* (1781, partially written by Thomas Young) extended and popularized the same arguments. Franklin, who once declared himself "a thorough deist," recounted his conversion to rational religion in his *Autobiography;* Freneau wrote deist poetry, while Barlow translated Volney's *Ruins* (1791), a French deistical tract, and assisted in spreading its doctrines in America. John Fitch, Palmer, and others organized deist clubs, and journals such as *The Beacon* and *The Temple of Reason* popularized deist principles. John Adams concluded later that "the principles of Deism made considerable progress" in America before the Revolution, and, to judge by the number of ministers who inveighed from their pulpits against "infidelity" after 1790, its expansion continued afterward.[16]

The clearest exposition of the rational, scientific approach to religion in the later eighteenth century is that of Thomas Paine, whose "natural bent of mind," he once said, "was to science." Only science, Paine believed, could sweep away the dusty cobwebs of authority, prejudice, and tradition from the true doctrines of Christianity, revealing nature's laws

---

[16] G. H. Koch, *Republican Religion* (New York, 1933), and H. M. Morais, *Deism in Eighteenth Century America* (New York, 1934), are excellent studies of deism.

and with them nature's true religion. His own religious faith he constructed on four major premises, each derived from Newtonian science: first, that nature, viewed by reason, is the only valid source of God's revelation to man; second, that nature so viewed is a "harmonious, magnificent order" which is natural law; third, that man and his society may partake of this order; and fourth, that the duty of man is to bring his life and society into harmony with natural law. From these premises Paine drew the conclusion that God is eminently rational and benevolent, and that man is rational and altruistic. To find religious truth, Paine believed, one must judge religion by the standards of reason as a scientist finds truth in nature; one rejected myth, mystery, and irrationality, meeting God through nature, and finding in nature those laws which God placed there to serve as guides to man. The *Age of Reason,* in which Paine explained his scientifically orientated theology, was in his view an attack on the false in Christianity and an attempt to validate the true.[17] Deists hoped to find a theology which reason could accept, a system of religious principles and laws derived from and congruent to those of science.

Not all of the men of the American Enlightenment were deists, of course—a minority, rather—nor did all deists pursue scientific rationalism so far as Paine or Allen. Nevertheless, the impact of science on theology during the period, qualitatively and quantitatively, was a powerful influence in changing the patterns of American religious thinking, in contributing to the decline of the older Calvinism, in encouraging independence in theological speculation, and in introducing new (or relatively new) religious trends. Because of science, the emphasis in theology shifted from Scripture to nature as a source of Divine revelation. Through science, men looked to nature and natural law, instead of to ecclesiastical authority and tradition, for guides and standards of human thought and conduct. The era's interest in science emphasized the primacy of reason in religious thought, as against the "affections" or intuitions of Methodism and the Great Awakening. Most of all, since the thinkers of the time called religion to the account of individual reason, they gave to the individual a much more important and central position in theology than he had possessed before.

Since the physical sciences were so much more highly developed than

[17] Harry Hayden Clark, *Thomas Paine* (New York, 1944), Introduction.

the biological sciences in the eighteenth century, their impact on theology was much more marked. The Newtonian method and viewpoint, deriving from physics, mathematics, and astronomy, pointed toward deism and the religion of reason, since the physical sciences provided the most understandable pattern by which God and nature might be explained. The gradual decline of deistic rationalism after 1800, however, did not settle the traditional conflict between naturalism and supernaturalism, between science and theology. Beginning about 1820, developments in the biological sciences precipitated another argument between scientists and theologians, for the new theories of biology and geology seemed also to deny certain orthodox religious doctrines.

There were certain differences, however, in the pattern of this later conflict of science and theology. The argument was less over the efficacy of the rationalistic method, as it applied in religious matters, than over the theological implications of the evidence this method produced. Did or did not the findings of science deny Scripture, and did or did not those findings support orthodox Christian doctrine? The controversy over "igneous" versus "aqueous" theories of the earth's formation created a dispute in the 1820's and 1830's between geologists and theologians as well as among geologists themselves. Benjamin Silliman, as already noted, found geological evidence to support Biblical accounts of the Flood. Thomas Cooper of South Carolina College, did not, and said so in his pamphlet, *On The Connection Between Geology and the Pentateuch* (1833), opening a war between science and theology that involved at first such eminent men as James Dwight Dana and Louis Agassiz, and that later drew in Lyell, Spencer, Darwin, Huxley, and many others before the end of the nineteenth century.

Between science and political thought, the eighteenth century saw certain close connections.[18] American political thinkers conceived of government as the science of society, analogous to the science of nature, subject to similar methods of investigation and productive of similar laws. Men possessed reason to locate these laws of society. They had a scientific method by which to pursue them. And they had the harmonious, orderly model of the universe itself to serve as a pattern for their government. The political philosopher, therefore, like the scientist, studied man in society to find those natural principles of political association

[18] G. N. Clark, *Science and Social Welfare*, pp. 330–336, and Hindle, *Pursuit of Science*, pp. 377 ff.

upon which an enduring and just government could be built. In this manner, he hoped to discover something of the fundamental natural law which governed the relations of men with each other. "All great laws of society," remarked Paine, "are laws of nature," therefore discoverable by science and reason.

The scientific spirit permeated much of the political thinking of the time. Franklin referred to the Revolution, the Confederation, and the Constitution as "experiments in politics," much as he would refer to laboratory experiments. Thomas Paine saw a close relationship between science and the new American political experiment, writing in *The Rights of Man* that "The revolution in America presented in politics what was only theory in mechanics." Thomas Cooper, the eminent chemist and geologist, in his *Propositions Respecting the Foundation of Civil Government* (1791), supported the doctrine that the aim of government is the greatest good for the greatest number with what he considered impeccable scientific proof. Dr. Samuel Latham Mitchill, an authority in several scientific fields, approached political problems in the true scientific manner. Analyzing the flaws of past governmental systems, he concluded that "the perfection of political wisdom . . . consists not in encumbering the machine of government with new contrivances," but rather in "removing gradually and imperceptibly the obstacles which disturb the order of nature." These men were by no means isolated cases.

The aim of government, they assumed, was to provide a framework of law in which men might live and move with the same harmony that characterized the planets in their courses. The analogy between political society and the Newtonian universe was quite obvious to the eighteenth century. As early as 1728, Desaugliers in France published an allegorical poem to show *The Newtonian System of the World, The Best Model of Government,* a principle that a number of Americans such as John Winthrop and Isaac Greenwood (who had heard Desaugliers lecture) popularized in the colonies.[19] Paine believed the best government to be that which most resembled "the unerring regularity of the visible solar system." "The representative system [of government]," he continued, "is always parallel with the order and immutable laws of nature, and meets the needs of man in every part." Freneau saw nature as a "model to man," providing for him

[19] On this matter, see Chap. 2 of Carl Becker, *The Declaration of Independence* (New York, 1922).

The pattern how to reign
With equal sway, and how maintain
True human dignity.

Most Americans approached their post-Revolutionary political problems in this rationalistic, scientific mood, confident that their duty was to find those laws of human society analogous to natural law, and to materialize them in legislation. Freneau, writing five years before the Revolutionary War, believed that "fair science . . . transplanted from the eastern skies" to America, could make it "a land of liberty and life, sweet liberty," whose "laws, copying those of Nature," made "a pattern to the world beside." Joel Barlow subtitled his poem *The Canal* (1802) "A Poem on the Application of Physical Science to Political Economy" and predicted that the combined powers of science and politics, as displayed in America, would "raise, improve, and harmonize mankind." Five years later in *The Columbiad* Barlow analyzed the American Revolution in clear Newtonian terms. At the beginning of creation, he explained, all was chaos until God sent "Order . . . in her cerulean robes/And launched or rein'd the renovated globes" into a harmonious universe. In the same way, he continued, kings and tyrants had created political chaos to "convulse the moral frame." The Revolution represented a restoration of natural law and order from political chaos, similar to God's own first creation of order in nature. The construction of an American government based on Newtonian natural order became thus to Barlow the first step toward "a general congress of all nations, assembled to establish the political harmony of mankind," which would reflect in political society the mechanistic perfection of the universe.

The men of the time had reason to believe that problems of state and society were in a real sense quasi-scientific problems, subject to scientific investigation. In this spirit a group of Virginians in 1784 founded a Constitutional Society to study government scientifically, much as the American Philosophical Society studied the natural world, while Franklin and his Philadelphia friends established the Society for Political Inquiries for the same purpose. Benjamin Rush could see no reason why American political problems could not be solved by controlled experimentation, and with Franklin and Francis Hopkinson was one of three first-rank scientists to sign the Declaration of Independence. Since the Creator, reasoned Rush, had made "the beauty and harmony of the universe" contingent on "the universal and mutual dependence" of its component parts, was this not an indication that any government like-wise must be "dependent on those for whose benefit alone all government should exist"? There was good scientific basis, therefore, to Rush's mind, for the establishment in the American system of the principle of popular sovereignty in governmental affairs.

It was not accidental, of course, that many of the leaders of American political thought before and after the Revolution were men of scientific interests—Jefferson, Paine, Franklin, Freneau, Noah Webster, Rush, Rittenhouse, Barlow, Priestley, and Hopkinson, to name a few.

Franklin was generally conceded by the mid-eighteenth century to be one of the two or three great scientific minds of the world. In the next generation Thomas Jefferson nearly attained the same eminence; certainly after 1800 he was the best-known American intellectual, familiar to statesmen, philosophers, and scientists in every land as America's dominant scholar. His importance in political affairs has tended to obscure his significant place in early American science. Modern scholars recognize him as a pioneer researcher and theorist in such fields as paleontology, ethnology, botany, geography, agriculture, and meteorology, as almost every important learned society recognized him in his own time. Even more important, however, to early American science, was the example he set. To him science, the pursuit of knowledge, was man's most important quest. Scientific knowledge, he believed, should be useful in social, moral, legal, cultural, and spiritual affairs, reaching into "the mass of mankind . . . [to] circle the extremes of society, beggars and kings." But at the same time Jefferson knew the excitement of the quest of truth for its own sake, the search in the universe for fundamental principles. "There is," he once wrote, "not a sprig of grass that shoots uninteresting to me."[20]

It was not by chance that Samuel Latham Mitchill, William Maclure, Adam Seybert, and other professional scientists held seats in Congress or posts in government. Yet there was a significant difference in the approach to politics of gifted amateurs such as Jefferson or Paine, and that of professionals like Priestley, Rush, or Franklin. Paine began his political thinking with certain a priori assumptions about man and society, derived from science, and used science as an aid in developing

---

[20] The best account of Jefferson's scientific interests and accomplishments is Edwin T. Martin, *Thomas Jefferson: Scientist* (New York, 1952). The quotation is on p. 13. See also Charles A. Browne, "Thomas Jefferson and the Scientific Trends of His Time," *Chronica Botanica,* VIII (1944), 363–426.

their political implications. Rush and Franklin were much less certain of the reliability of a priori assumptions, much more carefully inductive, and much less self-assured about their conclusions. Samuel Latham Mitchill[21] would only conclude from his scientific studies that man was "a rapacious and overbearing animal," and that to control him required a strong government of law based on force. The whole problem of how man behaved in society, remarked Joseph Priestley, is "so complex a subject that nothing can be safely concluded *a priori* with respect to it. Everything that we can depend on must be derived from *facts.*"

Verifiable facts about human nature, it seemed, were extraordinarily hard to find. If, as Freneau and Barlow and Jefferson assumed, man could be trusted under proper conditions to govern himself, he could also construct a political society as harmoniously balanced as nature's own machine. But could the essential altruism of human nature be established as a scientific fact? If, as Hamilton suspected, "the passions of men will not conform to the dictates of reason and justice," the analogy of government with nature had far less meaning and value to the political thinker than some scientists believed. Something of both attitudes found its way into contemporary political theory—in the checks and restraints of the Federalist system on the one hand and in the open, optimistic spirit of Jeffersonianism on the other.

[21] For an illuminating biography of this interesting man, see Courtney R. Hall, *A Scientist in the Early Republic: Samuel Latham Mitchill* (New York, 1934).

CHAPTER 4

The Organization of Scientific Knowledge

AMERICAN science faced great difficulties after the close of the Revolution. Scientific work had been badly disrupted by the war. New York, Philadelphia, and Charleston had been occupied by British troops, travel curtailed, colleges closed, libraries ransacked or destroyed, journals suspended, communication with Europe slowed or stopped. A good many scientists had been absorbed into war activities—Rittenhouse, for example, served as president of the Pennsylvania Council of Safety, while Jefferson and Franklin spent their entire time in governmental and diplomatic duties. Rush was Surgeon General of the Continental Army. The majority of scientists who chose the Loyalist side had departed by 1783 (among them such men as Benjamin Thompson, Joseph Galloway, and the eminent South Carolina botanist Alexander Garden), a severe loss only partially balanced by the gain of a few wartime visitors who decided to stay, among them L'Enfant, De Brahm, and Albert Gallatin. Later a larger number of immigrant arrivals helped to swell the ranks of acquisitions, notably Joseph Priestley (the discoverer of oxygen), Thomas Cooper, the Scots geologist William Maclure, and Constantine Rafinesque, the Italian botanist.

After the war, American scientists lacked leadership, libraries, laboratories, equipment, scientific organizations and journals, even college training. At the same time there was a tremendous amount of work to be done in collecting, classifying, and systematizing scientific knowledge. Merely collecting and naming American flora and fauna was in itself a huge task, complicated by the fact that terminology in most of the biological sciences was inexact and shifting. Fields of science still remained more or less undifferentiated, with few limits marked out; a scientist in the course of a single investigation might encounter unclassified and unnamed materials in several different fields. These problems were, of course, not uniquely American, but they were particularly pressing in American science during the postwar period.[1]

The first major step in launching American science on a new path after the Revolution was the reactivation of the older scientific societies and the creation of new ones.[2] Perhaps more than any other single thing, American science needed to establish a co-operative approach to scientific knowledge, and proper channels of communication and co-ordination among the various sciences. Conditions were good for scientific activity—increased wealth and leisure, the growth of urban communities where men of scientific interests congregated, a resurgence of scientific education in colleges and universities. There were many talented Americans deeply concerned with science, a wide popular interest in scientific affairs, and a tremendous amount of scientific activity in Europe ready to be channeled to America. Organization of American scientific resources was clearly of primary necessity.

Of the established scientific societies, two were particularly important in the development of American scientific work after the war. The American Philosophical Society (first organized in 1743–44) was a union of Franklin's old Junto, the American Society for Promoting and Propagating Useful Knowledge, and the Philadelphia Medical Society. Its influence on the development of American science from the time of its founding can hardly be overestimated; in 1771 the Society listed 242 members, 25 of them in Europe, and not only did it include every major American scientist (Franklin, Rittenhouse, and Jefferson served as its presidents) but it gave memberships to such eminent Europeans as Lavoisier, Buffon, Linnaeus, and Condorcet. In addition, the Society's *Transactions* and meetings served as the chief medium of communication among Americans and as their most important channel of scientific exchange with Europe. Nearly as influential was the American Acad-

[1] Brooke Hindle, *The Pursuit of Science in Revolutionary America* (Chapel Hill, 1956), Chaps. XIV, XV, is an especially good discussion of the postwar scientific situation.

[2] Scientifically minded colonists, of course, had long been connected with the Royal Society of London; Cotton Mather, for example, sent thirty-seven communications to the Society as well as specimens of plants, bones, berries, birds, and snakes. See F. E. Brasch, *The Royal Society of London and Its Influence on Scientific Thought in America* (Washington, D.C., 1931). For a complete discussion of scientific societies during the period, consult R. S. Bates, *Scientific Societies in the United States* (New York, 1945).

emy, organized in 1780 by John Adams and other New Englanders, "to cultivate every art and science which may tend to advance the interest, honor, dignity, and happiness of a free, independent, and virtuous people." Between them these two societies dominated American scientific inquiry throughout the Federalist and Jeffersonian periods.[3]

During the postwar years there was also a proliferation of smaller scientific societies. These were primarily of narrower interests than the two older groups, indicating the growing trend toward specialization in research. The earliest were the medical societies, since the study of medicine had been greatly stimulated by the war. The Medical Society of New Jersey (1766) and the American Medical Society of Philadelphia (founded 1773, reactivated 1792) were already in existence. The Boston Medical Society, established in 1780, was followed by similar societies in Massachusetts (1781), New Haven (1784), the Philadelphia College of Physicians (1787), Delaware (1789), South Carolina (1789), New Hampshire (1791), Connecticut (1792), the Philadelphia Academy of Medicine (1792), and the Medical Society of New York (1806). By 1830 all states except Pennsylvania, Virginia, and North Carolina had state medical societies which attempted with varying success to investigate nostrums, control quackery, and police the profession.

Other scientists organized too, though not so swiftly as the medical men. The Chemical Society of Philadelphia, founded in 1792, was the first of its kind in the world; the Columbian Chemical Society of Philadelphia (1811) and the Academy of Natural Sciences (1812) followed later. The Massachusetts Historical Society (1791) was the first of its kind in the new nation. The Philadelphia Society for Promoting Agriculture (1785) provided a model for agricultural societies in five other states before the turn of the century. The Pennsylvania Society for the Encouragement of Manufacture and Useful Arts (1787) was the first of several similar groups. Through the closing decades of the eighteenth century and into the opening years of the nineteenth century, American scientists slowly organized, began their publications, and con-

[3] Mention should also be made of the Columbian Institute, organized in 1816, which served as an advisory body to Congress and the federal government in scientific matters, and which counted fifteen senators and twenty-eight representatives among its members. In 1828 it reorganized as the National Institution, which in turn assisted in the formation of the Smithsonian Institution in 1846. See Richard Rathburn, *U.S. National Museum Bulletin 101* (Washington, D.C., 1917), and G. B. Goode, *Genesis of the National Museum,* Smithsonian Institute Report XLVI (1890–91).

fidently hoped to equal or surpass Europe in the discovery of new knowledge—all the while awaiting the appearance of an American Newton or Buffon.

The history of medical science during the Revolution itself was a classic example of confusion, frustration, and ignorance. Hospitals were few and bad; medical care scarce and incompetent; the administration of military medicine shockingly inept, shot through with bickerings and politics. Congress set up medical establishments but rarely provided funds for them. Disease killed thousands, malpractice and stupidity probably more. "Disease," wrote John Adams, "has destroyed ten men for us where the sword of the enemy has killed one." Dr. Benjamin Church, the first medical Director General of the Continental armies, turned Loyalist. Dr. John Morgan, the second, became so involved in intraprofessional squabblings that he was dismissed, as was his successor, Dr. William Shippen. Dr. Cochran, who finally lasted out the war, was no more than competent. Dr. Benjamin Rush, the most brilliant American medical scholar, served as Surgeon General of the Armies of the Middle Department, where he too faced jealousy and red tape. Still, though men died needlessly, physicians and surgeons learned something, albeit slowly, from the wartime experience.[4]

"The sick flow in regular current to the hospitals," wrote Dr. James Tilton in 1779. "These are overcrowded so as to produce infection, and mortality ensues too affecting to be described." Smallpox, dysentery, malaria, yellow fever, and "camp fever" (typhoid and typhus) were common in both armies, and at times sickness was so prevalent as to virtually suspend military action. Cornwallis' army was so sick in the summers of 1780 and 1781, during its occupation of the Carolinas, that any large-scale action was impossible. The Seventy-first British Regiment, for example, reported two-thirds unfit for duty through the summer of 1781, and at one point Cornwallis and his entire staff were so ill that his army was almost without command.[5] In prison camps, hospitals, and especially in the British prison ships, the toll was frightful. Of two hundred American militiamen captured from Gates's army, 150 died in two months on a prison ship moored in Charleston harbor, chiefly

[4] See "Health, Hospitals, and Medicine," Chap. XX, Vol. II, of Henry S. Commager and Richard B. Morris, *The Spirit of 'Seventy-Six* (New York, 1958), for an account of wartime medicine.

[5] Maurice Bear Gordon, *Aesculapius Comes to the Colonies* (Ventnor, N.J., 1949), pp. 307, 429.

from smallpox and dysentery. In one American hospital in New Jersey, mortality exceeded 60 per cent consistently.[6] Dr. James Tilton, who supervised American military hospitals in Trenton and New Windsor, New Jersey, fought for reform in military medical organization and particularly for hospital reforms. He modified the current system by subdividing hospitals into smaller sections, and by dividing the sick into small groups, each in a well-ventilated, clean individual hut. His *Economical Observations on Military Hospitals* was one of the major pieces of constructive medical research to come out of the war, but unfortunately few paid much attention to it.[7]

The most active and still the most confused branch of science in the United States after the Revolution was medicine. First of all, neither American nor European medical scientists possessed a body of basic theory or trustworthy research techniques. Following the pattern of the physical sciences, researchers in medicine hoped to discover a set of general laws into which observable medical knowledge might be fitted; in the proper Newtonian spirit they attempted to find a framework of principles by which they could bring some order to a bewildering multiplicity of symptoms and diseases. The difficulty was that the quantitative method, which worked passably well in physics, simply did not operate in medicine and pathology. Not only did medical phenomena seem to resist precise measurement, but there was disagreement among medical men themselves as to whether the body was a machine (which might be studied by the same methods of observation and generalization that seemed to be successful in the physical sciences) or a vital organism that required a quite different kind of analytical approach.[8]

Medicine lacked much else besides general theory. In the 1790's the French physician Pinel suggested the possibility of analyzing clinical data by tracing them back to their origins in the body, thus introducing

---

[6] *Ibid.,* pp. 417–419, letter of Peter Fayssoix. The British army physician who examined the ship after American protests reported it was "perfectly wholesome and had no appearance of infection or disorder."

[7] Tilton was made Surgeon General of the Army in the War of 1812, serving with great distinction. Tilton's account of Revolutionary hospitals, and of his own sickness with "camp fever," is a horrifying document; see Gordon, *Aesculapius,* pp. 305–307, for excerpts from it.

[8] For extended discussions of medical science in the period, see Richard Shyrock, *The Development of American Medicine* (Philadelphia, 1936), and Henry B. Shafer, *The American Medical Profession 1733–1850* (New York, 1936). A good briefer summary is that of John Krout and Dixon R. Fox, *The Completion of Independence* (New York, 1944), pp. 290–310.

the clinical method into medicine—but the method itself was long in developing. Physicians lacked reliable medical statistics, instruments, even means of measurement; the thermometer, for example, though perfected 250 years earlier, did not come into ordinary usage until the mid-nineteenth century. There existed no system of classification for disease; nosology was an undeveloped branch of medicine. Though physicians of Rush's time could identify 1,500 different diseases, no one seemed able to find any principle or classifications by which they might be arranged. Physicians floundered in confusion; Rush himself, for example, decided that since no order could possibly be imposed on such variety, therefore *all* diseases must be simply variations of a *single* disease.

Nor was this all. Physicians faced such strong public hostility toward experimentation on the human body—something which hindered neither the physical nor biological scientist—that even elementary research in physiology was difficult. Much of a physician's research had to be done in the course of his practice, without laboratory equipment, opportunity to experiment, or leisure to speculate. Surgery and medicine were, in most medical practices, more or less separate, for few medical men recognized the value of co-ordinating research in both fields. Furthermore, lacking adequate professional organizations or scientific journals, medical men found it hard to obtain information concerning progress in their field or to pass on knowledge they had acquired in the course of their own practices. As a result, most physicians tended to rely on tried and true methods and outmoded information. Medicine in the late eighteenth and early nineteenth centuries needed a theory from which to generalize, verified data, reliable methods of investigation and measurement, systems of classification and nomenclature, and an efficient means of disseminating what knowledge it did possess.[9]

Between 1776 and 1820, medical science stood at a standstill, lingering halfway between medievalism and modernity, unable to move ahead until scientists discovered a workable theory of illness and disease. Before medical men could find what cured disease, they had first to find out what diseases were and what caused them. With an acceptable theory of disease they could begin to evolve and test methods of cure; without it they could do little. In order to begin they were forced first

[9] For comprehensive contemporary criticism of the state of the medical profession, see Benjamin Rush, *Observations and Reasoning in Medicine* (1791), and *The Progress of Medicine* (1801).

to develop a science of pathology, a system of nomenclature and classi-fication, and eventually a science of bacteriology.

All of these were slow to come. The eighteenth century, true, pos-sessed certain broad classifications of disesase—"inflammation of the chest," for example, was recognized as possibly several different illnesses —but not until the nineteenth did these vague categories begin to be broken down into specific maladies. The germ theory was unknown and unimagined, although scientists had tantalizing glimpses, now and then, of possible connections between the animalculae visible under the micro-scope and man's infirmities. Pathology and bacteriology did not emerge as sciences for another half-century or more, and American scientists had little to do with their emergence.

The physician of Rush's time found an amazing variety of theories on which to model his practice. Some still believed with Galen and Aris-totle in "humors" or "spirits," teaching that illness was the result of impurities or imbalances in body fluids. Others, believing that disease resulted from tensions in the vascular or nervous systems, relied on nar-cotics or stimulants for cures, in addition to the bleedings and sweatings of the "humors" school. Both of these theories, carried to extremes in practice, killed thousands of patients. If bleeding seemed to help in one case, physicians were likely to employ it in all; if a particular drug seemed to help in another, it was likely to be used for all. If no method seemed to work in all cases, physicians were equally likely to discard it as useful in none.

The most popular medical theories of the time were the "Cullenian" and the "Brunonian," named respectively after Dr. William Cullen and Dr. John Brown, both Scottish physicians. Disease, in Cullen's view, originated in debilitation of a "nervous force" or "life force" which emanated from the brain. Brown considered disease an imbalance of "excitability" in the body; health, he believed, was a perfect balance between stimuli producing excitability and the body's ability to compen-sate for it. Some diseases, Cullen and Brown agreed, required treatments to reduce tension or excitability (opium, bleeding, wine, aromatics) or to increase it (fasting, cathartics, sweating). As late as 1819, one physi-cian said, the majority of physicians were either "bleeders" or "sweaters," and most of them were willing to experiment with fearsome remedies in an attempt to find specific prescriptions to influence "excitability" or to restore "life force." Rush himself once recommended the removal of three-quarters of a patient's entire blood supply, and other doctors used concoctions containing such items as saliva, bile, crushed woodlice, tobacco juice, and maple sugar.[10]

If he disapproved of the Cullenian or Brunonian systems, a physician had many other alternatives. The phlogistic theory, borrowed from chemistry, assumed that when a person inhaled air he absorbed "free heat" from the inhalation and exuded "phlogiston"; too much or too little exchange of phlogiston for heat produced disease. Another group of medical men claimed that oxygen was the vital life force, and that disease arose from too little oxygen or too much. The Galvanists, copying contemporary researches in electricity, believed disease arose from the interruption or imbalance of electrical charges in the body. Hydropathy, the cure of disease by different kinds of baths, was a popular European import after 1700, and "steam doctoring," a hydropathic variation, was still in use at the time of the Civil War. The "botanic" doctors relied on such things as herbs, beaver tails, and rabbits' feet, while the "Thomsonians," following a system patented by Samuel Thomson in 1813, combined herb remedies with steam baths. The "calomel school" of physicians, who believed that most illnesses could be cured by mercury, sometimes prescribed it by the pound, often killing patients by mercury poisoning. Homeopathy, introduced in the 1820's and still popular in 1900, cured disease by prescribing medicines which caused symptoms similar to those produced by the disease itself; given in minute doses, homeopathic medicines cured in inverse ratio to the amount administered. Naturally enough, physicians in Europe and America sometimes combined elements of several theories of cure in the hope that some, at least, were partially right.

Considering the paucity of medical knowledge and the utter confusion of medical theory and practice, the average American of the time enjoyed fairly good health, chiefly because of an excellent food supply and a dispersed population. Brissot de Warville, traveling in the United States in 1788, listed the most common illnesses as "consumption," "sore throat," pleurisy, fever and ague (malaria), and influenza. American teeth, he noted, were far better than European. Epidemics, which scourged Europe during these years, were less frequent in the United States, but still were a constant threat. Scurvy and intestinal infections were endemic in the American population as they were in the European.

[10] See the discussions of contemporary medical theory in Shryock, *Development of Medicine,* and Shafer, *Medical Profession.* A good summary is that of Courtney R. Hall, *Samuel Latham Mitchill* (New York, 1934).

Smallpox, diphtheria, and yellow fever swept American cities as they did those of England, France, and Spain.[11]

Against epidemics medicine possessed few defenses, though experience indicated the usefulness of certain controls. If periodic waves of disease were caused by contaminated air, food, or water, as some thought, public sanitation provided an answer; if they were caused by individual contagion, their prevention required cleanliness and isolation of the infected. The great yellow fever epidemic of 1793 in Philadelphia, the "autumnal epidemic" of 1812–13 in Savannah, and others like them forced attempts at sanitation, street cleaning, food inspection, and sewage disposal, all leading to better public health measures. Most of all, recurrent epidemics focused attention on the necessity of basic medical research and helped to make medical progress a matter of public as well as private concern. After 1790, permanent boards of public health began to appear in both Britain and the United States.[12]

Some American physicians, at least, were no less well trained than their European counterparts, for a number of Americans studied medicine abroad. Edinburgh, the finest medical school in the Old World, listed forty-one American students before 1775 and seventy-six between that year and 1800. Benjamin Rush, for example, studied under the great Cullen himself, and a number of other young Americans studied at Paris or Leiden. For those unable to study abroad the usual method of entrance to the profession meant apprenticeship to an established practitioner and what reading the student could do—a system that produced both skilled and utterly incompetent young physicians.

American medical education, slow to develop at first, expanded after the Revolution. Before 1776 only King's College in New York and the College of Philadelphia offered really legitimate instruction. At Philadelphia, Drs. William Shippen and John Morgan offered degrees in anatomy and surgery in 1776; Adam Kuhn (a student of Linnaeus') became professor of botany in 1768 and Rush professor of chemistry in 1769. King's College in New York gave medical instruction after 1767, though it granted no degrees until 1793. Scattered over the decades came medical education at William and Mary (1779), Harvard and Pennsylvania (1783), Queens (Rutgers) (1793), Dartmouth (1798),

[11] John Duffy, *Epidemics in Colonial America* (Baton Rouge, 1953).
[12] Richard H. Shryock, "The Health of the American People: A Historical Survey," *Proceedings of the American Philosophical Society*, XC (1946), 251–261.

Transylvania (1799, 1812), Cincinnati Medical College (1817), Maine (1820), and Jefferson (1824). By 1803, in fact, the editor of *The Medical Repository* noted proudly that American medical schools were doing so well that not one American was graduating that year at Edinburgh.[13]

The establishment of medical organization, standards, codes of ethics, and media of communication came next. Since there was little state control over medical practitioners, the title of doctor was easily assumed by almost anyone, a fact that did not inspire public confidence in doctors. Certified physicians, apothecaries, ministers, and irregular quacks all prescribed for illnesses, leading one harassed medical man to complain in the 1770's, "Any man at his pleasure sets up as a physician, apothecary, or chirurgeon; no candidates are either examined or licensed, or even sworn to fair practice." Patent medicines, such as Columbian Syrup, Parker's Vegetable Panacea, and Swaim's Panacea, sold widely— to the detriment of both patient and physician. After the Revolution, however, there were sincere efforts by the medical societies to evolve standards of professional qualification and ethics. Confidence and prestige came slowly, nevertheless, to the profession. In 1836 the *Boston Medical and Surgical Journal* listed sixteen different types of "doctors" still in common practice (including root, herb, magnetic, hydropathic, and floral, but excluding mesmerists), and as late as 1845 only a few states exerted much control over medical education or licensing.[14]

The organization of medical societies was primarily a post-Revolutionary movement. The New Jersey Medical Society (1766) was perhaps the earliest, with Massachusetts (1781), New Hampshire (1791), Connecticut (1792), and Delaware (1789) following after the war. After 1800 the number of local and state medical societies increased swiftly, and with them the number of American medical journals. Before the turn of the century, since American medical literature was to all practical purposes nonexistent, American physicians depended for the latest medical knowledge almost solely upon the Royal Academy *Transactions,* a few British journals, and foreign study. Although several American medical books appeared after the Revolution (among them Rush's monumental five-volume *Medical Observations,* 1788– 1812), most of them were simply American editions of older European texts. The *Papers* of the Massachusetts Medical Society, which began publication in 1790, marked a pioneer effort which other societies

[13] Shafer, *Medical Profession,* p. 162.
[14] Krout and Fox, *Completion of Independence,* p. 293.

quickly copied. The first major American medical journal, Samuel Mitchill's *American Medical Repository*, began in 1797; by 1810 there were six others, and by 1835 thirty-five in all. The *Journal of the Medical and Physical Sciences*, founded in 1820 and edited by the distinguished Nathaniel Chapman, became in 1828 the *American Journal of Medical Sciences*, which is still published. The publication of the *United States Pharmacopeia* in 1820 represented another landmark. By the time of the founding of the American Medical Society in 1846, medicine was well on the way toward professional status, with an increasing number of medical schools, a fair number of journals, and an elementary licensing system.

American medicine, despite its comparative isolation from European colleges and hospitals, nevertheless developed some highly competent men. Physicians of the caliber of Mitchill, Shippen, Morgan, or Cochran could hold their own with nearly any of their British or continental counterparts. Benjamin Rush, who trained at Edinburgh and Paris in the 1760's, returned to practice in Philadelphia in 1769 and also to accept the chair of chemistry at the College of Philadelphia, the first such professorship in the colonies. His *Syllabus for a Course of Lectures* (1770) was probably the first American chemistry text: his broad interests in social reform and politics diverted some of his energies from science, but in 1789 he accepted the post of professor of the theory and practice of medicine at the University of Pennsylvania and for the rest of his distinguished (and stormy) professional career was a powerful influence on the development of American medicine. Benjamin Smith Barton, Rush's successor at Pennsylvania, studied at Edinburgh and Göttingen, and interested himself in anthropology, botany, zoology, and chemistry, in addition to his distinguished medical work. Benjamin Waterhouse, who in 1783 was made professor in Harvard's newly established medical department, made great contributions to research in vaccination and was rewarded by world-wide honors. There were many other American medical men of stature, whatever the uncertain state of the science itself.[15]

---

[15] See the sketches of American medical scientists in the *Dictionary of American Biography;* Nathan Goodman, *Benjamin Rush: Physician and Citizen* (Philadelphia, 1934); and Shryock, *Development of Medicine.* Waterhouse's *Rise, Progress, and Present State of Medicine* (1792) is an especially important view of contemporary science; however, his book on the evils of tobacco and drink, *Cautions to Young Persons* . . . (1805) was by far the most popular of his works.

Though the period saw no epochal advances in medicine in the United States or in Europe, foundations were laid during these years for the great discoveries of the next generation of medical scientists. Developments in the basic sciences of chemistry, biology, and physiology stimulated medical research and were absorbed into it. The application of mathematical knowledge to medical statistics and the beginnings of accumulated records meant progress later; for example, Laplace's work on the calculus of probabilities, done in 1808, had direct bearing on medical research, and the statistics kept on the Philadelphia yellow fever epidemic assisted scientists immeasurably in determining which methods of treatment were useless.

The scientific methods of the Age of Enlightenment, if they did not prove to be completely workable in medicine, at least encouraged the rejection of much occult and superstitious medical lore. Furthermore, the intellectual atmosphere of the times, with its emphasis on careful observation and experimentation, did much to create a favorable climate for medical research. Theorizing was on the way out, scientific investigation on the way in. Thomas Cadwallader of Philadelphia pointed the way toward the future when he commented that in medical research "All hypotheses, unless they agree with the facts, are delusive and vain." Physicians, he advised, must confine themselves to "practical observations" before developing theories.

So long as men trusted reason and its efficacy in medical research as well as in physics or chemistry, they kept trying to find acceptable theories based on observable facts, preparing the way for the great breakthrough that came a generation later with researches in pathology, surgery, antisepsis, and anesthesia, and with the proposal of the germ theory of disease. And though it was slow, there was some progress in medical research in the United States after the Revolution. Men discovered much about hygiene, sanitation, and public health. They found out much about drugs (ergot, quinine, morphine, calomel, among others) and made steps toward the development of preventive medicine. They gave final approval, long held in abeyance, to the practice of inoculation. Medical education improved and expanded; the growth of medical societies established professional standards, raised morale, and afforded the means of professional co-operation.

Achievements in other sciences during the period 1776–1820 in America were not great, but still were significant.[16] The great strides made

[16] Sketches of prominent scientists of the period and estimates of their work

by the scientists of the seventeenth and early eighteenth centuries, particularly in the physical sciences, gave their heirs a solid scientific foundation on which to build. None of them matched the work of their fathers in mathematics, physics, and astronomy, but there was much for them to do in testing, disseminating, and applying its implications. Other sciences, lagging far behind, advanced slowly. Lacking general laws, classification systems, and most of all sound bases in theory, biologists, geologists, geneticists, and chemists had to evolve a rationale for further research and investigation. The work of Darwin, Lyell, Huxley, Spencer, and others was yet to come, and though there remained much to do in consolidating the discoveries of Newtonian physics, much more remained to be done in the biological and earth sciences. The face of America was still largely unknown, and a great deal of energy went into the tremendous task of simply finding out what animals and plants there were on the continent. The problem of simply cataloguing American nature was in itself a huge job, but a necessary preliminary to basic scientific research.

American scientists were most actively interested in agriculture during the post-Revolutionary period, since farming was the cornerstone of the American economy.[17] Shortly after the war attempts were made to introduce new crops into the country—hemp, ginseng, mangel-wurzel, silkworms, and others—some of which were successful. Agricultural research centered chiefly on the improvement of crop yields, control of disease and pests, crop rotation, fertilizers, and harvesting methods. Learned farmers such as Jefferson, Washington, and Henry Laurens, scientists such as Samuel Latham Mitchill, and experimental agriculturalists such as Samuel Deane, Elkanah Watson, and John Bordley encouraged agricultural research and the formation of agricultural societies.[18] The New Jersey Society for the Promotion of Agriculture,

---

may be found in Jaffe, *American Men of Science* (New York, 1944); David Starr Jordan (ed.), *Leading American Men of Science* (New York, 1910); Clarence J. Hylander, *American Scientists* (New York, 1935); and the *Dictionary of American Biography*.

[17] Good general accounts of early American agriculture are William H. Clark, *Farms and Farmers* (Boston, 1945); Lyman Carrier, *The Beginnings of Agriculture in America* (New York, 1923); and Chaps. II and III of Joseph Schafer, *The Social History of American Agriculture* (New York, 1936). Ulysses P. Hedrick, *History of Agriculture in New York* (Albany, 1933), and Stevenson W. Fletcher, *Pennsylvania Agriculture and Country Life, 1640–1840* (Harrisburg, 1950), are mines of information.

[18] See Everett Edwards, *Jefferson and Agriculture* (Washington, D.C., 1943).

Commerce, and Art (1781), the Philadelphia Society for Promoting Agriculture, and the South Carolina Society for Promoting and Improving Agriculture (both founded in 1785) were particularly active, while the major scientific societies themselves established agricultural sections and urged their members to publish papers in the field. British handbooks and guides were reprinted and widely sold; Deane's *New England Farmer* (1790) and Bordley's *Summary View . . . of Crops . . . in England and Maryland* (1784), Squibb's *Gardeners' Calendar* (1787) and McMahan's *Gardener's Calendar* (1806) were popular and informative compendia of research for practical use. The agricultural societies, however, were far more successful in gathering scientific material than in disseminating it; almanacs remained still the most effective medium for transmitting the results of research to the average farmer, though almanac makers were not always fully aware of the latest and most accurate information.[19]

In New York and in a few other states, agricultural societies established model farms, planned experiments, and sponsored agricultural fairs. Except for a fairly large amount of practical information gained from American experiments, the majority of basic agricultural research derived from Britain and France, though in the United States, where land was plentiful and relatively cheap, European agricultural methods were not especially effective. At the same time, however, Americans learned from Europe that farming was to be considered not as an art or as a vocation, but as a science, amenable to an experimental approach and related to the materials and methods of other sciences, particularly to botany, zoology, and chemistry.[20]

Astronomy, by the time of the Revolution, was perhaps the most advanced of American sciences.[21] Colonial scientists such as David Ritten-

---

Elkanah Watson of Pittsfield, Mass., did pioneer work in sheep, pig, and cattle breeding, and also in 1810 organized what soon became the agricultural county fair.

[19] The Pennsylvania Society for Improving the Breed of Cattle, for example, began breeding experiments in 1809 with both cattle and sheep. du Pont de Nemours smuggled merino rams from Spain, and merinos were imported wholesale after 1810. Washington did pioneer work in soil conservation, seed testing, and livestock breeding. See John W. Oliver, *A History of American Business and Technology* (New York, 1956).

[20] Carrier, *Beginnings of Agriculture*, Chaps. XIX, XX, and XXI, summarizes experimentation and research in agriculture, 1760–1840. See also Hindle, *Pursuit of Science*.

[21] See John C. Greene, "Some Aspects of American Astronomy, 1750–1815," *Isis*, XXXV (December, 1954), 339–359.

house and John Winthrop had already established a strong research tradition and had attained more than colonial repute.[22] The *Transactions* of the American Philosophical Society printed more papers in astronomy than in any other field, testifying to American interest in the subject, while American astronomers kept up a steady stream of correspondence with their European counterparts. However, no important astronomical discoveries were made by Americans during the period, nor did Americans publish any papers of major scientific value, although their publications and observations undoubtedly added useful details to research. Rittenhouse's Philadelphia observatory, built in the 1780's, remained for more than a decade the only one of its kind in the United States, despite efforts to build others. By far the most useful work in astronomy appeared in the almanacs, which served as the chief channel of dissemination for astronomical knowledge.

Physics, despite the pioneering work of Franklin and Rittenhouse, was not one of the more advanced sciences in America. In both Europe and the United States men were busy pursuing those lines of research already sketched out by the great scientists of the preceding century, such as Descartes, Newton, Leibniz, Kepler, and Pascal, all of whom had made their major contributions to physical science before 1750.[23]

---

[22] Rittenhouse in 1769 built what is considered to be the first American-constructed telescope. His famous orrery, completed in 1770, he sold to Princeton. His work in astronomy included observations of the solar and lunar eclipses, and the transit of Mercury and Uranus. Rittenhouse did astronomical calculations for various almanacs for years; surveyed state boundaries, canals, harbors, and rivers; made spectacles for George Washington; helped Franklin build a telescope; and assisted Jefferson in establishing standards of weights and measures. He was also the first director of the United States mint. He died in 1796. See Jaffe, *Men of Science*, pp. 45–48, for a summary of his career. Edward Ford, *David Rittenhouse* (Philadelphia, 1936), is the standard biography.

[23] Mention should be made, however, of the eccentric physicist Benjamin Thompson, the New Englander who became Count Rumford (after Rumford, the original name of Concord, New Hampshire) of the Holy Roman Empire. Rumford, trained in medicine, joined the Loyalists in the Revolution and eventually went to Bavaria, where he became internationally famous for his experiments in heat, friction, and metallurgy, member of both the Royal Society of London and the American Academy of Arts and Sciences, and a well-known social reformer. Rumford was not too busy, however, to improve drip coffee pots, carriage wheels, fireplaces, lamps, and cooking utensils in his long and busy career. He also married Lavoisier's widow. See Jaffe, *Men of Science;* Jordan, *Leading Men of Science;* and Hylander, *American Scientists,* for sketches; J. A. Thompson, *Count Rumford of Massachusetts* (Boston, 1935); and Sanborn Brown, "Count Rumford: International Informer," *New England Quarterly,* XXI (1948), 34–49.

Mathematics as a separate scientific discipline was not well developed in the United States. It was chiefly of interest as a tool for physicists or astronomers, or useful for practical studies such as surveying, navigating, or engineering.

In the person of Nathaniel Bowditch, however, the self-taught New England mathematical genius, the United States had a first-class practical mathematician. Bowditch's experiences as a seaman led him to correct hundreds of errors in the most widely used navigational guides, and eventually to write his own book, *The New American Practical Navigator* (1801–2). Bowditch's book soon became standard for practically all navigation in the western world; in various forms it went through at least fifty-six known editions and uncounted others. Bowditch also developed new and more accurate actuarial tables for insurance companies (strongly influencing the development of the insurance business), and published twenty-three important papers on astronomy and meteorology.[24] Except for Bowditch, the United States lagged in mathematical study. The best mathematical instruction in the United States was that at West Point, where after 1807 Ferdinand Hassler and Claude Crozet, both French, taught mathematics to prospective Army engineers.[25]

Chemistry, both in America and in Europe, lagged behind physics, mathematics, or astronomy. The chief problem of chemists was to organize the scattered knowledge that had accrued since the days of Egyptian antiquity, and to build upon the recent work of great chemical researchers such as Black, Priestley, Cavendish, Lavoisier, and Berthollet. Chemical nomenclature itself was confused and loaded with jargon, with elements and compounds enjoying such names as "mercury of life," "butter of antimony," "salt of many virtues," and "liver of sulphur."[26] Like medical men, chemists were hampered by their lack of

[24] See the sketch of Bowditch in the *Dictionary of American Biography*. Bowditch's importance in American science has been peculiarly neglected.

[25] The influence of French mathematics was especially strong. See L. G. Simons, "The Influence of French Mathematicians at the end of the XVIIIth Century . . . in American Colleges," *Isis*, XV (1931), 104–124; David E. Smith and Jekuthiel Ginsburg, *A History of Mathematics in the United States before 1900* (Chicago, 1934); L. Page, "A Century's Progress in Physics," in E. S. Dana, Charles Schuchert, and others, *A Century of Science in America* (New Haven, 1918)

[26] Edgar F. Smith, *Chemistry in America* (New York, 1914); Samuel Miller, *Retrospect of the Eighteenth Century* (1803), I, 35 ff.; Courtney Hall, *Samuel Latham Mitchill*, pp. 3, 19, 20 ff. See also Edgar F. Smith, *Priestley in America 1794–1804* (Philadelphia, 1920).

workable basic theories, and much of their energy was dissipated in arguments over conflicting hypotheses. The most popular contemporary chemical theory was the "phlogiston" theory, developed in Germany and imported to America from French and British sources. According to this hypothesis, combustible substances contained an element called phlogiston, which escaped on the application of high temperatures. The more phlogiston the material contained, the more phlogiston it lost when burned or heated—coal and wood, for example, were assumed to be nearly pure phlogiston. Though no chemist ever succeeded in isolating phlogiston, its existence explained a good many chemical reactions otherwise inexplicable. And though some chemists pointed out that the products of combustion, carefully weighed, proved to be heavier than the original substance, the majority of chemists (including Joseph Priestley, the discoverer of oxygen) clung to the phlogiston theory for want of a better.

The French chemist Lavoisier, in his *Treatise on Elementary Chemistry* (1789), exploded phlogiston. The real basis of combustion, he claimed, was oxygen. Combustion itself was oxidation; a burning substance did not lose phlogiston, but instead gained oxygen.[27] After 1790 the phlogiston-oxygen battle raged hotly in America, involving such scientists as Robert Hare, Samuel Mitchill, Benjamin Rush, James Woodhouse, Benjamin Silliman of Yale (who was trained under Sir Humphry Davy), and John McLean of Princeton.[28] Samuel Latham Mitchill, professor of chemistry at Columbia, delivered in 1792 the first series of lectures in America on Lavoisier's theories, and his journal,

[27] Chap. I, "Priestley, Lavoisier, and the Chemical Revolution," in D. B. Hammond, *Stories of Scientific Discoveries* (Cambridge, Eng., 1933).

[28] Silliman, who at twenty-three became professor of chemistry and natural history at Yale, was a great influence in scientific education from 1802 to 1853. He was a popular lecturer, who drew audiences of thousands on lecture tours. He was also first president of the Association of American Geologists (1840). English-born Thomas Cooper, who came to the United States in 1794 to teach chemistry at Carlisle College (now Dickinson), Pennsylvania, and South Carolina College (where he became president), was another influential scientific educator. Robert Hare, who taught at William and Mary and Pennsylvania, developed an oxygen blowpipe for high-temperature laboratory work and wrote nearly two hundred papers for the journals. Scots-born John McLean came to the College of New Jersey in 1795 as professor of chemistry, later served also as professor of mathematics and natural philosophy, and in 1812 moved to William and Mary. See Jaffe, *Men of Science,* pp. 270–275, and sketches in Jordan, *Leading Men of Science;* Hylander, *American Scientists;* and the *D.A.B.*

The Medical Repository, became the chief forum of the debate.[29] Rush's Chemical Society of Philadelphia argued the issue, and James Woodhouse's book, *The Young Chemist's Pocket Companion* (1797), was influential in popularizing the new doctrine.[30]

The victory of oxygen overturned the entire prevailing concept of chemical analysis and forced a complete revision of the system of chemical nomenclature. What phlogistonists had assumed to be elements were discovered to be compounds; what they considered to be compounds were found to be elements. For years chemists had considered sulfur as a compound of sulfuric acid and phlogiston; yet according to Lavoisier, sulfur was the element and sulfuric acid the compound. Meanwhile, in the process of debating phlogiston, chemists were forced to do a great deal of basic research in the nature of combustion and gases, to develop more accurate apparatus for measurement, and most of all to relate the results of research, correct or incorrect, to chemical knowledge in general. Lavoisier's theory, together with Dalton's theory of atomic weights (propounded in 1808), initiated a thorough revision of chemical science, with the result that the work of the seventeenth- and eighteenth-century chemists, long fitted within an incorrect set of hypotheses, took on new and different meanings. By 1820 modern chemistry had begun in Europe and America.[31]

Biological and earth scientists in Europe and America were still in the stage of describing, gathering, and classifying materials. Motivation for basic research in these sciences in the United States was perhaps stronger than in Europe (though the important basic work was done in Europe), for the entire country was open to botanists, biologists, zoologists, geographers, and geologists in all its glittering newness and astounding multiplicity. Basic work in these sciences lagged far behind that of Europe, and American scientists realized it. "The botany of America," Jefferson told President Willard of Harvard, "is far from exhausted, its mineralogy is untouched, and its natural history or zoology totally mistaken."

[29] Robert Siegfried, "An Attempt . . . to Resolve the Differences Between the Oxygen and Phlogiston Theories," *Isis,* XXXVI (Dec., 1955), 327–337.

[30] Woodhouse's book was in effect the first students' laboratory manual. Woodhouse, a student of Rush's, taught at the University of Pennsylvania, where he did pioneer work in chemical analysis and isolated potassium. Jaffe, *Men of Science,* pp. 74–78.

[31] The first convention of chemists, held in New York City in 1831, attracted nearly five hundred delegates. Oliver, *Business and Technology,* p. 325.

Botanists of the postwar period had first of all the wearisome task of observing and classifying the flora of the continent, a matter not only of primary importance for fundamental research but of practical value for agriculture and medicine.[32] The French government sent André Michaux to America on a collecting expedition in 1787–89 (as Peter Kalm, the Swede, had come before him), and German and Italian naturalists came for the same purpose. Americans, who were particularly interested in the importance of new agricultural products, exchanged seeds, plants, and information with European botanists and made numerous experiments of their own. Cadwallader Colden of New York and John Bartram of Pennsylvania, both of whom died before the end of the Revolution, left a body of first-quality botanical knowledge on which the next generation built.[33] Alexander Garden (after whom the gardenia was named) was a friend of Linnaeus himself, and his departure from America as a Loyalist sympathizer was a loss to American science.

The most significant botanical work done in the United States was that of collecting and classifying. Humphrey Marshall's catalogue of American trees (1785), William Young's plant lists (1783), and Thomas Waller's catalogue of South Carolina flora (1788) were pioneer American botanical efforts, while Manasseh Cutler's botanical study of New England (1793) was the first complete regional study.[34] William Bartram, Jr., continued the family botanical tradition; Benjamin Smith Barton (Rittenhouse's nephew) did botanical work of excellent quality, culminating in his *Collections for an Essay Towards a Materia Medica* (1798).[35] The Reverend Henry Muhlenberg, a Lutheran minister, com-

[32] For information on the history of early American botany, see Andrew P. Rogers, *John Torrey: A Story of North American Botany* (Princeton, 1942); Ernest Earnest, *John and William Bartram* (Boston, 1940); Jaffe, *Men of Science;* S. W. Geiser, *Naturalists of the Frontier* (Dallas, 1937); and Henry C. Tracy, *American Naturists* (New York, 1930). A good brief treatment is G. L. Gondale, "The Development of Botany," in E. S. Dana, Charles Schuchert, and others, *A Century of Science in America* (New Haven, 1918).

[33] Colden, at his farm, Coldenham, near Newburgh on the Hudson, had a botanical garden as early as 1739. His daughter Jane was also a highly competent botanist.

[34] Other important works were Frederick Pursch, *Flora Americae* (1814); and Stephen Elliott, *Sketch of the Botany of South Carolina and Georgia* (1814).

[35] Barton, a Pennsylvania graduate who studied in Europe and Scotland, became professor of natural history, botany, and materia medica at the University of Pennsylvania. His *Elements of Botany* (1803) was the first important

piled a catalogue of nearly 1,400 species of plants in Lancaster County, Pennsylvania, alone. Benjamin Waterhouse, who was professor of natural history at Harvard, and the ubiquitous Dr. Mitchill at Columbia, both introduced botany into the college curriculum before 1800, while Mitchill did a large share of the botanical work for the first *U.S. Pharmacopeia*.

American botanists in general followed the classification arrangement developed by the Swedish scholar Linnaeus, whose system had virtually displaced that of the Englishman John Ray and which was contesting for recognition with the French system of de Jussieu. By the end of the century, botany had developed in the United States into an autonomous branch of natural history, dealing, as Waterhouse defined it, with "the anatomy, physiology, and economy of vegetables." When Barton published his *Elements of Botany* in 1803, standard systems of nomenclature and classification were nearly complete, formal college instruction in botany was expanding, scientific societies were publishing numerous botanical papers, and programs of botanical research by qualified scholars were under way.[36]

Zoology, until the opening decades of the nineteenth century, existed less as a specific science than as an element of a group of studies loosely classified under the name of "natural history." Systems of zoological classification and nomenclature were still somewhat fluid, with at least three in current use. The Linnaean system (applied in zoology as well as in botany) described animals by a generic name with the addition of a specific name; Cuvier's system grouped all animals in four classifi-

---

American botanical handbook. William Bartram's *Travels* (1791), an excellent account of his scientific travels through the southeastern states, had a greater influence on British and French poets; since Bartram was strongly affected by the Rousseauistic "noble savage" tradition, his anecdotes of the frontier gave his readers a curious picture of American life. Bartram has one of his backwoods settlers remark, as he lies beneath an oak tree smoking a pipe, "Welcome, stranger. I am indulging in the rational dictates of nature, taking a little rest, having just come in from the chace and fishing." Wordsworth, Southey, Coleridge, Campbell, Chateaubriand, and others drew much of their information about American nature from Bartram.

[36] The chief early botanical societies were the Charleston Botanical Society (1805), the Linnaean Society of Philadelphia (1814), the Washington Botanical Society (1817), the New York Horticultural Society (1818), and the Pennsylvania Horticultural Society (1822). There were botanical gardens at Flushing and Charleston, the American Philosophical Society gardens in Philadelphia, and the New York Elgin Botanic Gardens, all founded before 1810. Humphrey Marshall's at Marshalltown, Pennsylvania, was established in 1773.

cations (vertebrate, articulated, radiated, and branched); Buffon and Lamarck classified them in a hierarchy ranging from lower to higher forms. All of these systems were used by American scientists, with Cuvier's perhaps the most widely accepted.[37]

Like the botanists, American zoologists were concerned chiefly with naming, classifying, and describing the bewildering variety of native fauna. Perhaps the most distinguished American zoological contribution of the period was that of Alexander Wilson, a Scots weaver, born in 1766, who came to America at twenty-eight. Acquaintance with William Bartram, his neighbor, interested him in science, particularly in ornithology. In 1804 he began collecting and drawing bird specimens, proposing to make drawings and observations of all the birds of eastern North America. Volume I of his *American Ornithology* appeared in 1809, and before the appearance of the eighth volume, just before his death in 1813, he had traveled thousands of miles through the eastern states, down the Mississippi, and to the edge of the Southwest. John James Audubon, his successor, did perhaps better ornithological work, but Wilson's pioneering opened the way for many other American zoologists.[38] Mitchill, Silliman, Barton, and others were deeply interested in zoology, but the science itself did not come of age until the appearance in the next generation of such specialized scientists as Thomas Say, Thomas Nuttall, John James Audubon, Constantine Rafinesque, Robert Harlan, and William Cooper—and, of course, with the development of theories of evolution and natural selection by Charles Darwin, Alfred Wallace, and those who followed them.[39]

Geology was almost wholly a nineteenth-century science. Not until Werner's system of classification appeared in 1780 did it possess even an orderly nomenclature. Like the chemists and zoologists, geologists of the late eighteenth century and the early nineteenth could not agree on

[37] W. R. Coe, "A Century of Zoology in America," in Dana, Schuchert, and others, *Century of Science.*

[38] Hylander, *American Scientists,* and Jordan, *Leading Men of Science.* Though his poetry occasionally limps, Wilson's love of the American land bursts out in great sincerity in his epic poem, *The Foresters, A Description of a Pedestrian Tour to the Fall of Niagara of 1804,* a charming travel and nature poem. For a good estimate of Wilson, see Hans Huth, *Nature and the Americans: Three Centuries of Changing Attitudes* (Berkeley, 1957), Chap. II.

[39] Hall, *Samuel Latham Mitchill,* Chap. VII, and Jaffe, *Men of Science.* See also A. S. Packard, "A Century's Progress in American Zoology," *American Naturalist,* X (1876), 591–599, and Charles Schuchert, "A Century of Zoology," in Dana, Schuchert, and others, *Century of Science.*

a basic theory of causation. Scientists in America and Europe were divided into two schools of thought concerning the origins of the earth's structure; they agreed that the source lay in some catastrophic event but disagreed over the nature of the catastrophe. Followers of Karl Werner, usually called Neptunists, held that the earth's composition was the result of "aqueous deposition"; that is, that the earth had once been covered by water and that, by pressure, precipitation, and crystallization, the suspended minerals formed rocks, soil, and earth formations. The Vulcanists, followers of James Hutton of Scotland, held that the earth's surface was the result of heat, volcanic action, and condensation of gaseous combinations into water and minerals.[40]

The Huttonian theory, of course, had theological implications (related to the Biblical account of the Flood and the Creation) that disturbed scientists and laymen alike and muddied the course of geological research for another half-century. Thomas Cooper's remark that neither the Old nor the New Testament were "infallible guides in mineralogy and geology" stirred up a controversy that eventually cost him his academic position.[41] Beyond their theological implications, however, American scientists were about equally divided in allegiance to the two schools of thought, though few Americans could be called geologists *per se*. Until William Maclure's book, *Observations on the Geology of the United States* (1809), there were few publications in the field in the United States, and those chiefly American editions of European texts such as Phillips' *Mineralogy* and Cuvier's *Theory of the Earth*.

Maclure's book, a careful geological study of the eastern United States, marked the beginnings of an American geological science. A year later Archibald Bruce founded the *American Mineralogical Journal,* the first publication devoted to geology, followed by Silliman's *American Journal of Science,* which became the most important organ of geological research in the United States. In 1819 a group at Yale, at Silliman's urging, formed the American Geological Society, a bona fide scientific organization concerned solely with that science. Instruction and research in geology, however, remained for some years subordinate to other sciences. Silliman taught mineralogy at Yale in 1802, but he was primarily

[40] G. P. Merrill, *The First Hundred Years of American Geology* (New Haven, 1924).

[41] For a discussion of the theological argument over geological theory, see Charles C. Gillispie, *Genesis and Geology* (New York, 1951), Chaps. I–IV inclusive.

a chemist and his entire collection of specimens was less than a bushel. Mitchill, who did pioneer work on the geology of New York State from 1798 to 1801, was really a chemist and physician. Nevertheless, there were many American scientists who enthusiastically collected and classi-fied specimens (often wrongly), wrote papers, and speculated on the earth's composition and origin—providing masses of evidence, at least, for later scientists of higher professional caliber. Amos Eaton of Yale, for example, made one of the first geological surveys (of Albany and Rensselaer counties) at the request of the New York State Agricultural Society. With the appearance in England of the work of William Smith in 1815 and of Lyell's monumental *Principles of Geology* (1830, 1833), geology became a science in its own right.[42]

Americans were intensely interested in geography, for they had an entire continent to map and explore. Jedidiah Morse's *American Ge-ography* (1789) included a respectable amount of zoological and bo-tanical information, and the multitude of state histories that appeared after the Revolution had a strong geographical flavor, among them Jer-emy Belknap's study of New Hampshire (1784–92) and Hutchins' of Louisiana and West Florida (1784).[43] Geography, however, was of util-itarian rather than purely scientific interest to Americans because of the importance of land settlement. The greatest impetus to geographical researches came from the federal government. The admission of Ken-tucky, Tennessee, and Ohio to the Union, and especially the purchase of Louisiana, opened great new expanses of land for natural scientists to survey, examine, and investigate. Lewis and Clark's expedition to Oregon (1804), Sibley's to the Red River (1803), Pike's and Long's to the Rockies (1805, 1819, 1923), and Schoolcraft's to the upper Great Lakes (1831) were only a few of the government-sponsored expedi-tions that not only advanced geographical science but contributed botanical, zoological, meteorological, ethnological, and agricultural in-

[42] Eaton also did surveying for the Erie Canal route, helped plan Rensselaer Institute (1825), and delivered more than 6,000 popular lectures on science.

[43] Belknap (1744–98) was a Massachusetts minister whose interest in history led him and a group of like-minded scholars to form an "Antiquarian Society" in 1790 which three years later became the Massachusetts Historical Society. Jedidiah Morse (1761–1826), another Massachusetts clergyman, became the first prominent American geographer. Dissatisfied as a young schoolmaster with geography texts, Morse prepared *Geography Made Easy* (1795), *The American Gazetteer* (1797), and *The New Gazetteer* (1802). His books dominated Amer-ican geography for forty years. See W. B. Sprague, *The Life of Jedidiah Morse* (Boston, 1874).

formation of great value. Major Long's group, for example, included Thomas Say and Edwin James (both eminent botanists), a geologist, a painter, a taxidermist, and a naturalist.

Meriwether Lewis, whose name and that of William Clark are inextricably attached to the greatest of these scientific expeditions, was a Virginia-born neighbor of Thomas Jefferson's. Well-educated in science, languages, and mathematics, Lewis served in the Indian wars of the 1790's and was invited by Jefferson to become his private secretary after Jefferson's election in 1801. Lewis spent two years at the White House, and when Jefferson squeezed $2,500 from a reluctant Congress for an expedition to the Pacific, Lewis accepted the post of joint leader, with William Clark of Kentucky. Lewis studied astronomy, botany, mineralogy, cartography, zoology, and "Indian history" for a year before departure; Jefferson himself, a scientist of real attainment, spent weeks with Lewis and Clark preparing them for the expedition. In 1804 the group left St. Louis to follow the Missouri to its source. The journey was a carefully planned scientific expedition, charged with reporting on flora and fauna, minerals, weather, rainfall and rivers, fossils, making maps, observing Indian society, and collecting scientific specimens. After reaching the headwaters of the Missouri, the group followed the Columbia to the Pacific, returning in 1806 after one of the most important scientific surveys in American history.[44]

The years 1776–1820 marked a period of transition from old to new in the development of scientific thinking in Europe and America. Advances in the various fields of science during the eighteenth century were uneven and unco-ordinated, but by the early decades of the nineteenth century it is safe to say that in most areas of scientific knowledge the foundations of modern science had been established. In certain sciences, notably chemistry, biology, botany, and zoology, old theories had been virtually demolished and new ones substituted. In better-developed disciplines such as physics, astronomy, and mathematics, scientists were pursuing lines of inquiry already indicated by their predecessors, testing and extending accepted theories of research. The Reverend Samuel Miller, surveying the immediate past from the vantage point of 1802, concluded that by 1800 science had attained maturity. The first thirty-

[44] John Bakeless, *Lewis and Clark: Partners in Discovery* (New York, 1947), is a readable account. For the reports themselves, see Reuben G. Thwaites, *The Original Journals of the Lewis and Clark Expeditions* (New York, 1904–5).

five years of the century, he explained, were dominated by Newtonian physics; the mid-century decades by the natural history of Buffon and Linnaeus; and the period 1770–1800 (the age of chemistry) by Lavoisier, Priestley, and Cavendish. In science, he concluded, "such an immense variety and amount of *facts* and experiments have been laid before the public, so eminently to distinguish the eighteenth from all preceding centuries." However, as Miller admitted, American science still depended on Europe for its basic research, although Americans displayed in the post-Revolutionary years an increasing sense of self-reliance. The emergence of a distinctly native scientific tradition lay in the future.

At the time Miller wrote there had been several important changes in science itself, and in the attitude of men toward it, that he could not have been expected to understand. First of all, science in Europe and America was rapidly becoming a profession, no longer a hobby of talented amateurs but a field of inquiry and research requiring a great deal more than a man's leisure time and interest. The day of the "natural philosopher" who took all knowledge as his province had closed; scientists found so much to observe and assimilate that the pressure of information streaming in upon them forced them to specialize. Harvard's John Winthrop, who ranged through astronomy, geology, electricity, chemistry, and mathematics with ease, would have found it difficult in 1800 merely to classify the data pouring in from any one of these fields. Franklin, Jefferson, Silliman, Rush, Barton, Rittenhouse, and others like them represented an older scientific tradition; by the time of Jackson their kind of science was obsolete. Samuel Latham Mitchill, who wrote papers in chemistry, mathematics, geology, medicine, and botany, was possibly the last of the old jack-of-all-trades breed. Nineteenth-century science demanded specialists—men such as Agassiz, Asa Gray, Othniel Marsh, Joseph Henry, Matthew Maury, or James Dwight Dana—for there was too much to know about too many things for any one man to encompass it. Trends in science pointed inevitably toward ever-narrower research, toward paleontology, ethnology, genetics, electrical physics, inorganic and organic chemistry, entomology, ornithology, crystallography, and so on.

The drift toward scientific specialization reflected fundamental changes in the attitude of men toward science itself. The eighteenth century regarded science as an inclusive, unified body of knowledge through which the human mind could rove at will. But after 1770 the scientist found so much variety in the world, and such a wealth of detailed information, that the concept of a universe of unified natural law began to fly apart. Though Newton recognized variety as well as unity as a universal fact, the eighteenth century found mechanistic unity so convenient an explanation of natural phenomena that it neglected to treat diversity and change as equally important scientific principles.

The flood of data that inundated the later years of the eighteenth century and those of the early nineteenth put great strain on the static, mechanistic scheme of Newton. Must everything conform to the rigid Newtonian pattern? Must everything fit into the chain of being? Evidence piled up so alarmingly, especially in the biological sciences, that the neat categories of eighteenth-century science refused to hold them all. The world was a surprisingly complex place, it seemed, not to be reduced to an easily ordered, unified pattern of mechanistic relationships among things. Scientific discovery and speculation produced conflicts, paradoxes, and unresolved questions, while rationalization of them all became more and more difficult. If one assumed with the Enlightenment that the universe was inflexibly and absolutely rational, the frantic attempt of scientists to make everything fit into the universal pattern became in itself a kind of irrationality.

The fact was that science was losing its central concept of the mechanistic unity of the universe, and that there was evolving in its place a new central concept of organic development. The idea of evolutionary change, at least as old as the Greeks, was not unfamiliar to the times; Kant, Saint-Hilaire, Buffon, Cuvier, Lamarck, Coleridge, Erasmus Darwin, and other philosophers and scientists all expressed intimations of the concept in various ways. The proliferation of scientific information that strained the Newtonian mechanistic scheme forced the thinkers of the period to reactivate this developmental, organic concept of nature as a more satisfactory method of classifying and explaining phenomena. Possibly nature was not fixed, but fluid; as Holbach had remarked as early as 1770, perhaps "Nature contains no constant forms." Perhaps everything in the universe had a history, a pattern of change of its own. The relationships between things and ideas were possibly not mechanical, but developmental; the observed fact had organic relations with the observer.

Charles Willson Peale, in arranging his Philadelphia Museum,[45]

[45] Peale, who painted numerous portraits of Revolutionary officers, opened a gallery for display of these and other paintings after the war. His gallery

could organize his exhibits in categories which illustrated the relationships of the Great Chain of Being. Rittenhouse, in his observatory, could enjoy his astronomical observations of eternal, permanent natural law in the heavens. But Ralph Waldo Emerson, visiting a botanical garden in 1833, found the universe "a more amazing puzzle than ever," seeing in it not clear, fixed natural law, but "law alive," "conscious law," "a bewildering series of animated forms." Where Freneau saw nature "fix'd on general laws," moving "on one fix'd point," Emerson perceived it as flux and development, a place where created matter "mounts through all the spires of form," where all forms existed not as objective realities in themselves, but as subjective "expressions of some property inherent in man the observer." The new science had arrived.

---

shortly became a repository for oddments and natural curiosities and finally a museum, which Peale opened to the public. The American Philosophical Society gave him use of its hall for his collection, and in 1802 the Pennsylvania Assembly gave him free use of Independence Hall.

PART TWO

*The Growth of an American
Point of View*

CHAPTER 5

The Structure of a New Society

E UROPEANS who visited the United States after the close of the
Revolution agreed that the society emerging from it was new, na-
tive, and unique. Most foreign observers, while willing to concede that
American life was different, found it difficult to understand or to ex-
plain its differences. Since it was new and strange, they searched for
(and were usually able to find) evidence that it could not succeed. Most
British and Europeans were unable to grasp the fact that the United
States was not Europe, and did not ever intend to be.

Joel Barlow thought that there were probably not more than five
men in all of Europe who really understood the nature of American
society. Franklin, Jay, and Jefferson, all of whom had broad experience
with Europeans, all remarked on the widespread ignorance and misunderstanding of the United States. "The ordinary traveller" in America,
Henry Adams later wrote, "was apt to be a little more reflective than a
bee or an ant."[1] The reports about American society carried to Britain
and Europe in the first half of the nineteenth century were sometimes
so superficial and biased as to be useless in conveying any accurate conception of American life. Captain Marryat quite frankly stated that the
aim of his *Diary In America* (1839) was "to do injury to democracy,"
while Mrs. Trollope's *Domestic Manners of the Americans* (1832)
showed the English the dangers of "the wild scheme of placing all the
power in the hands of the people."

Precariously perched on the water's edge, faced by forest and savages

[1] Herbert Agar (ed.), Henry Adams, *The Formative Years: A History of the
United States during the Administrations of Jefferson and Madison* (2 vols.,
London, 1948), I, 85.

to the west, American society at the close of the Revolution possessed little culture of its own and only a doubtful unity. As Europeans were fond of pointing out, the United States—in the world of Goethe, Mozart, Goya, Kant, Blackstone, Cuvier, Thorvaldsen, and so on—had a little commerce, a little agriculture, a lot of undeveloped land, and not much else. Its government, founded on questionable and untested principles (however glowingly they were stated), stood apparently little chance for survival. Everything upon which European society had been taught to depend for safety and stability—church, army, aristocracy, monarchy—America had jettisoned in favor of a dubious trust in the average human being.[2]

The majority of American leaders believed none of these things. They possessed a deep confidence in the future of American society. Ten years before Lexington and Concord, John Adams, who was no dreaming visionary, wrote that he considered the settlement of the American colonies "as the opening of a grand scene and design in Providence for the illumination of the ignorant and the emancipation of the slavish part of mankind all over the earth." Franklin called the Revolution "a glorious task assigned to us by Providence"; Jefferson emphasized again and again that "it is impossible not to be sensible that we are acting for all mankind." "We feel," he wrote of himself and other leaders of the Revolution, "that we are acting under obligations not confined to the limits of our own society."[3] These men, and others like them, phrased what many other Americans felt but less clearly expressed—that the United States was "a bold, sublime experiment" to determine whether men could live together in a society founded on liberty, equality, and justice. "The human race puts this great question to the United States of America," Mirabeau wrote from France, "and if by chance they should answer badly, it would be necessary to ask it again of Reason."[4]

Fortunately for the United States, it could begin to build its new society with two distinct advantages. First, as Tocqueville pointed out, it was to the American's great benefit that he "arrived at a state of de-

---

[2] See Henry Adams' discussion, *ibid.*, I, 83–86, of European misconceptions of America, its society, and its aims.

[3] Hans Kohn, *The Idea of Nationalism* (New York, 1944), p. 273; Albert H. Smyth (ed.), *The Writings of Benjamin Franklin* (10 vols., New York, 1905–7), VII, 56; Merrill Jensen, *The New Nation* (New York, 1950), p. 88; Jefferson to Joseph Meskey, June 19, 1802.

[4] Jensen, *New Nation*, pp. 88–92, 125–127; Louis Hartz, *The Liberal Tradition in America* (New York, 1955), pp. 35–67, "The Perspectives of 1776."

mocracy without having to endure a democratic revolution, and that he is born free without having to become so." The Revolution did not have to destroy a feudal society in order to evolve a new one, for Americans already possessed a free, liberal tradition. The American Revolutionary leader and the post-Revolutionary statesman acted and thought within an *American*, non-feudal framework. No other western nation began its modern history with quite such an advantage.

Second, American society after the Revolution was—compared to that of Europe and England—much more open, fluid, and forceful. Power and position were more available to the majority of men in the United States in 1790 than anywhere else in the world. The average man (even the most ignorant and penniless) was consumed by the great challenge of American life; as Henry Adams later pointed out, each man knew that "every stroke of the axe and the hoe made him a capitalist, and made gentlemen of his children." In Europe, conservatism, authority, and entrenched power had the whole machinery of church and state behind them; in the new American society, men and institutions competed for mastery on more equal terms.

The American Revolution did not have to overthrow an established church which, in Europe, continued for two more generations to possess the power to destroy revolutionary movements. America had no entrenched nobility, no *ancien régime*. There were, of course, colonial aristocrats, but they were by no means a permanent feudal, titled group. By the time of the Revolution American society had already developed what Crèvecoeur aptly called "a pleasing uniformity of decent competence."[5]

To those engaged in constructing the new society the most immediate problems were political. The greater part of American thought after the Revolution was naturally concerned with trying to construct a government that would be workable, durable, and in harmony with those principles for which the Revolution had been fought. The problem was, William Miller wrote, to "make liberty . . . a *practical principle*, and to *prove* it."[6] Building such a political society posed a hard question— were men so possessed of wisdom that a majority of them could be trusted to govern society as a whole? Few of the Founding Fathers could

[5] Louis Hartz, "American Political Thought and the American Revolution," *American Political Science Review*, XLVI (June, 1952), 321–342, has an interesting discussion.

[6] Irving Mark and Eugene Schwab, *The Faith of Our Fathers* (New York, 1952), p. 49.

answer with certainty. On the one hand they had just won a war fought for principles of liberty and justice; on the other, they were realistic men of political experience. They wanted to establish a free society, but they hoped also to establish an enduring one.

Most of the men who met in Philadelphia in 1787 to evolve a constitution for that society had no reason to trust human nature in the mass. Elbridge Gerry spoke of democracy as "the worst of political evils." Henry Knox thought that one purpose of the meeting was "to clip the wings of a mad democracy" that had developed under the Articles of Confederation. Edmund Randolph feared "the democratic parts of our [state] constitutions." "Every page of history," John Adams wrote, showed that the unchecked masses were "as unjust, tyrannical, brutal, barbarous, and cruel as any king or senate possessed of uncontrollable power." "There is no maxim which is more liable to be misapplied," Madison agreed, "than the current one that the interest of the majority is the political standard of right and wrong." Hamilton was convinced that "the people are turbulent and changing; they seldom judge or determine right." Gloomy Fisher Ames defined democracy as "government by the passions of the multitude" and thought it would always be "the dismal passport to a more dismal hereafter." Since men were creatures of passion, credulity, and error, the novelist Hugh Henry Brackenridge wrote, they must be governed not by freedom but by fear, which is "the foundation of government of man, as much as of a horse, or ass."[7]

Nevertheless, the Founding Fathers were also the heirs of a great liberal British tradition and of a deep British hatred of tyranny and oppression. Having just completed a successful revolt against what they considered unjust and arbitrary rule, they knew that liberty was something more than merely a wartime slogan. People *were* worth something; men had dignity; men had rights. Even if men could not be wholly trusted to govern themselves wisely, they still ought to have all the liberty they deserved. And there was always the hope that men, properly educated and trained, would improve. George Washington, who was no leveler, confided to Lafayette that since the world was "evidently much less barbarous than it has been," there was some assurance

[7] N. M. Blake, *A Short History of American Life* (New York, 1952), p. 255; F. C. Prescott, *Hamilton and Jefferson* (New York, 1934), pp. 11, 39, 47–49; Merrill Jensen, *New Nation*, p. 125; Alan Grimes, *American Political Thought* (New York, 1955), p. 129; C. F. Adams (ed.), *Works of John Adams* (10 vols., Boston, 1856), IX, 59; H. H. Brackenridge, *Modern Chivalry*, C. M. Newlin, ed., (New York, 1935), p. 112; see also pp. 160, 165, 186, 519.

that "its melioration must still be progressive." Benjamin Rush wrote: "In the uncultivated state of reason, the opinions and beliefs of a majority of mankind will be wrong. In the cultivated state of reason, just opinions and feelings will become general."[8]

The stratagem was, then, to strike a balance in political society between what was and what ought to be, to adjust politics to human nature. This the makers of the Constitution attempted to accomplish by four devices. The first of these was the establishment of a central government of sufficient authority to insure the supremacy of the whole over any combination of its parts, and to keep order in the midst of conflicting interests. The second was the adoption of the mechanism of representation as a way of "refining and enlarging the public views," Madison said, "by passing them through the medium of a chosen body of citizens." Third, as John Adams explained in his *Defense of the Constitutions,* was the device of forcing aristocratic and democratic interests to neutralize each other by agreement or compromise in a bicameral legislature. Fourth, believing (as John Jay said bluntly) that "the people who own the country ought to govern it," the convention implicitly recognized property qualifications for voting by restricting the suffrage for electing representatives to persons qualified to vote for members of the lower houses of their respective states, and by providing for an electoral college to elect the President. Drawing from precedent, experience, and idealism, Americans tried to erect a state in which men might have as much freedom as they could safely be trusted with.[9]

It was a self-evident truth, according to the Declaration of Independence, that all men were created equal. This "glittering generality" of Jefferson's (as John Adams called it) was easier to repeat than to interpret. How it was interpreted was a matter of great importance to early American society. There was general agreement in that in a number of ways men were not at all equal, and there were those who doubted if it were the design of nature or of nature's God that they be so.

"There is a natural aristocracy among men," Jefferson wrote John Adams, based on "virtue and talent." Adams agreed that "a physical inequality, and intellectual inequality of the most serious kind is established unchangeably by the Author of Nature," since it is implicit in the

[8] Macklin Thomas, "The Idea of Progress in Franklin, Freneau, Barlow, and Rush" (Unpublished dissertation, Wisconsin, 1938), p. 236.

[9] Hartz, *Liberal Tradition,* pp. 67–71.

order of things that "no two men are perfectly equal in person, property, or understanding, activity, and virtue."[10] Inequality was inherent in the nature of mankind, and so ordered by a wise divinity. It was therefore of primary importance for men to consider this fact in designing a stable, orderly, just society. Thomas Green Fessenden, a New England poet, put this opinion into couplets:

> The greatest number's greatest good
> Should, doubtless ever be pursued;
> But that consists, sans disputation,
> In order and subordination. . . .
> Every man throughout the nation
> Must be contented with his station,
> Nor think to cut a figure greater
> Than was designed for him by Nature.[11]

What did Jefferson's ringing phrase mean to contemporary American society? It meant, John Adams said, that whatever differences of birth, wealth, and natural endowments existed among men, they were all equal before the law, before God, and in their possession of those inherent and inalienable rights enumerated by the Declaration. In this sense, Paine wrote in his *Rights of Man* (1791–92), "Man is all of *one* degree, and consequently . . . all men are born equal, and with equal natural rights." "As creatures of God," said David Rice, "we are, with respect to liberty, equal."[12] Barlow's *Columbiad,* among other aims, hoped to

> Prove plain and clear how nature's hand of old,
> Cast all men equal in the human mould.

"All men are equal in their rights," Barlow repeated in his *Advice to*

[10] Merle Curti, *The Growth of American Thought* (New York, 1943), p. 190; and *Works of John Adams,* VI, 9.

[11] Clinton Rossiter, *Seedtime of the Republic* (New York, 1953), p. 118; see Chap. 14, "The Pattern of Government," for a general discussion. David Humphreys, another New England poet, stated that "A God of order ne'er designed/ Equal conditions for the human kind," while Jeremy Belknap's novel, *The Foresters* (1792, 1796), repeated that "there is, and always will be, a superiority and an inferiority, in spite of all the systems of metaphysics that ever existed." Pennsylvanian George Logan, in giving advice to the common man in his *Five Letters to Yeomen* (1792), explained that there were two kinds of inequality ingrained in the natural order—that of personal talent, and that of fortune. These were "indispensable to the happiness of man . . . and the source of whatever is excellent and admirable in society." Dozens of similar quotations from the period could be added.

[12] Mark and Schwab, *Faith of Our Fathers,* p. 129.

the Privileged Orders (1792). "It is impossible to make them otherwise."

American society, therefore, was never intended to be egalitarian, despite its frequent but consistently loose use of the term "equality." Colonial settlers brought with them the graded British social system and traditional British respect for distinctions based on breeding, wealth, political influence, public service, learning, land, and other indices of position. The settlers themselves—Saltonstalls, Randolphs, Winthrops, Cabells, Dudleys, Lees, and the rest—were drawn almost wholly from the middle and lower classes of the mother country. It was, in James Truslow Adams' apt phrase, a social "cake with the icing left off."[13] The categories of colonial society were always much more fluid than those of eighteenth-century England—John Harvard himself, after all, was a butcher's boy. The son of a London brazier, after he made a fortune in Boston, placed a brass kettle on the roof of his fine house to show he "was not asham'd of his original."

Revolutionary society had its own kind of aristocracy (though not, as Crèvecoeur observed, really "aristocratical" in the European sense) founded on land and money. The Byrds, Blands, Lees, Carys, Fairfaxes, and Wyatts of Virginia; the Van Rensselaers, Van Cortlandts, Bayards, Livingstons, and Schuylers of New York; and the Saltonstalls and Dudleys of New England were landed families of sound social position. Equally at home in the upper stratum were the mercantile and banking dynasties, the Hancocks and Faneuils and Amorys of Boston, the Lows and Waltons and Wolcotts and Brockholsts and Jays of New York, the Browns and Wartons of Rhode Island, the Morrises and Binghams and Shippens and Whartons and Pembertons of Philadelphia, the Izards, Rutledges, Laurenses, and Pickneys of South Carolina.[14] John Adams was very clear about where they belonged in the social structure. "The poor are destined to labor," he wrote firmly, "and the rich, by the advantages of education, independence, and leisure, are qualified for superior status."[15]

Below these people in the scale came the professional men (law, medicine, clergy, civil servants), the lesser merchants and shippers, the up-

[13] *Provincial Society, 1690–1793* (New York, 1927), pp. 56–57 and *passim*.
[14] Dixon Wecter, *The Sage of American Society* (New York, 1937), Chap. II, is an exhaustive analysis of eighteenth-century American society.
[15] See the discussion of John Adams and social equality in Benjamin F. Wright, *American Interpretations of Natural Law* (Cambridge, Mass., 1931), pp. 152–153.

per-middle economic and educational group. These people had bigger and better homes than their lower-class brethren, wore clothes tailored on British models, sent their children to better schools at home and abroad, and found amusement in cards, dancing, salons, and theaters, as did their wealthier superiors. Social distinctions among these classes were carefully maintained, even in presumably "democratic" New England.[16]

The Revolution disturbed but did not fundamentally alter the class structure of American society. A surprisingly large number of wealthy and aristocratic families threw in their lot with the revolutionaries (Washingtons and Lees, for example), and French officers stationed in America, such as the Comte de Ségur, observed that "democracy has not banished luxury." Such things as Washington's advice concerning officer recruitment, "Take none but gentlemen," or the enlistment of the entire Philadelphia Silk Stocking Company in a war to show that all men were free and equal, made odd contrasts.[17] Whatever the language of wartime propaganda, the Revolution was not a leveling movement, nor were its leaders interested either in liquidating the upper classes or in destroying class lines. "They were not making war upon the principle of aristocracy," writes John C. Miller. "They expected, in other words, to achieve a 'safe and sane' revolution of gentlemen, by gentlemen, and for gentlemen."[18]

A gentleman was made not only by wealth or birth, but by his merit. In American eighteenth-century terms, he was produced by training, piety, talent, virtue, feeling, and a certain indefinable "natural worth." The Christian-hero of Steele had displaced the Restoration rakehelly aristocrat as a model in American society long before the Revolution— soon to be displaced in turn by the Richardsonian man of sensitivity, emotion, and morality. Both the Richardsonian and the *Spectator* concepts fitted contemporary ideals of "natural aristocracy" and served as examples for Federalist and Antifederalist alike. In practice, however, the example was difficult to realize. Real *aristoi* (such as Gouverneur Morris, Fisher Ames, or Thomas Green Fessenden) kept French valets,

[16] John Krout and Dixon R. Fox, *The Completion of Independence* (New York, 1944), Chap. II; Wecter, *Sage of Society*, pp. 44–45. An excellent essay is Harold U. Faulkner, *American Political and Social History* (New York, 1946), Chap. XIII, "Life at the Beginning of the Nineteenth Century."

[17] See Wecter, *Sage of Society,* Chap. III, "Aristocracy in Retreat."

[18] John C. Miller, *Origins of the American Revolution* (Boston, 1943), p. 498.

disliked disorder, and had vast contempt for the unwashed "moboc-racy." Equalitarians such as Paine and Freneau hated the haughty, tie-wig "Prigarchy" of the Morrises and Ameses.[19]

Between these extremes there existed that "natural aristocracy of worth" on which Jefferson and Adams could agree in principle if not in degree. Adams, a stout believer in social gradations, thought that to maintain order in a free society there must be, as he wrote in 1776, "decency and respect and veneration introduced for persons in author-ity, at every rank." Some men were better than others, not by birth or wealth or education (though these were factors), but by qualities of health, strength, and agility. Jefferson too believed in such "natural" aristocrats, expressing more optimism than Adams in their numbers and distribution.[20] Both Adams and Jefferson illustrated the tendency in American social thinking to separate "gentleman" from "gentry," to reconcile a theory of an American upper class with a practical American political and social situation. There could be, both believed, a democ-racy in which there existed a class of leaders.[21]

It was difficult after 1790 for any single group to monopolize eco-nomic opportunity. There were simply too many roads to success. And where there was an opportunistic economic democracy, there were bound to be the beginnings of social democracy and leveling of classes. American and foreign commentators usually agreed that the great dif-ference between America and Europe was America's almost unlimited economic opportunity. There were rich men and poor men in the United States, naturally, but it was generally remarked that the gap between them was considerably narrower than in England or Europe, and that the chance for a poor man to become rich was immeasurably greater. "In America," wrote Lafayette a trifle overenthusiastically, "there are no poor, nor even what we call peasantry." Franklin, in his *Information for Those Who Would Remove to America* (1782), ex-plained more accurately that "though there are in that Country few people so miserable as the Poor of Europe, there are also very few that in Europe would be called rich."

American society, travelers reported, displayed "a pleasing equality"

[19] See E. H. Cady, *The Gentleman in America* (Syracuse, 1949), Chaps. II, III.

[20] Prescott, *Hamilton and Jefferson,* p. 375.

[21] Frederick B. Tolles, "The American Revolution Considered as a Social Movement: A Reconsideration," *American Historical Review,* LX (1954), 1–12.

without sharply defined class distinctions. "The levelling principle here everywhere operates strongly," noted a British officer. A traveling Englishman of the 1790's complained that New England servants refused to say "master" or "mistress," and a French visitor wrote home with horror that "all servants, no matter what their sex or color, insist on having coffee, sugar, and soft bread!" William Cobbett found that American workmen did not "creep and fawn" as in England; Baron von Steuben noted half-humorously that "Here we are in a Republic, and Mr. Baron does not count a farthing more than Mister Jacob or Mister Peter."[22]

Americans themselves were quite aware of their disrespect for social distinctions and sometimes aggressively proud of it. "Dependence and Servility," according to the Constitution of Pennsylvania, were "unbecoming Freemen." Birth, Franklin wrote in 1782, is "a Commodity that cannot be carried to a worse market than America, where people do not inquire concerning a Stranger, *What is he?* but *What can he do?*"[23] "There are fewer distinctions of fortune and less of rank," C. C. Pinckney told the Constitutional Convention, "than among the inhabitants of any other nation."

This did not necessarily mean that American society after the war turned into an egalitarian, level, homogeneous group. Wealth counted, and so did education, lineage, attitudes, and dress—as always they had. James K. Paulding, himself a member of New York "Knickerbocker" society, expressed in 1819 what no doubt many felt: "In the eyes of the law, let all men be equal, but not in the drawing rooms or in the assemblages of well-bred people. The United States must keep certain distinctions founded in the immutable principles of reason."[24]

At the opening of the nineteenth century the United States, though

[22] See Robert E. Brown, "Economic Democracy Before the Constitution," *American Quarterly,* VII (1955), 257–285. Cf. also Brown's "Democracy in Colonial Massachusetts," *New England Quarterly,* XXV (1952), 290–313. James Truslow Adams, *The American* (New York, 1943), p. 88, cites the troubles of the British ambassador to Washington in 1834, whose servants were required to wear livery. He could find American servants who would take jobs at the embassy, but who would not wear livery out of doors and who were "sure to go away as soon as they can find any employment in which the wearing of livery is not requisite," a problem not found in Britain then or now.

[23] F. L. Mott and C. Jorgensen, *Franklin* (New York, 1936), pp. 450, 459.

[24] *Salamagundi Papers* (second series, New York, 1819), I, 206. Paulding's *Letters From the South* (New York, 1817) is an excellent source of social history; Paulding was a shrewd observer of American life as well as a skillful writer.

barely twenty years old as a nation, had nevertheless been settled territory for nearly two hundred years. Over the preceding century the colonies had begun to show certain marks of division, until by the time of the Revolution most Americans recognized the existence of clearly separate groupings.[25] Postwar geographers usually distinguished a central "middle" group of states, a "Northern" or New England group, a Southern bloc, and occasionally a "coastal" and "back" region. Members of the Continental Congress referred to themselves as delegates from Northern, Middle, or Southern states, while the Continental Army organization likewise divided the nation into three military districts—Eastern (the New England states), Middle (New York, Pennsylvania, Delaware, and Maryland), and Southern. After 1800 a fourth or "Western" division appeared in standard geographies. Jedidiah Morse, whose *American Geography* of 1793 listed the "grand Division of the United States" as Northern, Middle, and Southern, in 1819 added the "Western States and Territories" as a separate section.

Within these major divisions there were identifiable subdivisions, accepted by both geographers and the public—the two poles of New England (Boston and New Haven), upstate and urban New York, western Pennsylvania and the Philadelphia region, Chesapeake society and the deep Carolina South, the agrarian Northwest and the cotton Southwest.[26] Even in its infancy, American society exhibited tremendous regional diversity and fierce sectional loyalties, rooted deep in colonial culture, tradition, economics, and government. "By the close of the 1830's," one historian writes, "every one-horse planter in the cotton belt, every coonskin clad farmer along the western waters, every shopkeeper in the smoky mill towns of New England, was blindly loyal to the region where he lived."[27]

New England, with the exception of Maine and parts of New Hampshire and Vermont, was completely settled by 1800, populated by a relatively homogeneous group of people who believed in a unified the-

---

[25] Fulmer Mood, "The Origin, Evolution, and Application of the Sectional Concept, 1750–1900," in Merrill Jensen (ed.), *Regionalism in America* (Madison, Wis., 1951). Of primary importance, of course, is Frederick Jackson Turner, *The Significance of Sections in American History* (New York, 1932).

[26] A fascinating view of the United States in Jefferson's time is that of the British diplomat Sir Augustus John Foster, whose travel notes of 1805–7 and 1811–12 were edited by Richard B. Davis, *Jefferson's America* (San Marino, Calif., 1954).

[27] R. A. Billington, *Westward Expansion* (New York, 1949), p. 349.

ological system that still held powerful authority.[28] Its polity and society were controlled by a small number of sea traders, bankers, and merchants of wealth, both inherited and new. New England was rich. Its men and ships appeared in ports all over the world. The world, too, came to New England; the port of Boston alone in 1800 handled more than a thousand foreign ships a year. Farming, once the mainstay of New England economy, rapidly declined in importance after 1800, as cheap water power, machinery, and immigrant labor encouraged the growth of industry. Old ports such as Salem, Newburyport, and Marblehead faded in importance beside new factory towns like Lowell and Lawrence; cities grew, farms deteriorated. Two institutions, the Congregational Church and the town meeting, dominated New England's cultural life and gave it its distinctive Yankee flavor—a compound of moralism, pietism, conservatism, self-sufficiency, and democracy.

Politically, New England in 1800 was divided into Federalist and Jeffersonian, later into Whig and Jacksonian. The dominant Federalist-Whig group was a union of clergy, bar, magistracy, merchants, and bankers, an "organized social system," Henry Adams called it, founded on education, wealth, and religion, "capable of acting at command either for offence or defence, admirably adapted for the uses of the eighteenth century." Its leaders feared change, suspected the new, and hoped to retain as long as possible in the nineteenth century the hierarchical harmony and order of eighteenth-century society. "Let us guard against the insidious encroachments of innovation," pleaded the Reverend Jedidiah Morse of Charlestown, Massachusetts, in 1803, "that evil and beguiling spirit which is now stalking to and fro through the earth." Dozens of other New England divines doubtless preached the same message to generations of approving congregations.

The New England clergy still served, especially in smaller towns and rural areas, as a quasi-official agency of law enforcement and of education. The union of bench, pulpit, and schoolroom made respectability conservative and conservatism respectable. Jeffersonians (and later Jacksonians) had no caste in this society. Speculators, scoffers, social climbers, debtors, intriguing politicos, and atheists were all presumably

[28] Henry Adams, *Formative Years*, Chap. III, "The Intellect of New England," is the best essay, on which this analysis is largely based. See also Krout and Fox, *Completion of Independence*, pp. 6–8, 71–72, 426–27, *passim;* John Bach McMaster, *History of the People of the United States*, I: 18–26; and Turner, *Significance of Sections*, Chap. II.

followers of the dangerous Virginian who was, the Reverend Joseph Buckminster warned his parish, "a contemner of religious duty, void of religious principle." Thirty years later New England simply substituted Jacksonians for Jeffersonians. At the trial of Abner Kneeland (the last man to be tried for heresy in New England) the prosecuting attorney charged that "nineteen-twentieths of the followers of Kneeland are Jacksonmen. I have no doubt that Infidel party constitute at least one-third of the Jackson party."[29]

Emerson's comment that in New England from 1790 to 1820 there was "not a book, not a speech, a conversation, or a thought" worth noticing was harsh, but not wholly inaccurate. New England did not lack for ideas; it merely lacked new ones. Politically its thinking was represented by Fisher Ames, who believed the nation was "too big for union, too sordid for patriotism, and too democratic for liberty." Ames could see no hope for a nation ruled by "the tyranny of what is called the people"; his fear of the future, he wrote, made his friends' "days heavy with the pressure of anxiety and our nights restless with visions of horror." Ames, George Cabot, Timothy Pickering, Theophilus Parsons, and others (beside whom John Adams was a suspected radical) spoke for New England's turn-of-the-century generation in politics.

In theology, conservative Congregationalists and Presbyterians held control, though there were also a number of Unitarians among the educated. In literature, New England followed Pope and Addison (a few of the more daring read Burns and Wordsworth), and Timothy Dwight, John Trumbull, and the Hartford Wits wrote good imitations of English neoclassic verse. Yale, Harvard, Princeton, and the smaller colleges continued to turn out orthodox young ministers, lawyers, and politicians, not much different from those of 1750. The young rebels who were to light the fires of revolt under the congealed New England culture of Dwight and Ames—Channing, Emerson, Everett, Parker, Bancroft, and many more—were not yet old enough to strike the spark.

The society of the Middle States, polarized about New York and Philadelphia, showed no such frozen hierarchy as New England's.[30] There were men of birth, education, and property—Jays, Schuylers, Livingstons, Clintons, Spencers, Hamiltons—on both sides of the politi-

[29] Leonard Levy, "Satan's Last Apostle in Massachusetts," *American Quarterly,* V (1953), 18.
[30] Henry Adams, *Formative Years,* Chap. IV, "Intellect of the Middle States."

cal fence in New York State. The Yankee alliance of church, school, and state did not hold quite so tightly west of the Hudson, nor did the Middle Colonies have a single dominant theology or social philosophy. Their society was much more diverse, loose, and cosmopolitan than New England's. As Timothy Dwight exemplified the New England mind, so Samuel Latham Mitchill might have represented New York's —chemist, botanist, physicist, medical man, teacher, politician, a man capable of writing a chemical dissertation in octosyllabics (as he did) while campaigning for Jefferson.

Instead of Ameses and Cabots, New York produced men such as De Witt Clinton, who built the Erie Canal; Chancellor Livingston, who helped build the first steamboat; and Aaron Burr, the most astute politician north of the Potomac. Instead of the Hartford Wits, New Yorkers could read Joseph Rodman Drake, James Paulding, Fitz-Greene Halleck, Washington Irving, and others of the sophisticated, witty Knickerbocker group. New York was unconcerned with metaphysical speculation, uninterested in theological controversy, and neither so morally energetic nor intellectually earnest as New England. The state poured much of its energy into business and politics; in 1800 it was already outdistancing New England in agriculture, shipping, banking, and trading.

Pennsylvania, next to Virginia the most powerful of the states, contained no social hierarchy like New England's, no great political-commercial dynasties like New York's, no plantation oligarchy like the South's. Albert Gallatin thought that there was in the state not "a single family that has any extensive influence." "An equal distribution of property," he remarked, "has rendered every individual independent, and there is among us true and rare equality." Pennsylvania was tolerant; with twenty different religious creeds in the state, its theology could hardly be narrow or authoritarian. Pennsylvania's politics was neither so bitterly Federalist as New England's nor so split among factions as New York's. Gallatin, the sensible Swiss who served Jefferson as Secretary of the Treasury, was the only Pennsylvanian who left any mark in contemporary politics.

Philadelphia, the largest and finest American city, was run by solid, efficient, industrious merchants—lesser Franklins all—who shared political power in the state with the canny Scotch-Irish and Germans from the southern and western counties. Though Boston loudly disputed the claim, Philadelphia in 1800 was generally agreed to be the intellectual center of the nation. Journalists such as William Cobbett and James Duane; novelist Charles Brockden Brown; Matthew Carey the publisher; scientists William Bartram and Alexander Wilson; lawyers James Wilson, Alexander Dallas, and William Rawle; Philip Freneau the poet —these men and others like them helped to give Pennsylvania a sound and lively (if not brilliant) intellectual environment. The ill-tempered British poet, Tom Moore, who disliked nearly everything he saw in America in 1804, found in Philadelphia "the few agreeable moments which my tour through the states afforded me."

The social and intellectual lines which separated North from South were nearly as distinct as boundaries drawn on a map.[31] There were in reality two dominant Southern societies—Virginia's and South Carolina's—differing in details but both sharply in contrast to life north of the Potomac.[32] The South was predominantly rural and agrarian. It had no cities except Charleston, which by Northern standards was hardly more than a large village. Virginia society, still proudly modeled on England's, valued dignified simplicity, gentlemanly learning, direct manners, and friendly hospitality. Young William Ellery Channing, fresh from Massachusetts, found in Virginia "great vices" (sensuality and slaves) but also "great virtues" of manners, friendship, and generosity. The Duc de Liancourt noted Virginia's "love of dissipation" on the one hand and its "taste for reading" on the other. Social and political position depended not only upon birth and wealth in Virginia, but upon talent. The Masons, Lees, Fairfaxes, Pages, Carters, and Blands were feudally powerful, but the road upward in Virginia was always open to men of brains and humbler origin, such as John Marshall, George Mason, or George Wythe.

[31] For surveys of Southern life, see Blake, *American Life,* Chap. 9; Harvey Wish, *Society and Thought in Early America* (New York, 1950), Chap. 8; Parkes, *The United States,* Chap. 10; Krout and Fox, *Completion of Independence,* Chap. 6. Turner, *Significance of Sections,* Chap. III, and the relevant sections of Van Wyck Brooks, *The World of Washington Irving* (Boston, 1944), are also interesting reading.

[32] Carl Bridenbaugh, *Myths and Realities: Societies of the Colonial South* (Baton Rouge, 1952), is an exposition of the bases of Southern society. W. J. Cash's *The Mind of the South* (New York, 1941) is a brilliant interpretative study. Clement Eaton, *A History of the Old South* (New York, 1949), and U. B. Phillips, *Life and Labor in the Old South* (Boston, 1929), are excellent general histories. Henry Adams, *Formative Years,* Chap. V, "The Intellect of the Southern States," is again a key essay.

Such Virginians of property and talent, of whom Jefferson was perhaps the finest example, were representative men of the Enlightenment, educated, urbane, philosophically minded, conscious of their
responsibilities, "natural aristocrats" in the Jeffersonian sense. Without
a strong centralized church, a developed educational system, few colleges and no universities, little literature, and no really concentrated intellectual and cultural life, Virginia channeled its energies into politics
and law. Virginians did not argue about theology, at least in public; as
one of them said, "No gentleman would choose any road to heaven but
the Episcopal." And like the New England gentry, they lived in an
eighteenth-century world that was rapidly breaking up.[33]

Within two decades the Virginia dynasty lost leadership of the South
to the aggressive, emotionalized, cotton-and-slave aristocracy of South
Carolina and Mississippi.[34] There was already a great gap between Virginia gentlemen and their middle- and lower-class brethren. The small
farmers of the Piedmont and the artisans of the towns were rough,
proud, individualistic, turbulent people. They were Calvinist or evangelical in their religion, with little sympathy for the gentlemanly deism
or Anglicanism of the Tidewater. Few back-country farmers owned
more than a small farm, few raised much cotton, not many owned more
than two or three slaves, and some of them had strong moral scruples
against slavery.

North Carolina seemed hardly Southern at all in comparison with
its northern and southern neighbors. Virginians and South Carolinians
looked down on the state ("Lubberland," William Byrd had contemptu-
ously called it) and its people were criticized for "excesses of Freedom
and Familiarity," insolence toward aristocrats, and opposition to authority. North Carolina was a Jeffersonian stronghold of small farmers,
without an aristocracy of slaveholders, without a dynasty of ruling families, without sharp division between gentry and common folk, without
the strong class feelings which usually marked Southern society. The
state was, as it half-proudly described itself, "a valley of humiliation between two mountain peaks of pride."

South Carolina society, dominated by Charleston, retained more of

---

[33] See Henry Adams, *Formative Years,* pp. 19–24, 67–81, and McMaster,
History, I, 62–78, on Virginia.
[34] Turner, *Significance of Sections,* Chap. III, discusses the changes in
Southern leadership.

the flavor of early eighteenth-century life than any other portion of the country. Pinckneys, Rutledges, Laurenses, Lowndeses, Middletons, and a few other old families held tight control of South Carolina's social, economic, and political life. The city surpassed both Philadelphia and New York for glitter, show, and easy living. New Englander Jedidiah Morse wrote approvingly in his *American Geography* (1789 ed.) that "in no part of America are the social blessings enjoyed more rationally and liberally than in Charleston." Yet Charleston locked its doors and blinds at ten and frowned on giddy gaiety even more than Boston. No Charleston gentleman had much to do with ordinary farming or trade, with liberal theology, with radical politics, or with intellectual pursuits.

South Carolina bristled with contradictions. The values admired by its ruling class were those of an eighteenth-century England long dead; its sparse intellectual and cultural life existed in a vacuum with no visible sources of renewal; the tone of its politics, after the disappearance of the Revolutionary generation, was set by John C. Calhoun, whose ideas reflected little or nothing of its old traditions.

The South itself, of course, from 1800 to 1830, was in the midst of a drastic economic change which transformed its social and cultural patterns. Until 1790 the South raised a great deal of tobacco and little cotton. But tobacco wore out the land, improved textile machinery created a tremendous new demand for cotton, and Yankee Eli Whitney's cotton gin (1793) made cotton farming profitable in a way never known before. After 1820 the black-and-white threads of slavery and cotton twisted through every part of the pattern of Southern life. Southern culture after that date can be understood only in terms of its chief crop and its peculiar institution.

Ideas—beyond economics and politics—played little part in Southern life. Southerners, the saying went, "took seriously only cotton, oratory, horses, and elections." As slavery increased in importance, Southern society took on more and more of a feudal feel. Class divisions were most rigid there, social contrasts most sharply defined, prejudices most unyielding, emotions nearest the surface. As leadership of Southern society passed from Virginia to South Carolina, so the power center of Southern life passed to the Cotton Kingdom. The new group of Southern leaders—Calhoun, Hayne, and McDuffie of South Carolina, or Cobb and Crawford of Georgia—represented the cotton aristocracy, whose authority swiftly spread over Alabama, Mississippi, and the Southwest.

Southern life, based on a definite social and economic order, exhibited far more coherence than that of either of the other two major sections. At the top of the order, giving Southern civilization its distinctive complexion, stood the great planters, those who owned fifty or more slaves, one or more plantations, most of the South's best land, and three-quarters of its wealth. There were never many of them—by 1850, probably fewer than 50,000 out of the South's population of 8 million—but they provided the South with its intellectual, social, and cultural leadership.

Below the great planter in the scale was the small planter, who owned from four or five to twenty slaves. He held less land and that less fertile, owned a frame house (or a log one), and lived a simple life of hard work. Next to him came the yeoman farmer, who made up more than 75 per cent of the South's population. He owned no slaves, and his farm was often small and poor. In the lowest brackets were the "crackers," "poor whites," or "shandhillers," scattered on the poorest land, illiterate, shiftless, living on the bare edge of subsistence.

Such was the antebellum South, a varied yet peculiarly unified section, a state of mind as much as a geographical area, its pattern of life shaped always by cotton and slavery. During the first half of the nineteenth century the South became acutely aware of the fact that it was a section, with a tradition and interests of its own, and its leaders made strenuous efforts to preserve and develop them. It had a closely guarded set of values, a way of life it deemed worthy of protecting and defending. It had also an extremely difficult set of political, social, and economic problems, all tied up with slavery, the one-crop system, and a rigid social order.

John Jay, in 1785, remarked on the "rage for emigrating to the western country." The first wave of post-Revolutionary westward migration carried into the back country of the settled states, and beyond the mountains into western Pennsylvania, Kentucky, and Tennessee. Virginia had 400,000 people in 1775 and 750,000 in 1790, with most of the increase concentrated in its western counties; South Carolina had 150,000 in 1775 and 250,000 in 1790, distributed in almost the same manner. Kentucky, which had perhaps a few hundred people in 1770, showed 73,000 in the census of 1790; Tennessee grew from 7,700 to 35,000 in not quite twenty years. This first wave of migration was a mere trickle in comparison with the flood to come. The great magnet that drew men West, of course, was land. The Ordinance of 1785, coupled with the Northwest Ordinance of 1787, provided a pattern for surveying, selling, and

1. Second and Market Streets, Philadelphia, 1799, by William Birch
(New York Public Library)

2. Benjamin Latrobe's Chestnut Street Theater, Philadelphia, 1794
(The Metropolitan Museum of Art, Bequest of
Charles Allen Munn, 1924)

3. Sally Port, Fort Mackinac, Straits of Mackinac, construction begun 1780
(Michigan Historical Commission Archives)
4. Winter Scene in Brooklyn, 1817-20, by Francis Guy
(The Brooklyn Museum Collection)

5. Comic lithograph: A New England School-room Scene, 1830

(American Antiquarian Society)

6. Interior of the Park Theater, New York, 1822, by John Searle

(New-York Historical Society, New York City)

7. A Baptist Baptismal Scene, 1811, by Pavel Svinin
(The Metropolitan Museum of Art, Rogers Fund, 1842)

8. Bruff: Portrait of FRANCIS ASBURY
(Drew University Library, Madison,
New Jersey)

9. John Singleton Copley: Portrait of PAUL
REVERE

(Museum of Fine Arts, Boston)

10. Samuel F. B. Morse: Portrait of
BENJAMIN SILLIMAN, 1825
(Yale University Art Gallery)

11. The Greek Revival in the West. The Brooks house, Marshall, Michigan.
(Michigan Historical Commission Archives)

12. The Pingree house, Salem, Massachusetts, 1804. Designed by Samuel McIntire. The New England style at its best.

(Essex Institute, Salem, Massachusetts)

13.   Water color by E. H.: Detroit, 1794
(Burton Historical Collection, Detroit Public Library)

14.   Public Square, Cleveland, 1839, view of northwest corner. Water color by Heine.
(Western Reserve Historical Society Collections)

15. Eighteenth-century Creole architecture, St. Peter and Royal streets, Vieux Carré, New Orleans

(Bureau of New Orleans News)

16. William Whitley House, Kentucky, 1787-94. The first brick house west of the Alleghenies, near Crab Orchard, Kentucky.

(Kentucky Department of Public Relations)

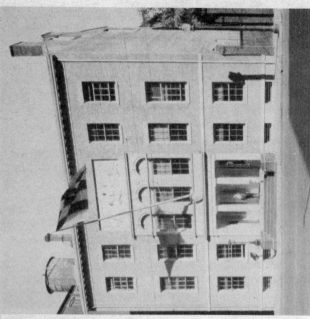

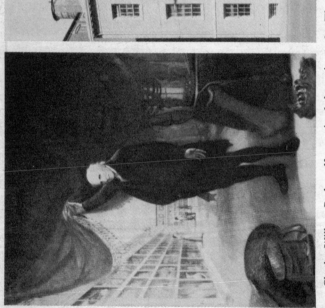

17. Charles Willson Peale: self-portrait of the artist in his museum

(The Pennsylvania Academy of the Fine Arts)

18. The Peale Museum, Baltimore, 1814, designed by Robert Cary Long, Sr. The first building in the United States, and the third in the world, to be designed as a public museum.

(Photo by A. A. Bodine, Courtesy of The Peale Museum)

19. Painting by Samuel F. B. Morse of the old House of Representatives, 1821-22, at candle-lighting time. Included are 86 portraits—House members, the Supreme Court (against the rear wall), and Benjamin Silliman, Jedidiah Morse, and a Pawnee chieftain in the gallery. (Corcoran Gallery of Art)

20. Football at Yale College, 1807. Engraving.
(Yale University Library)

21. Thomas Jefferson's plan for the University of Virginia. Sachse lithograph.
(The Old Print Shop, New York City)

22. A Camp Meeting, 1835. Kennedy and Lucas lithograph.
(The New-York Historical Society, New York City)

23. Frontispiece, William Billings' *Continental Harmony*, 1794. Billings believed all tunes were "compleat circles" and printed his music thus.
(New York Public Library, Music Division)

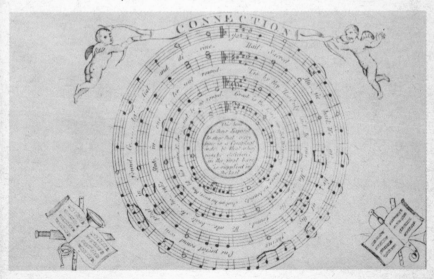

24. Military hospital, 1816, Fort Howard, Green Bay, Wisconsin
(State Historical Society of Wisconsin)

25. French influence in the Mississippi Valley. The Balduc house, Ste. Genevieve, Missouri, 1785.

(Photo, Martin Schweig, St. Louis)

26. Scene on the National Road. The Fairview Inn, 1801, near Baltimore.
(Maryland Historical Society)

27. The United States Capitol, 1824, by Charles Burton
(The Metropolitan Museum of Art, Joseph Pulitzer bequest, 1942)

28. Butcher shop sign, about 1820

29. Pieplate, Pennsylvania earthenware, 1805

(National Gallery of Art, Index of American Design)

30. A machine for generating static electricity, about 1825

31. Gilbert Stuart: Portrait of JOHN ADAMS (National Gallery of Art, Washington, D.C., gift of Mrs. Robert Homans)

32. Rembrandt Peale: Portrait of THOMAS JEFFERSON, 1805 (The New-York Historical Society, New York City)

33. John Trumbull: Portrait of TIMOTHY DWIGHT

(Yale University Art Gallery)

34. C. C. Ingham, N.A.: Portrait of WILLIAM DUNLAP, N.A.

(National Academy of Design, Permanent Collection)

35. Woodcarving, 1800. Ship's fig-
urehead, "Lady with a Rose"

36. Imported silk brocade dress, Boston, *c.* 1800

(National Gallery of Art, Index of
American Design)

37. Rhode Island tavern sign

settling the Western lands. Successive changes in land law led finally to the Act of 1820, which established the minimum size of grants at eighty acres and the minimum price at $1.25 an acre.[35]

Cheap land was lure enough, but the pressure of economic conditions in the crowded, war-dislocated cities of the East also helped to drive men West. American manufacturing, hurt by embargo and blockade, faltered after the War of 1812. Periodic business recessions, as the national economy adjusted to peace, were immediately reflected by increases in the westward flow, which was at its highest during the depression years of 1819 to 1821. From the seaboard South, where tobacco quickly wore out the soil, the lush bottom lands of the West attracted farmers who raised cotton and wheat. Southern yeomen and artisans often found the West an attractive escape from the planter-dominated economics and politics of the seaboard cities. The old conflict between back-country and coastal areas in Pennsylvania, New York, and the Carolinas helped also to drive back-country men farther West in search of personal independence and land. So, after 1800, America moved West.[36] An observer described it thus:

Generally, in all the western settlements, three classes, like the waves of the ocean, have rolled one after the other. First comes the pioneer, who depends for the subsistence of his family chiefly upon the natural growth of vegetation, called the "range," and the proceeds of hunting. His implements of agriculture are rude, chiefly of his own make, and his efforts directed mainly to a crop of corn, and a "truck patch." The last is a rude garden for growing cabbage, beans, corn for roasting ears, cucumbers and potatoes; a log cabin, and, occasionally, a stable and corn-crib, and a field of a dozen acres, the timber girdled or "deadened" and fenced, are enough for his occupancy. It is quite immaterial whether he ever becomes the owner of the soil. He is the occupant for the time being, pays no rent, and feels as independent as the "lord of the manor." With a horse, cow, and one or two breeders of swine, he strikes into the woods with his family, and becomes the founder of a new county, or perhaps State. He builds his cabin, gathers around him a few other families of similar taste and habits, and occupies till the range is somewhat subdued, and hunting a little precarious; or, which is more frequently the case, till neighbors crowd around, roads, bridges, and fields annoy him, and he lacks elbow room. The preemption law enables him to dispose of

[35] Jensen, *New Nation,* pp. 114–115; Turner, *Significance of Sectionalism,* p. 87; Krout and Fox, *Completion of Independence,* p. 139.

[36] Excellent studies of the westward movement are R. A. Billington, *Westward Expansion* (New York, 1949), and R. I. Riegel, *America Moves West* (rev. ed., New York, 1947).

his cabin and corn-field to the next class of emigrants, and, to employ his own figures, he "breaks for the high timber," "clears out for the New Purchase," or migrates to Arkansas or Texas, to work the same process over.

The next class of emigrants purchase the lands, add field to field, clear out the roads, throw rough bridges over the streams, put up hewn log houses, with glass windows, and brick or stone chimneys, occasionally plant orchards, build mills, school houses, court houses, etc., and exhibit the picture and forms of plain, frugal, civilized life.

Another wave rolls on. The men of capital and enterprise come. The "settler" is ready to sell out and take the advantage of the rise of property— push farther into the interior, and become, himself, a man of capital and enterprise in turn. The small villages rise to spacious towns or cities; substantial edifices of brick, extensive fields, orchards, gardens, colleges and churches are seen. Broadcloths, silks, leghorns, crapes, and all the refinements, luxuries, elegancies, frivolities and fashions, are in vogue. Thus wave after wave is rolling westward:—the real *el dorado* is still farther on.[37]

It seemed to the British traveler Morris Birkbeck in 1817 that the entire country "was breaking up and moving westward," along the Hudson-Mohawk valleys, or down the Ohio, or on the Cumberland Gap and Wilderness roads in a double-pronged invasion of the Northwest and Southwest. A farmer near Pittsburgh in 1810 counted 236 wagons on the way to Ohio; another in upstate New York a few years later counted 260 in nine days, all moving westward. In the spring of 1818 at Olean, New York, 3,000 families waited for the spring thaw to float them down the Alleghany River to Ohio. On the National Road, Birkbeck wrote, "We are seldom out of sight as we travel this grand track toward the Ohio, of family groups behind and after us."[38]

The violence and swiftness of this shift of population were shown in the national census figures. The population of Ohio doubled between 1810 and 1820; that of Indiana quadrupled. Two-fifths of the entire population of South Carolina, one-third of that of Virginia, and one-third of North Carolina's moved west. By 1821 the nine new Western states contained one-quarter of the total population of the United States. And during this mass movement, Americans were probing still farther west, toward the Pacific. Lewis and Clark's expedition crossed

[37] J. M. Peck, *A New Guide for Emigrants to the West* (Boston, 1837), cited in Harold U. Faulkner, *American Political and Social History* (New York, 1946), p. 231.

[38] Cited in Faulkner, *Political and Social History*, pp. 231, 233–234; Krout and Fox, *Completion of Independence*, p. 405.

the plains in 1804-6, Lieutenant Pike's crossed the mountains in 1807, and John Jacob Astor's private exploring parties set up his far-flung fur outposts on the Pacific coast in 1811 and 1812.

The West that emerged as a regional entity after 1810 was divided into Northwest and Southwest. The Northwest, bounded by the Ohio, the Great Lakes, and the Mississippi, was settled chiefly by the flow of migration from New England, New York, Pennsylvania, and the upland South. The Ordinance of 1787 banned slavery from the region. Conditions of soil, climate, and geography made it a land of grain, corn, cattle, and small farms—not of cotton and plantations—scattered among tremendous forests and huge tracts of fertile prairie land. The Ohio-Mississippi chain cut through it like a lifeline. Along the river banks cities buzzed with trade—Pittsburgh, Cincinnati, Louisville, St. Louis, dozens of bustling river towns in between. Detroit with 2,200 population in 1824, Cleveland with 1,000 or so, and Fort Dearborn (not yet Chicago) with fifty had yet to develop as trade centers. During the first three decades of the nineteenth century the Northwest sprouted wealth and towns, until by 1830 it was exporting $26 million of produce through the port of New Orleans alone.[39]

The Southwest developed differently.[40] Kentucky and Tennessee, settled primarily from back-country Virginia and the Carolinas, evolved their socio-economic pattern by the close of the War of 1812—small farms in the mountainous eastern counties, slaveholding planters in the western flatland, busy trade towns along the rivers. After 1814 population rushed into Alabama, Mississippi, Arkansas, and Missouri, at first small farmers, then planters who bought up huge tracts of land for slaves and cotton.

From 1782 to the end of the nineteenth century the West was a fact of primary importance—almost of dominant importance—in the development of American society. It took a long time, really, for Americans to accept the West and to recognize it for what it was. The seventeenth century had very little information about what lay to the west and little interest in it. It had seemed to the civilized East, as Michael Wigglesworth once called it, no more than "a waste and howling wilderness." Colonial eyes were turned toward Europe, toward English trade and English politics, not toward the exploitation of a continent,

[39] Krout and Fox, *Completion of Independence,* pp. 410–412.
[40] An interesting study is Everett Dick, *The Dixie Frontier* (New York, 1948).

and a good many Easterners in the eighteenth century saw no reason to do otherwise.[41]

Fisher Ames, who thought the West a useless appendage to the nation, termed the purchase of Louisiana a mistake that would send the country "rushing like a comet into infinite space." Timothy Dwight, who journeyed a little way westward in 1810, found the West dangerously unstable, full of men "who cannot live in regular society. They are all too ideal, too passionate, too prodigal and too shiftless to acquire either property or character." Gouverneur Morris, who believed that back-country pioneers could not be trusted, put his opinions quite bluntly in the Constitutional Convention—"If the western people get the power into their hands," he said, "they will ruin the Atlantic interests."[42]

Such men feared the West, its expanding society, its economic competition, its growing political power, and the unsettling effect its influence might have on national policies. The fact that in 1822 the Western states controlled more than one-quarter of the seats in the House and eighteen of forty-eight Senate seats did not escape notice in the East. As late as 1847 Horace Bushnell advised Easterners that the best way to protect their own interests was to civilize the West by making "the emigrant settlements of Minnesota and Oregon feel that they are just in the suburb of Boston."[43]

Yet other men caught glimpses of an empire, lying to the West, which fired their imaginations as truly as it had Hakluyt's or Raleigh's. Philip Freneau and Hugh Henry Brackenridge, in their youthful commencement poem at Princeton in 1771, visualized great "empires, kingdoms, powers and states" destined to rise from the "dreary wastes and awful solitudes" of the American wilderness. George Washington, who owned large tracts of Western land himself, hoped to ". . . let the poor, the needy, and the oppressed of the Earth and those who want land, resort to the fertile plains of our western country, the second Promise, and there dwell in peace." Jefferson visioned the United States marching

---

[41] For a discussion of American views of and attitudes toward the West, see Henry Nash Smith, *Virgin Land* (Cambridge, Mass., 1950), pp. 1–15.

[42] Krout and Fox, *Completion of Independence*, p. 191; Turner, *Significance of Sectionalism*, p. 26.

[43] Turner, *Significance of Sectionalism*, p. 71; R. H. Gabriel, "Evangelical Religion and Popular Romanticism," *Church History*, XIX (1950), p. 40; see also Albert Weinberg, *Manifest Destiny* (Baltimore, 1935), p. 104 and Chap. II, for a discussion of the relations between West and East.

across the plains and mountains, spilling into the Pacific, linking the western world with Asia.

Others saw the West as an enchanted land of rumor and legend, of Indians who spoke Welsh, of bushes that dripped honey, of a salt mountain a hundred miles long, of plains so fertile that trees died of growing too fast.[44] Even those who knew better found that the prospect of this unexhausted land, where everything was fresh, unspoiled, and open, quickened the fancy and intrigued the mind. The concept of a "new world of man" to be created beyond the mountains, Daniel Drake wrote in 1834, "started men from their slumbers and gave new impulses to action."[45] Thomas Nuttall, the ornithologist, as he watched the emigrants streaming westward, commented in his journals that they were all "searching for some better country, which lies to the West as Eden did to the East."

Americans thus saw the West as crudeness and revolt, as haven for the oppressed, as a great new empire, as Eden. There was a fourth image too, that of the West as the ideal agrarian society of the eighteenth-century philosophers, a republic of simple, intelligent, virtuous yeomen. So Crèvecoeur saw the frontier as a garden of democracy, as "asylum of freedom, the cradle of future nations." Freneau in 1782 predicted that in the West men could doubtless "discover those days of felicity . . . so beautifully described by the prophetic sages of ancient times." Six years later a traveler found Freneau's prophecy come true in Kentucky, exclaiming, "here was civil and religious liberty in perfection—here was independence, as far as the nature of human life would admit!"[46]

The great population shift that occurred after 1800 was not solely a movement of Americans from East to West. The westward flood was partially replaced by a substantial stream of immigration from Europe to the United States. The United States in 1800 was composed of $4\frac{1}{2}$ million white people and 1 million Negroes. The white population was a mixture of various national stocks, no more than 60 per cent English in origin, with heavy infusions of Swiss, Welsh, French, Scotch-Irish, and German. Religious persecution, war, and agricultural depression

---

[44] Krout and Fox, *Completion of Independence,* pp. 192–193; Washington's letter to David Humphreys, 1785.

[45] Perry Miller (ed.), Daniel Drake, *Discourse on the History, Character, and Prospects of the West* (1834) (Gainesville, Fla., 1955), p. 10.

[46] Smith, *Virgin Land,* p. 11; see especially Chaps. I and II.

sent numbers of Germans to America from the Rhineland after 1750, until by 1775 it was estimated that one American colonist in every ten came from Germany. The Scotch-Irish were nearly as numerous. In 1774–75, the emigrant lists showed between 1,000 and 2,000 persons leaving Scots and Irish ports for America, a rate which apparently continued for some years.[47] One Pennsylvania newspaper in 1786 reported that 20,000 Germans and Scotch-Irish had arrived in Pennsylvania in the previous three years. The French Revolution, and the revolts in the French West Indies, sent a good many Frenchmen; depressions in Wales, abortive Irish rebellions, and Swiss economic troubles sent contingents from those countries. However, since the years 1775–1815 were years of war and disturbance both in America and Europe, migration to the new country was not large, probably not more than a total of 250,000 for the entire period.[48]

After 1815 the rate of arrival rose rapidly. Peace, economic upturn, and cheap land in the United States, combined with worsening conditions in Europe, brought thousands of foreigners streaming into American ports. Land prices were low in America and labor prices high. A whole farm in the United States cost no more than a year's rent in Germany. Ninety-nine of every one hundred parishes in England had no land for sale large enough to support a cottage, and land taxes in the United States were so ridiculously low in comparison to Europe's as to seem nonexistent.[49]

Employment was good, wages good. A common mechanic could ask a dollar a day and board, or skilled workmen two dollars a day or more, in money whose purchasing power was at least four times that of Europe's. It was quite possible, one immigrant wrote back from western Virginia, for a workman's family to "adorn the table three times a day like a wedding dinner—tea, coffee, beef, fowls, pies, eggs, pickles, good bread. . . ." But passage to this New World was no pleasure jaunt. The boats which left Liverpool, Le Havre, and Bremen (the most popular embarkation ports) were small, dirty, and cramped. A voyage to America might take twelve weeks; typhus, smallpox, and "ship fever" claimed hundreds of lives en route.[50]

[47] An authoritative study is Henry J. Ford, *The Scotch-Irish in America* (Princeton, 1915).
[48] Blake, *American Life,* Chap. 12; Krout and Fox, *Completion of Independence,* pp. 376–378, 403; Wish, *Society and Thought,* pp. 133–141, 185–186.
[49] Blake, *American Life,* pp. 212–213; Krout and Fox, *Completion of Independence,* p. 3; Jensen, *New Nation,* pp. 122–123.
[50] Steerage passage, which cost £10–£12 in 1817, was reduced to £3–£10

American immigration policy, as John Quincy Adams explained it in 1818, was that any immigrant could come to America to compete with a citizen for his job if he wished, but he would receive neither help nor hindrance in so doing. Some states and localities, however, especially those with large tracts of land, made active appeals to European immigrants. Between 1815 and 1820 nearly 100,000 immigrants arrived in the United States. The majority went to the cities of the Middle States and to the West. Few of them went South, where they faced the competition of slave labor and where cotton agriculture demanded more initial investment than most immigrants possessed. New England's small farms and high land prices drew very few. New York State quadrupled its population between 1790 and 1820, while Connecticut gained very little. By 1836 an average of 80,000 immigrants were making the long sea crossing each year, a tide that swelled every year after that for the next half-century.[51]

The cumulative impact of this flood of immigration on American society was very large. It helped make possible the tremendous territorial expansion that marked American history in the first half of the nineteenth century. For its conquest of continental space the United States needed new population at a rate far faster than the birth rate could ever increase it; to get it, the new nation practically drained the surplus population of western Europe. The United States needed also a huge labor force to exploit its agricultural and industrial potential, and a market to absorb its products. Immigration helped to supply both, and by the time of Jackson the melting pot was at full boil. A large percentage of the new immigrants were non-English; all were blended into "this American, this new man," of whom Crèvecoeur had once written so glowingly. The landless wanted land. Others, here to escape taxes, military service, landlords, creditors, and churches, wanted a free and open society. It is no wonder that Federalists complained that every new boatload brought more votes for Jefferson, and that the Whigs shuddered at every Irish vote that landed at New England or New York wharves. Such people exerted tremendous influence on the shaping of American ideas and on the course of American institutions in the years to come. The development of American society would not have been the same without them.

---

by 1830, but captains packed their ships so tightly that the British government finally required four cubic feet of space per passenger by law. See Krout and Fox, *Completion of Independence,* p. 5; Blake, *American Life,* pp. 218–219.

[51] Krout and Fox, *Completion of Independence,* pp. 8–9.

CHAPTER 6

Emerging Patterns of Social Life

THE United States at the beginning of the nineteenth century was an overwhelmingly rural society.[1] No more than 4 or 5 per cent of the population lived in communities of more than 8,000 people, yet city life, in America as in Europe, formed the core of its civilization, and the phenomenal growth of cities after 1800 gave urban society a disproportionately large influence in the formation of American culture. The major social, intellectual, and political movements of the early nineteenth century developed in the cities, and in them the new republican society was shaped and directed.[2] In 1800 there were only five American cities of more than 10,000 population. Philadelphia, the largest with 70,000, was also the second largest city in the English-speaking world. New York with 60,000 stood second in the United States, Boston third with 25,000, Charleston fourth with 18,000, and Baltimore fifth with 13,000. How fast these cities grew is shown by the fact that Philadelphia gained 30,000 people in the next ten years; by 1830 New York and Philadelphia both had passed 150,000, while such cities as Albany, Pittsburgh, Cincinnati, and St. Louis grew at an even swifter rate.[3]

Allowing for regional differences, life in American cities was much

---

[1] Kenneth and Anna Roberts (eds.), *Moreau de St. Méry's American Journey* (Garden City, N.Y., 1947), is a mine of information on American life in the 1790's, written by a French refugee.

[2] Henry Adams' survey of American city life in 1800, *The Formative Years*, I, is brilliant. See also Blake's informative Chap. II, *American Life;* Krout and Fox, *Completion of Independence*, Chap. XIV; and Faulkner, *Political and Social History*, pp. 206–208. John Bach McMaster, *History*, I, Chap. I, is also useful.

[3] Krout and Fox, *Completion of Independence*, p. 10; Jensen, *New Nation*, p. 115.

the same everywhere. During the Revolution the conservatives and radicals argued bitterly over the nature of city government, and the conservatives, who favored incorporation, mayoral government, and council or aldermanic organization, generally won. Charleston incorporated shortly after the war, Philadelphia and New York somewhat later; Samuel Adams almost single-handedly kept Boston under a town-meeting government which the city retained until 1822, long after Adams' death. These city governments exercised rigid control over local affairs, particularly over trade, specifying by law the number of apprentices in a certain trade, licensing shops, and controlling standards of measure and grade in commodities such as wood, bread, hay, meat, and so on.[4]

Despite its tight hold over urban economic life, city government did not assume responsibility for much else. Police protection was almost unknown. During the day sheriffs and constables were presumably available, while at night city watchmen with lanterns and rattles cried the hours, tried doors, and watched for fires. In the majority of cities private citizens took turns patrolling their own neighborhoods, or hired watchmen to do so. It was neither uncommon nor unwise for those who went abroad at night to carry pistols or a sword cane. A few large cities lit their main streets by oil lamps, which were not used in rain or bright moonlight. After Baltimore put in gas lights in 1816, other cities followed suit, though Philadelphia did not convert until 1837. Fire, however, was perhaps a greater urban hazard than crime. Large cities averaged one fire per night. Moreau de St. Méry, from October 1794 to October 1795, counted seventeen major fires in Philadelphia; as late as 1838 a visitor to New York reported at least one alarm per night for twenty-nine consecutive weeks. Cities depended either on volunteer fire companies (which sometimes fought pitched battles at fires or looted the buildings) or on "mutual" companies which fought fires only on the property of members. Half of Boston's fire engines were privately owned and most of Philadelphia's belonged to insurance companies.[5]

All American cities had narrow dirt or cobblestoned streets, laid out in haphazard European fashion—except Philadelphia, which was built on Penn's gridiron pattern. No city possessed an adequate sewage disposal system, and only Philadelphia had municipal street cleaners. Garbage lay in the streets to be picked over by human and animal scav-

---

[4] Jensen, p. 118; Krout and Fox, p. 22.
[5] Faulkner, pp. 207–208; Krout and Fox, pp. 24, 26; Moreau de St. Méry, pp. 308–309, 331–333.

engers; the gutters of poor sections ran with sewage. Water was supplied by cisterns, private wells, community pumps, and street vendors, until the great epidemics of the 1790's forced cities to consider the purity of their water supplies. Philadelphia began piping water in wooden conduits from the Schuylkill into portions of the city, and in 1822 a system of iron pipes was completed to service the entire city. Aaron Burr's Manhattan Company established a water system for New York in 1799, using log, stone, and lead pipes leading from a reservoir which was badly polluted within a decade. Finally, in 1835, New York began work on the publicly owned system that eventually developed into the Croton Reservoir.[6]

Each of the major American cities in 1800 had a flavor and a temperament of its own. Boston resembled an old-fashioned English market town, with crooked, narrow streets, dark and badly lighted at night, paved with round cobbles. It was a town of shops and artisans, chandlers, wigmakers, tailors, ship suppliers, trade and import houses, and banks, of wharves lined with ships and seafront streets busy with merchants and sailors. In 1794 Charles Bulfinch began construction of some attached brick houses on Tontine Crescent, stamping the city's architecture thereafter with the Boston "Federal" style, just as his State House building, India Wharf, Federal Street Theater, remodeled Faneuil Hall, and the New South Church gave Boston its distinctive style of public buildings. Like other American cities, Boston had no well-defined "quarters" for poor, middle class, and rich, though wealthy residential areas and what shortly were to be slums had begun to appear by 1810. A settled, conservative city, Boston had more than its share of civic pride; few Bostonians would have disagreed, perhaps, with George Cabot, who stoutly believed that his city possessed "more wisdom and virtues than any other part of the world."[7]

New York City underwent tremendous growth between 1783 and 1820, when it became the nation's first city in both population and commerce. "The quaint old Dutch town into which Irving was born," remarked William Cullen Bryant, had by his time "become transformed into a comparatively gay metropolis." New York often reminded trav-

[6] Blake, *American Life*, p. 209; Faulkner, *Political and Social History*, pp. 23–24. Moreau de St. Méry, who visited Boston, New York, Philadelphia, and Baltimore in 1793–98, took copious notes which make fascinating reading. See also Carl Bridenbaugh, *Cities in Revolt* (New York, 1938).

[7] Henry Adams, *Formative Years*, pp. 12–13; Krout and Fox, *Completion of Independence*, pp. 10–13, 26–27, 133; McMaster, *History*, I, pp. 11–17.

elers of Liverpool. It had badly paved streets, brick sidewalks and curbs, and managed to be "as foul a town," Henry Adams wrote, "as a town surrounded by the tides could be." Wall Street in 1800 was begining to rival Philadelphia as a banking and trading center, and the Tontine Coffee House at the corner of Wall and Water housed stock exchanges and insurance offices. More than a mile of warehouses on the East River side of the island pointed to the city's future; so too did the floods of immigrants pouring into the lower East Side. By 1840 New York had slums that surpassed London's and shocked even Charles Dickens. Not until after the Civil War were the city's famous "foraging pigs" driven from the streets.

There were strong traces of Dutch influence still evident in early nineteenth-century New York street names, yellow brick houses, bilingual church services, and so on—but New York was by far the most cosmopolitan of the American cities. As early as 1750 it was possible to hear any of eighteen different languages spoken on its streets, and by 1850 almost half of its total population was foreign born. New York was an urbane, sophisticated city with a well-bred, gay, hospitable social life of theaters, parades, clubs, balls, lectures, and literary groups. There were famous local hangouts like Fraunces Tavern or the City Hotel or Wiley's Bookshop, clubs like the Sub Rosa or the Turtle, and more serious literary groups like the Uranian or Calliopean Societies. This was the bright, brittle, witty Knickerbocker city of Irving's *Salamagundi*.[8]

Philadelphia, which served as the national capital until 1800, was generally agreed to be the cleanest, best-governed, healthiest, and most elegant of American cities. Neither London nor Paris, thought Jefferson, was quite so handsome as Philadelphia, and travelers rarely failed to remark its solid, prosperous atmosphere of sober well-being. It had the finest church in the nation (Anglican Christ Church), the largest public building (the State House), the most bookshops and publishing houses, the most banks, and the largest public market. It was the center of American medical and scientific study, and, with the possible exception of Boston, the nation's foremost educational center. Philadelphia had a planned street system (with even-numbered houses on one side, odd on the other), street-cleaning and watering services, excellent street

[8] Henry Adams, *Formative Years*, pp. 15–17; McMaster, *History*, I, pp. 54–57; Krout and Fox, *Completion of Independence*, pp. 14–26, 219–223. See also Kendall Taft, *The Minor Knickerbockers* (New York, 1947), Chap. I, and Sidney I. Pomerantz, *New York: An American City, 1783–1803* (New York, 1938).

lamps, a patrol and watch system, a good water supply with a steam pump, and a strong tradition of civic responsibility that derived from the days of Franklin. Its buildings, the traveler Charles Janson wrote in 1799, "are well built, chiefly of red brick, and in general three stories high. A great number of private houses have marble steps to the street door, and in other respects are finished in a style of elegance." Three-fifths of Philadelphia's streets were paved and had brick sidewalks with gutter and curb. High Street (later Market) was 100 feet wide, Broad Street 113 feet. The Philadelphia Market, an arcaded one-story building a half-mile long, was undoubtedly the finest in the world.[9]

Washington, the new capital to which Jefferson moved his administration, was a raw, half-finished city in the fever-ridden swamp. The real estate boom-and-bust had left some crumbling relics of houses near Pennsylvania Avenue, which in 1801 was not much more than a causeway across an alder swamp and Tiber Creek. The single wing of the Capitol faced seven or eight boardinghouses, and a mile away, near the President's house, was a cluster of residences and shops. Nearby Baltimore had clean, broad streets on a grid plan like Philadelphia's, with distinctive wooden houses built flush to the street and painted in white, yellow, and blue. Charleston, the southernmost of the American cities, was a prosperous trading town, the center of the West Indies trade and also the largest cotton port—as early as 1801, before the cotton boom, it was shipping 20 million pounds of cotton each year. A wealthy, proud city dominated by an oligarchy of old mercantile families and landed gentry, Charleston had an atmosphere unlike that of any other American city. Its brick and stone houses, faced with delicately shaded stucco in pink, green, blue, or yellow, its moss-hung trees and filigreed ironwork, decorated gates and bricked streets, its gardens of oranges and palmettos, gave it an exotic, Mediterranean flavor that was distinctively Charlestonian.[10]

The majority of Americans in 1800, however, lived in small towns or on farms. The smaller the town, or the nearer the farm to the Western edge of civilization, the simpler life became. The most distant settler might live in a cave or a lean-to (as Lincoln's family once did) or at most in a crude log cabin. A habitable one-room cabin could be con-

[9] Henry Adams, pp. 16–18; McMaster, pp. 64–68; Krout and Fox, pp. 16–19. See also Carl and Jessica Bridenbaugh, *Rebels and Gentlemen* (New York, 1942).

[10] Henry Adams, p. 18; McMaster, pp. 83–85; Krout and Fox, pp. 19–20, 132, 185–188, 370.

structed with a few tools and without nails in about two days and finished for occupancy in four or five. The majority of all American buildings west of the Alleghanies in 1810 were built of logs—and much better built, William Cobbett thought, than most English farm cottages. In New England, where it was easier to obtain nails and finished lumber, the farmer usually built a two-story frame house with adz-hewn beams and shaved shingles, a steep roof for snow, a protected lean-to at the rear, and a dirt-floored cellar to store barrels of salt pork, brine beef, potatoes, and apples. Pennsylvania and New York State farmers used brick or plastered masonry, but their plans varied only slightly from the New England pattern. From Maryland southward the farmer added a veranda and built a central hallway for summer ventilation. The tremendous Greek Revival plantation houses or imitation chateaux were for wealthy planters only.[11]

Wherever he lived, the farmer made his living by hard, backbreaking labor that involved his entire family. Some observers claimed that American farmers worked much harder than British or European, and it seems to be true that few Englishmen lasted on American farms when they emigrated. In the beginning the farmer cleared his land by burning, by girdling and felling trees, and by grubbing out stones, brush, and stumps by hand. After he cleared it and put in a crop, he battled against a trying and capricious climate, armies of new weeds and insects, and a variety of unfamiliar plant and animal diseases. His farm was supposed to provide for practically all his needs, with a surplus for sale or export, and it usually did. On the frontier it had to, for stores were few and distances great. Except for $10 spent for salt and iron, one farmer in 1797 in New Jersey "bought nothing to eat, drink, or wear, as my farm provided all."[12]

City man and countryman in America ate well, for soil and seas provided food in God's plenty. America possessed virtually unlimited acreage of good grazing land for cattle. Pigs and chickens, which could forage for food, were raised everywhere, including the most crowded sections of cities. Fish were plentiful along the coasts and inland rivers. Because fish and pork could both be easily preserved (by salting or smoking), they were staple in American diet. American farmers raised few goats or sheep, since both required supervision and were subject to diseases.

[11] George R. Stewart, *American Ways of Life* (Garden City, N.Y., 1954), pp. 152–154; Krout and Fox, pp. 19–20, 99–101, 140–141.
[12] Henry Adams, p. 23; McMaster, p. 19.

The first colonists planted wheat, barley, rye, and oats; Indian corn or maize shortly became an even more popular crop. Farmers also raised the usual English vegetables (peas, beans, cabbage, marrow) and added a few of their own, such as squash, pumpkins, and yams. Potatoes were not widely planted until the nineteenth century; tomatoes, considered by many to be poisonous, were practically unknown. Apples, peaches, and pears were extensively cultivated, while bananas, figs, pineapples, and other fruits were imported from the West Indies.[13]

Nowhere in the world did people have such a variety of food, and such quantities, as in the United States. A visitor to the New York City market in 1796 counted sixty-three kinds of fish, fourteen kinds of shell-fish, fifty-two kinds of meat and fowl, and twenty-seven kinds of vege-tables for sale. The price of a whole pig in 1798 was half a dollar.[14]

Contemporary accounts show that the American appetite was impres-sively large. Count Volney, who was almost hospitalized by an American breakfast of fish, steak, ham, sausage, salt beef, and hot breads, gave a horrified account of an American gastronomic day:[15]

In the morning they deluge their stomachs with a quart of hot water im-pregnated with tea, or so slightly with coffee that it is mere colored water; and they swallow, almost without chewing, hot bread, half-baked toast soaked with butter, cheese of the fattest kind, slices of salt or hung beef, ham, etc., all which are nearly insoluble. At dinner they have boiled pastes under the name of puddings, and the fattest are esteemed the most delicious; all their sauces, even for roast beef, are melted butter, or fat; under the name of pie or pumpkin, their pastry is nothing but a greasy paste, never sufficiently baked. To digest these viscous substances they take tea bitter to the taste, in which state it affects the nerves so powerfully that even the English find it brings on a more obstinate restlessness than coffee. Supper again introduces

[13] The most complete study is Richard Osborn Cummings, *The American and His Food* (Chicago, 1940). See also Arthur Train, *The Story of Everyday Things* (New York, 1941), pp. 239–240.

[14] Moreau de St. Méry, *American Journey*, pp. 156–158.

[15] Thomas Gwatkin reported that for breakfast in Virginia he had hot cakes, hash, hominy, eggs, cold beef, ham, and tea, and for dinner fish, fowl, beef, pork, veal, Madeira, hot toddies, and rum punch. Moreau de St. Méry had broth, beef, eggs, pork, fish, peas, cabbage, pastry, fruit, cheese, cider, beer, and white wine for dinner in Philadelphia. John Adams, while attending the Continental Congress in Philadelphia, wrote his wife of a dinner of "ducks, hams, chickens, beef, pig, tarts, custards, creams, jellies, fools, trifles, floating islands, beer, porter, and wine." W. E. Woodward, *The Way Our People Lived* (New York, 1944), 140 ff.; Moreau de St. Méry, pp. 265–266.

salt meats or oysters. As Chastellux says, the whole day passes in heaping in-
digestions on one another. . . .

Though Americans had food in quantity and variety, the average diet
was likely to be ill-balanced and monotonous. Frontier meals leaned
heavily on game (a frontiersman could kill three to eight deer a day in
western Pennsylvania), "hawg and hominy," cornmeal mush, molasses,
bear oil for frying, and beans and peas. A Kentucky dinner, one traveler
wrote in 1806, consisted of "bacon, hominy, squirrel broth, and whiskey," though the settled farmer of course set a better table.[16] The dietary base of most farm diets was corn, in the form of meal, mush, cakes,
hominy, and (after the wheat blight of the 1790's) "rye and Injun
bread," baked from a mixture of rye and corn flours. There were regional food preferences, naturally—in New England cod and beans, in
the West wheat and game, in the South yams and cowpeas—and dietary
differences based on food habits imported by Dutch, German, Scotch-
Irish, and other immigrant groups. Farm wives served meat at every
meal, usually salted or smoked; farm families, in fact, ordinarily preferred salted or cured meat to fresh. Farmers sweetened their food with
molasses or brown sugar, spiced it with herbs from their gardens, and
purchased only salt from a store.

The city man's diet was not markedly different from the farmer's,
though he usually had less chance to eat fresh vegetables. It was difficult to preserve meats in the city (a freshly killed chicken lasted about
eighteen hours in New York), so cattle were driven to the markets and
slaughtered on the spot. City laborers lived chiefly on bread and meat,
usually salt pork, pickled beef, fish, or sausage. A typical supper for an
ordinary man, according to a young New York lady in 1830, was salt
pork, beets, potatoes, and cabbage. Wealthier city people had much
more varied meals, of course, with white bread, fowls, shellfish, fruits,
and a wider range of vegetables. Like their country cousins, the majority of city dwellers lacked milk, fresh vegetables, and fruit in their
diets. Poor diet was common in all walks of life, scurvy and rickets
endemic among the urban workers.[17]

A great change in American dietary habits came after 1820, when
the introduction of refrigeration and new canning methods solved the

[16] Henry Adams, *Formative Years,* p. 30.
[17] Richard O. Cummings, *The American and His Food* (Chicago, 1940), pp.
25–43.

ancient problem of food preservation. The principles of heat canning were known in 1800, though it was forty more years before canning came into wide commercial and home use. Two firms in New York began commercial canning in 1819, while the substitution of tin containers for glass in the 1830's made the process cheaper and more satisfactory. New England farmers had stored ice in icehouses since the late seventeenth century, and it had long been used by the wealthy for cooling drinks and making ice cream. Though Thomas Moore of Maryland patented an efficient refrigerator in 1803, the cost of ice cutting and storage left ice refrigeration still too expensive for the average family. An improved ice cutter, developed in 1820, cut the cost by more than half and made ice available in quantity for the first time. Ice companies flourished in the cities, and by 1840 a refrigerator, according to the New York *Mirror*, was "as much an article of necessity" as a kitchen table. As methods of refrigeration, food preservation, and transportation improved, both rural and urban families enjoyed more diversified and better-balanced diets.

The American of 1790 dressed much the same as a Britisher of corresponding economic and social station. American styles, observers noted, usually lagged about a year behind the British, which in turn were about a year behind the French. Some gentlemen still wore red coats in church and at the theater, carried small swords or sword canes, and wore tight white doeskin breeches. There were sharp distinctions in dress between upper-class city men and laborers, and between city workers and farmers. The well-to-do merchant might dress in velvet, or imported woolens, wearing silk stockings, a linen stock, knee breeches, and a satin waistcoat. The mechanic wore buckskin breeches, a leather apron, a flannel jacket, felt hat, wool stockings, and cowhide shoes with leather buckles. The farmer wore homespun breeches and jacket, cut and sewn at home, heavy boots or moccasins, a homemade shirt of linsey-woolsey or deerskin, and wool stockings, with a broadcloth or corduroy suit for weddings, christenings, and burials.[18]

The best satins, brocades, damasks, woolens, and cottons were imported, which put them beyond the reach of most American pocketbooks. Since the preparation of cotton and woolen cloth was a laborious

[18] Krout and Fox, *Completion of Independence*, pp. 33–35; Faulkner, *Political and Social History*, pp. 210–211. The most complete treatment is that of Alice M. Earle, *Two Centuries of Costume in America* (2 vols., New York, 1903).

process, the loom and spinning wheel were standard equipment in every household. Preparing linen was especially difficult, requiring as many as thirty bleachings to produce a white cloth. Pennsylvania Germans apparently specialized in linens, for according to a popular couplet

> Where live High German people and low Dutch
> There trade in weaving linen cloth is much,

and the Scotch-Irish reportedly loomed the best woolens. Most clothes, however, were made from a combination of materials. Linsey-woolsey, a combination of linen and wool, was popular in the North for warmth and durability. Fustian, a cotton-flax mixture, was widely used in the South. Jeans, a wool and cotton mixture, was another popular mixture.[19]

The introduction of looming and spinning machinery, and the rise of the textile industry in the early nineteenth century, changed the entire clothing industry within a few years. Cheap and plentiful cloth, combined with the development of factory-made, ready-to-wear clothing, revised American clothing habits. By the time of the Civil War class distinctions in style, cut, or fabric had practically disappeared. It was virtually impossible of a Sunday, foreign travelers observed by 1830, to distinguish a mechanic from a banker or a factory hand from a clerk.

Until about 1790, American men dressed in a combination of French and English styles, the more sophisticated following Paris fashions. A well-to-do city man's dress might consist of beaver hat, a blue cutaway coat with high collar and broad lapels, striped waistcoat, white linen stock, ruffled cuffs, light-colored breeches buttoning below the knee, and high boots with turned-down tops. By 1800 the full-length pantaloon, a French import, was beginning to replace knee breeches and had done so by 1810—the first patent for suspenders, issued in 1804, was an omen of change. By 1830 men's clothes had developed a broad-shouldered coat with a tight waist, rolled collars, frilled shirts, cravats, and tight trousers with bootstraps. A few men, notably clergymen, still wore wigs in 1800, though most men wore long hair tied in a queue—all but five of the fifty-six members of the New York legislature wore their hair thus in 1798. James Madison was the last President to wear a queue, and the fashion was completely gone by another decade.[20]

---

[19] Krout and Fox, *Completion of Independence,* pp. 104–105; W. C. Langdon, *Everyday Things in American Life* (New York, 1941), I, pp. 205, 251.

[20] Krout and Fox, *Completion of Independence,* pp. 33–34; Train, *Everyday Things,* pp. 235–236; Woodward, *Way Our People Lived,* pp. 160–162. John

Women's fashions reflected a strong French influence and, in time-honored tradition, changed rapidly. In the late 1790's a trend appeared toward light, sheer, clinging materials, with shorter and narrower skirts, sleeveless or puff sleeves, low-cut neck, and an absence of petticoat or whalebone supports. The tremendous hair arrangements of the preceding decade (some mounted on wire forms) gave way to loosely curled hair, shoulder length, secured with ribbons or combs, sometimes lightly powdered. By 1800 hair was even shorter, plastered into tight curls with pomade. In comparison to the fashions of 1790, turn-of-the-century dresses were extremely revealing, leading to warnings about health and morals. By 1806 the French "Empire" fashion was in full swing—long narrow dresses, narrow sleeves, high waistlines, low-cut neck, classically long hair curled into loose tendrils and decorated with ribbons, leaves, and flowers. In another decade stays and stomach boards began to appear, along with French pantalettes, leg-of-mutton sleeves, and a full skirt, soon to become the hoop skirt.[21]

American colonists brought with them the contemporary middle-class British code of social behavior, itself adapted from the French. Despite the pressures of colonial and frontier life, Americans maintained—far from centers of elegance—at least minimum European standards of civility and deportment. As gradations of class, parallel to those of British society, emerged in the eighteenth century, upper-class Americans strained to acquire and maintain manners as polished as those of London. There were dozens of handbooks for the eager to follow—Henry Peacham's *Complete Gentleman,* Allstree's *Whole Duty of Man,* the anonymous *Friendly Instructor or Companion for Young Ladies and Gentlemen* (an especially popular reprint), and even children's manuals such as *A Pretty Little Pocket Book,* which advised the proper number of times to rise on one's toes before a curtsy.[22]

The number and popularity of such books reflected the self-conscious effort of a young, uncertain society to achieve urbanity and sophistication. Washington and Franklin, who as youths carefully set down rules

---

Quincy Adams was presumably the first President to wear pantaloons habitually, though Justice John Marshall stubbornly clung to knee breeches long after Jackson's men had defeated the Federalists.

[21] Krout and Fox, p. 35; Train, pp. 237–239.

[22] Dixon Wecter, *The Saga of American Society* (New York, 1937), pp. 161–165; and A. M. Schlesinger, *Learning How to Behave* (New York, 1946), pp. 6–7, 9–10; see also Chap. III, "Republican Etiquette."

of behavior and trained themselves to follow them, were typical young American colonial gentlemen. Lord Chesterfield, though popular as a gentleman's guide, was often attacked by moralists (Abigail Adams thought he inculcated "immoral, pernicious, and Libertine principals into the mind of a youth") and was finally expurgated and revised into *The American Chesterfield* (1827). *The Family Companion,* falsely ascribed to Chesterfield, went through forty editions between 1751 and 1800. Lady Pennington's *Unfortunate Mother's Advice to Her Daughters,* Moore's *Fables for the Female Sex,* Fordyce's *Sermons to Young Women,* and other guidebooks appeared serially in the magazines, read by the same young ladies who swooned over Samuel Richardson's *Pamela,* which was, of course, the most popular parable of behavior and manners of them all. These books all emphasized the traditionally religious basis of proper social behavior, and related manners to morals.[23] How one acted, and by what code, in the contemporary view reflected one's inner virtues and shaped one's moral course of action.

By the turn of the century it was evident that there was a slow shift of emphasis from morality as the standard of manners to propriety and custom. Behavior became what one's class did—not what moral standards one's class adhered to. The French Revolution and the slave rebellions in the West Indies sent thousands of French to the United States, adding Gallic spice to city society. Louis Philippe himself taught French in America; Rouchefoucald lived with a barber; Talleyrand, the Viscomte de Noailles, and hosts of lesser nobility took up residence in American cities. On Broadway, a New Yorker wrote, one could "jostle ex-kings and ex-empresses and ex-nobles any day."[24]

The French, assisted by a number of wealthy Americans, changed the style of American behavior.[25] Washington's administrations were marked by a gay and sophisticated social life that was almost Parisian in flavor. Mary Allen wrote happily in her diary of the "crowds of foreigners of highest rank and ministers with their suites from all parts of the world" who graced Philadelphia society, and young Mary Binney twittered to her diary, "I have not one minute to spare from French, music, balls, and plays. Oh dear, this dissipation will kill me!"[26]

[23] F. L. Mott, *Golden Multitudes* (New York, 1947), pp. 29–32.
[24] Krout and Fox, *Completion of Independence,* pp. 31–33, 102–109.
[25] Howard Mumford Jones, *America and French Culture* (Chapel Hill, 1927), Chaps. VII and VIII, "French Manners in America."
[26] Anne Wharton, *Social Life in the Early Republic* (Philadelphia, 1902), p. 110.

The New England temperature of the Adams administrations, however, was quite different from the Virginia life of the Washingtons, and as Mrs. Stoddert, a capital hostess, remarked sadly, "had not half the gayety." The removal of the capital to Washington City and the arrival of the Jeffersonian Republicans brought an even more abrupt change to political society. Though Jefferson was a great lover of good company, good talk, and good wines, he limited form and ceremony severely. The Federalist-Jeffersonian political conflict, the rise to influence of the business class, and the growing importance of the American middle class all helped to produce great changes in American manners after 1800. Distinctions of dress, speech, and behavior lessened visibly; mass education began its leveling effects; caste and birth lines counted for less and less. Emergent nationalism called for the development of "American manners," not foreign, to fit the democratic society over which Andrew Jackson was soon to assume authority.

British manners were of course severely criticized during and after the Revolution. Timothy Dwight in 1785 lampooned those "travell'd apes" who returned from London with Anglicized manners, "of worth bereft, of real sense forlorn." So too Royall Tyler's popular comedy, *The Contrast* (1787), contrasted Billy Dimple, an imitation English fop, with Colonel Manly, a true-blue native American gentleman. The intense nationalism of the War of 1812 convinced many Americans of the need for a "republican" code of behavior, consistent with the American philosophy of liberty and equality. "Native" books of etiquette poured from the presses to replace British reprints, while popular magazines exhorted American ladies and gentlemen to "get rid of *imported superfluities* of etiquette" and to "promote sensible and easy changes of good will and sensibility." "We should all be glad," wrote Nathaniel P. Willis, "to see a distinctively American school of good manners, in which all useless etiquettes were thrown aside."[27]

These "native" and "democratic" manners, augmented by an aggressive Jacksonian equalitarianism, baffled and irritated British and European visitors to the United States after 1820. English travelers remarked on the independence of servants and menials, the invasion of privacy by inquisitive strangers, the alternation of "cold civility" with undue familiarity, the failure to follow form, the lack of social finesse,

[27] Edwin H. Cady, *The Gentleman in America* (Syracuse, 1949), is an authoritative study of the development of American manners and social ideals.

the aggressiveness of crowds, and the rudeness of women and children.[28] Mrs. Trollope, whose *Domestic Manners of the Americans* (1832) showed her in an almost constant state of shock during her travels, exemplified the classic British reaction to American society. Neither she nor the dozens of other foreign travelers who preceded and followed her could quite understand that the purpose of the American social code as it developed after 1820 was not to set groups apart, but rather to merge them.

American attitudes toward sexual morality were much the same as those of contemporary England except for minor differences arising from history and environment.[29] The powerful Calvinistic tradition (plus an Anglicanism more rigid than England's) produced a stricter kind of morality in the American colonies than in the parent society.[30] The lack of sharp class distinctions made moral relationships among social classes quite different from those of Britain or Europe; the victimized servant girl and the rakish aristocrat of Richardsonian fiction meant little, for example, to American experience. A national shortage of women, especially acute in rural and frontier areas, gave women much more independence than they possessed in Europe and consequently greater freedom. Moreau de St. Méry, commenting on the Philadelphia of the 1790's, found its morals no looser than Europe's, though he was continually amazed at American frankness concerning sex.[31] Crèvecoeur thought "a general decency" prevailed everywhere in America; Alexis de Tocqueville, writing a generation later, thought American morals stricter than British or French.

Such observations, of course, were based on limited experience. The European custom of keeping mistresses, while unusual in America, was not unknown in wealthy urban groups. St. Méry observed a profusion

---

[28] Jane Mesick, *The English Traveller in America 1785–1835* (New York, 1922), "Manners and Customs," pp. 64–108.

[29] Stewart, *American Ways*, pp. 184, 186, *passim;* Arthur W. Calhoun, *A Social History of the American Family* (Philadelphia, 1917–19), II, Chap. II.

[30] See H. B. Parkes, "Morals and Law Enforcement in Colonial New England," *New England Quarterly*, V (1932), 431–452. Parkes concludes that "sexual morals were probably stricter in New England than in any other community of equal size that ever existed." See also Edmund Morgan, "The Puritan and Sex," *ibid.*, XV (1942), 541–607; and Emil Oberholzer, *Delinquent Saints* (New York, 1956).

[31] Moreau de St. Méry, *American Journey*, pp. 285, 295.

of "young and pretty streetwalkers" in Philadelphia, saw a bevy of attractive sailors' girls in Baltimore, and found an entire section of New York City, called "Holy Ground," set aside for prostitution. There were large numbers of illegitimate children born each year in Philadelphia, he noted, and the easy virtue of the city's servant girls shocked him.[32] However, Philadelphia was not unusually immoral. Charles Francis Adams' study of Massachusetts church records showed that of two hundred couples married over a fourteen-year span, sixty-six confessed to premarital relations. "Bundling," though never so widespread as later supposed, was a natural result of frontier conditions and its innocence no doubt varied with the persons involved. Nearly all travelers commented on the surprising amount of freedom granted to American youth; at the same time many of them agreed that there was probably less extramarital activity after marriage than was customary in Europe. St. Méry noted that though girls "enjoy unlimited liberty" before marriage, an American wife "lives only for her husband, to devote herself without surcease to the care of her household and her home."[33]

Negro slavery complicated Southern problems of morality and created special moral patterns characteristic only of the slaveholding South. As early as the 1750's, travelers commented on the effects of the slave system on white morals. "Fundamental morality," one social historian has remarked after reading contemporary accounts of Southern life, even in colonial days was "a very scarce commodity among people of the ruling class."[34] The presence of a completely subject race in the South, some believed, had a weakening effect on white morality and developed certain character traits among the masters. Thomas Jefferson, in his *Notes on Virginia,* noted how the absolute authority of white over Negro seemed to encourage arrogance, lack of self-control, and bullying in the master, giving "loose rein to the worst passions," an observation confirmed by later commentators. The freedom of sex relations among white youths and Negro girls worried many parents and clergymen, though such relationships apparently often received tacit social sanction. After 1790 this kind of relationship became a distinctive pattern in the Southern social system.[35]

[32] *Ibid.,* pp. 284–285; 123, 315, 302–304.
[33] *Ibid.,* pp. 316, 286–287.
[34] Calhoun, *American Family,* I, 328–329.
[35] *Ibid.,* II, 286–290. The North Carolina Supreme Court even ruled that a white man could not be punished for fornication or adultery with a Negro slave woman, since she had no legal standing in court; *ibid.,* p. 291. See also

"Marriages in America," Franklin wrote in 1782, "are more general, and more generally early, than in Europe." With cheap land available and his labor belonging to himself, no young American need wait for capital in order to marry, as in Europe he often must. Nor did a young woman need to stay unwed, since women were in short supply and each wife could have her own independent household. And American marriages were unusually fecund. Families of more than ten children were common, and David Ramsay, the South Carolina historian, found one woman with thirty-four living children.[36]

British and French travelers were always astonished that in America the delicate and important business of marriage contracts was either neglected or left to the principals. The "arranged marriage" never found much acceptance in the United States. A few colonial families tried to preserve the custom (as Samuel Sewall did with his daughter Betty, who would have none of it), but the dowry, the *dot*, the marriage articles, and other European nuptial apparatus were all virtually non-existent in the United States before 1780. Brides and bridegrooms, of course, might recognize the benefits of a good match, but American marriages, most observers agreed, were usually made without reference to economic advantage. All this produced a different attitude toward marriage and divorce from that current in Europe.

Divorce in the United States seemed to be somewhat more frequent than abroad (except in Catholic or strict Anglican circles) and somewhat easier to obtain. Divorce laws varied by states, but cruelty and desertion, in addition to adultery (and at least eighteen other reasons) were recognized in the United States as grounds for divorce much earlier than they were in Europe. In frontier areas, where courts met infrequently, couples sometimes separated without bothering about legal formalities. On the other hand, some couples might live together without benefit of clergy for months until a circuit-riding parson arrived, or might neglect for years to legalize their union. In the absence of ministers there were also what the frontier called "left-handed marriages" by militia captains, doubtful justices of the peace, and even by the bride's father. As organized churches and the agencies of civil govern-

the discussion in W. J. Cash, *The Mind of the South* (New York, 1941), of the Negro woman in Southern life, pp. 95–96, and of violence in the South, stemming from "ideas of superiority to the Negro and the peerage of white men," pp. 55–56.

[36] Calhoun, *American Family,* "Marriage and Fecundity in the New Nation," II, 11–27.

ment gradually caught up with the waves of westward settlement, there was less of such casualness.[37]

The institution of slavery again caused certain modifications in the pattern of Southern family life. The availability of servants, and the evolution of a strict hierarchical pattern of domestic duties in an upper-class home, made household arrangements in the South quite different from those above the Mason-Dixon line.[38] Courtship and marriage were, in all but the lower economic white groups, highly formalized and ritualistic, bound by accepted restrictions, with much energy and attention expended on the rules of pursuit. In theory, at least, woman was idealized in a manner which, by 1800, had begun to take shape as the "Southern womanhood" ideal of nineteenth-century Southern chivalric romanticism. Whatever the ideal type, however, it was obvious that the Southern woman varied from it as considerably as her Northern or Western sisters. The English traveler Harriet Martineau, who was vitally interested in such things, found in the South some of "the strongest-minded and most remarkable women I have ever known," and others who were "the weakest women I have anywhere seen . . . , languid in body and with minds of no reach at all."[39]

One clearly identifiable characteristic of Southern family life was its tighter patriarchal control, at least in upper- and middle-class households. There was also in the South an unusually strong sense of consanguinity, since the family, in a status-conscious society, was the chief custodian of status. The avid interest in family trees, and the careful cultivation of second and third cousins once removed, which provided much material for later jests, was apparently a well-developed Southern trait by 1800. Intermarriage and family relationships were, of course, an important means of consolidating and retaining economic and political power in a semi-feudal, agrarian society.[40] The influence of a wealthy

[37] *Ibid.,* II, 32–34, and "Sex Morals in the Opening Continent," II, 149–161.

[38] The psychological effect on Southern children of being reared by a Negro "mammy" and familiar with Negro playmates under one set of relationships, and of shifting to a completely different set at adolescence, has still to be fully explored—particularly as regards the attitude of the nineteenth-century white male toward Negro and white women. See *ibid.,* II, 311–315.

[39] *Ibid.,* II, 321. See Cash, *Mind of the South,* pp. 97–98, for a discussion of Southern "gyneolatry."

[40] Calhoun, *American Family,* II, 335–336. Families sometimes kept up close relationships with thirty to sixty relatives. One old lady in Georgia in 1825 recalled very few dinners in her girlhood at which there were less than twenty-five at the table.

family connected with a dozen other families by blood and marriage, all holding a common point of view, is hard to overestimate.

Foreign travelers who commented on American family life often remarked that it seemed to lack the close-knit unity of the European family. There was no doubt some truth in the observation, though the American colonial family was unified in a somewhat different way. The New England settlers were family men rather than adventurers, and so too were the later Southern settlers. While the tight patriarchal structure of the European family was not justified by frontier conditions, the American family was nevertheless a strong unit, with important educative, protective, religious, and economic functions. It was, however, notably less father-directed than in Europe, especially on the frontier, where women had higher social and economic status, dowries were unimportant, and younger sons had equal opportunities with older ones.[41]

In European society the father was admittedly the head of the family unit, since he owned the land and had clear and traditional legal and social status. In colonial America and in the new United States, his sons might easily have an economic domain larger than his, and his daughters might just as easily leave his home to set up households of their own. Family wealth, social caste, and parental influence counted much less in a society as open and as fluid as that of the United States. The mobility of American society meant that the family no longer need be the chief unit of social continuity; the spread of popular education meant that it was no longer the sole medium of educational and cultural transmission.

European family traditions and customs fell by the wayside very early in American history, among them the superior position of the eldest son, deference to parental orders, responsibility for relatives, teaching of craft or professional skills, and so on. Equal division of property among children under American law tended to prevent the formation of family wealth; rapid dispersion of population in a new country relieved the necessity for accumulating large family acreages of land. In the United States, children could and did leave home at a very early age for frontier farm or city factory. Sons and daughters could, by hard work and a bit of luck, "go on their own" and spectacularly outdo their parents. When good land was cheap in the West, the matter of who inherited the family plot at home was often of little importance. In a society that

[41] Sister Frances Jerome Woods, *The American Family System* (New York, 1958), pp. 71–97.

demanded more and more skilled and unskilled labor of any sort, it was not at all necessary for fathers to teach sons how to make a living.

British and Europeans were also puzzled by the responsibilities placed on children in the United States and by the lack of strict parental restraints.[42] At twelve or thirteen, one Britisher wrote, "female children rejoice in the appellation of 'Misses' and begin to enjoy all the privileges of self-management." Some attributed this to the American feeling for equality, which counted a son's vote equal to the father's; others saw it as laxness of discipline or oversentimentalization of children. Much more likely, however, was the fact that in the United States, as in any society where population is sparse and resources great, children played a significant role. In a frontier society, boys and girls had to make their own way in life as soon as possible. Children of the late eighteenth and early nineteenth centuries reached maturity swiftly because they had to.[43]

The American society of the period, of course, was still predominantly built about and for the adult male. The legal position of women in the post-Revolutionary period was little different from that of women in England. Since American law followed Blackstone's dictum that "the husband and wife are one and that is the husband," a woman was therefore the ward of her husband or nearest male relative. Her right to hold property was narrowly restricted; she had no right to make a will, enter into contract, or sue in court without her husband's consent. She had no vote, was generally denied entrance to higher education or the professions, and could appear in public only under carefully supervised conditions. "The power of a woman," the Congregational clergy of Massachusetts resolved piously, "is in her dependence, flowing from the consciousness of that weakness which God has given her for her protection."[44]

The American ideal of womanhood in the early nineteenth century was still officially that of the seventeenth. Pride, intellectuality, hardness of mind—these were to be eschewed by ladies. "Politics, philosophy, mathematics, or metaphysics are not your province," the Reverend John Burnet told the women of his Massachusetts congregation. Women, he added, must recognize "that consciousness of inferiority which, for the

[42] Except in the Southern middle- and upper-middle class, where the attitude toward child training seems to have been fairly conservative. Calhoun, *American Family*, II, 336–337.

[43] *Ibid.*, II, 51–79.

[44] Blake, *American Life,* pp. 283–284.

sake of *order*, the all-wise Author of Nature manifestly intended for them."[45]

In actual practice American women had higher social position, greater responsibilities, and greater freedom than their European sisters. Under frontier conditions in a new land, women had key economic and social roles to play, and their shortage made their position even stronger. Wives were at a premium on the frontier, where a single woman (if she wished) could marry within a few weeks or even days after her arrival in a new community. One New York family, before moving to Illinois, hired the ugliest servant girl obtainable; nevertheless, a lonesome settler married her within ten days. In the cities, as the factories sprang up, women became an important part of the labor market. Though they were shamefully exploited, mill girls could earn enough to maintain independence regardless of their marriage chances.[46]

By the time of Jackson the contrast between the position of women in America and in Europe was sufficiently sharp to provoke comment from a number of foreign visitors. Tocqueville thought that American women, compared to European, showed "a masculine strength of understanding and manly energy," adding gallantly that they nevertheless possessed "great delicacy of personal appearance" and "the manners of women." But nowhere in the world, he believed, did women occupy "a loftier position." Harriet Martineau, who looked closely at the status of women in the United States, concluded that they were much better treated than Englishwomen. In America, another British lady noted with satisfaction, a wife did not have to black her husband's boots as a matter of course.[47]

Early American colonists had little time for play or amusement. There was much to do in a rough, hard-working society, and the colonists from the beginning held "a detestation of idlenesse." As life grew less rigorous and society more settled, they paid more attention to diversion and recreation.[48] On the frontier and farm there were log rollings, barn rais-

[45] Schlesinger, *Learning How to Behave.*
[46] Calhoun, *American Family*, II, Chaps. IV, V; Mary S. Benson, *Women in Eighteenth Century America* (New York, 1935), Chaps. IV–VI.
[47] Wecter, *American Society*, "Women in American Society," 289–348; Calhoun, *American Family*, II, 113; H. B. Parkes, *The United States of America: A History* (New York, 1953), p. 255.
[48] Foster Rhea Dulles, *America Learns to Play* (New York, 1940), and Jennie Holliman, *American Sports 1785–1835* (Durham, N.C., 1931), are thorough treatments of the subject. See also briefer treatments in Faulkner, *Political and*

ings, corn-husking and stump-clearing bees, harvesting celebrations, quilting parties, spinning bees, and so on. Farm boys and men hunted, skated, fished, and sometimes held competitive hunts. They wrestled, held foot races, shooting matches, and now and then fought savage, eye-gouging fights in "rough-and-tumble" or Yorkshire style. New England communities frowned on horse racing, though young men with pacers and trotters could hardly be expected to refrain from a test or two of a Sunday. Timothy Dwight listed the favorite New England sports in the 1780's as fishing, hunting, quoits, skating, bowls, shooting, and sailing. New England boys also played informal football, using a sawdust-filled bag or a leather-covered bladder, although the Reverend William Bentley of Salem wrote that "the bruising of shins rendered it disgraceful to those of better education." In the South, except for foxhunts, occasional cockfights, and horse racing, the list was much the same.[49]

City society placed greater emphasis on such diversions as balls, sleigh rides, picnics, parlor games, and theater parties. City men and boys played "fives" (a game resembling handball), battledore and shuttlecock, and bowls. New Englanders played "town ball" (a variation of English stool ball) and Philadelphians played cricket (as they still do). Larger cities had archery and tennis clubs. Swimming was popular in the seaboard states, and swimming schools enjoyed heavy patronage— John Quincy Adams learned diving in one of them at the age of sixty-one. Billiards, backgammon, and chess were popular parlor games. Gambling at cards and dice was widespread; even in Boston men and women played for high stakes. Cockfighting and bear- and bullbaiting still survived (though clandestinely) until the Civil War, some years after they had lost popularity in England.[50] Though both city and frontier were tolerant of fighting, commercial pugilism was never very successful in the United States until later in the nineteenth century. Tom Molyneaux, the freed Negro who claimed the American championship, had to do a good deal of his fighting in England.[51]

In both city and country by far the most popular of all recreations was dancing, which ranged from the genteel cotillions of Charleston's

---

Social History, pp. 58–60; Blake, American Life, pp. 350–352; Wish, Society and Thought, II, 275–278.

[49] Dulles, America Learns to Play, pp. 67–79, 136–145; Krout and Fox, Completion of Independence, pp. 386–388; Henry Adams, Formative Years, p. 38.

[50] Dulles, America Learns to Play, pp. 137–145.

[51] Ibid., pp. 144–145; Krout and Fox, Completion of Independence, p. 391.

St. Cecilia Society Ball to robust "bran dances" (barn dances) where country folk danced to exhaustion to the strains of "Worse to Better," "Ragged Jacket," or "Running Home." New dance steps spread rapidly, though ministers frowned on some of the more daring of them. Jedidiah Morse called dancing "the principal and foremost amusement" of the age, nor should one forget General Washington's famous feat of dancing for three consecutive hours with Mrs. Nathanael Greene.[52]

Until about 1820 city and farm people enjoyed much the same recreations and pastimes as their colonial grandfathers. The growth of cities, and the consequent concentration of a large laboring and artisan class in urban areas, soon provided a huge new market for commercialized sports and amusements. The county fair, a New England invention, developed by 1827 into a national institution, complete with spectacular commercialized entertainment. English equestrian shows, popular in the post-Revolutionary years, added clowns, tumblers, and jugglers for their American tours; there were perhaps thirty or more such shows touring the Eastern states before 1820. Animal menageries, which had already appeared in American cities by 1780, joined with the equestrian shows to become traveling circuses.[53]

Foot races, boat races, and walking races attracted thousands of spectators in the early decades of the nineteenth century, but horse races drew the largest crowds of all. Boats ran from New York and Philadelphia to Charleston for the racing season, and it was jokingly claimed that the demise of the great racer Diomed in 1808 caused as much national grief as Washington's death. The South, of course, had supported racing since the early eighteenth century, and after 1820 the Northern cities took it up enthusiastically. The Union track on Long Island regularly drew crowds of 50,000, while in 1823 nearly 100,000 watched Eclipse race Sir Henry. Trotters and pacers raced, too, at famous tracks such as Long Island's Jamaica or Philadelphia's Hunting Park.[54]

Possibly as a result of the frontier feeling that leisure time was wasted time, and perhaps too as part of the Old Calvinistic aversion to idleness, the American attitude toward sports in pre-Civil War years had a tinge of moral earnestness. Horse racing, popular as it was, never received unanimous social sanction. Recreation, a good many Americans seemed to feel, should add to one's virtue or moral power; play, as one minister

[52] Krout and Fox, pp. 180, 119, 140–141.
[53] *Ibid.*, pp. 399–400.
[54] *Ibid.*, pp. 390–392; Dulles, *America Learns to Play*, pp. 139–140.

put it, should be "useful and innocent." Physical development, relaxation, sporting competition, and healthful exercise were worthy goals, true, and Franklin himself had written that life was "a kind of game in which we have points to gain and competitors or adversaries to contend with." But too much sport, the *New York Magazine* remarked in 1794, could lead to excess in other things—"the path of amusement can become the Broadway to destruction."[55] During the great burgeoning of spectator sports in the nineteenth century, this was a common theme. Neither mass commercialism nor mass hero worship had yet arrived on the American sporting scene, but neither was far off.

The development of American society in the period 1776–1830 was characterized by the extension of a number of trends, already visible since 1700, toward an identifiably American way of living. During these years there emerged the beginnings of an American *style,* a distinctly American social pattern, expressed in a thousand and one major and minor variations from the British and European. In effect, what had been a particular kind of British-colonial way of life now became an American way—a change naturally accelerated and emphasized by political independence, but one that no doubt would ultimately have emerged without it. There had been for some time, in 1776, discernible differences between America and Europe in dress, manners, mores, classifications, speech, and so on. These were, of course, only the superficial, external aspects of society. There were also differences of a more fundamental nature, differences of attitudes and point of view, which separated America from Britain and Europe. Three of these differences arose from the American outlook on its past and its future; two were more directly concerned with those American social problems of mobility and diversity which would normally arise in a new society in a new state and in a new and empty continent.

First, American society during these years was evolving a strong sense of its own past, despite European and British gibes that it had no history nor an awareness of one. The men of the early Republic realized that they were products of a long British and European historical process; they were proud of it and respectful of it. But once having recognized this, they did not look back at it with exaggerated veneration, nor did they feel quite so deeply responsible to it as some of their transat-

[55] Holliman, *American Sports,* p. 67.

lantic contemporaries. No American intellectual, for example, was more indebted to European books, ideas, and history than Thomas Jefferson —and no one less bound by them.

Americans did not reject the past, but they were far more concerned with building a new society than in perpetuating the qualities and values of the older ones. They had a past of their own, so recent as to be within the memory of almost every American, but still a sense of their own roots. They did not think of themselves as cut off from the experience of other nations, nor from the universal heritage of western civilization, in all of which they shared. But they did declare themselves free agents, exempt from the forces of the past that played on other nations and immune to *others'* pasts; there were to be no dead hands laid on American society. The social ideals and practices, then, of the new United States grew in a time when everything was being done for the first time, when everything was a starting point. The British and Continental heritage and the colonial experience all pointed at the present, the here and now. So American society began with a sense of *the* past and of *its* past, which it blended and used in its own way as a base for constructing its own new society.

Closely coupled with this attitude toward the past was the contemporary American feeling of breaking away, of leaving behind, of beginning anew. This is one of the most easily identifiable attributes of American society after 1776.[56] Americans after the Revolution were keenly conscious of their separateness, of the necessity of placing their society in correct relation to the rest of the world. There was but one standard against which the American social experiment could be measured; that was, naturally, the standard of England and the Continent. It was continually necessary therefore, during these formative years, to ask of any American social attitude, institution, or experience, "Is it better than what was before in colonial times, or than what is now in England and Europe?"

Britain and Europe were always points of reference for American social developments and judgments. Ways of acting and thinking in America were to be classified as American or non-American, approved, declined, or assimilated. American society thus possessed from the early decades of its independence the feeling of having been constructed,

[56] See Max Lerner's provocative discussion, "The Slaying of the European Father," in his *America as a Civilization* (New York, 1957).

rather than gradually derived, with the implication that it was volun-tarily formed of selected materials for American purposes. No other society in the western world was evolved by this method of constant acceptance, modification, and rejection, nor any in such a pervasive atmosphere of deliberate choice.

A third characteristic of social thought during the period was its distinctively American attitude toward the future. American society after 1776 (and to some extent before) was permeated by an assurance of its ultimate superiority (though admitting temporary inferiorities in some areas) over all other societies in the world. American society had a sense of commitment to the future which produced a peculiarly Amer-ican kind of social dynamism. There was never, in most Americans, any real doubt of their ability to master their society, control it, and direct it to good and admirable ends. They might rebuke themselves for their tardiness in so doing, or criticize the manner in which some hoped to do it, but they had no doubts of their eventual success. American society of the late eighteenth and early nineteenth centuries derived from its sense of the future its own metaphysic of promise; it was to them a per-petually unfinished society, always making and never made.

A fourth characteristic of American society, as it was formed in the years 1776–1830, was its mobility—physical, social, and ideological. What was to be a durable theme in American life—movement, change, fluidity—was already apparent by the time of the Revolution. This was partially the result of geography; in a frontier nation one could always move. Movement, therefore, often became an American means of solv-ing (or merely postponing) social problems, for if things were unsatis-factory one place, they might be better somewhere else. This mobility was partly too the result of rapid technological change; the Ameri-can economy after 1782 was as much a frontier, and as mobile and flexible, as the westward edge of geographical settlement. And it was also partly the result of a curiously American kind of political and social expansionism. Instruments of government and their interpretations in the new United States were always changing; there were constant shifts of political power and economic interests. American society was always spreading outward to include (never to exclude) something. In their society Americans moved always outward toward limits, and the limits were wide.

A fifth characteristic of American society in the period 1776–1830 was its combination of unity with diversity, in aim, tone, and detail.

The creation of solidarity out of variety was a vital task for the new society, as its shapers clearly realized; their adoption of the Roman *fasces* as a national symbol had real pertinence to their problems. The men of the period were acutely aware of the need for creating a stable, cohesive society. They knew that the individual was important, and that so was the group. They knew that similarity and difference were both sources of social strength; that neither should be cultivated at the expense of the other. The colonies themselves had already developed a collective sense of difference toward England as well as a groping sense of unity in their own affairs. Each of the new states had a common English heritage, but a different colonial history. There were wide geographical variations among them, yet they were juxtaposed on one side of the ocean, connected by natural communication systems. Politically all of the new states were equal in a common cause, but each had its own constitution as well as a national instrument of government; even most of their veterans had been state troops in a "continental" army.

The United States was, at its beginning, both a nation and a collection of states and sections. Its society, during the period 1776–1830, produced a quite complicated set of multiple allegiances, bound up in the term *American*. Unlike any other western nation, the United States was by 1830 a tangled skein of loyalties to sentiments, symbols, sections, localities, groups, political divisions and subdivisions, and to economic, ethnic, ideological, and other interests, all of which held the individual citizen in a sort of loose social orbit. *E pluribus unum* was not an idly chosen motto for the society of the new Republic.

CHAPTER 7

The Training of Free Minds

LIKE their other institutional and cultural patterns, the American colonists brought with them European education, its aims, and its methods, which were immediately modified by the colonial, frontier environment. The Enlightenment's belief in the worth and perfectibility of the individual; its interest in nature and science; its faith in the ability of man to progress—these influenced the growth of the eighteenth-century American educational system. If men were to improve themselves, they must be educated. The school was society's most important tool, Jefferson wrote, for "ameliorating the condition, promoting, and virtue, and advancing the happiness of man." Whatever their doubts about the frailties of humanity, Americans of the Enlightenment agreed that men were educable. Weak as they might be, men who did not by themselves know how to find truth could still be taught how to do so. "Many people lead bad lives," remarked Franklin, "that would gladly lead good ones, but know not *how* to make the change."[1]

Eighteenth-century America was the heir of four distinct educational traditions. The ideal of education as a means of producing the scholar-gentleman derived from the Renaissance of Elyot and Milton. The scientific, utilitarian ideal of education as a means of mastering the physical world for man's progress and betterment (a bequest from the tradition of Bacon and Comenius) had especial appeal to a colonial people engaged in subduing the rim of an empty continent. The ideal of education as a function of the church, as a means of moral, ethical, and religious development, was their heritage from the Reformation. And

[1] Albert H. Smyth (ed.), *The Writings of Benjamin Franklin* (10 vols., New York, 1905–7), IV, 12.

during the eighteenth century there developed a fourth strain of educational theory, based on the premise that education was a function of the state, to train citizens for their civic, social, and intellectual responsibilities—the tradition of Locke, the French Revolution, and of the young American republic. None of these, it was believed, excluded the others.[2]

From its colonial beginnings, however, American education stressed religious and moral aims. The schools of seventeenth-century New England, of Dutch New York, of the royal colonies of the South, and the church schools of the Middle Colonies, were all considered to be primarily agencies for preserving religious faith, developing the spiritual capacities of the individual, and implanting in him a sense of moral and ethical values. "Where Schools are not vigorously and Honorably Encouraged," wrote Cotton Mather, "whole *Colonies* will sink apace, into a Degenerate and Contemptible Condition, and at last become horribly Barbarous."

The flood of eighteenth-century science and rationalism failed to submerge the older concept of the religious function of education. "Colleges," the President of Yale said flatly in 1760, "are societies of Ministers for training up Persons for the Work of the Ministry." Under the terms of Dartmouth's charter, granted in 1769 by George III, the college was to "supply a great number of churches and congregations . . . in that new country, with a learned and orthodox ministry." King's College in New York proposed to "teach principles of Christianity and Morality generally agreed upon." Samuel Johnson, president of King's, felt that the aim of education was to lead students "from the Study of Nature to the Knowledge of themselves, and of the God of Nature, and their duty to him, themselves, and one another, and everything that can contribute to their true Happiness, both here and hereafter"—a view more liberal than Yale's, but one equally respectful of religion and morality. Both private and public schools continued to emphasize religious teachings into the nineteenth century. No educational leader before the Civil War would have placed intellectual above religious values.[3]

The religious cast of the schools was shown in the reluctance of many schools to throw off ministerial control. In Massachusetts, where the

[2] See J. P. Mulhern, *A History of Education* (New York, 1946), Chap. I.

[3] Merle Curti, *The Social Ideals of American Educators* (New York, 1935), pp. 4–15, 20; Samuel Brown, *The Secularization of American Education* (New York, 1912), p. 18; George P. Schmidt, *The Old Time College President* (New York, 1930), p. 153. A. A. Holtz, *A Study of Moral and Religious Elements in American Education up to 1800* (Menasha, Wis., 1917), is a thorough study.

loosening of church connections with the schools began with the law of 1691, ministers gradually disappeared from school boards to be replaced by laymen, but religious tests for teachers continued. It was not until 1827 that ministers finally lost their authority both to inspect and license schools and teachers. In the North and the South the churches retained control of the local schools to a large extent, extralegally perhaps but still effectively, well into the nineteenth century. If a community possessed a dominant church sect, its schools were very likely to reflect its religious bias—an Anglican teacher would not ordinarily be hired in Massachusetts, nor a Methodist in Tidewater Virginia. In private schools, apprentice schools, charity schools, and town schools, pupils studied the Catechism, the Bible, and imbibed moral teachings from their primers. By an Ohio law of 1814, for example, though the public schools could not teach "religious tenets peculiar to any Christian sect," religion could still be taught on a non-sectarian basis.

American schools from their beginnings also displayed a strong class bias. Colonial schools, it was assumed by parents in the upper social and economic brackets, existed to produce citizens much like themselves. Eighteenth-century American schools, therefore, like European, provided dual systems for rich and poor. Youths of middle-class origin learned their letters, trades, and crafts at apprentice schools. Youths from the upper social stratum learned the classics, reading, writing, elementary science, and moral philosophy in private or parish schools, in addition to a cultured accent in speech and a properly adorned prose style. The lowest class, at charity or "free" schools, learned only the rudiments of literacy, with heavy stress on those studies which might tend to impart habits of obedience, thrift, and industry. Thus William Smith, provost of Philadelphia Academy, divided education for "gentlemen" from education "for the Mechanic Professions, and all the remaining people in the country."[4]

The tremendous growth of seventeenth- and eighteenth-century science had strong influence on education, in Europe as well as in America. Demands for a scientific, utilitarian education bulked large in the educational writings of Franklin, Rush, Paine, and others. Paine placed astronomy as "the queen of the sciences" and the first requirement of an educated man; learning ought to consist, he wrote, "as it originally did, in scientific knowledge." "There is nothing to be learned," he once re-

---

[4] Max Savelle, *Seeds of Liberty* (New York, 1948), pp. 258–259; Curti, *Social Ideals*, pp. 4–15.

marked scornfully, "from the dead languages," while Philip Freneau advised a "Student of Dead Languages" to free his mind from "the fetters of Latin lore and heathen Greek" and pursue "the kindling ray" of science. Rush's plan for a national school system emphasized the study of natural science; Franklin's plans for an academy (1749) stressed the usefulness of English, physical culture, gardening, modern languages, and science over classical study and "dull divinity." History, geography, English grammar, optics, surveying, mathematics, and modern languages, in addition to general science, consistently appeared in the curricula of the grammar schools and academies after 1790.[5]

Though educators and parents never lost sight of the moral and religious values of education, the schools of the later eighteenth century showed a marked trend toward secularization. Science, utilitarianism, and the secularization of American life itself, with its expansion of business, trade, and political interests, led to demands for a useful, secular education, in contrast to that of the "scholar-gentleman" or the minister. As church and state separated after 1750, the influence which the church could bring to bear on American schools lessened proportionately. Education became more an attempt to understand man as a social and biological being, and less an attempt to discipline his morals or to sanctify his soul.[6]

Maryland's act of 1723, for example, though it recognized the importance of "a liberal and pious education of youth," emphasized that schools should also fit them "for their duties in the several stations and employment they may be called to, or employed in."[7] The majority of eighteenth-century colleges had no religious tests for admission, and even Harvard's aim, as *New England's First Fruits* (1643) had explained, was not simply to produce ministers but to "advance learning and perpetuate it to posterity." The secularization of knowledge meant that the aim of education was enlightenment, as well as moral discipline. It meant, too, that education had public implications, and was therefore of primary importance to the state; the state, as well as the church, had a stake in the training of its citizens.

The gradual shift of control of education from sectarian to secular

[5] H. H. Clark, *Thomas Paine* (New York, 1944), Chap. V; R. Freeman Butts, *A Cultural History of Western Education* (New York, 1955), pp. 49–53.

[6] E. P. Cubberley, *Public Education in the United States* (Boston, 1934), pp. 519–529.

[7] Brown, *Secularization of Education*, p. 16.

hands, and the development of public rather than ecclesiastical aims in education, can be clearly traced after 1700. By the time of the Revolution, American schools were chiefly under local control, where both federal and state constitutions afterward left them. Six of the sixteen state constitutions framed before 1800 contained clauses setting forth the educational authority and responsibility of the state (Pennsylvania, North Carolina, Vermont, Massachusetts, New Hampshire, and Delaware), though little was actually done to implement them. The educational provisions of the Ordinances of 1784, 1785, and 1787, relating to the Northwest Territory, and the subsequent grants of land (eventually 80 million acres) allotted to its schools, reaffirmed the position of the federal government. The constitutions of those states carved from the Northwest Territory all contained provisions for public education, while in the older states the legislatures after 1783 passed a number of laws requiring the establishment and maintenance of at least some schools. The idea that education was a prerogative and responsibility of the state, though it was neither fully accepted nor implemented for another half-century, was clearly acceptable to the late eighteenth century.[8]

The belief that education was a phase of civil policy was not new, of course, to Americans—Yale's early charter spoke of preparing youths for "public employment, both in Church and Civil State"—but the development of the concept was chiefly a post-Revolutionary phenomenon. Here French influence was especially strong. Rousseau, Rolland, Turgot, Diderot, and the French *philosophes* had all explained that the primary function of education was, as Turgot phrased it, "to study the duties of citizenship," in order to reform society by educating those who formed society.[9] For the young American Republic, imbued with nationalistic fervor, this concept of education had great appeal. Education, wrote Franklin, was essentially service; it increased one's ability "to serve mankind, one's Country, Friends, and Family," and would "supply the succeeding Age with Men qualified to serve the Publick with Honor to themselves, and to their Country."

Nearly every prominent American of the postwar decades gave priority to the problem of building a distinctively American educational

[8] *Ibid.*, Chap. VIII; Cubberley, *Public Education*, pp. 521–535, *et seq.*
[9] E. P. Cubberley, *A History of Education* (New York, 1920), Chap. XX, is a discussion of European influences on eighteenth-century American educational theory. See also the relevant sections of Edgar W. Knight, *Twenty Centuries of Education* (Boston, 1940).

system in harmony with the needs and goals of American society. It was imperative, Jefferson wrote in 1779 in presenting his Virginia Bill for the More General Diffusion of Knowledge, for those "whom nature hath endowed with genius and virtue" to be educated for public service, so that they might be "worthy to receive, and able to guard the sacred deposit of the rights and liberties of their fellow citizens." "A general diffusion of knowledge among all classes of men," agreed Noah Webster, "is the necessary consequence of the genius of our Governments." "Without learning," wrote Dr. Benjamin Rush, in his essay, *Education Agreeable to a Republican Form of Government* (1786), "men are incapable of knowing their rights, and where learning is confined to a few people, liberty can be neither equal nor universal."

John Adams believed that the nation should provide for "the instruction of people in every kind of knowledge that can be of use to them in their moral duties as men, citizens, and Christians." John Jay considered "knowledge to be the soul of a Republic"; James Madison warned that "a people who mean to be their own governors must arm themselves with the power which knowledge gives"; Washington, in his Farewell Address of 1796, agreed that "in proportion as the structure of a government gives force to public opinion, it is essential that public opinion should be enlightened." The leading men of the new Republic were convinced that men could be educated to be good citizens, and must be so educated if they were to remain free ones.[10]

The postwar decades produced dozens of plans for nationalized educational systems, by which, Benjamin Rush wrote in his essay *On Education* (1798), the Republic might "convert men into republican machines . . . to perform their parts properly in the great machine of government of the state." Charles Pinckney, speaking at the Constitutional Convention, suggested the creation of a national university and tried unsuccessfully to establish congressional power over education. Joel Barlow planned a National Institute to educate scientists, civil servants, and artists. Rush in 1788 proposed to establish a Federal University to "prepare our youth for civil and public life," and advocated a law forbidding public office to any person who did not possess a Federal

[10] See A. O. Hansen, *Liberalism and Education in the 18th Century* (New York, 1926), for an excellent survey of the educational philosophy of this period. Ervin C. Shoemaker, *Noah Webster: Pioneer of Learning* (New York, 1936); Thomas Woody, *The Educational Views of Benjamin Franklin* (New York, 1931); and R. J. Honeywell, *The Educational Work of Thomas Jefferson* (Cambridge, Mass., 1931), are also useful studies.

University degree. Robert Coram, Samuel Knox, Nathaniel Chipman, Noah Webster, James Sullivan, Samuel Smith, and others evolved similar plans. The French philosopher and scientist Pierre du Pont de Nemours in 1800 wrote a book on national educational systems at the request of Jefferson, and the American Philosophical Society in 1795 sponsored a contest to encourage plans for just such a system. Quesnay de Beaurepaire, another Frenchman, drew up a plan for a national university and actually laid its cornerstone in 1786 in Richmond. A Congressional Committee in 1811 investigated the possibility of establishing a federal university (reporting it of doubtful constitutionality), and Congress defeated a similar proposal in 1816.[11]

The framers of the educational plans submitted in such profusion during the postwar decades held three principles in common: they regarded education as a public responsibility of the federal government; they considered education as a bulwark of American security and freedom; and, in true eighteenth-century fashion, they believed the diffusion of knowledge through a nationalized system of education to be essential to individual and social progress. None of the plans succeeded, for the popular suspicion of centralized government prevented widespread support of any federalized educational organization. Education still had, in the mind of the general public, strong theological and moral connotations. The powerful religious interests were unwilling to relinquish control of the schools, and conservative leaders showed great reluctance to place them in the hands of a government that, under Jefferson or his successors, might be too liberal for the *status quo*.[12] Despite the popular clamor for a better-educated citizenry, state-controlled and state-supported education for the average man did not appear in the United States for more than another quarter-century, and then in a different guise and under different sponsorship.

Throughout the first half of the eighteenth century, American school-

[11] G. B. Goode, "The Origin of the National Scientific and Educational Institutions of the United States," *Papers of the American Historical Association*, IV (April, 1890), discusses many of these plans. One such, proposed by "A Private Citizen of Philadelphia," outlined a curriculum including government, history, mathematics, commerce, "natural history and chemistry," "the natural history of animals, vegetables, and fossils," philology, rhetoric and criticism, the "construction and pronunciation of the English language," German, French, and "athletic and manly exercises" (Appendix A). See also Hansen, *Liberalism and Education*, pp. 110–120, for these plans for universities.

[12] Curti, *Social Ideals*, pp. 24–26.

books were commonly reprints of British texts.[13] After the Revolution, American presses poured out a flood of texts, specifically aimed at American uses; between 1804 and 1832, the number of different schoolbooks published in the United States increased from 93 to 407. At the same time the expansion of the school curriculum and the emphasis on practicality in education produced changes in the content of the texts themselves. The *New England Primer,* still standard for elementary pupils after dozens of editions since 1690, contained the alphabet, illustrated couplets, the Shorter Catechism, selections from Watts's *Hymns,* and various rules for behavior. There were dozens of such primers, of course, of much the same pattern—*The ABC with the Church of England Catechism* (1785), *The Fortune Teller; or an Alphabet without Tears* (1793), Matthew Carey's *American Primer* (1813), and others, including *The Instructive Alphabet* (1814), which drove home temperance lessons with the alphabet.[14]

After learning his A B C's the child moved on to grammar—usually Latin, not English. Culman's *Sententiae Pueriles Anglo-Latinae* (1702) and Nathan Bailey's *English and Latin Exercises for Schoolboys* (1720) remained widely used until 1800. Bailey, mindful of the moral values of education, so constructed his Latin exercises that as pupils translated they might "suck in such Principles as will be of use to them afterwards, in the manly Conduct and ordering of their Lives." So too Whitehall's *Short Introduction to Grammar* (1762) explained in its preface that the study of Latin was[15] "the Sacrist that bears the Key of Knowledge by whome alone admittance can be had into the temple of the Muses, and Treasures of Arts, even whatever can enrich the Mind, and raise it from the level of a Barbarian and Ideot, to the Dignity of an Intelligence."

Mid-century demands for the study of English, instead of what Franklin called "the useless classics," brought English grammar into the curriculum, though some schoolmasters feared that neglect of Greek and Latin might cause students to "sink into absolute barbarism, and the gloom of mental darkness."[16] Thomas Dilworth's *New Guide to the*

[13] Clifton Johnson, *Old Time Schools and Schoolbooks* (New York, 1904), is an excellent source of information.

[14] Monica Kiefer, *American Children Through Their Books 1700–1835* (Philadelphia, 1948), pp. 139 ff.

[15] *Ibid.,* pp. 120–122.

[16] R. Freeman Butts, *The College Charts Its Course* (New York, 1939), p. 117.

English Tongue (published in England in 1740 and reprinted by Franklin in 1747), which served as a basic text for several decades, included alphabets, spelling lists, illustrated stories, selections for reading, and examples of Biblical literature. Noah Webster, alert to the prevailing nationalistic trend, drove Dilworth and other British imports from the market with his *American Spelling Book* (1783), to which he later added an *American Reader* and an *American Grammar*. His "blue-backed speller," said Webster, was designed "to diffuse a uniformity and purity of language in America . . . and to promote the interests of literature and the harmony of the United States," which it did along with sound moral aphorisms and conservative politics.[17] There were other spellers, such as *The Youth's Instructor in the English Tongue* (1770), Watts's *Complete Spelling Book* (1770), containing "Portions of Scripture, a Short History of England, and Directions for Writing the Round Hands and the Italian Hand," James Greenwood's *Philadelphia Vocabulary* (1787), and Picket's *Juvenile Spelling Book* (1823), but Webster left his competitors far behind. The spelling book, until 1820, was the most common, and often the only, book used in elementary school instruction.[18]

British arithmetic texts, such as Hodder's *Arithmetick* (1719), continued to be used in American schools throughout the eighteenth century. Arithmetic was not usually taught from texts, but more often from manuscript "sum books" kept by the master, from which he gave out problems. However, sections of other texts were often given over to arithmetic, such as Daniel Fenning's *American Youth's Instructor* (1795), or Franklin's *American Instructor, or Young Man's Best Companion* (1748), which contained chapters not only on arithmetic, but on reading, writing, bookkeeping, surveying, navigation, wills, contracts, medical advice, and "Prudent Advice to Young Tradesmen and Dealers." Nicholas Pike's *Arithmetic* (1788) dominated its field nearly as completely as Webster his. Pike simply printed rules and problems,

---

[17] A good biography of this amazing man is Harry R. Warfel, *Noah Webster: Schoolmaster to America* (New York, 1936). An excellent brief article is Henry Steele Commager, "Noah Webster, 1785–1958," *Saturday Review,* October 18, 1958. In addition to his schoolbooks, which sold in the tens of millions for fifty years, Webster edited magazines; ran a newspaper; wrote essays on government, language, banking, insurance, and taxes; compiled a two-volume history of epidemics; edited histories; and even published a revision of the Bible. As for the *Speller,* writes Commager, "No other secular book had ever spread so wide, penetrated so deep, lasted so long."

[18] Kiefer, *Children Through Their Books,* Chap. VI.

leaving explanations to the instructor. In one edition, he listed 360 rules to be memorized without a single word of comment—among them rules for calculating measures of beer and ale, for finding the Gregorian Epact, the number of bushels in a strike, and the number of quarters in a caldron.[19] Erastus Root's *Introduction to Arithmetic* (1796), Daniel Adams' *Arithmetic* (1801), and Walsh's *Mercantile Arithmetic* (1807) were also widely used texts.

Requests for the study of history in grammar schools, to give (as Franklin said) "a connected Idea of Human Affairs," met little response from the textbook publishers. Webster's *Grammatical Institutes* included "short stories of the geography and history of the United States," and he also wrote a historical sketch for Jedidiah Morse's *American Geography* (1788). Webster's *Chronological Table of Remarkable Events from the Creation of the World and Adam and Eve, 4004 B.C., to the Death of Lord Nelson, October, 1805,* was hardly a suitable history text for elementary schools. John M'Culloch published the first text in American history in 1787, and another edition in 1795; other American histories for school use began to appear after 1800. The intense nationalism that followed the War of 1812 stimulated the study of American history in the academies, and, beginning with Massachusetts in 1827, various states passed laws requiring it in the public schools. Geography, which entered the curriculum in the Revolutionary period, was taught from texts such as Robert Davidson's *Geography Epitomized, or a Tour Around the World* (1784) and Nathaniel Dwight's *Short but Comprehensive Geography of the World* (1795).[20]

The function of the history and the geography text was more often filled by the reader, a new kind of multipurpose text that appeared after 1800, which gathered together in one book what amounted to a generalized school course. *The Franklin Primer* (1802), which had no connection with Benjamin Franklin, included not only the usual reading selections and spelling lists but "tales, moral lessons, and sentences, a concise history and geography of the world, appropriate hymns, Bible readings, and the Assembly of Divines' catechism." Noah Webster's *Grammatical Institutes, Third Part,* his *Reader's Assistant,* his *Ameri-*

[19] H. K. Beale, *A History of Freedom of Teaching in American Schools* (New York, 1941), pp. 41–43.

[20] Kiefer, *Children Through Their Books,* Chap. VI. For a complete study, see Henry Johnson, *The Teaching of History* (New York, 1940), pp. 42–44, 49–51, and Alice W. Spieseke, *The First Textbooks in History and Their Compiler, John M'Culloch* (New York, 1938).

can Reader, and Caleb Bingham's *American Preceptor* were advanced readers for older children. The next step, a series of graded readers, was taken later by the famous William McGuffey.[21]

Though editions of schoolbooks multiplied rapidly after the Revolution, schoolmasters decried the lack of sound texts in specific fields of learning. "Our whole system of education," wrote Noah Webster in his *Elements of Useful Knowledge* (1807), "is still defective in the number of sciences taught. Many of the most useful sciences and arts are not taught at all, or very imperfectly—nor have we books well calculated for the purpose." Some students studied in no more than two books during their entire elementary and secondary schooling. Schoolbooks were handed down from generation to generation within families, with the result that the texts used in a single class might vary a hundred years or more in age. In 1810, for example, there still were arithmetic texts in common use which phrased problems in shillings and pence, or gave problems in measures obsolete since the sixteenth century.[22] The concept of the graded text, fitted to the child's stage of development, or of separate texts for separate fields of study, was still to come.

The colonists modeled their secondary schools on the British "Latin" or "grammar" school, whose chief function was to prepare boys for entrance into the university. The first of these, Boston Latin School, which opened in 1635, taught Latin and Greek solely, and in 1789, when it shortened its course from seven to four years, its students still studied only Latin and Greek and conducted all recitations in Latin. Other grammar schools during the eighteenth century included work in English and arithmetic, but for the most part their curricula remained preponderantly classical. Narrow as the range of studies was in the grammar school, it must be remembered that Boston Latin School alone produced John Hancock, Samuel Adams, Robert Paine, Franklin, James Bowdoin, Emerson, Edward Everett, and dozens of other educated leaders of New England society. The grammar school did not, however, meet the needs of the rising middle class in the eighteenth century, whose sons did not always enter college but might instead go

[21] Johnson, *Teaching of History,* Chap. IX. Richard D. Mosier, *Making the American Mind: McGuffey's Readers* (New York, 1947), is interesting and informative.

[22] One of Walsh's problems in his *Mercantile Arithmetic* (1807) deserves to be remembered: "How much will ten ferons of cochineal come to, weighing neat 724 okes, 73 rotalas, at 80 piastres per oke?"

directly into business or a skilled craft. "The Counting House and counter," remarked the Philadelphia *American Weekly Mercury* in 1735, "require different qualifications from those which fit a man for the Pulpit and Bar," while a Boston committee complained that boys "spent two, three, or four years or more" in Latin schools with "little or no benefit as to their after accomplishments."[23]

Parallel to the Latin school, therefore, there existed the private "English school," offering instruction of a utilitarian nature which, as Franklin wrote of his own proposal in *The Idea of an English School* (1751), would fit youth "for learning any business, calling, or profession." One such Boston school in 1709 advertised instruction in "writing, arithmetic in all its parts, also geometry, trigonometry, surveying, drafting, gauging, astronomy, and the use of mathematical instruments," while another taught "mathematics of chances" for use in figuring insurance, annuities, lotteries, and games. New York City's English Grammar School, opened in 1732, offered mathematics, algebra, geometry, navigation, geography, and bookkeeping, in addition to Latin. Franklin's Philadelphia Academy, established in 1751, and Dummer Academy in Connecticut, opened in 1763, were forerunners of the academy, which by 1790 had virtually displaced Latin and grammar schools in the field of secondary education.[24]

Academies had two specific educational functions: to prepare youths for college, and to prepare those who did not attend college for entrance in business and the lesser professions. Until the beginnings of the public

[23] I. L. Kandel, *History of Secondary Education* (Boston, 1938), pp. 111–128, 168–175; Walter Monroe and Oscar Weber, *The High School* (New York, 1928), pp. 29, 30, 50. For additional information on the Latin school, see Adolph E. Meyer, *An Educational History of the American People* (New York, 1957), pp. 20 ff.; H. G. Good, *A History of American Education* (New York, 1956), pp. 49–51, 56–58; R. Freeman Butts and L. A. Cremin, *A History of Education in American Culture* (New York, 1953), pp. 75–81, 86–89, 101–104, *passim;* E. P. Cubberley, *Public Education in the United States,* pp. 29–30, 243–252; Edgar Knight, *Education in the United States* (Boston, 1951), pp. 112 ff.; Stuart G. Noble, *A History of American Education* (New York, 1951), pp. 28–32.

[24] Vera M. Butler, *Education as Revealed by New England Newspapers Prior to 1850* (Philadelphia, 1935), pp. 218–220. For discussions of academies, see Meyer, *Educational History,* pp. 89, 129, 189; Noble, *History of Education,* pp. 72–73, 118–120; Good, *History of Education,* pp. 110–119; Knight, *Education,* pp. 373–384; Cubberley, *Public Education,* pp. 111–113, 246–268; Butts and Cremin, *Education in American Culture,* pp. 77–81, 126–128, 196–198; and Leonard V. Koos, *The American Secondary School* (New York, 1922), 31.

high school, academies dominated the educational scene. New York in 1800 had nineteen academies, Virginia twenty-one; Massachusetts had seventeen that year, thirty-six in 1820, and sixty-eight in 1830. Some 6,000 academies were in operation in the country in 1850. By 1800 the standard academy curriculum offered mathematics, algebra, geometry, trigonometry, surveying, geography, logic, public speaking, English, commercial studies, and usually a course in science—physics, biology, botany, or geology.

Many academies had a four-year "classical" curriculum to prepare graduates for college, a three-year "English" curriculum for those entering business, and a teacher-training course to provide teachers for lower schools. A few of the early academies accepted girls, and after 1800 there were a number of them open to girls only. The quality of education offered by the academy varied with the school's financial resources and the desires of the governing board. Some were excellent. Others were no more than finishing schools which produced, Timothy Dwight complained, "Not a man or a woman, but a well-dressed bundle of accomplishments."[25]

Despite the academy's adaptability, it too failed to meet fully the educational needs of early nineteenth-century society. The academy charged tuition, and since it was governed by a self-perpetuating board of trustees, it was not directly responsible to the community. Then too, with the disappearance of the Latin school, the academy was forced to take over the college preparatory function, sometimes to the detriment of its non-preparatory courses. What the United States needed, wrote John Griscom, was "a system of education congenial with our republican institutions, and commensurate with our means and wants." The answer was the public high school, to prepare boys, said the High School Society of New York, "for such advancement and such pursuits in life as they are destined to after leaving it."[26]

The English Classical School, established in Boston in 1821, and the Portland School in Maine, founded the same year, were the first of the new "high" schools wholly supported by public funds, controlled by the public, and open to the public. The English Classical School, according

[25] N. M. Blake, *A Short History of American Life* (New York, 1952), pp. 302–304.

[26] Kandel, *Secondary Education*, p. 430; Monroe and Weber, *High School*, p. 37.

to its founders, intended to fit a youth "for active life," and gave courses which "shall serve as a foundation for eminence in his profession, either mercantile or mechanical." Therefore it offered English, mathematics, trigonometry, French, geography, history, science, navigation, surveying, logic, forensic discussion, moral philosophy, and drawing. Massachusetts, in 1824, required the establishment of a high school in each town of more than 500 families, with a curriculum including American history, algebra, geometry, surveying, and English grammar. If the town's population exceeded 4,000, the high school was required to offer a college preparatory course. Other states followed suit, and though the laws were often evaded, by 1860 public high schools had virtually displaced academies as instruments of secondary education.[27]

The quality of teaching in the late eighteenth- and early nineteenth-century school depended on the interests and finances of the community. Professional training for teachers did not exist. Town meetings, church boards, and parish officials hired whom they pleased and with what qualifications they pleased—college students earning extra money, ministers, itinerant tutors, and occasionally women, though the influx of women into teaching did not arrive until the expansion of higher educational facilities for girls. Teaching school could hardly be considered a career for able men, since the teacher enjoyed little social status in the community and received extremely low pay. One Connecticut teacher in 1798 received 67 cents per week, and as late as 1834 teachers in New England received $12–$14 per month with board and room, slightly more than a farm laborer. Amos Kendall, in 1810, was paid $8 a month in Massachusetts for teaching eighty-six pupils in a one-room school, while Bronson Alcott in 1820 received $135 for four months' teaching of eighty students.[28]

Teaching therefore did not always attract men of the highest type, and contemporary school-board minutes show numerous references to alcoholics, thieves, sadists, and plain ignoramuses. John Trumbull,

[27] For additional information on high schools, see Noble, *History of Education*, pp. 178–179; Knight, *Education*, pp. 384 ff.; Good, *History of Education*, pp. 237 ff.; Cubberley, *Public Education*, pp. 245–264; Butts and Cremin, *Education in American Culture*, pp. 197–198, 201–209; Meyer, *Educational History*, pp. 189 ff. Koos, *Secondary School*, and Monroe and Weber, *High School*, are thorough studies.

[28] Johnson, *Teaching of History*, p. 126; Monroe and Weber, *High School*, p. 32, *passim;* W. S. Elsbree, *The American Teacher* (New York, 1939), pp. 118 ff.

in his *Progress of Dulness* (1772–73), drew a picture of the country schoolmaster at his worst:

> Procured for forty pounds a year,
> His ragged regiment round assembles,
> Taught not to read, but fear and tremble.
> Before him rods prepare the way,
> Those dreaded antidotes to play . . .
> He tries, with ease and unconcern,
> To teach, what ne'er himself could learn.

Since a one-room school might contain pupils ranging in age from six to thirty, even the most skillful teacher found discipline sometimes difficult, and the ferrule (which was sometimes a three-foot club) was a normal remedy. Records exist to show the use of the cat-o'-nine-tails in 1800, while Sunderland, Massachusetts, had a whipping post in its school yard as late as 1793.[29]

Wealthier communities, or those with strong educational interests, naturally kept good schools and demanded teachers of "good moral character, a certificate from a learned person, and exemplary conduct." New York in 1829 passed one of the first state certification laws, requiring of a teacher "unimpeachable character" as well as "the requisite literary qualifications." Some communities were less attentive. The parents of Wythe County, Virginia, protested in 1820 that their schoolteachers were "entirely ignorant of the art of teaching, and a terror to their pupils." A committee of Philadelphians in 1829 reported that the schools of that city were taught by persons "destitute of all moral character, often grossly ignorant." One irate Massachusetts parent in 1824 thought that "if a young man can be moral enough to keep out of State prison, he will find no difficulty in getting application for a schoolmaster." It is heartening to read in the report of a New Jersey committee of 1821 that some teachers, at least, were "stated to be what they should be, competent, and of good moral character." Despite the numerous criticisms leveled at teachers in contemporary records, there obviously were also many who were writers and authors of note, holders of university degrees, and well-educated men.[30] And whatever the hand-

[29] Johnson, *Teaching of History*, pp. 44–45, 123.

[30] Beale, *Freedom of Teaching*, pp. 40–43; Kiefer, *Children Through Their Books*, p. 138; Kandel, *Secondary Education*, p. 125; Butts and Cremin, *Education in American Culture*, pp. 131–136. See also the documents in R. F. Seybolt, "Source Studies in American Colonial Education," *University of Illinois Bulletin*, Vol. 23, No. 4 (Urbana, 1925).

icaps of the profession, there were many intelligent and dedicated teachers who did an excellent job of educating the young. A teacher had few administrators to contend with, little interference in his work, few reports or records to keep, and a surprising amount of freedom in the classroom.

Seventeenth-century elementary and secondary education was based on the theory that children were miniature adults, and that the aim of education was to instill in them the attitudes and habits of an adult world. Children were regarded as fractious, undisciplined, mentally and morally undeveloped, possessed of all the evils of unregenerate human nature without any of the saving experiences of the adult. Though this theory of child psychology was already outmoded in Europe by 1750, American educators lagged far behind British and European thinkers until the closing years of the eighteenth century.[31]

Eighteenth-century secularization and liberalism, true, brought some softening of this older view. The Anglican Society for the Propagation of the Gospel instructed its teachers in 1720 to "use all kind and gentle methods in government of their Scholars, that they may be loved as well as feared by them," and Samuel Johnson's *Elements of Philosophy* (1752) suggested that educational experiences should be pleasant as well as useful. The concept of the learning process, however, remained one of discipline for some decades to come. American schools continued to be based on the psychology of Hobbes and Locke—the belief that the life of the mind was an association of ideas, and that ideas were units arising from sensation, bearing within themselves the powers of association by which knowledge was created. Education therefore should provide experience for the mind, develop associations of ideas, and implant good habits. "The end of education," a New England newspaper editor wrote in 1785, "is to direct the powers of the mind in unfolding themselves." This view harmonized with the traditional "faculty" psychology, which assumed that the mind contained inherent faculties of reason, memory, logic, imagination, and so on. Education disciplined and developed these faculties, training the mind for the ethical and moral decisions which must be made in later life.[32]

The revolution that occurred in American educational theory and practice after 1800 was chiefly the result of the delayed acceptance in America of eighteenth-century European educational theories. Rousseau

[31] Butts and Cremin, *Education in American Culture,* p. 67.
[32] *Ibid.,* p. 68; Butler, *Education Prior to 1850,* p. 439.

challenged the traditional assumptions of educational psychology by asserting that the child was not a miniature adult, but an individual organism that developed by stages according to natural laws. An effective system of education, he wrote, "must be in harmony with the nature of children"; education was a "natural development of mind" by contact with nature and experience, not solely through books and externally imposed disciplines.

Rousseau's theories had two important effects on educational thought in Europe, and later in America. First, they led to an increased emphasis on the study of educational psychology, for if education were to be framed in terms of the child's mental and emotional development, it was vitally important to understand the learning process. Second, if education were to be redirected, the schools needed professionally skilled teachers, specifically trained for a new kind of teaching. Johann Pestalozzi of Zurich in 1800 opened a school at Yverdon in Switzerland that attracted attention everywhere, but especially from the United States. The problem of teaching, as he conceived it, was "how to bring the elements of every art into harmony with the very nature of the mind, by following the psychological mechanical laws by which mind rises from physical sense impressions to clear ideas."[33]

Joseph Neef, a retired French officer and an avowed Pestalozzian, opened a school in Philadelphia in 1809, and a few other experimenters introduced Pestalozzi's methods into their schools. In 1818 Professor John Griscom of New York toured Britain and the Continent, and his subsequent report, *A Year in Europe* (1819, reprinted, 1824), in the opinion of Henry Barnard became "the single most influential educational work of the nineteenth century." After Griscom, dozens of Americans visited the Yverdon school, among them Alexander Bache of Girard College, Horace Mann, Henry Dwight, Henry Barnard, George Bancroft, William Woodbridge, Calvin Stowe, and Joseph Cogswell, all of whom later wrote or lectured on German and Swiss educational theories. In addition, a report on German education, published by the French philosopher Victor Cousin and translated in 1834, was widely read by American educators, who gained from it familiarity with Pestalozzian principles. Educational journals, such as the *American Journal*

[33] Frank D. Graves, *Great Educators of Three Centuries* (New York, 1912), contains useful summaries of the major ideas of educational philosophies. See also the relevant sections of the histories of American education cited in the Bibliography, especially Knight, *Twenty Centuries of Education*, pp. 746–750, and Cubberley, *History of Education*, pp. 532–540.

of Education (1826–31), its successor, *American Annals of Education,* the *Quarterly Register* (1829–43), and Horace Mann's *Common School Journal* (1838–48) discussed the new education with enthusiasm and assisted in disseminating its theories.[34]

Pestalozzi's insistence on the training of skilled teachers particularly impressed his American disciples. The Reverend Samuel Hall opened a private teacher-training institute, the first of its kind in America, at Concord, Vermont, in 1823. Four years later the New York legislature appropriated funds for the establishment of similar institutions; in 1839 Massachusetts opened the first state-supported teacher-training school in Lexington.[35] But despite the popularity of Pestalozzi and his circle, the principles of the new education took hold slowly, and there is little evidence to show general acceptance of them in American schools before 1830. Still, by that date, American educators were beginning to recognize that the learning process was psychologically complex, that the teacher was a guide rather than a taskmaster, and that teaching was a specialized profession. Education, said Bronson Alcott in 1835, consisted of "leading the mind by its own light to the perception of truth." The object of education, in the opinion of a contributor to the *American Annals of Education and Instruction* in 1832, was to bring young people "as early and rapidly as possible to *self-instruction, self-government,* and *self-education*"—a far cry from the educational philosophy of a half-century before.[36]

During the eighteenth century, the education of a girl clearly reflected her family's economic and social status. Daughters of poor parents were fortunate if they were taught to read and write by a parent or wandering tutor; girls of wealthier families received a hardly better (but more polite) education from a tutor, a dame school, a church school, or a girl's seminary. In New England, girls were admitted to grammar schools at "separate hours" (sometimes from five to seven in the morning) to study reading, writing and spelling. There were also, during the

---

[34] B. A. Hinsdale, "Notes on the History of Foreign Influences upon Education in the United States," *Report of the Commissioner of Education,* I (1897–1898), 618–621; S. C. Parker, *Modern Elementary Education* (Boston, 1912), pp. 297–298.

[35] Knight, *Education,* pp. 752–754.

[36] A complete treatment is W. S. Monroe, *A History of the Pestalozzian Movement in the United States* (Syracuse, 1907). Alcott is quoted by Odell Shepard, *Pedlar's Progress* (Boston, 1937), p. 182; see also Dorothy McCuskey, *Bronson Alcott, Teacher* (New York, 1940), for a complete account of this brilliant and fascinating educator.

eighteenth century, a number of private girls' schools; some 200 of them existed between 1722 and 1776. Nevertheless, perhaps 50 to 70 per cent of all women in the eighteenth century were either illiterate or barely literate.[37] "'Tis quite enough for girls to know," wrote John Trumbull in his *Progress of Dulness* (1772–73).

> If she can read a billet-doux,
> Or write a line you'd understand,
> Without a cipher of the hand.
> Why need she learn to write or spell?
> A pothook scrawl is just as well.

Jefferson's outline of studies for his daughter Martha, including music, dancing, drawing, French, English, and letter writing, was probably typical of a wealthy girl's education in 1783. Since, as Timothy Dwight remarked in his *Travels,* "the employments of the women of New England are wholly domestic," their educational needs were few and simple.[38]

On the other hand, the middle class in the late eighteenth century demanded for its daughters an education equal to that granted the children of the wealthy—and they had money to pay for it. The rising feminist movement, combined with the natural-rights tradition (which, after all, applied to both sexes), created demands for a better female education, while the movement of men into factories created a need for educated women teachers. Men such as Benjamin Rush, noting the increased importance of women in eighteenth-century life, advocated an education for girls adapted to "the state of society, manners, and government of the country."[39]

Academies were opened to girls in the 1790's, though boys and girls

[37] Kandel, *Secondary Education,* pp. 514–519; Monroe and Weber, *High School,* pp. 33–35.

[38] *Travels* (1821–22), IV, 474.

[39] *Essays Literary, Moral, and Philosophical* (1798), p. 75. Rush's *Thoughts upon Female Education* (1782) is an excellent essay. The Reverend Samuel Miller, however, thought (1803) that acceptance of the idea that "women are equal in mind to men" was "to renounce reason, to contradict experience, to trample on divine authority, and to diminish the usefulness, the respectability, and the real enjoyment of the female sex." *Retrospect of the Eighteenth Century,* II, 279. The Reverend John Todd thought that "As for training young ladies through a long intellectual course, as we do young men, it can never be done. They will die in the process. . . . For the sake of having them 'intelectual,' must we make them puny, nervous, and their whole earthly existence a struggle between life and death?" Quoted in George P. Schmidt, *The Liberal Arts College* (New Brunswick, 1957), p. 129.

were rigidly separated and the female curriculum much less demanding
—music, drawing, painting, light reading, English, perhaps French—
leading Dwight to complain that "girls sink down to songs, novels, and
plays."[40] In the opening decades of the nineteenth century, academies
for girls, or "female seminaries," multiplied, though tuition fees restricted attendance to daughters of more prosperous families. Girls of
lesser means were allowed to attend public grammar schools in the
summer months. With the emergence of the women's-rights movements,
and the appearance of feminist leaders such as Emma Willard, Catherine Beecher, and Mary Lyon, equal education for women became a
lively issue. The editor of the Springfield, Massachusetts, *Republican*
still believed in 1828 that "the most acceptable degree" for any young
lady was "the degree of M.R.S."[41]

Emma Willard's Female Seminary, opened at Troy, New York, in
1821, was one of the first institutions to offer an education for girls equal
to that offered boys. Catherine Beecher founded a girls' school in Hartford, Connecticut, in 1820, and when her family moved to Cincinnati
she founded another there for the training of teachers. Mary Lyon, who
financed Mount Holyoke by collecting $27,000 in gifts, opened her
school in South Hadley, Massachusetts, in 1837, with a curriculum as
solid and stiff as that of any man's college. Oberlin College in 1834 enrolled forty girls in its Female Department, though not for college work;
in 1837 four girls entered at the college level and in 1841 three of them
graduated. Collegiate coeducation, however, was long in arriving. Wom-
en's education remained for another generation as the responsibility of
separate seminaries or colleges.[42]

The revolution in American education that occurred during the latter
decades of the eighteenth century and the early decades of the nineteenth irrevocably altered the nature of the American school. It firmly
fixed education on the state as a public responsibility, and initiated the
development of the public school system. Education, after 1820, found
itself expected to assume a variety of responsibilities—for individual self-
development, for civic duty, for economic security and self-improvement, for the moral and ethical training, for social betterment. Since

[40] *Travels*, I, 514–515.
[41] Butler, *Education Prior to 1850*, p. 190.
[42] Wm. Goodsell, *Education of Women* (New York, 1923), and Thomas
Woody, *A History of Women's Education in the United States* (2 vols., New
York, 1929), are standard sources. An excellent brief explanation is that of
Schmidt, *Liberal Arts College*, Chap. VI, pp. 124–145.

that time no other educational philosophy in the world has been marked by such diversity of purpose.

The early nineteenth-century belief that public education was the prerogative of all citizens left its mark on subsequent educational theory and practice in the United States. If the public paid for education, it therefore owned it; prejudices of the majority could (and did) develop into threats to intellectual freedom and educational efficiency. The Jefferson who "swore upon the altar of God eternal hostility against every form of tyranny over the mind of man" would have found relatively few supporters in Jacksonian America. The trend toward utilitarianism, characteristic of an expanding, commercial society, led to a stress on practicality rather than ideas in the educational process; as Alexis de Tocqueville noted in 1835, "the spirit of Americans is averse to general ideas, and it does not make theoretical discoveries." The belief that education meant all things to all men, which had its origins in the society of the late eighteenth and early nineteenth centuries, continued to influence American educational theory and practice for many years to come.

CHAPTER 8

The Idea of an American University

EDUCATION at the collegiate level came relatively late to the North American English colonies, for Latin America possessed twelve universities before the English colonies had one. When the first American institution of higher education was founded at Cambridge, Massachusetts, in 1636, it was (unlike its European counterparts) a frontier institution. The American university began as a center for the radiation of religion and culture outward into an undeveloped, expanding society, a fact which has influenced the development of American higher education from that day to this.

Early American colleges were predominantly religious in aim. Of the "colonial nine" in existence at the opening of the Revolution, seven were founded by Protestant church groups under sectarian control.[1] The sectarian, denominational nature of the colonial colleges established a clear pattern for the subsequent development of collegiate education in the eighteenth and nineteenth centuries.

The first American colleges were modeled on British universities as they existed in the seventeenth century. Though William and Mary, Princeton, and Pennsylvania showed traces of Scottish university influence, the other colonial colleges tended to follow the examples of Oxford or Cambridge.[2] However, the pressures of American conditions

---

[1] Harvard (1636, Congregational); William and Mary (1643, Anglican); Yale (1701, Congregational); Princeton (1746, Presbyterian); Brown (College of Rhode Island, 1765, Baptist); Dartmouth (1769, Congregational); Rutgers (Queens, 1770, Reformed). Columbia (King's, 1754) and Pennsylvania (College of Philadelphia, 1755) were nondenominational. Catholic Georgetown was founded in 1789.

[2] See W. H. Cowley, "European Influences on American Higher Education,"

quickly forced the colonists to modify the traditional British university pattern. The American university, unlike the British, was not composed of "colleges" grouped about a center, but developed rather as an autonomous, free-standing institution. Its sponsorship was privately denominational, with control usually vested in a board of ministers and lay persons who were not academic. The colonial college existed under a charter, granted by the Crown or a legislative body, with authority for its government and operation vested in a board or corporation. Harvard had a system of dual control, involving both a corporation composed of a president, treasurer, and teaching fellows and a board of overseers comprised of church and state officials. A board of trustees, of which the Bishop of London was chancellor, governed William and Mary. Yale, until the Revolution, possessed a single governing board composed of the president and fellows.[3]

Faculty government of the European type could not exist in the early American college, since it often opened with a faculty of no more than a president and tutor or two. Not until the mid-eighteenth century, for example, did regularly appointed faculty at Yale, Harvard, and Princeton outnumber transient tutors. Boards of control, therefore, granted a great deal of authority to the president, who was in many cases the single faculty member of permanence and professional standing. American colleges and universities enjoyed none of the financial security of their British brethren, and far less public or state support. Since colonial students often entered college with scanty academic preparation (because of the paucity of good pre-college schools) and at a very early age, American colleges provided training of a much less advanced nature than that of British or Continental universities. As a result of these factors, the American university system by the time of the Revolution was markedly different from that of Britain and Europe, with its own characteristic aims, standards, and organizational patterns.[4]

Educational Record, XX (1939), 165–190; A. B. Cutts, "The Educational Influence of Aberdeen in Seventeenth Century Virginia," *William and Mary Quarterly*, XV (1935), 229–249. Charles Thwing, *A History of Higher Education in America* (New York, 1900), has several relevant sections.

[3] Richard Hofstadter and W. F. Metzer, *The Development of Academic Freedom in the United States* (New York, 1955), pp. 114–116; George P. Schmidt, *The Old Time College President* (New York, 1930), pp. 46–51, and *The Liberal Arts College* (New Brunswick, N.J., 1957), pp. 20–23.

[4] An interesting general article is R. H. Shryock, "The Academic Profession in the United States," *American Association of University Professors Bulletin*, XXXVIII (1952), 32–70.

American universities during the eighteenth century drifted gradually toward secular education. The impact of the Enlightenment, the emergence of a powerful middle class, the separation of church and state, the controversy over independence and revolution, all contributed to the secularization of American education and loosened the ecclesiastical grip on universities. From 1750 to 1800 the control of American colleges passed from the church, to the church layman, and finally into predominantly nonsectarian hands.[5]

The spirit of religious toleration that characterized eighteenth-century thinking helped, of course, to loosen the denominational grasp on higher education. Franklin, Jefferson, Rush (all of whom founded colleges), and others like them condemned religious partisanship in education, while the gradual collapse of theological authority over American life during the eighteenth century meant less and less sectarianism in the colleges. After the mid-point of the eighteenth century, politics—not theology—provided the major topic of discussion in America. By the time of the Revolution the pattern of administrative control in American higher education (except for Harvard) was fairly standardized on the Yale pattern, with authority resting in a board of trustees, usually composed of ministers, state officials, and laymen in varying proportions, while the college president served *ex officio* as the board's executive officer for the administration of the institution's day-to-day affairs. This administrative organization, unique among the universities of the world, placed the major decisions concerning educational aims, financial policy, and academic standards almost wholly in nonacademic hands.

The drift toward secularization in American higher education during the eighteenth century was also reflected by changes in the college curriculum.[6] Courses of study in the early colleges were adapted directly from those of British universities, which in turn were based on the medieval concept of a university education. Harvard's first curriculum, which remained virtually unchanged for nearly a hundred years, included the medieval *quadrivium*, Aristotelian philosophy, classical languages, and Hebrew, all aimed at producing cultured, literate, orthodox Congregational ministers. Admission requirements in the majority of colonial col-

[5] Hofstadter and Metzer, *Academic Freedom*, pp. 120–130. For additional information on the evolution of American university administration, see E. H. Reisner, "The Origin of Lay Boards of Control in the United States," *Columbia University Quarterly*, XXIII (1931), 60–69, and J. E. Kirkpatrick, *Academic Organization and Control* (Yellow Springs, Ohio, 1931).

[6] Hofstadter and Metzer, *Academic Freedom*, pp. 186, 191 ff.

leges consisted of competence in Latin and Greek, perhaps arithmetic; a good tutor could easily prepare a bright boy for any American college in a reasonably short time.

Science, in the form of mathematics, astronomy, or "natural philosophy," began to appear in the curriculum in the early eighteenth century, though what science was taught had a strong theological flavor. Mathematics, beyond arithmetic or simple geometry, was fairly rare and usually taught in some practical form (surveying, navigation, mensuration, projectiles). The average graduate of the first half of the eighteenth century usually emerged from college with a good knowledge of Latin, Greek, and perhaps Hebrew, a solid foundation in philosophy and theology, and a smattering of science.[7]

The curriculum of the colonial college reflected rather accurately the prevailing concept of what an education should be and do. Built about a central core of classics, logic, philosophy, theology, and moral training, its course of study was intended to provide for young gentlemen a body of knowledge that would assure them of entrance into a community of educated leaders. This body of knowledge was assumed to be relatively fixed, with science lying somewhat beyond, but yet related to it. Higher education had nothing to do with vocational, pre-professional, or commercial education; an acquaintance with the fine arts was considered ornamental but not essential. The idea of knowledge as an expanding, dynamic thing was quite foreign to the early eighteenth century, nor was it then conceived that education might be preparation for the creation of new ideas.[8]

The first revolt against the traditional curriculum began in the middle of the eighteenth century. Expanding horizons in both scientific and nonscientific knowledge called for a broader collegiate education for broader purposes; American colleges had failed to reflect the changing character of American life, the expansion of trade and commerce, the emergence of regional cultural interests, the growth of urban society, the shift of class demarcations. Students in 1750 no longer entered college chiefly to prepare for the ministry or the bar; whereas Harvard had sent 70 per cent of its graduates into the church in 1650, it sent only

[7] See R. H. Shryock, "American Indifference to Basic Science During the Nineteenth Century," *Archives Internationales d'Histoire des Sciences* (Paris, 1940), No. 5, for an excellent study of science in education.

[8] R. Freeman Butts, *The College Charts Its Course* (New York, 1939), pp. 47–49, 63–68.

45 per cent in 1750 and fewer thereafter, with the same true of Yale and Princeton.[9]

The political struggles of the eighteenth century meant that the young man ought to study Locke, Grotius, Montesquieu, and Pufendorf; that he must debate taxation, the compact theory of government, and resistance to political authority rather than free will and predestination. The great burst of scientific knowledge sent him to Newton and Descartes. The spread of theological controversy meant he should read Watts, Woollaston, Shaftesbury, and others. By 1788 nine colleges had professors of mathematics, astronomy, or physics, or chairs of "natural philosophy." The curriculum of the College of Philadelphia, founded at the high tide of the Enlightenment, contained mathematics, physics, astronomy, zoology, French, and botany in addition to the usual logic, philosophy, and classics. Jefferson, at William and Mary in the late eighteenth century, suggested a reorganization of its curriculum intended to abolish professorships of divinity and Oriental languages in favor of law, medicine, and modern languages.

The Revolution itself had a powerful effect on the college curriculum. Since most educational institutions were located in cities, and since all major cities were occupied by the British, most colleges were closed for the greater part of the war. One-quarter of all college students entered some form of military service. Both Harvard and Princeton were used as Army barracks, while William and Mary served first as Cornwallis' headquarters and later as a French military hospital. What little financial help a few colleges enjoyed from British sources was abruptly cut off, importations of books ceased, and wartime inflation made college financing almost impossible.[10]

The Revolution infused the colleges with a powerful nationalistic spirit. If education were necessary to the success of the Republic, as its founders unanimously asserted, education to produce national leadership was a public responsibility. Education, wrote Robert Coram in his *Political Inquiries* (1791), must "not be left to the caprice, or negligence of parents, to chance, or confined to the children of wealthy citizens; it is a shame, a scandal to civilized society, that part only of the citizens should be sent to colleges and universities."

---

[9] See B. B. Burritt, *Professional Distribution of College and University Graduates* (Washington, D.C., 1912), pp. 14, 22, 75, *passim.*

[10] Thwing, *Higher Education,* pp. 165–175. The French alliance also brought renewed interest in French educational ideas; see *ibid.,* pp. 192–203; Hinsdale, "Foreign Influences," pp. 594–597.

After the war, the nation demanded new responsibilities of its institutions of higher education. Those universities which already existed in 1783, it was assumed, should not only train cultured gentlemen, ministers, and leaders, but must produce useful, intelligent, patriotic citizens. Those states which did not have institutions of higher learning within their borders set about at once to charter them—North Carolina (1789), South Carolina (1801), Georgia (1783), Maryland (1784), Tennessee (1794), and Vermont (1791). Colleges proliferated wildly in the postwar decades. Whereas nine colleges had been established over the period from 1636 to 1776, at least sixteen—some of them short-lived —were established in the closing decades of the eighteenth century and the first few years of the nineteenth.[11]

The expansion of collegiate education in the postwar period brought into focus the long struggle for control, implicit in the development of eighteenth-century American education, between the church-related college and the publicly supported university. Although the European concept of education as a function of the state was not unknown to the United States, the colonial concept that education belonged to the church, and that the aims of education were primarily religious, was by far the stronger of the two. There were colonial precedents for state support of higher education (Harvard and William and Mary were founded by church and state together), but in all of the colonial colleges the state had only an indirect relationship to their actual administration.

The drift of eighteenth-century society toward secularization, coupled with the spread of new ideas of natural rights, political freedom, and individual equality, put the church colleges on the defensive. In five of the thirteen states, a particular church denomination virtually dominated society (Virginia, New York, Massachusetts, Connecticut, and New Hampshire), and in them the established universities (William and Mary, Harvard, Yale, Columbia, and Dartmouth) held exclusive rights over higher education. With the exception of Columbia all these universities had deep religious roots and powerful church connections.[12]

[11] Washington, Maryland (1782); Hampden-Sydney (1776); Washington and Jefferson (1780 ff.); Transylvania (1783); Dickinson (1783); St. Johns (1784); Charleston (1785); Georgia (1785); Franklin (1787); North Carolina (1789); Vermont (1791); Williams (1793); Bowdoin (1794); Greenville, Tenn. (1794); Blount, Tenn. (1794); Union (1795); Middlebury (1800).

[12] D. G. Tewkesbury, *The Founding of American Colleges and Universities Before the Civil War* (New York, 1932), pp. 62–67.

The majority of colleges founded after 1783, following the colonial tradition, were intended to produce, if not ministers, at least Christians. To turn control of higher education from the church over to the state seemed unthinkable to many Americans, steeped as they were in a long tradition of religious education—particularly since after 1796 it seemed the state might sometime be controlled by deists, rationalists, and Jeffersonian "infidels."

State politicians made several attempts to secure control of the private, denominational colleges after 1785. Harvard, Princeton, Yale, Columbia, Pennsylvania, and William and Mary stood them off, and the settlement of the Dartmouth College case of 1819, ably argued by Daniel Webster, finally gave a legal victory to the forces of private sectarian education. The Dartmouth case established two principles: that state institutions were subject to state, not denominational, control; and that denominational colleges established by minority sectarian groups, once having obtained a charter, were to be free from state interference. The way, therefore, was opened for public and private institutions of higher education to develop separately, with the victory to the most powerful. In the ensuing struggle for educational dominance of the United States, the religious institutions had by far the heavier guns.

There were several reasons for their victory. The religious impulse in American society was too powerful, and the orthodox churches too firmly entrenched. State legislatures, on which state colleges and universities depended for support, understandably reflected the religious attitudes of the electorate. Most of the state institutions were staffed by products of the older church colleges; of seventy-five college presidents in 1840, thirty-six were Yale men and twenty-two Princeton.[13] The state educational institutions, during the first half of the nineteenth century, never managed to gain sufficient financial support or administrative autonomy to establish themselves as serious rivals to the church-related colleges.[14] The churches fought them in the legislature, in the public prints, and in the local governments, and usually won. By 1830 all universities, public or private, had common moral and religious (if

[13] Schmidt, *Old Time College President,* p. 96.

[14] State legislatures were notoriously pinchpenny in their appropriations to state universities. The University of Georgia got 40,000 acres of land and a loan, and nothing else. The University of Missouri waited twenty-eight years for its first state appropriation, and the University of Michigan twenty-three. See Schmidt, *Liberal Arts College,* pp. 15–16.

not wholly sectarian) purposes, reflected in their curricula, administration, and faculties.[15]

The most important factor in the victory of religion in higher education after 1800, however, was the wave of evangelistic fervor that swept over American churches during the first forty years of the nineteenth century. The revitalization of religion, under the impact of a second Great Awakening, led to a sharp reaction against the liberal, tolerant educational thinking of the eighteenth century. Orthodox churches, as well as the strong new evangelistic sects, recognized the importance of education as protection against deism, "infidelity," Jeffersonian liberalism, and "French radicalism." Dozens of church colleges, dedicated to propagating the faith, sprang up overnight. Of the seventy-eight permanent colleges and universities existing in the United States in 1840, thirty-five were founded after 1830, almost all of these under religious sponsorship.[16]

The Baptist Convention of 1820 amended its constitution to make education a function of the church, with the slogan "Every state its own Baptist college." Four years later the Methodist Conference voted to place a college within the boundaries of each Annual Conference, leading to the Wesleyan Universities of Ohio, Illinois, Dakota, Iowa, and Nebraska. The nondenominational Society for the Promotion of Collegiate and Theological Education at the West (sponsored chiefly by Congregationalists) threw its support to new, struggling church colleges. For each sect, a college represented an outpost of faith, a seed of religion planted on the frontier, and in them dedicated young men attacked their task with holy zeal. "The sun shines not on such a missionary field as the valley of the Mississippi," wrote one of them, and "bands" from the American Home Missionary Society, the American Educational Society, and the eastern churches spread over the West, leaving log-cabin colleges scattered behind them on the plains.[17]

[15] State universities, or those partially state-supported, chartered or founded after 1800 included Ohio (1802), Miami (1809), Virginia (1819), Missouri (1820), Alabama (1821), College of Louisiana (1825), Nashville (1826), Indiana (1828), Mississippi (1830), Delaware (1833), and Michigan (1837). See Tewkesbury, *Founding of Colleges,* Chap. III, for an extended discussion; also Hofstadter and Metzer, *Academic Freedom,* pp. 220–230, 248–450.

[16] For an excellent account of the religious impulse in higher education prior to the Civil War, see Schmidt, *Liberal Arts College,* Chap. II, "Higher Education, The Child of Religion." See also Butts, *College Charts Its Course,* Chap. VII, and Tewkesbury, *Founding of Colleges,* pp. 9–14, 70–72, 89 ff.

[17] The rate of failure among these hastily founded colleges was extremely high.

Congregational and Presbyterian institutions were usually established for the explicit purpose of producing ministerial leadership for the frontier. Wabash, its charter said, was founded to "remedy the painful destitution of educated ministers in the state," while Western Reserve, its founders wrote, would provide "an able, learned, and pious ministry for the infant churches . . . and a missionary Establishment for planting the Gospel upon a new Field."[18] The production of clergy was less urgent to Baptists and Methodists, who felt that a young man's "call" to the ministry was likely to be more important than his educational qualifications. As one Methodist Conference told its ministers in 1784, "gaining knowledge is a good thing, but saving souls is better. If you can do but one, let your studies alone." The early Baptist and Methodist colleges in the West were therefore not solely ministerial training schools. De Pauw (Indiana-Asbury), founded in 1837, was not, the Indiana Methodist Conference said, merely "a manufactory of which preachers are to be made."[19]

State institutions in the Western states fared poorly in the race for educational supremacy. The new states were thinly populated; the cost of public education was high. In 1800 there were no more than 800,000 people in the entire Northwest Territory, of whom almost half lived in Ohio. The major share of the West's resources were instead channeled into the denominational colleges which sprang up in profusion after 1815—Alleghany (1812), Centre (1819), Kenyon (1824), Western Reserve (1826), Georgetown (Kentucky, 1829), Marietta (1835), Denison (1831), Oberlin (1833)—and farthest west, De Pauw (1837), Hanover (1827), Wabash (1832), Shurtleff (1827), McKendree (1828), Illinois College (1829), Albion (1835), Hillsdale (1844), Knox (Prairie College, 1837), and Jubilee (1839). These colleges were aggressively orthodox, prone to label themselves as "Yales of the West" and to copy their Eastern brethren with devoted care. The Catholic Church, during the same period, founded St. Mary's (Baltimore, 1805), St. Joseph's (Bardstown, Kentucky, 1824), and St. Louis (1833).[20]

Southern states had no tradition of state-supported education, though

---

Of forty-three founded in Ohio between 1790 and 1860, twenty-six failed; in Georgia, thirty-nine out of forty-six; in Missouri, sixty-five out of seventy-seven. Schmidt, *Liberal Arts College,* p. 11.

[18] Tewkesbury, *Founding of Colleges,* pp. 83–84.

[19] W. W. Sweet, *Religion in the Development of American Culture* (New York, 1952), pp. 173–180.

[20] Thwing, *Higher Education,* pp. 210 ff.

one was in the making. Wealthier families sent their sons North (Harvard in 1820 had fifty Southern students, Princeton forty-two, and Yale forty-two), and poorer families sent theirs to the church colleges which dominated the South and Southwest. The Presbyterians supported Hampden-Sidney (Virginia), Davidson (North Carolina), Erskine (South Carolina), Oglethorpe (Georgia), and Centre (Kentucky). The Baptists founded Richmond (Virginia), Wake Forest (North Carolina), Furman (South Carolina), Mercer (Georgia), Howard (Alabama), and Union (Tennessee). The Methodists had Randolph-Macon and Emory-Henry in Virginia, Trinity in North Carolina, Emory in Georgia, and La Grange in Alabama. Even in the East, where older church colleges already existed, the impetus of renewed religious enthusiasm led to the founding of Waterville, Colby, Amherst, Washington (later Trinity), Asbury, and Wesleyan. Of the total number of colleges in existence in 1860, Presbyterians controlled forty-nine, Methodists thirty-four, Baptists twenty-five, Congregationalists twenty-one, Catholics fourteen, Anglicans eleven, and Lutherans six.[21]

The tremendous expansion of collegiate education after 1800 and the rivalry between state and sectarian institutions caused serious deterioration in the quality of American higher education. The proliferation of colleges scattered educational enterprise and strained the limited financial resources available to education. Colleges sprang up everywhere, wrote President Philip Lindsley of Nashville in 1829, "like mushrooms on our luxuriant soil."[22] The evangelistic reaction against the Enlightenment's rationalism, tolerance, and unhindered search for knowledge turned many of the new colleges into defenders of the faith against theological subversion rather than true educational institutions. Sectarian rivalries and religious imperialism prevented the growth of state universities and restricted the church colleges themselves to narrow goals. The majority of religious colleges were too often expected to produce devout church members, missionaries, or ministers—not young men interested in science, humanities, the arts, government, or the free pursuit of truth.

The rapid expansion of educational institutions brought lower academic standards, for there were not enough qualified faculties to supply

[21] *Ibid.*, Chap. XI. It is also significant that of all college presidents who held office before 1860, 90 per cent were ordained ministers. Schmidt, *Old Time College President*, pp. 130–132.

[22] Hofstadter and Metzer, *Academic Freedom*, p. 212.

the need nor sufficient money available to attract them. Many of the smaller colleges were hardly the equal of mediocre academies; their aim, said Lindsley bitterly, was usually "to finish off and graduate, in double quick time."[23] In 1815 the entire faculty of Dickinson College resigned in protest against an order to revise the curriculum so that a student could finish all his work in a single year.[24] In their quest for students and tuition fees, colleges admitted applicants of widely varying ages and preparations—as low as thirteen, as high as forty-five—and since tuition represented the major share of college finances, admission requirements sometimes tended to be extremely flexible. The result was a general lowering of faculty qualifications, academic standards, and discipline.[25]

Most colleges were inadequately financed. The history of American higher education after 1800 is one of constant, wearying struggle against bankruptcy. In 1839 only eleven American institutions enrolled more than 150 students (Yale, Dartmouth, Princeton, Pennsylvania, Harvard, Virginia, Union, Brown, Amherst, South Carolina, and Bowdoin), while the average college enrollment was approximately half that number. Yale, in 1830, received less than $3,000 a year from its endowments, while Columbia, in 1850, still had a debt of $68,000. Gifts and bequests occasionally provided aid, but they were infrequent and remarkably small. Some colleges resorted to lotteries; Yale, Harvard, Rutgers, and Princeton all used this device, and the legislature of New York in 1841 approved lotteries for Hamilton and Union. Princeton in 1821 showed a deficit of $753 for the fiscal year, which it promptly made up by reducing the salaries of two professors. The faculty of Amherst averted one crisis by teaching for several weeks with no pay at all.

In the log-cabin frontier colleges a yearly "begging tour" by the college president was an established custom. During the 1830's, Eastern colleges discovered the value of alumni as a source of finance, with results not always quite as anticipated.[26] State institutions, of course, obtained funds from legislatures, which were rarely noted for generosity, though some state institutions enjoyed certain advantages through tax exemptions and land grants. Colleges depended primarily on tuition fees

[23] *Ibid.*, p. 213.
[24] See the account in J. H. Morgan, *Dickinson College* (Carlisle, Pa., 1913), pp. 130–145.
[25] Hofstadter and Metzer, *Academic Freedom,* pp. 224 ff.
[26] Princeton's Alumni Association, the first, was founded in 1826, Pennsylvania's in 1835. Schmidt, *Liberal Arts College,* p. 13.

for solvency, though many students could afford to pay only modest sums. Harvard in 1825 charged $55 per year, Yale $33, and Columbia $90, and others down to $5 per year at some small Western schools.[27]

The administrative pattern of American colleges that had developed in the eighteenth century continued, with a few exceptions, in the new institutions founded in the nineteenth century. The supreme authority was ordinarily vested in a board of nonacademic trustees, who were appointed (or elected) by the controlling group—church, legislature, corporation, or electorate. Since the trustees were not always residents of the college community and met only at stated times, boards tended to delegate authority to the college president, or to committees of trustees who lived nearby. The office of president therefore took on a unique importance in American higher education. He set the curriculum and academic standards, hired and fired faculty, supervised admissions, officiated at graduations, enforced discipline, collected fees, bought college supplies, counseled students, and raised money.

The president of Princeton in 1802 presided at all college functions and ceremonies, taught the senior class, and held a regular ministerial post. At North Carolina, in addition to his other duties, the president examined each student every Sunday evening on the state of his religious beliefs. At Columbia, the president was responsible for such things as purchasing books, providing coathooks for classrooms, and taking attendance at faculty prayers. President Samuels of Vermont taught all classes offered at the College, supervised the construction of college buildings, and helped to chop down the trees to build them. President Humphreys of St. Johns in one year lectured fourteen times on political economy, twenty-seven on classic literature, twenty-seven on chemistry and geology, thirty-four on natural philosophy, and six on astronomy.[28] For such labors college presidents received a salary of $800 to $1,800 per year, a house and garden, and permission to augment their incomes by outside preaching.[29] The eighteenth- and nineteenth-century Ameri-

[27] Hofstadter and Metzer, *Academic Freedom*, pp. 311 ff.; 121–123; Thwing, *Higher Education*, Chap. XIV, pp. 323–334; Schmidt, *Old Time College President*, pp. 63 *et seq.*

[28] Schmidt, *Old Time College President*, pp. 74, 105; Thwing, *Higher Education*, pp. 325–335, and Chap. XII. Schmidt's book is a mine of information.

[29] Salaries ranged from $800 at Miami (1832), $1,600 at Princeton (1828), $1,400 at Columbia (1828), $1,700 at Rutgers (1810), $1,300 at Indiana (1832), to $1,800 at Hamilton (1812). Thwing, *Higher Education*, pp. 330–332.

can college thus reflected in large measure the personality and qualities of its president.

The growth of college enrollments, consequent increases in staff, and the function of the college president gradually changed after 1820. During the early years of a college, when the faculty numbered three to five and the student body fifty to seventy, the president's relations with his faculty and students could be personal and intimate. However, as faculties grew to twenty and forty, and as the curriculum broadened, this relationship changed. In larger institutions the president tended to serve as intermediary between board and faculty, as administrator rather than teacher and counselor; at the same time faculty opinion on matters of salary, tenure, appointments, and curriculum became of greater importance. At well-established colleges with powerful faculties, clashes between faculty and board, or faculty and president, were frequent, and in a few cases (such as that of President Kirkland at Harvard) a faculty virtually forced a president's resignation. In smaller colleges the president maintained more or less complete authority, and it was not until after the Civil War that any systematized relationship among faculty, administrative officers and governing boards was established.[30]

Faculty members were ordinarily hired without tenure at the pleasure of the president, at an average salary in 1800 of $600 per year, reaching $1,000 by 1860—an income about equal to that of a clergyman in a small parish or of a skilled workman. In smaller colleges, the president was usually the sole professor, with a tutor or two to assist him. In large universities there were professors in various subject-matter areas, as well as tutors (at $100 per year) to handle elementary instruction. The requirement for a professorship was customarily the B.A., or a divinity degree, though smaller colleges did not always insist on a degree at all.[31]

The college teacher was presumed to be a guide and model to his students, rather than a scholar. "Learning, in a professor," wrote one educator, "though universal, is but a secondary qualification." There was little to encourage the specialist or the researcher, and very few facilities for him. Harvard's library, in 1781, had 11,000 volumes; Yale's

[30] Hofstadter and Metzer, *Academic Freedom,* pp. 232 ff.
[31] Joseph Caldwell, when he became president of North Carolina at twenty-four, found a faculty composed of a French ex-monk, an ex-actor, and a British navy deserter—admittedly an extreme case. Schmidt, *Liberal Arts College,* p. 93.

in 1808 had 5,000; Princeton's in 1770 had only 1,200. An English visitor to Princeton in 1800 judged its library to be "most wretched, consisting for the most part of old theological books, not even arranged with any regularity." George Ticknor in 1816 noted that Göttingen had 200,000 volumes compared to Harvard's 20,000, while Ticknor eventually himself possessed 13,000 books, a collection larger than any owned by three-quarters of the libraries in the United States.[32]

The university faculty member had little chance for creative work in his dreary round of teaching. C. C. Felton, one of the nation's great Greek scholars, taught twelve classes of beginning Greek for twenty-three years before he had an opportunity to lecture in his special field. College teaching was likely to be monotonous and unimaginative. Student diaries of the early nineteenth century were filled with bitter criticisms of faculty; according to Henry Adams, Harvard's curriculum was suited to a boy of fourteen, "the instruction itself was poor, and the discipline was indifferent."[33] Most teaching was done by the recitation method (occasionally by lecture or demonstration), in which the student studied a text, memorized it, was drilled on it, recited it, and was checked by the teacher for correctness. "It scarcely ever entered the heads of our teachers," wrote the Reverend Warren Burton, "to question us about the ideas hidden in the great long words and spacious sentences of the texts."[34] There was little time for discussion, and whatever original thinking the student did was usually on his own time. College teaching methods, like those of the lower schools, were based on the traditional "faculty" psychology, which assumed that the mind was composed of certain elements which could be developed and strengthened, like muscles, by constant exercise. Education, wrote President Day of Yale in 1828, consisted of "the *discipline* and *furniture* of the mind; expanding its powers, and storing it with knowledge. The former of these, perhaps, is the more important of the two. A commanding object, therefore, in a collegiate course should be to call into daily and vigorous exercise the faculties of the students."[35]

Collegiate instruction in the early nineteenth century was based on

[32] Thwing, *Higher Education,* Chap. XIX; H. U. Faulkner, *American Political and Social History* (New York, 1948), 215; Hofstadter and Metzer, *Academic Freedom,* pp. 227 ff.

[33] *Education of Henry Adams* (Cambridge, Mass., 1918), p. 55; Hofstadter and Metzer, *Academic Freedom,* p. 229.

[34] Butts and Cremin, *History of Education,* p. 270.

[35] Hofstadter and Metzer, *Academic Freedom,* p. 15.

three assumptions: that scholarship was less important than ethico-religious learning; that students required strong moral guidance; and that the aim of education was to discipline the mind. All decisions concerning knowledge rested with the professor; what students thought was of little importance and not worth discussion.[36] There was much of the deadly, the dull, and the niggling about the system—yet in the hands of gifted teachers it produced its share of brilliant, well-educated men, whatever its shortcomings and handicaps. And it was also true that good teachers of the time encouraged hard work, considered learning a serious endeavor, and respected care, precision, and sincere effort.

The right of the scholar to pursue truth in an impartial, objective manner was by no means fully recognized by the nineteenth-century university.[37] College teachers were expected to be politically sound and theologically orthodox; those who were not usually found themselves in trouble. Church-related colleges, in particular, tolerated little deviationism, and state universities, conscious of prevailing political winds in the legislatures, could not afford much liberalism.

The discipline, morals, and religion of students were considered by universities to be the primary concern of faculty and administration. Rules governing behavior were numerous and rigorously enforced. Since a student body might range in age from fourteen to forty-five, there was perhaps need for stiff discipline, since the laborious monotony of classroom work tended to engender undergraduate explosions. At Union College in 1802, for example, the rulebook to be memorized by every student contained eleven chapters of seven to twenty-three sections each; on the other hand, it is also true that the things which the rules forbade seem to have been done.

The college student lived a vigorously regimented life, with fixed times for rising, prayers, study, church, recreation, and bed.[38] At Am-

---

[36] *Ibid.,* p. 279.

[37] *Ibid.,* pp. 207, 238 ff., 262 ff.; Schmidt, *Liberal Arts College,* Chap. 12. Howard K. Beale, *A History of the Freedom of Teaching in American Schools* (New York, 1941), Chaps. II and III, provides a careful account of academic freedom during the years 1776–1830. Clement Eaton, "Southern Senators and the Right of Instruction, 1789–1860," *Journal of Southern History,* XVIII (1952), 303–319, discusses the particular Southern problem. See also Eaton's *History of the Freedom of Thought in the Old South* (Durham, N.C., 1940).

[38] Costs for a college education varied widely. At Princeton in 1804 the average yearly cost per student was $171.23, though John Rutledge of South Carolina thought $600 a year more likely for costs at Harvard at about the same time. Schmidt, *Liberal Arts College,* p. 77.

herst, students were forbidden (among other things) to dance, play cards, drink, race horses, swear, duel, break furniture, or lock instructors in their rooms, on pain of fine or expulsion. At Georgia students might be fined, suspended, or expelled for profanity, fighting, smashing doors, playing billiards or "any other unlawful game," associating with "idle or dissolute persons," noisiness, loud singing, "ringing the bell without permission," traveling more than two miles from the campus, keeping dogs, striking a teacher, forgery, defacing walls, robbery, fornication, "refractory behavior," and, if no rule could be found for any other offense, "the faculty might proceed at their discretion." At Union, fines varied from 3 cents for missing chapel to $3 for drunkenness; at Harvard, students were fined $3 for attending a Boston theater.

Larger institutions gradually reduced the number of rules and the severity of punishments, but the smaller, church-related schools retained the demerit system of discipline well into the late nineteenth century. Punishments ranged from small fines, to large ones, to "rustication" or temporary suspension, to expulsion, which could be "ordinary" (private) or public. Enforcement of the rules took much faculty time and effort. At Brown, for example, faculty members were required to visit a student's rooms twice every twenty-four hours. President Caldwell of North Carolina patrolled the campus nightly on the lookout for offenders, and President McLean of Princeton, who caught some students out after hours, chased them up a tree.[39]

Harsh discipline, added to the rigorous demands of classroom work, sometimes produced bitterness and insubordination. The cow in the chapel, the dining-hall shambles, and asafoetida in the classroom stove were routine pranks, traditional in colleges since time immemorial. But pranks occasionally erupted into riots, and the history of almost any nineteenth-century college shows at least one serious outbreak. In 1807, 125 of Princeton's total enrollment of 200 were expelled for rioting. Harvard freshmen and sophomores in 1817 smashed all the college crockery; that same year Princeton students broke the dormitory windows and threw wine bottles and firewood at the faculty. At Hobart students rolled red-hot cannonballs down a dormitory corridor and seriously injured a faculty member. At North Carolina students shot out windows with guns, and at Virginia the high-spirited Southern boys horsewhipped several faculty members. In 1814 Princeton students

[39] *Ibid.*, pp. 77–84.

constructed a giant firecracker with a hollow log and two pounds of gunpowder and nearly blew up Nassau Hall. The class of 1824, in preparation for graduation at Dartmouth, "burnt one barn, stoned Professor Chamberlain, burnt him and tutor Parley and hung the President in effigy." Three Bowdoin students were expelled and a score of others disciplined in 1827 for setting off powder charges under tutors' chairs.[40]

But there were also serious young men in college who worked hard, starved on a pittance, and educated themselves well. Even in New England, the most educationally conscious section of the nation, the ratio of college students to population was only 1 to 513, and in 1840 the national college enrollment of college-age persons was perhaps less than 2 per cent. Education was not a luxury but a serious undertaking, and the majority of students realized its importance.

There was little organized student life in the pre-Civil War college or university. Sports were considered to be the student's own business, though colleges hoped that he would keep himself fit. Richard Henry Dana, Jr., reported to his parents in 1831 that Harvard students played cricket, had informal football games, and boxed, fenced, and swam for exercise. These sports, plus a few others such as footracing and an early version of baseball, were popular on most college campuses. Americans who traveled abroad were tremendously impressed by the German system of physical education, and Harvard in 1826 established its first gymnasium in an empty dining hall, where Dr. Follen, a German scholar, taught exercises. The European "manual labor school," in which a student worked for pay and exercise on college projects, was particularly popular in the West—Oberlin, Western Reserve, Marietta, Illinois College, Knox, and others retained the system for several decades. Students at older universities founded societies, clubs, debating, or "literary" groups to provide an organized social life; by the 1840's the majority of colleges had Athenian Societies, or Greek Clubs, or Singing Clubs of some description. Phi Beta Kappa, the first Greek-letter society, formed at William and Mary in 1776, was originally a literary club.[41]

[40] Schmidt, *Old Time College President*, pp. 85–87; Hofstadter and Metzer, *Academic Freedom*, pp. 307–308; E. M. Coulter, *College Life in the Old South* (Durham, N.C., 1928), pp. 60–62; N. M. Blake, *Short History of American Life*, pp. 309–310; Butler, *Education Prior to 1850*, p. 104.
[41] Thwing, *Higher Education*, pp. 115, 377–379; John Krout and D. R. Fox, *The Completion of Independence* (New York, 1944), p. 275; Butler, *Education Prior to 1850*, pp. 31, 73.

The college curriculum of 1800 showed very little change from that of 1750. Samuel Miller, in a survey of collegiate education in 1802, described Harvard's offerings as:

First Year: Greek and Latin writers, Rhetoric, Universal History, Arith-
               metic, English Grammar, French, Hebrew, Logic, Geography.
Second Year: Greek and Latin writers, French, Hebrew, Logic, Geography,
               Arithmetic, History, Algebra, Mensuration, Philosophy (Locke
               and Blair).
Third Year: Greek and Latin writers, History, Euclid, Trigonometry, Conic
               Sections, Mensuration, English Composition, Forensic Dispu-
               tations.
Fourth Year: Greek and Latin writers, Elements of Natural and Political
               Law, Paley's Philosophy, Spheric Geometry and Trigonometry,
               Astronomy, Theology, English Composition.

Yale's and Dartmouth's curricula looked much the same, except for chemistry in the fourth year at Dartmouth. Columbia offered two years of chemistry in the third and fourth years. William and Mary required the study of Jonathan Edwards in addition to Locke, and placed greater emphasis on history, law, and science.[42]

Until the late eighteenth century, degree work was fairly well standardized about the central core of classical, philosophical, and theological study, on the Harvard-Yale-Princeton pattern. Smaller colleges, of course, tended to copy the curricula of the larger, older institutions, since their faculties were overwhelmingly drawn from them, and since the newer colleges wanted to offer no less of an education. Mathematics, which began to appear in the curriculum in the early eighteenth century, was consistently offered after 1750, usually taught from translations of French or Latin texts. The physical and biological sciences, though occasionally taught in the seventeenth century, did not enter the college curriculum as full-fledged disciplines until the late eighteenth century as physics, chemistry, or astronomy, with isolated courses in botany, zoology, and geology taught in a few colleges.[43]

Harvard, under the influence of Winthrop and Greenwood, and Yale, with Thomas Clap, offered courses in mathematics and astronomy at

[42] Samuel Miller, *Retrospect of the Eighteenth Century* (New York, 1803), II, Appendix.
[43] *Ibid.*, pp. 300–303; Butts and Cremin, *Education in American Culture*, pp. 179–181. See also John C. Schwab, "The Yale College Curriculum, 1701–1901," *Educational Review*, XXII (1901), 1–17.

fairly advanced levels as early as 1720, while the contemporary veneration of Newton firmly fixed physics in the curriculum by the mid-eighteenth century. Chemists and botanists such as Waterhouse at Brown,
Mitchill at Columbia, Silliman at Yale, and Rush and Woodhouse at
Philadelphia all gave instruction in science in the post-Revolutionary
years, while Bowdoin, Dickinson, and William and Mary were teaching
science by 1800. However, few colleges could count well-qualified scientists on their faculties, and though science might be offered by smaller
colleges, it was obviously not on the level of those institutions which
possessed men of the caliber of Mitchill or Silliman.[44]

For the most part, the sciences (with the exception of mathematics)
tended to be superficially taught, or taught as adjuncts of theology or
philosophy by way of illustrating the beneficence of divine providence.
There were very few competent research scientists in colleges at all—
Benjamin Silliman, one of the few, worked for fifteen years in a small,
damp cellar constructed fifteen feet below ground level.[45] There was
some suspicion, even among scientists themselves, that too much scientific study in colleges might lead to impiety or unorthodoxy.

History, ordinarily taught as a corollary of classical studies, appeared
in the curriculum as a separate discipline in the late eighteenth century.
William and Mary in 1822 established the first professorship of history;
Harvard appointed the great Jared Sparks to its faculty in 1839. Yale,
however, had no history professorship until 1865, nor was it until 1847
that Harvard and Michigan, the first two universities to do so, recognized history as a subject for college entrance. Isolated courses in political science and economics, combined as "political economy," were
taught after 1800 at Columbia, William and Mary, South Carolina (under the German refugee Francis Lieber), and a few other institutions.

Similar courses appeared at Harvard in 1820, Yale in 1824, Dartmouth in 1828, and Princeton in 1830, although the first legitimate text,
Thomas Cooper's *Lectures on Political Economy*, was not published
until 1826. French suffered a temporary decline during the French Revolution and the Napoleonic period. Bowdoin in 1825 established a chair

---

[44] Schmidt, *Liberal Arts College*, p. 51. Since no universities or colleges
trained scientists before 1810, the teachers were self-taught or trained abroad.
Silliman, for example, was trained as a lawyer.

[45] For an interesting account of scientific study at one American university,
see L. W. McKeehan, *Yale Science: The First Hundred Years 1701–1801*
(New York, 1947), especially Chap. II.

of modern languages, with young Henry Wadsworth Longfellow as its occupant, and Harvard followed with the creation of the Smith Chair. German, long taught in the denominational colleges of Pennsylvania, failed to excite interest until Harvard, at the urging of the young Americans who studied in Germany after 1816, added it to its curriculum in 1825.[46]

The college and university curriculum, during the years 1780–1830, was in a transitional stage. Essentially, it still retained the classical-theological emphasis inherited from the seventeenth century, with accretions of the scientific, utilitarian studies demanded by the society of the Enlightenment. In the hands of gifted teachers, the course of college study could and did produce brilliant, well-educated men, but the whole drift of contemporary social and intellectual change had passed the colleges by. The education of 1812, while it may have fitted the needs of the eighteenth century, most assuredly did not meet those of the rapidly industrializing nineteenth. The curriculum of the institution of higher education in 1820, still based on the concept of education as the absorption of a fixed, traditional body of knowledge, had broadened only slightly over the preceding century. It made little provision for the pursuit of personal interests, little for pre-professional or vocational education, and none for technical education. For example, until the Civil War every engineer trained in the United States was a product of the United States Military Academy (1802), Rensselaer Polytechnic Institute (1824), or the United States Naval Academy (1846). Most of the men who built the bridges, turnpikes, canals, machines, and buildings of the period were either self-trained on the job or learned engineering abroad. The Erie Canal, a prime training school, produced practically all of the civil engineers in the United States before 1860. Not until Abbott Lawrence gave Harvard $50,000 in the 1840's did any American college or university consider any kind of technical education as its academic responsibility.[47]

The college curriculum, of course, had been under continual attack since the middle of the eighteenth century, but the force of educational

[46] Butts, *College Charts Its Course*, Chap. V; Louis F. Snow, *The College Curriculum in the United States* (New York, 1907); Theodore Hornberger, *Scientific Thought in American Colleges 1638–1800*, Chap. V. (Austin, Tex., 1945); Hofstadter and Metzer, *Academic Freedom*, pp. 283–284.

[47] Thwing, *Higher Education*, pp. 421–422; Hofstadter and Metzer, *Academic Freedom*, pp. 27–28.

tradition, with help from the churches, managed to maintain the *status quo* until well into the nineteenth century. However, the heritage of the Enlightenment's critique of education still remained, and after the turn of the century the educational liberals received aid from new and more powerful sources. One such source was a new generation of scholars, many of them trained in Europe, who found much to criticize in the American system. The impact of Germany was especially powerful on those young men who either studied at or visited German universities. Though Franklin visited Göttingen in 1766, and Benjamin Smith Barton took a medical degree there in 1799, German universities were relatively unknown to Americans until 1812. After that, a stream of students flowed to Göttingen, Berlin, Jena, Halle, and Heidelberg, returning with new and radically different concepts of what higher education should be and what it should do.

Fifteen Americans studied at Göttingen before 1830, two at Halle, six at the Royal Friedrich Wilhelm University, and two at Leipzig. Ticknor, George Bancroft, Edward Everett, Joseph Cogswell, F. H. Hedge, Theodore Woolsey, and others took German degrees or spent considerable time in German schools. The majority of them brought back glowing reports of German universities, finding in them a scholarly tradition and an intellectual energy in teaching and research apparently lacking in America. The respect in which learning was held, and the high standards of attainment demanded by German professors, imbued the young Americans with enthusiasm for scholarship. The tremendous demands made by German scholars on their students (Everett and Bancroft usually studied twelve hours every day) made American university habits seem childish, and Bancroft very nearly precipitated a full-scale student riot when he made such Teutonic demands on his Greek class at Harvard.[48]

Theodore Woolsey, after his return to Yale, revised Yale's classical course on the German plan. Ticknor, after his return to Harvard, sharply criticized its curriculum and advocated a freer, elective system of study (as Jefferson had so recommended in 1779), lectures rather than monotonous recitations, and much higher standards of student attainment. Though Ticknor resigned in 1835, despondent over his failure

[48] See O. W. Long, *Literary Pioneers* (Cambridge, Mass., 1935), for accounts of these young men in Germany. Also Butts, *College Charts Its Course*, pp. 97 ff. Henry A. Pochmann, *German Culture in America* (Madison, Wis., 1957), treats American students in Germany, pp. 66–79.

to effect any real reforms, by the 1840's some universities allowed a limited choice of courses, divided classes on the basis of proficiency rather than age, and began at least to recognize the merits of good teaching and of scholarship. Such reforms came slowly, and against bitter opposition.

The greatest demand for reform in the college curriculum, however, came as a result of changes in the economic, intellectual, social, and political climate of nineteenth-century America. There was simply so much more to know than ever before—in science, politics, economics, philosophy, and in almost any area of knowledge one might name—that the traditional curriculum could not possibly contain it. No course in "natural history" sufficed to cover all that was known, or was being discovered, in science. No course in "moral philosophy" could teach the new psychology, politics, or economics. For that matter, college enrollments grew so swiftly after 1800 that it was no longer possible for one man to teach all students in all subjects, or even in one. And with the influx of students into college, fewer came with the intent of entering law, the ministry, or public service. The traditional curriculum plainly failed to satisfy contemporary needs; it was not, as Francis Wayland of Brown remarked, "adapted to the wants of the whole community." Education, according to a New England newspaper editor, "must necessarily have a relation with the state of society, and the wants and condition of the community for which it is intended as a preparation."

Some colleges showed an inclination to move with the times; others resisted. Union College in 1802 allowed the substitution of French for Greek; its President Nott in 1828 expanded the range of choice to include any modern language and established a "scientific" curriculum parallel to the classical course. Amherst allowed its students some flexibility in the choice of required languages, and like Union offered a parallel scientific curriculum, which did not succeed.[49] Experiments of this nature created consternation at other colleges. President Maxcy of Brown thought that abandoning the classics as required study might lead to "mental insanity," and Samuel Miller predicted that the decline of the classics would "discourage one important means of supporting

---

[49] Butler, *Education Prior to 1850,* pp. 112, 115. Nott, however, did not dare to award A.B. diplomas to those graduates who had substituted modern languages for Greek and Latin, but merely certificates. Schmidt, *Liberal Arts College,* p. 60.

and defending" true Christianity.[50] North Carolina, as early as 1795, planned a curriculum which allowed a student to "apply himself to those branches of learning in science alone which are absolutely necessary to fit him for his destined profession or occupation in life," though it never went into full effect. Trinity, in 1823, offered courses in science and practical studies, as did Hobart in 1825. These were, however, isolated experiments.[51]

The most radical experiment was Virginia's, where in 1826 the majority of Jefferson's cherished educational theories came to fruition. Virginia required no standardized entrance requirements, no fixed period of residence, and allowed a student to graduate when he had satisfactorily completed his work. Virginia students had, Jefferson wrote Ticknor, "uncontrolled choice in the lectures they choose to attend," though they were expected to concentrate their work in one or more of eight departments—ancient languages, modern languages, mathematics, natural philosophy, natural history, anatomy and medicine, moral philosophy, or law.

Virginia's plan, however, was unique, and Philip Lindsley, when he proposed a similar reorganization at Nashville, was rudely disillusioned. Yale, Harvard, and Princeton, those fecund mothers of college presidents and faculties, stood fast.[52] Harvard successfully resisted the Germanism of its young scholars; Princeton maintained its old curriculum against student attacks; Yale, under President Day, quelled a revolt in 1827 by reaffirming its traditional stand. Wrote President Day: "The great object of a collegiate education . . . is to give that expansion and balance of the mental powers, those liberal and comprehensive views, and those fine proportions of character, which are not to be found in him whose ideas are always confined in a particular channel."[53]

Education, as Day wrote and as the majority of other college presidents would have agreed, was and would continue to be "mental discipline," the training of those faculties of the mind "that fix the attention,

[50] Schmidt, *Old Time College President*, p. 98; Miller, *Retrospect*, II, 37, 43.

[51] Butts, *College Charts Its Course*, Chap. VIII, has a thorough discussion of these experiments.

[52] Thwing, *Higher Education*, pp. 311–316.

[53] Quoted in Butts, *College Charts Its Course*, p. 120. See pp. 118–125 for an account of the Yale rebellion and also Schmidt, *Liberal Arts College*, pp. 54–56. The Yale committee soundly rejected any vocational aims, proudly proclaiming that "We have on our premises no experimental farm or retail shop, no cotton or iron manufactory."

train thought, arrange the treasures of memory, and guide the powers of genius." They carried the day. The major changes in college and university curricula came after 1860, concurrent with the rise of the state university and the redirection of the aims of higher education for the needs of another age and of another kind of society.

CHAPTER 9

The Building of an American Church

A MERICAN Protestantism of the late eighteenth century was divided into three relatively stable categories. There were those who, like Franklin, paid their church dues and went to Sunday services because it was socially profitable and correct to do so. Tolerant, urbane, rationalistic, these men found a sort of easy Christianity in those "essentials of religion," as Franklin called them, to which all educated men could agree. Second, there were traditional, orthodox Calvinists who, despite their acceptance of the spirit of Enlightenment, still retained (as Timothy Dwight did) the hard core of seventeenth-century theology, its discipline, its piety, and its authoritarianism. The tradition of the Great Awakening, still strong, created still a third variety—an evangelical, personalized, individualized Protestantism, often rebellious, intense, and emotional.

Until the last half of the eighteenth century these three groups maintained a kind of uneasy theological alliance. They could agree on the need for resistance to external authority, on the necessity of protecting individual rights of conscience in religion, and on the right of Americans to choose their own church as well as their government. Yet, once the common end of political independence had been gained, their theological and temperamental differences were bound to create disharmony and controversy.[1]

There were in 1775 some 3,000 churches in the American colonies. Of these the two most powerful were the Congregational and Presby-

[1] Sidney Mead, "American Protestantism during the Revolutionary Epoch," *Church History*, XXII (1953), 279–297.

terian, whose differences were less in creed than in government.[2] The major American Protestant sects (with the exception of some Anglicans) supported the revolutionary cause, but the Congregationalists and Presbyterians were especially active in promoting resistance to Britain.[3] The worst incendiaries of all, complained Loyalist Joseph Galloway in 1774, were "Congregationalists, Presbyterians, and Smugglers." The New England clergy prepared their congregations for revolution with dozens of election sermons which, especially after 1750, inveighed against Parliamentary acts that subverted American "Rights, Liberties, and Privileges." Parliament's attempt to establish an American Episcopate in the mid-eighteenth century, in John Adams' opinion, contributed "as much as any other cause to arouse the attention, not only of the inquiring mind, but of the common people, and urge them to close thinking on the constitutional authority of Parliament over the Colonies." Freedom of religion, as well as political and economic rights, was from the American point of view clearly at stake in the revolutionary struggle. "There is not a single instance in history," wrote Presbyterian John Witherspoon, "in which civil liberty was lost, and religious liberty preserved entire. If, therefore, we yield up our temporal property, we at the same time deliver the conscience into bondage."[4]

The Presbyterian Synod of New York and Philadelphia resolved in 1783 that its churches "possessed a general and universal attachment . . . to the cause of liberty and the rights of mankind."[5] In their roles as community leaders, colonial ministers prayed and preached for the American cause until their pulpits, a New England Loyalist remarked bitterly, "were converted into Gutters of Sedition," filled with

[2] There were 658 Congregational churches, 543 Presbyterian, 498 Baptist, 480 Anglican, 251 Reformed, 295 Quaker, 151 Lutheran, 50 Catholic, and 6 synagogues, though such statistics are necessarily only approximate. W. W. Sweet, *Religion in the Development of American Culture* (New York, 1952), pp. 2–26, 50–55, discusses American churches and the Revolution. Church census figures are from N. M. Blake, *A Short History of American Life* (New York, 1952), p. 77.

[3] For a full account, see Alice M. Baldwin, *The New England Clergy and the American Revolution* (Durham, N.C., 1928). See also "Organized Christianity and the American Revolution," in T. C. Hall, *The Religious Background of American Culture* (Boston, 1930), and Edward F. Humphrey, *Nationalism and Religion in America 1774–1789* (Boston, 1924).

[4] Baldwin, *New England Clergy*, pp. 122, 123; Humphrey, *Nationalism and Religion*, pp. 25, 88.

[5] Andrew Zenos, *Presbyterianism in America* (New York, 1937), p. 62.

"wicked, malicious, and inflammatory harangues." The Reverend Charles Inglis of New York could not find a single Congregational or Presbyterian minister in the city "who did not, by preaching and every effort, promote all measures of the Continental Congress, however extravagant."[6] Whole congregations, wrote the Reverend Ammi Robbins of Norfolk, Connecticut, went to war with "their ministers of the Gospel to encourage them in their duty." The Calvinist preachers of New England echoed the triumphant cry of the Reverend John Cleaveland, "King George the Third, adieu! No more shall we cry to you for protection."[7]

The Anglican Church in America was seriously split by the Revolution, furnishing on the one hand the largest number of Loyalists of any church, and on the other the majority of the signers of the Declaration of Independence. Virginia, the center of Anglicanism, produced as many revolutionary leaders as Calvinist New England; New York and New England produced more Anglican Tories than Virginia. The Anglican clergy and laity had strong sentimental and organizational ties with the British mother church, and consequently strong loyalties to their British rulers. Usually allied with urban, mercantile, conservative interests, and often directly involved in royal administration, New England and Middle Colony Anglicans tended either to remain aloof from the controversy or to support the Crown. Jonathan Odell and Samuel Seabury, both Anglican divines, received pay from General Howe for their support of the British cause. "The principle of submission and all lawful authority," wrote Thomas Chandler of New Jersey in 1774, "are as inseparable from a sound genuine member of the Church of England, as any religious principle whatsoever," an opinion with which some prominent Anglicans, such as Washington and Madison, apparently disagreed.[8]

The first accredited Methodist missionaries arrived in the colonies in 1769, followed by others (among them the great Francis Asbury) in 1771. The sect grew rapidly, counting more than 15,000 members by 1784. Though neither John nor Charles Wesley favored American inde-

---

[6] A. P. Stokes, *Church and State in the United States* (3 vols., New York, 1950), I, 727.

[7] C. P. Smith, *Yankees and God* (New York, 1954), p. 287; and Baldwin, *New England Clergy*, p. 122.

[8] William W. Manross, *A History of the American Episcopal Church* (Milwaukee, 1935), Chaps. 1–4, and Sweet, *Religion in American Culture*, 14–24.

pendence,[9] they advised American Methodists to avoid politics, a policy that produced mutterings of protest among Virginia and Carolina Methodists. American Baptists, who suffered a good many indignities as a minority in Calvinist New England and Anglican Virginia, had much to gain and little to lose by independence; they championed the revolutionary cause with great enthusiasm. The Lutheran and Reformed churches, whose membership lay chiefly in the German and Dutch populations of New York and Pennsylvania, had no ties either to a British government or a British church.[10]

The small number of Catholics in the colonies could hope for very little civil or religious liberty from the British if the Crown prevailed. At the same time, since the radical wing of the revolutionary group was strongly anti-Catholic, Catholics could likewise expect little relief from civic and religious discrimination if the colonists won. "One cannot escape the conviction," writes one Catholic historian, "that to the average colonial, Roman Catholicism was an evil fiercely to be hated, deeply to be feared, and unremittingly to be fought."[11] However, the Carrolls of Maryland, the most powerful Catholic family in the colonies, threw in their lot with the revolutionists and other Catholics tended to follow them. Charles Carroll wrote frankly in his old age, "When I signed the Declaration of Independence, I had in view not only our independence of England, but the toleration of all sects professing the Christian religion, and communicating to them all equal rights."[12] Congress' desire during the war to neutralize Canada led to promises of Catholic toleration. However, Tory journals played rather effectively on the general American fear of Catholicism in an attempt to split the Franco-American alliance, and Benedict Arnold used the claim that Congress was "the dupe of Rome" as partial justification for his defection. Nevertheless, wartime professions of toleration and the alliance of America with the world's most powerful Catholic nation did much to relieve some of the traditional colonial fear of "Popery."[13]

The most urgent practical problem faced by American churches after

[9] W. W. Sweet, "John Wesley: Tory," *Methodist Quarterly Review,* LXXI (1922), 255–268.

[10] Sweet, *Religion in American Culture,* pp. 26–40.

[11] Sister Mary Augustana (Ray), *American Opinion of Roman Catholicism in the Eighteenth Century* (New York, 1936), p. 309. See also R. A. Billington, *The Protestant Crusade, 1800–1860* (New York, 1938), pp. 17–20.

[12] Humphrey, *Nationalism and Religion,* p. 493.

[13] W. W. Sweet, *Religion in American Culture,* pp. 40–45; Stokes, *Church and State,* pp. 785–787; Sister Augustana, *Opinion of Catholicism,* Chap. IX.

the Revolution was that of reorganization. Presbyterians had the easiest task. The New York and Philadelphia Synod established itself as an independent body in 1785, adopted a new constitution at the first General Assembly held at Philadelphia in 1789, and modified its Westminster Confession to suit American needs. The Dutch and Reformed churches, whose theology was essentially Presbyterian, separated from the mother church in Holland in 1792 and 1793.[14] The Lutherans, who had created an American Synod in 1748, adopted a new constitution in 1792 and erased the last vestiges of European control. Since Congregational churches had in theory broken their ties with the Old World long before the Revolution, their reorganization too was easy. Methodists, embarrassed by Wesley's anti-Americanism, expected some difficulty in severing British connections, but Wesley himself prepared a special liturgy for American use and encouraged American leaders to organize a semi-independent church. At Baltimore in 1784 the Methodist Conference founded the Methodist Episcopal Church, with provisions for American deacons and elders, thereby creating what was in effect an independent American Methodism. Baptists found themselves in an excellent position at the close of the war. Because of their aggressive wartime activity, they no longer lived under a stigma, and the distribution of their church membership throughout the country gave them strength in every section.[15]

The Church of England faced the most difficult problem of all. It was "too far gone," thought John Marshall after the war, "ever to be revived." Wartime divisions between patriots and Tories left the Anglican organization seriously weakened, while the flight of Tories decimated the Anglican clergy. In Virginia, the center of Anglicanism, two-thirds of its ministry had departed by 1783, leaving more than half of Virginia's parishes vacant or extinct. In Pennsylvania there was only one Anglican clergyman, in North Carolina two, in New Jersey four. Independence not only stopped financial support from Britain, but cut off every Anglican church from the authority of the Bishop of London.

In each section of the nation, however, Anglicans set out to reorganize independently. Representatives from Pennsylvania, New York, and New Jersey met at Annapolis in 1783 to establish the Protestant Episcopal Church and to draw up new articles of church government. New England Anglicans, chiefly from Connecticut, met the same year and

14 Zenos, *Presbyterianism,* Chap. III.
15 Sweet, *Religion in American Culture,* pp. 54–67.

voted to send Samuel Seabury to London to receive consecration as an American bishop. Seabury, after some difficulties, was finally consecrated by Scottish bishops and returned in 1785. Meanwhile William Smith, the leader of the Middle Colony Anglicans, proposed a national convention of all Church of England delegates. The convention eventually met in Philadelphia to adopt a revised liturgy and to draw up new articles of church government. Smith was consecrated as a bishop by the Archbishop of Canterbury in 1787, and in 1789 the Connecticut Anglicans joined the Protestant Episcopal Church.[16]

Independence placed American Catholics in a curious position. There was still considerable intolerance, for Foxe's *Book of Martyrs* had been favorite reading in American homes for generations and "burning the Pope" on Pope's Day was still a popular diversion in New England. Every state except Rhode Island had laws depriving Catholics of full civil and religious rights; during the war some states either deliberately disarmed Catholics or exercised rigid control over their militia service. Though revolutionary principles of natural rights and liberty helped somewhat to make religious toleration respectable, and though the war had been won with French Catholic help, American Catholics continued to live after it in the shadow of discrimination.[17]

There were perhaps twenty-five priests in America in 1782, but the Church at Rome provided them with very little guidance. Since all ties with British Catholicism had been broken by war, French Catholics planned to place the United States under French control. John Carroll, however, brother of Charles, sent a petition to the Pope requesting, in effect, the formation of an American Catholic Church with an American Bishop. As a result Carroll was appointed head of American missions and served, until his own elevation to bishop, as Prefect Apostolic in the United States, marking the inception of an American Catholicism.[18]

Negro slaves numbered nearly 20 per cent of the total population at the close of the Revolution. In the seventeenth and early eighteenth centuries, both slaves and freedmen attended white services, and in some cases belonged to white congregations. By the time of the Revolution separate Negro churches with Negro ministers began to appear, though presumably Negro congregations could exist only under white

[16] *Ibid.*, pp. 67–75.
[17] *Ibid.*, pp. 75–80.
[18] Sweet, *Religion in American Culture*, pp. 120–126; Humphrey, *Nationalism and Religion*, pp. 233–235.

sponsorship. Baptist and Methodist missionaries were particularly active among Negroes in the slave states; the first organized Negro church, formed in South Carolina between 1773 and 1775, seems to have been Baptist. Both Baptists and Methodists organized Negro churches in Virginia and North Carolina a few years later, and in the early 1790's a convention of Negroes founded what became the African Methodist Episcopal Church—New York, Philadelphia, Baltimore, and Boston all had thriving Negro churches after 1800.[19] The spread of organized religion among Negroes before 1860 is difficult to estimate; records are scanty and a number of informally organized churches apparently existed. According to a recent estimate, perhaps 7 per cent of all American Negroes in 1797 were church members, though their precise affiliations are impossible to ascertain.[20]

The problem of church reorganization in the period after Yorktown was no more difficult than that of establishing the proper relationships between church and state in the new republic.[21] Since each colony had its own religious history and its own particular political and ecclesiastical problems, the postwar generation inherited a mixed tradition of church-state relationships. In the colonies of New England and the South, bonds between church and state had always been traditionally strong; at the opening of the Revolution all of them had official, established state churches. At the same time, all of the colonies possessed an equally strong tradition of religious freedom, dating from Anne Hutchinson, Roger Williams, William Penn, and other dissidents, reinforced by heavy migrations of nonconformist Germans, Swiss, French, Dutch, and Swedes in the seventeenth and eighteenth centuries. The Great Awakening of the 1740's weakened religious authoritarianism in New England; the wartime Protestant suspicion of the Quebec Act of course exacerbated the widespread fear of any established state church.[22]

[19] The first nine chapters of Carter G. Woodson, *History of the Negro Church* (Washington, 1921), cover the development of Negro churches up to 1860. Briefer discussions are Chaps. I and II of Ruby F. Johnston, *The Development of Negro Religion* (New York, 1954), and Harry V. Richardson, *Dark Glory* (New York, 1947), Chap. I.

[20] K. S. Latourette, *A History of the Expansion of Christianity* (New York, 1937–41), IV, 325–330.

[21] The most thorough study is Stokes, *Church and State*, I, Chaps. IV–VIII especially.

[22] W. G. Torpey, *Judicial Doctrines of Religious Rights in America* (Chapel Hill, 1948), Chap. I.

Prewar legislatures almost unanimously affirmed, as New York's did in 1775, the "free enjoyment of the rights of conscience," while the act of independence itself released all American churches from any Parliamentary or legislative authority. It seemed clear to the Revolutionary generation that the right to pursue happiness must necessarily include the right to worship in one's own way, since (as Madison phrased it) the right to religious freedom "is in its nature an inalienable right." Samuel Williams of Vermont expressed the prevailing view in good eighteenth-century terms: "What then has society to do in matters of religion, but simply to follow the laws of nature, to adopt these and no other, and to leave to every man a full and perfect liberty to follow the dictates of his own conscience, in all transactions with his Maker?"[23] There was too, of course, the plain fact that no single established church could possibly satisfy the needs of a diverse, scattered, expanding population that already, in 1776, worshiped God under seventeen different creeds. By the close of the Revolution the separation of church and state in America was virtually complete, and subsequent legislation confirming it was primarily a formulation of existing practices.

The Continental Congress wisely left matters of church-state relationships to the states, some of which (Pennsylvania, Maryland, Rhode Island, North Carolina, New York, and Delaware) had already provided in their constitutions or bills of rights for clear separation of civil and ecclesiastical authority. In Virginia, a law requiring non-Anglicans to pay church taxes was repealed, but Jefferson's 1779 bill for the separation of church and state lost. His Statute of Religious Freedom, finally passed in 1786, took what he called "the hardest struggle of my life." New York, with its great mixture of sects, made provision for separation of church and state in its Constitution of 1777, as both New Jersey and Maryland had done in their Constitutions a year before.

In Massachusetts, Connecticut, and New Hampshire, however, the Congregational Church successfully resisted disestablishment for several years. To dissolve the bonds between religion and government, wrote Simeon Howard of Boston, seemed to many New Englanders "a daring affront to Heaven." Samuel West of Dartmouth no doubt spoke for a majority of Congregationalists and Presbyterians in his plea for laws "for maintaining public worship" as "absolutely necessary for the well-

[23] James Madison, *Memorial and Remonstrance to the Virginia General Assembly* (1785). Williams is quoted in Ralph N. Miller, "The Historians Discover America" (unpublished dissertation, Northwestern, 1946), p. 326.

being of society."[24] These three states reaffirmed the old laws requiring support of their established churches by public taxes—Anglicans and Quakers exempted. Connecticut held out until 1818, New Hampshire until 1819, and Massachusetts until 1833.[25]

The Constitutional Convention reaffirmed the prevailing belief in governmental noninterference in religious affairs.[26] Like Madison, the majority of delegates believed that religion "must be left to the conviction and conscience of every man." Reflecting the secular spirit of the lawyers, merchants, bankers, and businessmen who wrote it, the Constitution simply abolished religious qualifications "to any office or public trust under the United States."[27] However, in the state ratifying conventions, the religious issue appeared to be of much more importance. Massachusetts, New Hampshire, Virginia, both Carolinas, and Rhode Island all recommended that a similar clause be inserted in their constitutions and in a federal Bill of Rights. The First Amendment to the Constitution, with its guarantees of free speech, free press, and rights of assembly and petition, bore directly on religious freedom. So, too, in the Northwest Ordinance of 1787, Congress included the guarantee that "No person, demeaning himself in a peaceful and orderly manner, shall be molested on account of his mode of worship, or religious sentiments in said territory."[28] Reflecting the spirit of the Enlightenment, most of the statesmen of the postwar years—from rigidly Presbyterian John Witherspoon to Roman Catholic Charles Carroll—would have agreed with Jefferson's statement that "Religion is a

[24] J. L. Diman, "Religion in America, 1776–1876," *North American Review,* CXXII (1876), 12.

[25] On postwar disestablishment, see Marcus Jensen, *The New Nation: A History of the United States Under the Confederation* (New York, 1950), pp. 130–134; and Willard Sperry, *Religion in America* (New York, 1946), pp. 44–48.

[26] See Sweet, *Religion in American Culture,* pp. 85–90; Stokes, *Church and State,* II, Chaps. VII, VIII.

[27] Further information may be found in R. C. Harnett, "The Religion of the Founding Fathers," in F. E. Johnson (ed.), *Wellsprings of the American Spirit* (New York, 1938).

[28] Omission of direct reference to God in the Constitution caused comment at the time, but, as Chancellor Kent explained in 1811, many believed that the delegates assumed that "we are a Christian people" and saw no necessity for so stating. On the other hand, the treaty of 1796 between the United States and Tripoli, which opened with the words, "As the government of the United States is not in any sense founded on the Christian religion . . ." was ratified by the Senate without protest. Torpey, *Judicial Doctrines,* pp. 32–33, and Hans Kohn, *American Nationalism* (New York, 1957), p. 312.

matter which lies solely between man and his God." Foreign travelers in the United States rarely failed to remark on the apparent harmony of American religious sects, just as one Englishman visiting in Philadelphia was amazed at the sight of "Papists, Episcopalians, Moravians, Lutherans, Calvinists, Methodists, and Quakers passing each other peacefully and in good temper on the Sabbath."[29]

Nevertheless, there were still doubts whether religious toleration could be fully and immediately extended to Jews and Catholics.[30] The majority of states required religious tests or qualifications for full civil and political rights, which discriminated against Catholic, Jewish, or nonconformist Protestant sects. New Jersey's 1776 constitution restricted candidacy for civil office to "Protestant inhabitants"; the constitutions of New Hampshire, Connecticut, Georgia, South Carolina, and North Carolina contained similar provisions. Delaware, Pennsylvania, North Carolina, and South Carolina required all officeholders to affirm the divine inspiration of the Bible. Pennsylvania and South Carolina added the requirement of a belief in heaven and hell, and Delaware a belief in the Trinity.[31] All of the early state constitutions, with the exception of New York's and Virginia's, contained clauses which discriminated against Jews, though there is little evidence to indicate that these were narrowly interpreted. Georgia, Pennsylvania, and South Carolina removed these provisions by 1790, and other states followed; Rhode Island was the last to do so, in 1842.[32]

Ministers of the postwar years generally believed American Christianity to be in "a low and declining state." The Presbyterian Assembly of 1798 noted "with pain and fearful apprehension a general dereliction of religious principles and practice among our citizens, a visible and prevailing impiety," and others thundered the theme from hundreds of pulpits. Church buildings had been destroyed by war, congregations split, parishes disbanded. New Salem, Massachusetts, supported no church services at all for twenty years; of New York City's nineteen churches, the Reverend John Rodgers reported, ten were unfit for use in 1784. Congregations were restive and less inclined than before to

---

[29] Diman, "Religion in America," p. 12.

[30] On religious toleration in the colonies, see Sweet, *Religion in American Culture,* Chap. II, and Hall, *Religious Background of American Culture,* Chap. XI.

[31] E. F. Humphrey, *Nationalism and Religion,* pp. 483–501.

[32] Stokes, *Church and State,* I, Chap. XIII; Rufus Learsi, *The Jews in America* (Cleveland, 1954), pp. 26–50.

accept ministerial leadership in political and social affairs. Stanch New England Calvinist though he was, even John Adams was irritated at "the ecclesiastical synods, conventions, councils, decrees, confessions, oaths, subscriptions, and whole cartloads of trumpery that we find religion encumbered with these days."[33]

Severance of the bonds between church and state encouraged denominationalism and a proliferation of sects, while postwar financial inflation made support of any church difficult for the ordinary man. There was also, as many ministers noted, a disturbing interest in religious liberalism, in "natural religion," in skepticism, in those "infidel doctrines" which (wrote the Reverend Timothy Dwight) "are vomited upon us from France, Germany, and Great Britain." Church membership declined, particularly among younger people. At William and Mary, William Hill reported "rudeness, ribaldry, and infidelity" among the students, and a visitor to Princeton in 1799 likewise found only a few undergraduates who "made any pretensions to piety." "The name of God is blasphemed," cried the Reverend Lyman Beecher, "the Bible denounced, the Sabbath profaned, the public worship of God is neglected."[34]

Churchmen prayed for strength to combat indifference and irreligion, called for fast and prayer, and hoped for divine assistance in reenergizing American faith. But the fact was that Calvinism was losing its grip on contemporary American society. The Congregational and Presbyterian churches, long the most powerful in America, were in decline (membership dropped to 6.9 per cent of the population in New England and the Middle Colonies in 1800), and apparently they could do little to arrest a trend evident since 1750.[35] The reasons, external and internal, for this trend lay deep in the colonial past as well as in the postwar present.

Seventeenth-century Calvinism was an all-embracing faith, "an organization," as Professor Perry Miller has called it, "of man's whole life, emotional and intellectual." It prescribed, as John Cotton said, not only "perfect rules for the right ordering of a private man's soule," but for "the right ordering of a man's family, yea, for the commonwealth too." If the aim of life was "to glorify God and enjoy Him forever," as

---

[33] C. C. Cleaveland, *The Great Revival in the West* (Chicago, 1916), p. 32; Sweet, *Religion in American Culture*, p. 53; Stokes, *Church and State*, p. 654; Hall, *Religious Background of American Culture*, p. 174.

[34] Sweet, *Religion in American Culture*, pp. 92–94.

[35] K. S. Latourette, *Expansion of Christianity*, IV, 355.

Cotton Mather believed, this principle must pervade every aspect of living.[36] Throughout the seventeenth and the early eighteenth centuries American Calvinists had constructed a comprehensive theological system which encompassed, in an integrated intellectual unit, all the affairs of science, politics, ethics, economics, and social life. By 1750, this structure had begun to disintegrate from within.[37]

Calvinism, in its American phase, was a synthesis of contradictory elements maintained in balance by constant scrutiny, compromise, and agreement. By the late eighteenth century the Calvinist system was held together by pure logic, and its logic no longer convinced. Its theology was too rigid to adjust, its organization too closely planned to allow adaptation. "A change in the solar system," John Adams remarked in 1774, "might be expected as soon as a change in the ecclesiastical system of Massachusetts."[38]

American Calvinist sects might differ among themselves on matters of church government or even minor matters of doctrine, but in general they agreed in theology. They believed that God was all-powerful; that in their fall Adam and Eve stained their progeny forever with the touch of sin; and that unless cleansed by the intervention of Christ and God's mercy men were condemned to eternal punishment in hell. They believed that men must at all times do all that lay within their power to honor God, glorify Him, and attain salvation so that at death they might enter Paradise. How that salvation might be attained, and how that worship and glorification of God might be realized, might be matters of argument among the Calvinist sects, but in fundamental principles they rarely differed. The Enlightenment, however, held far more optimism concerning God, human nature, and the efficacy of reason than Calvinism, and much higher and more attractive estimates of man's abilities and potential. Locke, Newton, and Rousseau had easier and clearer answers to the old Calvinist questions of free will, fate, evil, revelation, progress, and sin.[39]

Calvinist apologists found it particularly difficult to deal with the eighteenth century's concept of reason. John Wise in 1717 believed it

[36] Perry Miller and Thomas Johnson, *The Puritans* (New York, 1938), pp. 4, 209.

[37] H. W. Schneider, *History of American Philosophy* (New York, 1946), pp. 59–69.

[38] Diman, "Religion in America," p. 9.

[39] Miller and Johnson, *Puritans*, Introduction, is an excellent explanation of Calvinist theology.

unnecessary to discriminate among divine truths received through the reason, the Bible, and the outside world, "for that each is equally an emanation of His Wisdom." John Cotton could not quite agree, since "in the blindness of our minds . . . we cannot rightly judge of moral or civil things," man must depend for truth on God's own revelations. The Enlightenment's deification of reason, however, forced the Calvinist into a dilemma. What if reason denied Scriptural revelation? And if men were inherently depraved, could their reason be trusted to reveal divine truth? Jonathan Edwards, and others who had wrestled earlier with the problem, found beyond reason or Scripture a supra-rational revelation in "a Spiritual and Divine Light, immediately imparted to the soul by God, of a different nature from anything that is obtained by natural means"—or, as Thomas Shepard defined it, "A spirit of light, illumination, or revelation let into the mind."[40]

The conflict between revelation from within, through reason or "a spirit of light," and revelation from without, through Scripture, continued through eighteenth-century Calvinist theology. Nor was it fully resolved by Calvinist logicians. Jonathan Edwards' conclusion—that inner revelation really "teaches no new thing . . . not taught in the Bible" but merely deepens understanding of the Bible—was not satisfactory. The Reverend William Bentley of Salem, writing in 1790, conceded the failure of the Edwardean compromise by admitting that "the will of God is made known to us" not only through Scripture, "which acts merely as an auxiliary capacity," but rather by "natural" or rational means. By thus emphasizing the validity of individual revelation, either by reason or intuition, the liberal eighteenth-century Calvinist leaders struck at a key principle of the carefully balanced Calvinist system. On the other hand, those who argued, debated, and counted votes to discover an acceptable doctrine ran the risk of creating a structure of compromises which, like Dr. Holmes's one-hoss shay, might suddenly crumble if one small proposition collapsed within it.

Confronted by the swift expansion of science, Calvinism chose to absorb it rather than oppose it. Indeed, during the seventeenth century the great discoveries of science seemed at first to reinforce orthodox Calvinist belief in God's sovereignty and beneficence, and to prove beyond a doubt (as they did to Newton) the existence of a Divine First Cause. Colonial ministers found much in science on which to sermon-

[40] For an account of the evangelistic movement of the 1740's and 1750's, see E. S. Gaustad, *The Great Awakening in New England* (New York, 1957).

ize; the Reverend Ebenezer Gay of Hingham, for example, discovered "a spiritual gravitation" within the soul that attracted men to God exactly as Newton's law drew falling bodies to earth.

But science eventually betrayed the Calvinists by tending to supplant, rather than reinforce, their faith. If God is visible in nature and natural law, of what use is Scripture? If truth may be perceived by the application of man's reason to nature, of what use is a Bible, a minister, or an organized church? "Rational" religion, a key phrase in the Enlightenment, obviated belief in many of the contradictory, hard-wrought doctrines of Calvinism and opened up avenues of exploration that Calvinists dared not follow. Instead of restricting theology to "the study of human opinions and human fancies concerning God," why not, as Thomas Paine asked, find "the true theology" in "the study of God Himself in the works that he made"?[41]

In effect, Calvinism gradually lost touch with the secular spirit of eighteenth-century life. Americans were growing rich, amassing a goodly share of the world's profits, and the theocentric piety of an older Calvinism seemed to have very little relevance to an expanding mercantile society which believed in natural rights, social contracts, and foreign trade. The Puritan preoccupation with the state of one's soul and the next world did not fit the Bostonian's or Philadelphian's interest in the state of his pocketbook and the pleasures of this world—which impressed him as a rather good one. Since the facts of American life seemed to have little relationship to Calvinistic theology, a growing number of Americans simply ignored it as a matter of small consequence for practical living. To John Cotton in 1636, theology embraced all of life. Benjamin Franklin, when he planned an academy a little more than a century later, left religion to be studied for its "usefulness to the public," as a means of gaining "the advantage of a religious character among individuals."[42]

The first great threat to Calvinism in the late eighteenth century came from deism, a religio-philosophical movement imported from Europe. Rooted in the Enlightenment's faith in reason and its belief in science, deism provided the latter half of the eighteenth century with a

[41] Ernest S. Bates, *American Faith* (New York, 1940), Chap. 15, provides further discussion of this point.

[42] A brilliant discussion of postwar Calvinism is C. H. Faust, "The Decline of Puritanism," in H. H. Clark (ed.), *Transitions in American Literary History* (Durham, N.C., 1954). See also Joseph Harotunian, *Piety vs. Moralism* (New York, 1932).

theology which harmonized with the secular, rationalistic temper of the age. In addition to Locke, Hume, Tillotson, Shaftesbury, Bolingbroke, Woollaston, and other liberal British thinkers, colonial deists read the French philosophers and skeptics too, developing a native American strain of deism that appeared in its early form in the writings of Franklin.[43]

American deism recognized no accepted creed of belief. "I am a sect by myself," wrote Jefferson, echoing Paine's "My own mind is my own church." Flexible as their beliefs were, the majority of eighteenth-century American deists would probably have agreed that:

Men are not inherently evil, but at least capable of benevolence and possessed of some degree of free will. "Human nature," said Paine, "is not of itself vicious," and "the great mass of people are invariably just" if properly educated and indoctrinated. "Man is possessed," wrote Elihu Palmer, "of moral and intellectual faculties sufficient for the improvement of his nature." "Morality, compassion, and generosity," Jefferson told Dupont de Nemours, "are innate elements of the human constitution."

There is one God, a First Cause of Law, "the Origin of All Science, the Author of All Knowledge, the God of Order and Harmony."

Jesus was not necessarily divine, but the greatest of ethical philosophers, he preached "a most excellent morality and the equality of man," and his life is the perfect model for men to imitate.

The most appropriate service to God is serving one's fellow man, since "a practical imitation of the goodness of God," as Paine phrased it, "is no other than our acting toward each other as he acts toward us all." "A benevolent disposition, and beneficent actions," wrote Elihu Palmer, "are fundamental duties of rational beings." Doctrine, creed, and dogma are less important than living a good and useful life, allowing others to believe as they wish according to the dictates of their own reason.

All men are equal in the sight of God, and equally possessed of certain natural rights. "Civil and religious liberty," in Palmer's definition, "are equally as essential to their true interests."

There are no mysteries or miracles in Christianity. "Mystery, Miracle, and Prophesy," according to Paine, "are appendages that belong to the fabulous and not to the true religion."

Man may find divine truth through study of God and His Works as exemplified in "the harmonious, magnificent Order of Nature." By "Reason's aid," Freneau wrote in 1786, man sees in nature "One Sole God, prime

[43] Stephen Girard, the eccentric Philadelphia millionaire, owned seventy-five editions of Voltaire and named three of his merchant ships after Voltaire, Rousseau, and Montesquieu.

source of wisdom, at whose command all worlds their circuits run." "The Word of God," Paine reaffirmed, "is the Creation we behold; and it is in this Word, which no human invention can counterfeit or alter, that God speaketh universally to man."

Reason, the "choicest gift of God to Man," is the primary source of revelation, by which man may perceive "the power and wisdom of God in his works." "It is only by the exercise of reason," explained Paine, "that man can discover God," and deist Ethan Allen titled his book *Reason the Only Oracle of Man.* "Fix reason firmly in her seat," Jefferson advised young Peter Carr, "and call to her tribunal every fact, every opinion. Your own reason is the only oracle given you by heaven."

If men would but live and think by these principles, Ethan Allen concluded, "they would in a great measure rid themselves of blindness and superstition, gain more exalted ideas of God . . . make better members of society, and acquire more powerful incentives of morality."[44]

Deism's attack on Calvinism was double-pronged. First, following the French rationalists, some of the more extreme American deists regarded organized churches, like monarchs, as highly dangerous to man's freedom. The churches, wrote Jefferson, had perverted Christianity, "the purest of all moral systems, for the purpose of deriving from it pence and power," while they had twisted the religion of Jesus "into an engine for enslaving mankind, and aggrandizing their oppressors in church and state." Paine, even more bluntly, called churches "no other than human inventions, set up to terrify and enslave mankind, and monopolize power and profit." It was not Christianity, therefore, that the deist opposed, but the ecclesiastical misuse of organized religion as an agent of unreason and a weapon of oppression. His *Age of Reason,* Paine carefully explained, was written to preserve "true theology" from the wreckage of the French Revolution. Jefferson's personal edition of the Bible, stripped of all that he considered false and irrational, contained "the pure religion of Jesus" as institutionalized Christianity, he believed, did not.

Second, deists atacked the orthodox Calvinist view of revelation by Scriptural and ecclesiastical authority, since it was by its jealous guardianship of what was presumably God's word that the church held dominion over man. If, as the deist claimed, each man possessed reason by which he could find truth revealed in Nature, the authority of the

[44] "Religion and Science," in H. H. Clark, "The Influence of Science on American Ideas, 1775–1809," *Transactions of the Wisconsin Academy of Arts and Sciences,* XXXV–VI (1943–44), 305–349.

church over man was forever shattered. Such books as Allen's *Reason the Only Oracle of Man* (1784, written partially by Thomas Young), Paine's own spectacular *Age of Reason* (Paris, 1794), and Elihu Palmer's *Principles of Nature* (1802) struck at Biblical revelation in strong terms, affirming that man himself, without the intervention of ministers, prelates, or other authoritarian interpreters, could find God's word in the world about him and in his own experience.[45]

There were, of course, varying shades of deism. Paine, Allen, Palmer, and a few others, claiming that nature and reason alone provided truth, rejected both institutionalized religion and Scriptural authority. Others, such as Franklin, Jefferson, George Mason, and James Madison, found it possible to remain within a traditionally organized church and to accept a somewhat more orthodox Christianity. But deists in general agreed that the basis of true religion was personal rather than institutional, that it was more concerned with reason than faith, and that it was rooted in science and nature rather than in Biblical or ecclesiastical authority.[46]

The reaction of the orthodox churches to the threat of the so-called "natural" religion was swift and energetic. Whatever their doctrinal differences and rivalries, the major Protestant sects could make common cause of their battle against deism, which not only undermined each creed but apparently threatened Christianity itself. The deist's claim that he attacked not *true* Christianity, but rather an authoritarian "institution" that hindered man's social and intellectual progress, was far too subtle and sophisticated for the majority of Americans to grasp. Whatever Paine's intent, he (and Allen, Palmer, and others) seemed to the popular mind to endanger the basic doctrines of every Christian sect. Deism had little attraction for the ordinary man, whatever its appeal to the philosopher. No matter how logical the deist system nor how rational its theology, its cold, intellectualized concept of the Great Architect was not a satisfactory God to Calvinist or Methodist. "No heart was ever won," wrote Presbyterian Timothy Dwight in his poem *Greenfield Hill*, "by reason's power alone," showing that Dwight knew the psychology of religious belief better than the deists did.

Ministers of all faiths preached stoutly against deist "infidelity."

[45] G. H. Koch, *Republican Religion* (New York, 1933), and Herbert M. Morais, *Deism in Eighteenth Century America* (New York, 1934), are complete and careful accounts on deist theology and activity.

[46] The best brief introduction to deism, and to the thought of its most famous proponent, is Harry Hayden Clark's *Thomas Paine* (New York, 1944).

There were more than thirty-five replies to Paine's *Age of Reason,* ranging from calm to hysterically scurrilous, while the Harvard Corporation in 1796 distributed a copy of Bishop Watson's *Apology for the Bible* to every student as an antidote to it. In the colleges, particularly, Calvinists expended great effort to counteract deism's appeal to the young intellectual. Dozens of professors leveled their theological guns at "natural religion" in sermons, courses, lectures, and discussions.[47] President Timothy Dwight of Yale devoted almost 200 sermons to "infidelity," starting the series anew every four years so that no student should miss one. These he collected in *Theology Explained and Defended* (1795), carrying the fight to the public in *The Nature and Danger of Infidel Philosophy* (1798) and in his savagely satiric poem, *The Triumph of Infidelity* (1788) which, he wrote, would come as deism:

> New gates of falsehood opened on mankind,
> New Paths to ruin strew'd with Flowers divine,
> And other aids, and motives, gain'd to sin.[48]

Deism's most vulnerable point was its presumed debt to "certain skeptical philosophers of France," as Samuel Miller called them, "who were always ready to believe anything which might release them from the obligation to believe in Christianity."[49] The excesses of the French Revolution struck real fear in the hearts of American conservatives, who feared, as Thomas Fessenden wrote in *Democracy Unveiled* (1805), that its

> . . . principles, alas, will flood
> Columbia's happy land with blood,
> Unless kind Providence restrain
> Those demons of a hurricane.

The French sympathies of Jefferson, Paine, Barlow, and other religious

---

[47] James D. Hart, *The Popular Book in America* (New York, 1950), pp. 35–37. Morais, *Deism,* Chap. VI, has an account of the warfare against infidelity in the colleges.

[48] Dwight's exhortations must have had some effect, for in 1802 one-third of Yale's student body professed conversion; in 1803 Benjamin Silliman found Yale "a little temple," where "prayer and praise seem to be the delight of the greater part of the students." For a biography of this amazing personality, see Charles E. Cuningham, *Timothy Dwight* (New York, 1942). Ralph H. Gabriel, *Religion and Learning at Yale* (New Haven, 1958), Chap. IV, "Timothy Dwight," is a superb brief essay.

[49] *Retrospect of the Eighteenth Century* (New York, 1803), II, 88.

and political liberals aroused suspicions of an organized "infidel plot," engineered by French radicals and their American agents, to seize the government of the United States.[50]

There was in the United States, Jedidiah Morse believed in 1789, a well-planned "conspiracy against *all* Religions and Governments," involving deists, Antifederalists, Freemasons, rebellious farmers, and restive debtors. The conservatives had not far to look for its leader—Thomas Jefferson, "the archapostle of irreligion and freethought." If the forces of Jefferson won in the election of 1800, warned one New England minister, "Thus would political atheism suspend the kind attration of heaven upon us, and let out a store of guilty passion, and by one disastrous move from stem to stern, make a clear breach over us."

It was "the duty of all our Christian fellow citizens," said another clergyman in his election sermon, "to honor the Lord Jesus Christ and promote Christianity by electing and supporting as public officers the friends of our blessed Savior." The war against deist "infidelity" thus became an important aspect of the Federalist-Jeffersonian political struggle after 1800. "Calvinism and Federalism," wrote a Methodist circuit rider, "are yoked together," as Republicanism and liberal theology were equally so.[51]

The extent to which deism actually influenced American religious thought after 1783 is not easy to estimate. Deist enthusiasts tended to claim more followers than they possessed, while clergymen were prone to exaggerate the threat of deism in order to impress their congregations with its dangers. Elihu Palmer in 1804 spoke of "thousands and tens of thousands of deists," and Congregational or Presbyterian ministers reported "infidelity" everywhere.[52] Baptist missionary J. M. Peck in 1794 feared that "French infidelity" would "sweep away every vestige of Christianity" in the Ohio Valley, and another alarmed missionary found several North Carolina back-country debating societies in 1797 "furnished with a circulating library replete with infidel philosophy." Frontier freethinkers argued Paine and Volney in taverns, college students devoured Voltaire and Locke, and in the East a few deist societies sprang up, including John Fitch's Philadelphia group (1791),

[50] Howard Mumford Jones, *America and French Culture* (Chapel Hill, 1927), pp. 410 ff.; John C. Miller, *Crisis in Freedom* (Boston, 1951), p. 63; and Merle Curti, *The Growth of American Thought* (New York, 1943), p. 188.
[51] Stokes, *Church and State*, p. 676.
[52] Morais, *Deism*, Chap. V, *passim*.

Elihu Palmer's "Deistical Society of New York," and his "Society of Druids."[53]

Palmer, who proposed to build a Temple of Nature "for the worship of One God Supreme and Benevolent Creator of the World," published a deist periodical, *The Temple of Reason*, and later another, *The Theophilanthropist*. Voltaire, whose works passed through six American editions before 1800, was favorite deist reading; Volney's *Ruins* (1791), an essay on comparative religion translated by Barlow, ran through three American editions. Paine's *Age of Reason*, the most popular deist work of all, had eight editions in 1794, seven in 1795, and two in 1796. Franklin Bache, Franklin's grandson, sold 15,000 copies of the 1796 edition in his Philadelphia bookstore; Parson Weems, who noted that "divinity, for this climate, sh'd be very rational and liberal," considered Paine a staple of his itinerant booktrade.[54]

Yet deism's popularity was brief, and confined to a relatively small minority of American intellectual leaders. It had no creed, no church organization, no missions, no preachers other than its militant pamphleteers, and a limited appeal to the common man. The orthodox counterattack thoroughly discredited its theology and its leaders. Paine, though a Revolutionary hero and friend of Jefferson and Franklin, was greeted on his return to the United States in 1800 as "a lying, drunken infidel," "a drunken atheist and scavenger of fashion," nor has deism's chief pamphleteer gained full respectability in our own time. Deism, like Paine's own reputation, diminished swiftly.[55] A few men kept on with the freethinking tradition, such as George English with his *Grounds of Christianity Examined* (1813), William Munday with *An Examination of the Bible* (1808), and Abner Kneeland of Boston, who in 1834–35 had the distinction of being the last man to be prosecuted for blasphemy in New England.[56] Timothy Dwight, who in 1800 be-

[53] J. M. Mecklin, *The Story of American Dissent* (New York, 1934), p. 350; Hart, *Popular Book*, p. 35; and Albert Post, *Popular Free Thought in America* (New York, 1943), pp. 24–27.

[54] Morais, *Deism*, Chap. IV; Hart, *Popular Book*, pp. 36–38.

[55] Deism "brutalizes man, degrades him from his rank, makes him a being of the moment, existing without an intelligent cause, or moral end, the sport of accidents, and the everlasting victim of death." "A Review of the Eighteenth Century," *Monthly Anthology*, II (1805), 175. See also the attacks on Paine, quoted in Bates, *American Faith*, Chap. 20.

[56] Post, *Free Thought*, pp. 29–33; also H. S. Commager, "The Blasphemy of Abner Kneeland," *New England Quarterly*, VIII (1935), 29–41. Samuel Gridley Howe, "Atheism in New England," *New England Magazine*, VII (1834), 500–509, and VIII (1835), 53–62, is a useful contemporary essay.

lieved deist "infidelity" to be the supreme enemy of "civil and domestic government, the right to private property, chastity, and decency," in 1822 no longer thought it a threat, for "the common people had caught it up."[57] "Happily," wrote President Lindsley of the University of Nashville in 1830, "the reign of atheism has passed away, and the fopperies of infidelity are no longer in fashion."[58] Deism died in the Second Great Awakening that revitalized American Protestantism after 1800.

[57] Bates, *American Faith,* pp. 304, 307.
[58] George Schmidt, *The Old Time College President* (New York, 1930), p. 191.

CHAPTER 10

The Great Revival of American Faith

B Y 1800, American Protestant churches were ripe for a revival of religious piety, after two decades of apathy and bickering, the shock of war, and the confusions of postwar social and economic readjustment. There had been indications, as early as 1790, that the religious evangelism of the Great Awakening of the 1740's, which had left its mark indelibly on eighteenth-century theology, might once again become a powerful religious force. Many of the pious orthodox battlers against deist "infidelity" fervently prayed that it would.

The new revivalism appeared first in New England in the 1790's, welcomed by such men as Timothy Dwight and Jedidiah Morse as a weapon against deism. Neither Methodist nor Baptist evangelists, however, were ever really popular with the orthodox Calvinist churches. Evangelists were sometimes ducked, stoned, or whipped, and those who conducted services in New England often found it safest to hold them at night. Nevertheless, Methodists and Baptists gained converts in Calvinist territory against powerful opposition, though Francis Asbury remarked that "there were not a few who were ashamed to be seen going to a Methodist meeting." Though there were an increasing number of such revivals, the Second Awakening found its emotional outlet in New England through the Presbyterian and Congregational movements led later by Beecher and Finney.[1]

On the frontier, after 1800, matters were different. Unlike the churches of the East, where church and state had long existed in close relationship, the frontier church was a communal, free-standing institu-

[1] J. M. Mecklin, *The Story of American Dissent* (New York, 1934), pp. 312–317.

tion from the beginning. With little or no ministry to keep theological order, frontier Methodism and Baptism became almost folk religions; pioneer congregations chose and discarded among theological elements much as they wished. Most of all, the emotional element of evangelism exerted a powerful appeal to a rude, scattered, lonely, and energetic people. The camp meeting, which had never been a vital principle of evangelical religion, took on an importance on the frontier that it never possessed in the settled East.[2] By 1800 a number of itinerant evangelists were attracting huge crowds in the back country, particularly an evangelist named James McGready.[3]

McGready, a Presbyterian from Scotch-Irish country in Pennsylvania, began preaching in South Carolina in the 1790's, finally creating such disturbances with his hellfire sermons that he was asked to move West. In 1796 he appeared in Logan County, Kentucky, where in three years he gathered a large following among Presbyterians, Congregationalists, Baptists, and Methodists alike. McGready, wrote an eyewitness, "could so array hell before the wicked that they would tremble and quake, imagining a lake of fire and brimstone yawning to overwhelm them." Barton Stone, whose rhetoric matched McGready's, set a similar blaze in Bourbon County. Other exhorters adopted McGready's and Stone's techniques and a wave of emotional religious revivalism swept across Georgia, the Carolinas, Pennsylvania, Tennessee, and Ohio. In 1811 Bishop Francis Asbury counted 400 revivals, most of them in the West and South.[4]

The typical Western revival, or camp meeting, began on a Thursday or Friday and lasted until the following Monday or Tuesday, day and night, with continuous praying, preaching, and singing by the light of huge bonfires in the darkness. Those who attended brought bedding and food, lived in tents or improvised huts in the fields, and stayed for the duration. As the meetings wore on, the familiar phenomena of mass religious emotionalism often appeared—men and women falling insensible, barking like dogs, rolling, climbing trees, dancing to ex-

---

[2] R. H. Gabriel, "Evangelical Religion and Popular Romanticism in the Early Nineteenth Century," *Church History*, XIX (1950), 34–47. Church life on the frontier is depicted in Edgar D. Branch, *Westward: The Story of the American Frontier* (New York, 1930), pp. 204–220.

[3] W. W. Sweet, *Religion in the Development of American Culture* (New York, 1952), pp. 146–149, and *Revivalism: Its Origin, Growth, and Decline* (New York, 1945).

[4] *Ibid.*, p. 155. See also C. C. Cleaveland, *The Great Revival in the West* (Chicago, 1916), pp. 45, 55–58, 90–104, 154–156.

haustion, or, the most common, the "jerks"—though such extravagances were not always encouraged by the ministers. The Reverend John Lyle, who observed a Kentucky revival in 1805, described the "jerks" as follows: "The hands of the jerking patients flew, with wondrous quickness, from side to side in various directions, and their necks doubled like a flail in the hands of the thresher. Their faces were distorted and black, and their eyes seemed to flash horror and distraction. Numbers of them roared out in sounds the most wild and terrific."[5]

Attendance at the Cane Ridge, Kentucky, revival of 1801 (probably the largest ever held) was estimated at between 10,000 and 20,000, with forty ministers (eighteen of them Presbyterian) to preach to the crowds. "From Friday until the following Thursday," a witness wrote, "night and day without intermission," people "engaged in some religious act of worship." At one time there were more than a hundred "sinners" laid out unconscious in orderly rows, while "the solemn hymns, the impassioned exhortations, the earnest prayers, and the sobs, shrieks, or shouts bursting from persons under intense agitation" surged about them. Colonel Robert Patterson, reporting on the case of a girl who attended a camp meeting at Paris, Kentucky, in 1801, described her "fall into hell" thus: "She was struck down fell stiff heer hand and arm also became as cold as Death heer fingers cramp'd recov'd heer speech in 2 hours was haled home on a sled continues in a state of despare which has lasted 3 weekes."[6]

Neither Methodists nor Baptists considered the spread of such revivals dangerous to their faith. Presbyterian synods, however, were sharply divided. A decade of debates, heresy trials, suspensions, and argument led to the formation of the independent Cumberland Synod in 1813, composed of those who favored revivalism and a loosening of strict Calvinist doctrine. During this controversy, another schism appeared among Presbyterians in Pennsylvania and Virginia. Thomas Campbell and his son Alexander were conservative Presbyterians who deplored not only revivalism but the bewildering variety of Presby-

[5] Quoted in N. M. Armstrong, L. A. Loetscher, and C. M. Anderson (eds.), *The Presbyterian Enterprise* (Philadelphia, 1956), p. 113. See also Jerald C. Brauer, *Protestantism in America* (Philadelphia, 1953), Chap. VII, for a brief account of the Western revivals; and Chap. X, "Revivalism," of Elizabeth Nottingham, *Methodism and The Frontier* (New York, 1941).

[6] See the descriptions of witnesses in Cleaveland, *Great Revival*, pp. 55–56, 90–104, 183–190; also Sweet, *Religion in American Culture*, pp. 229–230.

terianisms which appeared under its influence. In 1808–9 the Campbells organized a "Christian Association," not to form a new church, but to discover some common ground on which all Presbyterians could unite. Rejected by the orthodox, they made an alliance with the Baptists, and after his father's death Alexander became an influential Baptist leader. After arguments over the doctrine of immersion and over revivalism, Campbell's followers and some sympathetic Baptist groups joined to found a church of their own, the Disciples of Christ.[7]

The Second Great Awakening had immediate and lasting effects on American churches and their place in American society. First of all, it meant that the Methodists and Baptists became the two most powerful American sects. During the period 1800–1830, Methodist membership increased sevenfold, Presbyterian quadrupled, Baptist tripled, and Congregational doubled. The Methodists gained 6,000 new members in the Western Conference in two years during the height of revivalism, and the Baptists added 10,000 to their rolls in Kentucky alone in three years. Presbyterian gains, while large, were more than offset by the divisions and schisms that beset them. Second, the Awakening meant that the United States, despite the shocks of eighteenth-century rationalism and "infidelity," remained predominantly a religious-minded nation, with an emotional, pietistic, moralistic spirit that would color its social, political, and economic thinking for generations to come.[8] The shrewd French traveler, Alexis de Tocqueville, noted this primary fact of American life in 1831, after the Awakening had run its course. "There is no country in the world," he wrote, "in which the Christian religion retains a greater hold over the souls of men than in America. . . . Religion is the foremost of the institutions of the country."[9]

The resurgence of American religion had at least two significant social and political effects in the early nineteenth century. There was a clear connection, in the opinion of contemporary observers, between the extension of revivalism into the West and the elevation of moral standards in frontier society. The Reverend David Rice noted in 1803 that after a few camp meetings in Kentucky "drunkards, profane swearers, liars, quarrelsome persons, etc. are remarkably reformed. . . . Some neighborhoods, noted for their vicious and profligate man-

[7] Sweet, *Religion in American Culture,* pp. 221–226.
[8] A. P. Stokes, *Church and State in the United States* (3 vols., New York, 1950), pp. 655–657.
[9] *Democracy in America,* ed. Phillips Bradley (New York, 1948), I, pp. 303–304.

ners are now as much noted for their piety and good order." Another minister reported with some awe that after its wave of revivals "Kentucky was the most moral place I had ever been."[10]

The churches left behind by the circuit riders, evangelists, and missionaries were (with the schools) powerful moral forces in a society where whiskey sold at 25 cents a gallon, eye-gouging fights were common, gambling endemic, illiteracy high, and restrictions on sexual activity casual. Baptist conferences for years meted out stiff discipline to their members for fighting, drunkenness, gossip, adultery, horse racing, stealing, and dishonesty; Presbyterian presbyteries and Congregational congregations punished their recalcitrant members in much the same manner.[11]

The Methodist Discipline contained a code of conduct which Methodists were expected to follow to the letter, and the Quarterly Conferences functioned as moral courts for ministers and members alike. Churches could and did bring powerful moral pressures to bear on frontier society, and preachers such as Peter Cartwright were quite capable of personally manhandling transgressors or scoffers who refused to see the light.[12] The church became the social and intellectual center of the frontier community. People attended church, said Peter Mode, "almost as much to meet each other as to attend upon the means of grace." It provided a place for wives to gossip, young people to court, men to argue and trade, and for children to learn the manners and mores of their society. American society, as it moved westward, found the church a point at which it could coalesce.

Politically, the victory of evangelical religion in the West helped to prepare the way for the triumph of Andrew Jackson. There were many factors involved in the rise of Jacksonian democracy, but as early as 1800 political observers noted that Methodists and Baptists usually leaned toward Antifederalist politics, and that Jefferson's ministerial supporters seemed to be chiefly in evangelical pulpits. Baptists and Methodists formed the bulk of Republican strength in New England; it was Baptist minister John Leland who escorted a 1,300-pound cheese, a gift to Jefferson from the Berkshire farmers, on its journey to Washington in 1808, preaching seventy-four rousing Baptist sermons on the

[10] W. W. Sweet, *Story of American Religion* (New York, 1950), p. 231.
[11] *Ibid.*, "The Moral Force of Revivalism," pp. 129–154.
[12] W. W. Sweet, *The Rise of Methodism in the West* (New York, 1920), pp. 112 ff.

way.[13] "Infidelity and liberalism are combined," a New England
Calvinist reported in 1802, and missionaries in the West after 1820
found "strongly democratic" trends among the evangelical congregations of Kentucky and Tennessee.[14]

Significantly, the revivalist preachers made the amusements and
vices of the wealthy and the conservative into sins—card playing,
horse racing, dancing, billiards, gambling, cockfighting, theaters—thus
giving morality a class bias that had obvious political connotations.[15]
Frontier preachers, writes Professor Sweet, "brought home to the
pioneers the fact that they were masters of their own destiny, an emphasis that fitted in exactly with the new democracy rising in the West,
for both emphasized the actual equality among men."[16] Evangelical
churchmen and Jacksonians agreed that government and religion were
both rooted in the individual; that both were matters that lay between
man and his God, and man and his rulers. Both admired simplicity,
directness, and common sense in religion or politics, and neither had
much patience with dogma, authority, or tradition. Both regarded
institutional rigidity as evil—Old Hickory and Peter Cartwright would
have agreed that politics and religion should be kept flexible, personal,
and close to the people. It was no accident that much of Jackson's
strength came from the areas "burned over" by Beecher, Finney, Mc-
Gready, and the others who lit the fires of the Second Great Awakening.

Beginning in the early eighteenth century, a series of revolts shook
Calvinism from within. The "revivals" of the 1740's and 1750's split
the Congregational churches of New England into orthodox "Old
Lights" and liberal "New Lights," who lived together in uneasy compromise through the revolutionary years. The leaven of liberalism,
nevertheless, was still at work, and wartime arguments over church
doctrine continued to be sharp and numerous. The most serious
controversy arose over the introduction into Congregational Calvinism
of so-called "unitarian" doctrines, which emphasized the rights of
private conscience over Scriptural and ecclesiastical authority, stressed

[13] Mecklin, *Dissent*, pp. 320–325.
[14] A Western circuit rider reported in 1800, "The great mass . . . of the
Methodist church and her adherents are Republicans." Stokes, *Church and
State*, p. 676.
[15] Mecklin, *Dissent*, pp. 360–362.
[16] Sweet, *Religion in the Development of American Culture*, p. 97.

the inherent capabilities of man, claimed the unity (not trinity) of the Deity, and questioned the actual divinity of Jesus. Such Arian and Socinian doctrines were, of course, centuries old, but after the loosening effects of revivalism in the 1740's, they made swift headway among orthodox Calvinist sects.

A smooth transition was taking place, in the decades immediately following the Revolution, from the legalism of eighteenth-century Calvinism toward an ethico-humanitarian Christianity which disregarded many of the more rigid Calvinist doctrines.[17] By 1800 there were three discernible groups within the Congregational churches. Conservatives held fast to the older orthodox creed, extending it by ceaseless exposition and defense. The moderates, the largest group, preached a vaguely mitigated Calvinism which de-emphasized some of the harsher orthodox doctrines. Liberals, many of them in clerical or academic positions clustered about Cambridge and Boston, tacitly accepted unitarian doctrines. The chief points of conflict concerned revelation, the authority of the Scriptures, and the proper method of Biblical interpretation.

Liberals, moderates, and conservatives all considered the Bible as revelatory of God's truth, but differed concerning the degree of its validity. Liberal Calvinists regarded the Bible as a source of revelation—but not an infallible source, since it was a human record subject to human error and misunderstanding. To comprehend Biblical truth one must, they said, interpret it rationally; reason and revelation must "speak with one voice." The liberals argued with the orthodox (and among themselves, too) over a correct definition of "reason," and over what course to follow if the findings of reason could not be reconciled with Biblical teachings.

Henry Ware, an avowed liberal, told his Harvard students that in deciding a conflict between Biblical statement and human reason, one had best trust the Bible, since "you can never be so certain of the correctness of what takes place in your mind as of what is in the Bible." William Ellery Channing, another liberal Congregationalist, took the opposite view. "I am surer of my rational nature from God," said Channing, "than that any book is." Stressing the validity of the in-

[17] For general accounts of religion in New England in the period, see F. H. Foster, *A Genetic History of the New England Theology* (Boston, 1907), and the histories of Unitarianism by Wilbur, Cooke, and Wright cited in the Bibliography. For a briefer, general account, see "The Revolt Against Calvinism," in Sweet, *Religion in American Culture*, pp. 190–230.

dividual reason as a guide to truth, most liberals agreed with Channing's belief that "the ultimate reliance of a human being is, and must be, on his own mind." Though never fully resolved, the controversy over the reason and its function in religion led directly, within a decade, toward transcendentalism.

As liberals interpreted the Bible, it taught the unity, not the trinity, of God, an interpretation which to conservative minds implied that Christ was merely a human teacher. The deity whom liberals found in the Bible was not a God of wrath, but a God of mercy, compassion, and love. "We maintain," said Channing, "that God's attributes are intelligible, and that we can conceive as truly of his goodness and justice as of these qualities in men; a doctrine that contradicts our best ideas of goodness and justice cannot come from a just and good God." Where the orthodox found proof of man's innate depravity in the Bible, the liberals found evidence that man, if not completely pure, at least possessed certain powers of reason and conscience. By cultivating these human attributes, men *could* be good, for, as Channing wrote, "Virtue and benevolence are *natural* to man. . . . The idea of God is the idea of our own spiritual nature, purified and enlarged to infinity." If men respected their reason, followed their consciences, and educated their minds, they could make progress. In contrast to the orthodox Calvinist view that since man was depraved, salvation could come to him only by God's grace, the liberals replied that the essential powers of spiritual regeneration were already in human nature, and needed only to be awakened and emancipated. "We can fix our eyes on perfection," wrote Channing, "and make almost everything speed us toward it."

By 1800 the lines of battle between liberal and conservative theology in New England were clearly drawn. The first break in the long truce came with the appointment of a professor to the Hollis Chair of Divinity at Harvard in 1805. The death of the incumbent professor, David Tappan, left the chair vacant in 1803. One group of Harvard theologians, who wanted the vacancy filled by a "liberal," proposed the name of Henry Ware of Hingham, a young Harvard minister of unitarian leanings. But President Willard of Harvard, a stanch conservative, declared that he "would sooner cut off his hand" than make such an appointment, and there the matter rested. Willard's death brought into office a new acting president, Professor Eliphalet Pearson, who was equally opposed to Ware's appointment. After a good deal of electioneering and politicking, the overseers, by a very narrow margin, chose Ware. They also passed over Pearson for the presidency, choosing instead the Reverend Samuel Webber and marking a tremendous victory for the "liberals"—at Harvard, the mother of Calvinistic orthodoxy, the home of the Mathers, the great Puritan center of learning.[18]

With Ware's appointment, it seemed to many New Englanders, the great globe itself cracked. Within four years four other professorships were filled by liberals and Harvard was accepted as the center of "unitarian" Christianity. In 1808 a group of conservative ministers withdrew from Harvard to found Andover Theological Seminary, thus symbolizing the division on Congregational ranks. For thirty years the argument persisted over who should control Harvard Divinity School and the Congregational Church in New England, dividing friends, families, and communities.

The break between liberal and conservative was further widened in 1815, when Thomas Belsham, an English preacher, published *American Unitarianism,* a laudatory account of the spread of unitarian doctrines in the United States. Belsham's pamphlet brought swift and heated replies from conservative theologians, and in their defense the liberals for the first time accepted the name Unitarian. The result was a lively pamphlet war, with conservatives such as Jedidiah Morse, Moses Stuart, Leonard Woods, Samuel Worcester, and Nehemiah Adams attacking the "infidelity" of the new doctrines, and men such as Andrews Norton, John Lowell, Edward Everett, and James Freeman asserting, as Lowell said, their "doctrinal independence" of the old faith.

The most effective proponent of the liberal position was William Ellery Channing, pastor of Boston's Federal Street Church.[19] Though not an argumentative man, Channing's keen mind and facile pen forced him into a debate with Samuel Worcester of Salem and Moses Stuart of Andover, the most vocal of the conservatives. From disagreements over Scriptural revelation the argument moved into a more

---

[18] A good account of the controversy is that of Samuel Eliot Morison, *Three Centuries of Harvard* (Cambridge, Mass., 1936), pp. 187–190. The argument, said William Buckminster, caused "much embarrassment and false refinement from the ingenuity and subtility of its professors," producing "scholastick theologues, hairsplitting metaphysicians, and long-breathed controversialists." *Monthly Anthology,* II (1805), p. 418.

[19] A good recent biography is Arthur W. Brown, *Always Young for Liberty: A Biography of William Ellery Channing* (Syracuse, 1956). Chap. VIII treats Channing's part in the Unitarian controversy.

general discussion of the "tendency" of unitarian doctrines to increase "infidelity." Unitarianism, said Samuel Miller, was a negative system, a theology of "not believing," and a step on the path to pure skepticism. In subordinating Scripture to reason (however defined) the liberals were, like the deists, "stealthily undermining the foundations of true Christianity." Not so, replied Channing. Unitarian Christianity protected true faith—if orthodox Calvinism was so irrational that thinking men were forced to doubt it, ridding its theology of errors and "corruptions" preserved the true. As for the Bible, the unitarian liberals were perfectly willing to believe, as Channing wrote, what the Bible "*clearly*" said." If orthodox Calvinism could be discovered in the Bible, they would believe that too, if the evidence to support it met the test of reason.[20]

Despite the sturdy defense of orthodoxy by the Andover group and their followers, the liberals steadily gained ground in New England. "All the literary men of Massachusetts were Unitarians," lamented Lyman Beecher, "all the trustees and professors of Harvard College were Unitarians. All the elite of wealth and fashion crowded Unitarian Churches."[21] Channing's sermon at the ordination of Jared Sparks as minister of a Baltimore church in 1819 put the Unitarian position so convincingly that it gained him a national reputation. A year later Channing and others called together a "Conference of Liberal Ministers," which in 1826 became the American Unitarian Association, a separate sect with 125 churches (120 of them in Massachusetts), including twenty of the twenty-five oldest Calvinist churches in the United States. "Calvinism, we are persuaded," Channing wrote, "is giving place to better views. It has passed its meridian, and is sinking to rise no more."

[20] For a careful analysis of the Calvinist-Unitarian controversy, see J. Harotunian, *Piety Versus Moralism* (New York, 1932), and C. H. Faust, "The Background of Unitarian Opposition to Transcendentalism," *Modern Philology*, XXXV (1938), 297–334. Among the representative items of the pamphlet war are Channing's *Letter to Samuel Thacher* (1815), *The System of Exclusion and Denunciation in Religion Considered* (1815), *Unitarian Christianity* (1819), and *Objections to Unitarian Christianity Considered* (1819); Henry Ware, *Letters Addressed to Trinitarians and Calvinists* (1820); Andrews Norton, *Statement of Reasons for Not Believing Doctrines of Trinity* (1819), William Peabody, *Come and See* (1823), and Jared Sparks, *Inquiry into the Comparative Moral Tendencies of Calvinism and Unitarianism* (1822). For the conservatives, see Samuel Worcester, *Letters to Dr. Channing* (1815); Leonard Woods, *Letters to Unitarians* (1820); Samuel Miller, *Letters on Unitarianism* (1823); and George Cheever, *The Spirit of the Pilgrims* (1823).

[21] *Autobiography* (New York, 1864), p. 73.

Congregational moderates, unwilling to accept either extreme conservatism or unitarian liberalism, tried to find a middle way. Nathaniel Taylor of Yale hope to revise Calvinistic theology in such a way as to keep liberals within the fold and to satisfy those conservatives whose rigidity had driven them out. Since one of the major arguments between liberal and conservative concerned the nature of man and his will, Taylor virtually repudiated the orthodox doctrine of predestination by declaring that man, as a free and thinking creature, had the power to accept goodness and reject evil, and that his salvation depended upon his own choice. In addition Taylor seemed willing to accept what was essentially the Unitarian position concerning revelation, declaring that Calvinism was after all "a rational faith of rational human beings" and that the Bible "ought to be tried at the bar of reason."[22] Since Taylorism, or "the New Haven theology," went at least part of the way with the Unitarians, it failed to satisfy the orthodox while it alienated liberals by its refusal to go the whole distance. Yet Taylor's compromise had its adherents; preached by the powerful Presbyterian evangelist Lyman Beecher,[23] it succeeded in creating another division in Calvinism's shattered ranks.

As if Channings and Taylors were not enough, Congregationalism was plagued by still another schism. Universalism, which appeared concurrently in New England with Unitarian doctrines, denied the Calvinist principle of eternal damnation; there might be punishment after death for sins committed in life, the Universalists believed, but for disciplinary purposes only, with eternal salvation accorded by God to all. The universal salvation of believers had been preached in mid-century England and New England by occasional Calvinists, but the arrival in the colonies in 1770 of John Murry, a British Universalist, gave the movement a new impetus. Murry, after nine years of missionary work, organized a Universalist chapel at Gloucester and later moved to the pulpit of Boston's First Universalist Society. After Murry's death Hosea Ballou, a New England Baptist, became the

[22] See Sidney E. Mead, *Nathaniel William Taylor, 1786–1858* (Chicago, 1942). For a summary of Taylor's theology, see Sweet, *Religion in American Culture,* pp. 197–201.

[23] Beecher, the father of Harriet Beecher Stowe, was a major figure in Eastern evangelism, often called "the Presbyterian Pope." Charles Beecher (ed.), *The Autobiography and Correspondence of Lyman Beecher* (New York, 1864), is still interesting reading about an interesting man.

leader of the movement. Ballou and his followers in 1805 decided to accept the central doctrines of Unitarianism,[24] and although Universalists and Unitarians maintained separate identity as sects, they agreed, as Zephaniah Swift of Connecticut wrote, "that religion was not instituted for the purpose of rendering [men] miserable, but happy, and that . . . the condition of men in the future state will not be dependent on the speculative opinions they may have adopted in the present."

Universalism drew its converts chiefly from the rural and working classes and had particular success in frontier territory. Though the Free Will Baptists created a less serious division within Congregationalism, they too served to indicate the trend of disintegration in the old order. Benjamin Randall of New Hampshire, a Congregationalist who was strongly influenced by Baptist doctrine, left the church with a group of followers to join the Baptists, but soon seceded to form a separate Free Will Baptist Church in 1781. After Randall's death the Free Will Baptists rapidly gained momentum, until by 1830 they claimed 450 churches with a membership of 21,000.[25]

While controversies raged within Congregationalism, the Presbyterians were plagued by internal revolts caused by the intrusion of Unitarian-Universalist and Methodist doctrines into their own churches. "Old School" Presbyterians counseled strict adherence to the tenets of the Westminster Confession. "New School" Presbyterians were willing to accept liberalized modifications, or to adopt semi-Methodist interpretations of some of Calvinism's more rigid rules. The problem of the moderate, caught between right and left, was best expressed by President Horace Holley of Transylvania, who hoped that his church might find a faith that was "liberal without indifference, evangelical without fanaticism, simple without crudeness, natural without licentiousness, and pious without the spirit of exclusion or tolerance."[26] Like Holley, too, most Presbyterians found the task impossible. Beginning in the 1820's the division between Old and New Schools widened perceptibly, culminating in a series of heresy trials involving such prominent Presbyterians as Lyman Beecher's son Edward and even Beecher himself. Eventually, in 1837, the New

[24] The best explanation of Ballou's theology is his own *Nine Sermons on Important Doctrinal and Practical Subjects* (Philadelphia, 1835).
[25] Sweet, *Religion in American Culture,* pp. 196–206.
[26] *Ibid.,* p. 213.

School Presbyterian Church seceded from the General Assembly to form a separate body.

The "perfectionism" of Charles Grandison Finney posed a serious threat to both Congregational and Presbyterian conservatives. Finney committed himself about 1820 to a doctrine of "free and full salvation," really a Methodist-Universalist principle, and after some difficulties obtained ordination as a Presbyterian minister.[27] He immediately began preaching his new theology, adopting in the process a number of evangelistic techniques usually associated with frontier Methodism. His creed, which he named "Perfectionism," defined sin as simply selfishness, virtue as "disinterested benevolence." In Finney's system conversion was a normal experience, accomplished by the sinner himself with the aid of ministerial exhortation. Salvation or "perfection," therefore, was available to every person by reason of his own intent and efforts. Furthermore, said Finney, those converted to grace must act to help others; all must aim at "being useful in the highest degree possible." Finney's theology clearly violated the chief Calvinist doctrines of sin, salvation, election, and predestination. In addition, reports from western New York indicated that Finney's own preaching techniques were apparently not in harmony with orthodox dignity and decorum. He "postured and groaned," it was claimed, mentioned sinners by name, instituted an "anxious seat" for repentant sinners, and permitted women to pray publicly.

Finney, with the aid of a band of eager young disciples, blazed a trail of camp meetings through the West. Lyman Beecher, the most powerful of Eastern Presbyterians, arranged a conference with Finney in an attempt to win him back into more acceptable channels of theology. Finney, however, refused to compromise and carried his campaign into New York and New England. His phenomenal success forced the Presbyterian Assembly to give him qualified approval, after which he accepted the presidency of the newly established Oberlin College. Following out his doctrine of "usefulness," numbers of his disciples entered various reform movements; it was no accident that the famous "Seventy" agents of the American Antislavery Society were nearly all Finney converts.[28]

[27] Whitney R. Cross, *The Burned-Over District* (Ithaca, 1950), pp. 158–205, contains an excellent account of Finney's early evangelism and his theology.

[28] See Finney's own *Memoirs of the Reverend Charles G. Finney* (New York, 1876). The impact of Finney on the antislavery movement is treated by G. H. Barnes, *The Antislavery Impulse* (New York, 1933).

The overwhelming religious issue of the period 1776 to 1830 was the contest for the West. The thrust of population into Kentucky, Tennessee, Missouri, Mississippi, and the vast expanse of the Northwest Territory meant that a whole new empire was open to religion, and all the churches of the East recognized the challenge. Early reports from the West, furthermore, were not encouraging. Samuel Mills, who toured the frontier in 1812–15 to "learn its moral and religious state," found frontiersmen generally illiterate, ignorant, blasphemous, and irreligious. Even the pious Connecticut Congregationalists who settled Ohio's Western Reserve, a missionary reported, had "fallen away" from their faith like "freed prisoners." All of the Eastern churches, therefore, girded themselves for the task of conquering the West.[29]

The Episcopal Church was not well equipped for frontier missionary work. Suspicion of its British connections still clung to it, and its hierarchical church organization appealed very little to frontiersmen. Episcopal ministers were college-trained and tied to their parishes; there was neither a sufficient supply of ministers for the West nor sufficient settlement in new territories to support them. In 1820 there were but six Episcopal pastors in Ohio, four in Kentucky, and none at all in Indiana, Illinois, or Tennessee.

Of the older Calvinistic churches, the Presbyterians were best situated for westward advance, since the last wave of eighteenth-century migration carried numbers of Scotch-Irish Presbyterians into the Pennsylvania and Virginia back country and across the mountains into Kentucky and Tennessee. Though the Congregational Association of Connecticut created a Missionary Society in 1798 to "extend charitable assistance . . . to the new Christian settlements," the Congregationalists were not well adapted to the task. Congregationalism's strength lay chiefly in New England, its political affiliations were conservative, and its pattern of autonomous church government did not suit the frontier's need for a firm, centralized church polity to tie together a loose, scattered society.[30] Congregationalism and Presbyterianism, however, had much to gain from extending their faith into the West. In 1801, therefore, the General Association of Connecticut (later other Congregational groups) and the Presbyterian General Assembly

[29] Sweet, *Religion in American Culture*, pp. 99–135, is a detailed account of the religious history of the West, from which much of the ensuing discussion is drawn. Quotations, unless otherwise noted, are from Sweet's account.
[30] Stokes, *Church and State*, pp. 652, 660 ff.

adopted a Plan of Union. Under the agreement, settlers of either sect could form a church under a minister of either faith. Such "Presbygational" churches would then be officially recognized by both.[31]

Both Presbyterian and Congregational churches found it difficult to supply ministers in sufficient quantities to meet frontier needs. The numbers of college graduates entering the ministry dropped from 30 per cent to 20 per cent during the three decades from 1762 to 1792, and continued to decline. As a result, both Presbyterian and Congregational groups founded theological seminaries in an attempt to keep up with the increased population—Andover (1808), Bangor (1816), Auburn (1822), Western at Pittsburgh (1827), Hanover in Indiana (1830), and Lane in Ohio (1832). In addition, private "log colleges" run by ordained ministers trained other theological students; Joseph Bellamy of Connecticut produced more than a hundred young ministers from his training school and Nathaniel Evans nearly as many in Massachusetts.

Methodists and Baptists were much better prepared for the westward push. Migrations west from Virginia and Carolina back country carried Baptists swiftly into the Southwest and Northwest frontier. Baptist doctrine was easily understood and easily preached; the informal Baptist organization and its democratic church polity were attuned to frontier sentiments; the Baptist system of lay preachers was particularly well suited to pioneer conditions. Lay preachers need not be college-trained, received no salary, and made their own way as farmers or mechanics. They lived closely with the people they served, and they could be licensed to preach by a congregation without formal ordination by a central church body. By 1810 Kentucky had 286 Baptist churches and Tennessee 102, with new ones springing up in Indiana, Ohio, and Illinois.

Methodism, like Baptism, quickly adapted itself to Western conditions. Its flexible polity, simplicity of creed, and stress on free will and individual responsibility appealed to frontiersmen in a fashion that Presbyterian or Congregational doctrine could not. Methodists too employed lay preachers or issued "exhorter's licenses" to enthusiastic church members who wished to preach. The Methodist circuit-rider system, developed by the Wesleys in England, fitted frontier needs perfectly. Under the system ministers traveled circuits of varying sizes, meeting "classes" or congregations at each stop. The circuit rider,

[31] Armstrong, Loetscher, and Anderson, *Presbyterian Enterprise*, p. 71.

as Peter Cartwright described him, "riding a hardy pony of a horse, and some travelling apparatus, and with his library at hand, namely Bible, hymnbook, and Discipline . . . through storms, wind, hail, snow, and swamps, wet, weary, and hungry," searched out the unconverted in the cabins and taverns of the crudest settlements.

In 1844 there were almost 4,500 traveling Methodist preachers on the road, paid an average of $64 a year, not including "horse and fixin's." Asbury himself, who never had a permanent parish and who spent forty-five years in travel, covered more than 5,000 miles a year by foot, boat, or horse, and crossed the Allegheny mountains sixty times. Peter Cartwright, that muscular, fearless servant of his Methodist God, baptized 8,000 children and 4,000 adults in his fifty years of service, founded two colleges, reared eight children of his own into the church, and died in the faith at ninety-seven.[32]

The history of American religion during the period 1776–1830 shows two marked characteristics: diversity and criticism. Historically, uniformity in American religion was the exception, never the rule. The original settlements were melting pots of faith as well as of national strains, a tradition of diversity which the colonies passed on undiminished to the new republic. What seemed to England and Europe to be American theological chaos was, as James Madison explained, a strength and not a weakness of its society. The freedom "that arises from that multiplicity of sects which pervades America," he wrote, "is the best and only security for religious liberty in any society." No better illustration could be found of the era's religious diversity than the wide spectrum of beliefs belonging to the Revolutionary leaders, ranging from the rockbound Calvinism of the Adamses to the free-running deism of Thomas Paine. Yet none of these men were against religion; all agreed that liberty and faith in God went together, that free men must be moral if they were to be awarded the right to operate their own society. "Religion and virtue," John Adams wrote, "are the only foundations, not only of republicanism and all free government, but of social felicity under all governments and in all combinations of human society."

These men, and the generation that followed them, valued religious diversity because to them it meant freedom. They wished to keep open the channels which directed their thinking toward their two major

[32] Sweet, *Rise of Methodism,* is a complete account.

religious problems: first, establishing the proper relationship between church and state; and second, finding the proper position of the individual in relation to both. Jefferson and Emerson—and other American religious philosophers between—feared the frozen attitude, the set mind, the chosen dogma which made it impossible to find answers. They wanted free outlets for speculation; religion could survive best, Jefferson was sure, when it did not have to be believed.

These years were also the scene of an astonishing paradox in the development of American religious thought. While New England, the ancient stronghold of Calvinistic orthodoxy, was swinging toward a looser, liberalized heterodoxy, exemplified most clearly in unitarian-transcendental Christianity, the South was moving toward an evangelized, neo-Calvinist orthodoxy. The eighteenth-century South, though it normally considered Anglicanism safe and fashionable, never really gave the Episcopal Church the dominance it was presumed to have. Beyond the seaboard cities, the theology of the eighteenth-century South was a broad, tolerant, almost freethinking kind of Christianity, represented perhaps best by the rationalized, deist-unitarian faith of a Jefferson or the easy-going Anglicanism of a Madison. There was even a good deal of "atheism and French deism" in rural and urban Southern society. Parson Weems reported a brisk market for Voltaire, Volney, and the like in back-country Virginia and the Carolinas, while the University of Virginia and the College of South Carolina, the South's most prominent educational institutions, were known to be lax in theology.

Yet there was, from the early days of settlement, a strong dissenting strain in Southern society, strengthened by the revivals of the 1740's (which struck the South almost as hard as New England) and by the Scotch-Irish and German migrations of the eighteenth century. Methodist and Baptist missionaries always found fertile soil below the Ohio River; the great revivals of the post-1800 years drew the greatest crowds there and produced the most effective evangelists. From the early eighteenth century to the mid-nineteenth, the religious philosophy of the South moved toward rigidity of creed, orthodoxy, Scriptural literalness, and moral earnestness. By 1830, had Jefferson been still alive, he would undoubtedly have found his religious principles highly unpopular in his native Virginia, just as President Cooper found himself expelled from his post at the College of South Carolina for heresy.

The controlling factor, of course, in this shift of Southern religious thought from liberalism to orthodoxy was slavery—the emergence of the slavery issue in politics and the growing importance of the institution within the South's political, economic, and social structure. The need for theological orthodoxy and for support of slavery ran together. Free thought, deviationism, or liberalism in theology might lead to embarrassing questions (and dangerous answers) about the slave system, something the South could not afford. Men could not be allowed the luxury of thinking for themselves in religion (or otherwise) lest slavery be damaged. The rigid theocratic ideal of seventeenth-century Calvinism, buttressed by the narrow emotional evangelism of the early nineteenth, fitted best with slavery—the two reinforced each other, in word and spirit. By 1850, ironically, Southern Protestantism was far closer in creed and temper to the ideals of the Massachusetts Bay Colony of 1650 than it was to Jefferson's Virginia of 1750 and after. By the time that the Unitarians had captured most of New England, in the South all the seminaries and universities (with the possible exception of the University of Virginia) were in the hands of evangelical faculties.[33]

Quite the opposite was taking place in New England. The theological argument from 1790 to 1830 in New England was at bottom an argument over the source of revealed religious truth. At its conclusion, the winners agreed that the *individual* (under proper conditions and safeguards) was the primary source and vehicle of God's truth. In accordance with the spirit of the Romantic movement, Northern Protestant theology accepted in one way or another a kind of individualistic metaphysic. God, as Bronson Alcott implied in his *Orphic Sayings* (1840, 1841), was always to be "privately perceived," a point of view which led inexorably from orthodoxy to individualism. In moving thus toward theological individualism, New England pointed toward Emerson, Beecher, and Finney as clearly as it did toward Garrison, Horace Mann, Dorothea Dix, William Ladd, and the great group of reformers who crusaded (from religious motives) for human, individual rights. The South, faced with the necessity of defending the *status quo,* was forced to reject the individualistic implications of the whole Romantic movement; indeed, it found it necessary instead to use its theology as an instrument to protect its vital, central institution. The South could not risk a Thoreau. Instead of Emerson, the religious

[33] Cf. the discussion of the shift in Southern theology in W. J. Cash, *The Mind of the South* (New York, 1941), pp. 65–73.

liberal, it produced Calhoun, the political conservative; instead of Brook Farmers, it yielded "fire-eaters."[34]

The late eighteenth and early nineteenth centuries in America were years of vigorous religious criticism and debate. The more men explored the universe without and the mind within, the more they wondered about first causes and inner awarenesses, which led them naturally to theological questionings. They intended to examine theology closely and carefully, just as they examined government, in order to find a sound bedrock of believable and workable doctrines—what Franklin called "the fundamental principles of all sound religion." Disregarding the limits of criticism set by their colonial forebears, some of them pushed hard at the boundaries of tolerance, but all of them—however their personal beliefs might differ—had a basically religious attitude. They never rejected religion, nor lost respect for it, nor doubted its validity. They felt rather that neither religious institutions nor theology had quite kept pace with the swift progress of human knowledge and technology, nor with the great expansion of belief in the powers of the individual himself. They wished to find out why. For this reason, the men of the times in the United States thought that one important aspect of the struggle for political rights was the need to create conditions under which a man could worship God as he wished. They questioned orthodox faith and criticized sectarian organization (at times with some heat), but it was with the view of opening the doors of churches, not of tearing them down.

---

[34] For a discussion of the Southern problem, see Clement Eaton, *Freedom of Thought in the Old South* (Durham, N.C., 1940), and R. B. Nye, *Fettered Freedom* (East Lansing, Mich., 1949), Chaps. III, IV.

CHAPTER 11

The Quest for a National Literature

AS THE United States took on shape and stability as a nation after the Revolution, Americans showed greater interest in the culture of Continental Europe. They accepted England for granted; they were part and parcel of the British tradition and were proud of it. At the same time, for patriotic reasons, they naturally wished to lean on it no longer quite so heavily as before, a reaction naturally heightened by the War of 1812. Increased immigration throughout the eighteenth century meant also that the British heritage was not the only cultural legacy Americans possessed. There were at least 40,000 French, for example, in the Northwest, half that many Spanish in the South, and perhaps three times that number of Germans in Pennsylvania, Ohio, or scattered along the seaboard states, to say nothing of thousands of frontier Scotch-Irish.

The actual cultural impact of Germany on American thought throughout the eighteenth century was never large, but by the time of the Revolution a well-defined tradition of German-American relations was firmly established.[1] The Reverend William Bentley of Salem, the most knowledgeable man of his time about Germany, served as the most important single influence in acquainting the United States with German culture after 1790. Bentley's *Impartial Register* (1800–1819), which published estimates and summaries of German scientific writing, philosophy, and art, was the primary channel of communication be-

---

[1] Henry A. Pochmann, *German Culture in America* (Madison, Wis., 1957), is the definitive study of German-American relations. H. S. Jantz, "German Thought and Literature in New England 1620–1820," *Journal of English and Germanic Philology,* XLI (1942), 1–46, is an informative brief study.

tween Germany and the United States during its existence. At the same time, the British were also discovering Germany, finding much in its art and philosophy to stimulate prevailing Romantic interests. By the turn of the century both British and American critics and writers were showing great interest in the German *Sturm und Drang* school, in the sentimentality of German poetry and drama, in the Gothicism of German tales, and in the rebelliousness of the early Goethe and Schiller.[2] William Dunlap, for example, introduced German sentimental drama to the American public by translating and presenting thirty of Kotzebue's plays between 1799 and 1820.

At the close of the War of 1812, American interest in things German began to climb swiftly. Madame de Staël's *Germany,* a survey of German thought that swept Europe, appeared in New York in 1814; the *North American Review* and other journals were filled for the next thirty years with translations of German poetry, philosophy, and criticism—sometimes not too well-informed perhaps, but enthusiastically received. Travelers and students, among them such men as George Ticknor, Edward Everett, George Bancroft, F. H. Hedge, Joseph Buckminster, Joseph Cogswell, James Marsh, and Henry Wadsworth Longfellow returned from Germany with new ideas, new theories of literature, fresh approaches to theology, education, criticism, and philosophy.[3] Throughout the first forty years of the nineteenth century there was in the United States, as one student observed, "an intense excitement about Germany."[4] The great wind of German thought was

[2] Despite their admiration for Goethe and Schiller, a good many American writers could not accept the moral implications of some of their works, when their individualism seemed to violate established social standards. See A. H. Everett's thoughtful review, "Life and Writings of Schiller," *North American Review,* XVI (1823), 397–410. Young George Bancroft found Goethe "too dirty, too bestial in his conceptions," though he later revised his opinions; Russel B. Nye, *George Bancroft* (New York, 1944), p. 40.

[3] O. W. Long, *Literary Pioneers* (Cambridge, Mass., 1935), contains excellent accounts of most of these young Americans who studied in Germany. In order to learn German, Ticknor borrowed a German grammar in French, found a German dictionary in New Hampshire, and tutored with an Alsatian mathematics teacher in Boston. Bancroft, a few years later, learned German from a Greek grammar published in German and tutored with Professor Willard of Harvard, who had taught himself to read but not speak German. Nye, *Bancroft,* pp. 31–32.

[4] Pochmann, *German Culture,* pp. 328–334. Between 1810 and 1864 almost one-third of all notes on German books in American journals were concerned with Schiller or Goethe. Following them, in order of popularity, came Jean Paul, Zschokke, Kotzebue, Herder, Lessing, and Bürger. In addition to Poch-

blowing hard through the United States by 1815, and after 1830 reached gale force in New England and New York.

The influence of France on American thought and culture throughout the eighteenth century was large, second only to that of England; indeed, during the latter decades of the century, France was perhaps a greater source of intellectual and cultural stimulation to the United States than Britain herself.[5] French Protestant literature, of course, was very much a part of the colonial heritage. Sylvester's translations of Du Bartas, Descartes, Ramus, Dumoulin, and other French theologians and philosophers were well known to educated colonists. The first great wave of influence, however, came in the years 1750–90, when Americans discovered in the earlier French Enlightenment, and in Voltaire, Montesquieu, the *philosophes,* and the encyclopedists, a host of new principles and substantiation for others in which they already believed. The French neoclassic ideal of "light" (*les lumières*) —of emphasis on reason, order, clarity, and intellect, and of an optimistic contemplation of nature—all these became integrated parts of the Anglo-American Enlightenment point of view. A second wave of French thought, less powerful perhaps but still strong, overlapped the first in America after 1790. This was the sentimentalism of Rousseau and Madame de Staël—its sentimental morality, its concern for the individual, its subjectivism, primitivism, emotionalism, its recognition of the complexities of nature and human experience—which provided such potent reinforcements for post-1790 American Romanticism.[6]

Before 1775 French culture was especially strong in those settlements of the Mississippi Valley and the Northwest where migrating French

mann's study, Stanley M. Vogel, *German Literary Influences on the American Transcendentalists* (New Haven, 1955), and Scott M. Goodnight, *German Literature in American Magazines Prior to 1846* (Madison, Wis., 1907), are useful studies. George Bancroft's three articles on "German Literature," *The American Quarterly Review,* II (1827), 171–186; III (1828), 150–173; and IV (1828), 157–190, which form the first comprehensive survey of German literature to be made in America, are still interesting reading.

[5] The definitive study is Howard Mumford Jones, *America and French Culture 1750–1848* (Chapel Hill, N.C., 1927).

[6] L. Cazamian, *A History of French Literature* (Oxford, 1955), pp. 216–293; for a more thorough study of French thought, see Daniel Mornet, *French Thought in the Eighteenth Century* (New York, 1929). Useful special studies of French influences include Paul M. Spurlin, *Montesquieu in the United States 1760–1801* (Baton Rouge, 1940); Mary M. Barr, *Voltaire in America 1744–1800* (Baltimore, 1941); Richmond L. Hawkins, *Mme. de Staël and the United States* (Cambridge, Mass., 1950); Adrian H. Jaffe, *French Literature in American Magazines 1740–1800* (East Lansing, Mich., 1952).

had settled long before, in Detroit, Vincennes, St. Louis, and of course New Orleans. The Revolutionary War, which turned American sympathies away from Britain toward the new French allies, brought crowds of French soldiers, diplomats, traders, and travelers into the new nation, so that French culture and politics became a focal point of American intellectual attention. French principles and arms, many believed, had contributed overwhelmingly to American success. After all, it was "Gallia great and good" who "Columbia's friend in fiery trial stood," as a poet in *The Universal Asylum and Columbian Magazine* pointed out in July, 1790, a sentiment echoed hundreds of times over after the war. At the onset of the French Revolution, which Americans generally hailed as the second great step in mankind's liberation, French ideas, manners, literature, fashions, and food were at their highest point of popularity. "O France!" wrote Philip Freneau ecstatically,

> The world to thee must owe
> A debt they ne'er can pay;
> The Rights of Man you bid them know,
> And kindle Reason's day![7]

But as the French Revolution continued, American enthusiasm for France cooled. Its political principles seemed dangerously anarchical, its religious ideas positively anti-Christian and atheistic. "Frenchified Freedom," Thomas Green Fessenden wrote in his poem *Democracy Unveiled* (1805), could ruin the United States, which must not countenance the principles of *"sans culotte* Frenchmen." John Adams, reflecting the opinion of many informed Americans, considered France "a nation of thirty million atheists."[8] The collapse of the Revolution and the appearance of Napoleon drove the two nations even farther apart. What had been suspicion and distrust in the 1790's had turned into active attack by 1812, and even after Napoleon's defeat and demise the American attitude toward French culture and French poli-

[7] "On the Demolition of the French Monarchy" (1792). See also Esther Brown, *The French Revolution and the Man of Letters* (Columbia, Mo., 1951). Howard Mumford Jones estimates that at this time perhaps one-fourth of all books imported into New York and Philadelphia were French, and one-eighth of all those imported into the nation at large. H. M. Jones, "The Importance of French Books in Philadelphia, 1750–1800," *Modern Philology,* XXVII (1934), 157–177, and "The Importance of French Literature in New York City, 1750–1800," *Studies in Philology,* XXVIII (1931), pp. 235–257.

[8] Merle Curti, *The Growth of American Thought* (New York, 1943), p. 199.

tics remained one of no more than indifferent interest until nearly mid-century.[9]

Spain, despite its deep penetration into the New World, exerted much less influence on the culture of the American colonies or on the Republic.[10] Pockets of Spanish settlement, of course, existed within the continental United States throughout the eighteenth and well into the nineteenth century—notably in Florida and Louisiana—but their influence on the American culture of Texas, California, and the Southwest came later. Spanish travel books were popular, while the history of Spain in the Americas, Columbus, the *conquistadores,* and the explorers appealed to many American novelists and poets. After 1820 the dedication to Spanish studies of a number of talented men, among them Irving, Prescott, Ticknor, Longfellow, and Bryant, awakened the United States to a wider realization of the depth and wealth of their Spanish heritage.

What Americans wanted most, naturally, was a culture of their own. Immediately after the Revolution, American critics, editors, and authors clamored for the immediate creation of a native, indigenous, original American art.[11]

"We are called to sing a New Song," said Nathaniel Appleton, "a Song that neither We nor our Fathers were ever able to sing before." "America must be as independent in *literature,*" Noah Webster wrote in the preface to his speller in 1783, "as she is in *politics.*" Having already proved its military and political genius, the United States must now demonstrate its eminence in art and literature. "Let our writers emulate the ambition, diligence, and zeal that have so eminently characterized our gentlemen of the sword," John Neal advised in *The Portico,* while Noah Webster's preface to his famous spelling book expressed his hope that the United States would "be as distinguished

[9] The most thorough study of the shifting popularity of French thought in the United States is Georges J. Joyaux, "French Thought in American Magazines 1800–1848" (unpublished dissertation, Michigan State University, 1951), especially pp. 13–105. Joyaux finds, however, great American interest in French science during the period, and significant interest in French philosophy, despite American suspicions of French political and religious thought.

[10] The best study is Stanley T. Williams, *The Spanish Background of American Literature* (New Haven, 1955), pp. 21–49, "Spanish Culture in Eighteenth Century America."

[11] The most thorough study of American literary nationalism is Benjamin T. Spencer, *The Quest for Nationality* (Syracuse, 1957). See also the articles by H. H. Clark, W. E. Sedgwick, E. K. Brown, Earl Bradsher, and J. C. McCloskey, listed in the Bibliography.

by the superiority of her literary improvements as she is already by the liberality of her civil and ecclesiastical institutions."[12]

The nation should have—nay, *must* have to prove its greatness—a literature commensurate with its glorious past and brilliant future, an art, wrote the dramatist James Nelson Barker, "to celebrate American achievements, and to record American events." Nor was there reason to doubt that such a literature might soon appear. Free men would produce great art; liberty, Samuel Gardner wrote in 1780, will always "unfetter and expand the human mind" to greater creative efforts. In free and independent America, David Ramsay predicted, "Every circumstance concurs to make it probable that the arts and sciences will be cultivated, extended and improved. . . . It is hoped that the free government of America will produce poets, orators, critics, and historians equal to the most celebrated of the ancient commonwealths of Greece and Italy." John Trumbull put the same thought into couplets:

> This land her Swift and Addison shall view,
> The former honors equalled by the new;
> Here shall some Shakespeare charm the rising age,
> And hold in magic chain the listening stage;
> A second Watts shall strike the heavenly lyre,
> And other muses other bards inspire.

So too Samuel Latham Mitchill, a generation later, predicted the day soon at hand "when the proficients in benign letters and arts . . . with harps and timbrels in their hands, and with crowns of glory on their heads," would sing in the new republic.[13] Literally hundreds of similar exhortations and predictions echoed through the journals in the years after 1776.

To encourage the creation of this national literature, literary clubs (such as New York's Friendly Club and Boston's Anthology Club) announced contests, magazines sponsored native authors, critics puffed native works, newspapers demanded greater production from domestic talent. *The Columbian Magazine,* edited by a group including Francis Hopkinson and Matthew Carey; Carey's *American Museum;* Charles Brockden Brown's *Monthly Magazine,* the Boston group's *Monthly*

---

[12] J. C. McCloskey, "The Campaign of Periodicals after the War of 1812 for a National American Literature," *PMLA,* L (1935), 262–273.

[13] *Discourse on the Nature and Prospects of American Literature* (Albany, 1821); the others are quoted in Brooke Hindle, *The Pursuit of Science in Revolutionary America* (Chapel Hill, 1956), Chap. XII.

Anthology, Aitken and Paine's *Pennsylvania Magazine;* Brackenridge's *United States Magazine;* and other journals published native authors and clamored for more. After 1800 such magazines as *The Portico* and the powerful *North American Review* (1815) hoped, in the words of the *Review,* "to foster American genius, and by independent literary criticism, instruct and guide the public taste." This fervent literary nationalism found reinforcements in contemporary Europe, especially Germany, from the Schlegels, Herder, Madame de Staël, and other influential critics. Edward Channing's belief, expressed in his essay "On Models in Literature" (1816), that literature must grow out of "differences of country, of habits, of institutions," and Edward Everett's statement of 1824 that literature is a product of "a state of society, its leading pursuits, and characteristic institutions," were but two of many such reflections of literary nationalism.[14]

It was easier to demand a great native literature than to produce it. No new Miltons or Addisons appeared in response to the call, no republican nests of singing birds. Some critics suspected that strident demands for a thoroughly native literature might be premature—that to be national, however laudable, was not automatically to be good. Others found it nonsense to reject Pope or Goldsmith because they were British, and equally silly to hail the wild and often faltering woodnotes of native bards because they were Americans.[15] Joseph Dennie, the editor of *The Portfolio,* warned enthusiasts that American literature, "still in its swaddling bands," should not be forced to grow too soon. Robert Walsh of the *American Quarterly Review* thought that American letters "must wait for improvements from abroad" before proclaiming itself great. Even Noah Webster, one of the most enthusiastic nationalists, agreed that cultural nationalism need not mean cultural isolation, especially if he had to give up Addison, whom he thought the greatest essayist of all time.[16]

American critics also realized that American literature labored under certain heavy handicaps which might well delay for some time the appearance of American Homers and Shakespeares. The "commercial-

---

[14] Spencer, *Quest for Nationality,* pp. 63, 82, 90.

[15] The critic calling himself "John Whittler," for example, wrote fulsomely in *The United States Magazine* of Newark, April 1, 1794, "The writings of a *Trumbull,* a *Dwight,* a *Barlow,* and an *Humphries,* are as highly esteemed even by foreigners, as those of a *Butler,* a *Milton,* a *Pope,* or an *Addison.*"

[16] McCloskey, "Campaign of Periodicals," p. 268; Spencer, *Quest for Nationality,* p. 36.

ized spirit" of a new nation, busily engaged in gathering land and wealth, stifled literature; John Quincy Adams remarked that it was impossible in the United States "to be a man of business and a man of rime," while Nathaniel Evans pitied all American poets, "in a climate cast where few the muse can relish." Bank shares and epics, said Joel Barlow, did not mix. Others doubted whether a society built on equality could yield genius; did not democracy produce mediocrity, a dead-level flatness of art?

"Where the spirit of democracy is everywhere diffused," a contributor to the Boston *Anthology* complained in 1807, "we are exposed, as it were, to a poisonous atmosphere, which blasts everything beautiful in nature and corrodes everything elegant in art."[17] Bitter political factionalism created an atmosphere unsuitable to the politer arts. Freneau, in his poem *To an Author,* warned poets that

> An age employed in edging steel
> Can no poetic raptures feel

and complained that the public preferred "the murdered victims" of political battle to poetry. Most serious of all, others pointed out, was what Irving called the United States' lack of "the charms of storied and poetical association . . . the accumulated treasures of age." In the United States, Cooper wrote in *Notions of the Americans* (1828): "There are no annals for the historian; no follies (beyond the most vulgar and commonplace) for the satirist; no manners for the dramatist; no obscure fictions for the writer of romance; no gross and hardy offenses against decorum for the moralist; nor any of the rich artificial auxiliaries of poetry."[18]

To be national, one must free oneself from cultural dependence on Europe, especially England. But having declared one's freedom of Britain and Europe, critics asked, what then does one retain of their great literary traditions? They decided upon two principles of selection. First, American authors must carefully avoid foreign models, lest

[17] Spencer, *Quest for Nationality,* pp. 112–114; Merle Curti, *Roots of American Loyalty* (New York, 1946), p. 194.

[18] Compare *Blackwood's Magazine* in England, in 1819, writing of America: "There is nothing to awaken fancy in that land of dull realities. No objects carry the mind back to contemplation of a remote antiquity. No moldering ruins excite interest in the history of the past. No memorials commemorative of noble deeds arouse enthusiasm and reverence. No traditions, legends, fables, afford material for poetry and romance."

by imitation they destroy their own native creativeness. Let there be, warned Webster, no "servile imitation of the language, manners, and vices of foreigners"; Benjamin Rush likewise advised young authors to stop imitating the European classics if they hoped to equal them. Second, American authors must reject that foreign literature which was immoral, untrue, or subversive of American principles. They should accept only "true and useful ideas of glory," wrote Barlow in *The Columbian*, and discard those "false and destructive ones that have degraded the species in other countries." For this reason there was strong contemporary suspicion of "vile foreign trash" which possessed no "moral utility."[19]

Simply to reject the derivative, imitative, and European, of course, was not enough. To create an *American* literature required the formulation of a body of critical theory on which such a native literature might be founded and by which it could be evaluated. The prevailing critical theory was based on the writings of Kames and Blair,[20] British pre-Romantic theorists who insisted that good and true art was based on "moral sense" and taste, and on "universal" principles commonly held by all men of all nations and ages. An American literature, in addition to being native and original, must therefore meet certain universally accepted standards of taste, beauty, and morality.

American writers therefore searched for an "American manner." Webster, Dennie, and Rush believed that the "plain style" of neoclassic prose, of Mather and Franklin, suited the American spirit better than the florid, ornamental style of Johnson and Gibbon. There was some feeling that British English itself was not an entirely suitable medium for such expression. Webster's famous speller was intended to institute "an American tongue"; James Kirke Paulding thought that the United States would never have its own literature until "we make our own books, and coin our own words." Walter Channing urged authors not to "describe Niagara in language fitted for the falls at London Bridge, or attempt the majesty of the Mississippi in that which was made for the Thames." On the other hand, some agreed with the editors of the *Monthly Anthology* that the notion of an *American* tongue was absurd, since it meant only that Americans might exchange "the language of

[19] Spencer, *Quest for Nationality,* pp. 39–43.
[20] William Charvat, *The Origins of American Critical Thought 1810–1835* (Philadelphia, 1936), finds thirty-one editions of Kames in America before 1835, thirty-nine of Blair, and nine of Alison.

Shakespeare and the Bible" for an "idiom from the mouths of il-
literates."[21]

What, then, might an American author write about, and in what
manner? How could an American, Timothy Dwight asked, "compen-
sate the want of ancient castles, ruined abbeys, and fine pictures?"
Quite possibly, Paulding suggested, Americans did not need such
things, nor any of the "ghosts, fairies, goblins, and all that antiquated
machinery" popular in Europe, for they had literary blessings yet
unrealized and uncounted.[22]

First, American literature had the Indian and the frontier. There
was disagreement at first concerning the Indian's suitability for literature, since experiences with the red man were too recent and unfortunate for native authors to see him as a "noble savage." An
anonymous critic in 1818 probably expressed the sentiments of many
American writers by saying that such "miserable barbarians, their
squaws and papooses," did not belong in literature at all. However,
Charles Brockden Brown, in his preface to *Edgar Huntly* (1799), had
already suggested that "the incidents of Indian hostility and the perils
of the Western wilderness" were very likely better materials than Gothic
castles. Paulding, in 1817, believed that the "active, hardy, vigilant,
enterprising, fearless" frontiersman was prime material for the novelist
(as James Fenimore Cooper soon abundantly proved), and the *North
American Review* in 1826 thought that an inventive poet "might discover the hint of an epic" in Indian life (as Longfellow shortly did).

Second, the United States had its own history. "Thy native land is
big with mighty scenes," Mercy Warren told young poets in 1782. The
North American Review assured American novelists in 1817 that
American history was "infinite, its characters innumerable, and the
scenery of its places full of beauty and grandeur." The Revolution, in
particular, provided poets and writers with distinctively native subject
matter, fraught with tragic, epic, and narrative possibilities, loaded
with heroes and villains. President Stiles of Yale thought that such a
great struggle would surely produce "future Homers, Livys, and
Tassos." Mrs. Susannah Rowson, the popular novelist, counted Ameri-

[21] Spencer, *Quest for Nationality*, Chap. I, discusses linguistic nationalism,
pp. 36–38, 56–59; Channing's "Essay on an American Language and Literature" appeared in *The North American Review*, I (1815), 307–314; Paulding's
essay, "A National Literature," in *Salamagundi Papers* (second series, 1819).

[22] See Spencer, *Quest for Nationality*, "Themes and Materials," pp. 39–53,
for a discussion.

can authors much more fortunate than Homer, who had only "barbarous chieftains" to write about, while they had "matchless Washington."

Every author of note made at least one attempt to use American history in a major literary work, but except for William Dunlap's play, *André*, nothing of consequence appeared. Not until Cooper's *Spy* (1821) did an author find a way to handle American historical materials with success. The difficulty seemed to be, in Dunlap's opinion, that the United States had no remote past, and that "recent events are unfit subjects for tragedy." James Hillhouse advised Yale's fledgling authors that American history was probably unsuitable for poetry, since it was too new and too much concerned with matters of "calmness and plainness of intellect" to "afford proper inspiration." Even Cooper complained in 1828 that in American history there was "scarcely an ore that contributes to the wealth of an author . . . in veins as rich as Europe"—while he was busily working several rich American veins himself.[23] Many Americans were aware of the existence of an authentic American past, but very few, by 1820, knew how to use it.

Third, the "events, customs, opinions, and characters of American society," according to James Nelson Barker, furnished enormous resources for a distinguished literature of manners, free from "corruptions of foreign tastes." Still, those novelists and dramatists who tried their hands at American social novels, or comedies of manners, found it extremely hard to carry off. What was authentically "native" or "tasteful" in American society? Was it sufficiently "elegant" and "genteel" to evoke the skill of an Austen or Sheridan? Cooper thought that American life lacked the variety and contrast that made British or European society literarily useful; the United States had no peasants, no aristocracy, no trappings of caste and class, no "wig for the judge or baton for the general." "I have never seen," he remarked, "a nation so much alike, in my life, as the people of the United States." American society had simply "too little variety for extended poetical efforts," wrote James Hillhouse, too few examples of "outraged affection, remorseless cruelty, or dire revenge."[24]

Not all American artists agreed with this view. William Cullen Bryant, in his famous review of Catherine Sedgwick's novel, *Redwood* (1825), pointed out that instead of uniformity, as Cooper claimed, the

[23] *Ibid.*, pp. 42–44.
[24] *Ibid.*, pp. 45–47; W. E. Sedgwick, "The Materials for an American Literature," *Harvard Studies and Notes in Philology and Literature* (1935).

United States displayed innumerable fascinating contrasts in its religion, manners, customs, politics, and characters, an "infinite variety of pursuits and subjects, this endless diversity of and change of fortunes . . . gathered and grouped into one vast assemblage." All that was needed to exploit it, Bryant concluded, was an author of "sagacity and skill."[25]

Critics were on surer ground when they pointed out a fourth category of available literary material—American nature, the vast, various, fascinating land itself. Fresh, unspoiled, "grand," "lofty," and "sublime" (in the critical vocabulary of the day), American nature could supply subject and inspiration for great literary art. Though America might lack "storied and poetical associations," Irving admitted, it possessed a matchless "simple beauty" and "wild magnificence" that Europe did not. Poets found American nature rich in "immense spectacles," "inspiring vistas," and "magnificent images." The Delaware, the Schuylkill, the Hudson, the Mohawk, the Ohio, and the mighty Mississippi were certainly as inspiring as the Thames, the Tweed, or the Avon—perhaps more so because they were bigger. "Compared with our own," boasted one enthusiastic reviewer, "Scottish rivers are but brooks and Scottish forests mere thickets." The robin, the whippoorwill, the firefly, the mockingbird, the wild honeysuckle, and the daisy were equally as worthy of artistic notice, Joseph Dennie believed, "as nightingales or skylarks, singles and dells." "Oak and elm," he said, "are as good wood to supply poetical fire as cypress and yew."[26]

The quest for literary nationalism was a search for a way to use the resources of the American land, the American past, and American society, to produce an art that was indigenous, new, universally beautiful, morally true, expressive of American ideals, and representative of the American spirit—an art "scarcely less wonderful," playwright Samuel Woodworth wrote, "than the growth of our physical and political greatness." It could not be created in artificial isolation; it must grow and mature, Paulding said, out of "the feelings, attachments, and associations of the people at large." To create it the writer must, as Brown believed, "examine objects with his own eyes, employ European models merely for the improvement of his taste and adapt his fiction to all that is genuine and peculiar in the scene before him." To find what John Neal called "the abundant and hidden sources of

[25] Reprinted in Tremaine McDowell, *Bryant* (New York, 1935).
[26] Spencer, *Quest for Nationality,* pp. 48–51.

fertility in our own beautiful brave earth" was, then, the aim of this first generation of American literary artists.[27]

The second great factor in the development of an American literature was the Romantic movement. The period 1776–1830 is not one of clear distinction between the receding neoclassicism of the eighteenth century and the approaching Romanticism of the nineteenth century.[28] Though neoclassicism was certainly the dominant literary strain during the years 1776–1820, it was obviously a steadily declining influence. There were, as Professor Heiser has pointed out, three kinds of American neoclassicists in the period: those who, like Dwight, Trumbull, and Wirt, followed eighteenth-century models with some care; those who, though not primarily literary men, partook of the characteristic neoclassic temper and spirit, such as Paine, Barlow, Rush, and Jefferson; and those such as Freneau, Cooper, and Paulding who used the older forms of expression to advance new, nonclassical ideas.[29]

The drift from neoclassicism to Romanticism in American letters is best illustrated by those differences in outlook, temperament, interests, and expression apparent among the three generations of American literary men who dominated the scene between 1750 and 1850. Dwight, Barlow, Brackenridge, and Trumbull, all born between 1748 and 1758, were the first to reach literary maturity after the Revolution. Irving, Cooper, Paulding, and Bryant, all born between 1783 and 1794, were products of a neoclassical background, who yet broke free into a new kind of creative art. The third generation, born between 1800 and 1820—Emerson, Longfellow, Thoreau, Poe, Lowell, Hawthorne, Whitman, Melville—brought American Romanticism to its highest and finest expression.

The Romantic movement, which spread through western culture during the latter half of the eighteenth century and the first half of the nineteenth, was an extension of certain principles of the Enlightenment and a rejection of others. It was, in general, an attitude of mind,

[27] *Ibid.*, pp. 76, 103. Brown's essay is in *The Weekly Magazine* (March 17, 1798). See also discussion of Neal and Woodworth (the author of "The Old Oaken Bucket") in Kendall Taft, *The Minor Knickerbockers* (New York, 1947), Introduction.

[28] For discussion of the prevailing literary trends of the period, see Norman Foerster's *Reinterpretation of American Literature* (New York, 1928); M. F. Heiser and G. H. Orians, in H. H. Clark (ed.), *Transitions in American Literary History* (Durham, N.C., 1954); and H. M. Jones' spirited essay in *Ideas in America* (Cambridge, Mass., 1945).

[29] Merrill F. Heiser, "The Decline of Neo-classicism," in Clark, *Transitions*.

deriving from a set of loosely related, sometimes overlapping ideas about the nature of Deity, man, and the external world. Literary historians have agreed that at the center of the cluster of beliefs included under the name Romanticism are the following:

An emphasis on the emotional and imaginative aspects of life and literature, with a corresponding emphasis on the "intimations," the "fancy," or the imagination, over the reason as a source of aesthetic and moral truth.

A recognition of the importance of individual and subjective values as equal to social values.

A belief (especially emphasized in American Romantic thought) in the dignity and worth of the common man, his freedom from restraints, and his capacity for improvement.

A new kind of interest in external nature, directly experienced, both in its spiritual and sensuous aspects.

A renewed interest in the literary uses of the past, particularly in the unique, colorful, primitive, exotic, and distant.

The most profound literary influence of Romanticism originated from its "organic" theory of literature, which assumed that a work of art, like a plant, grew naturally in response to its own inner laws, creating unity of idea, form, and execution. The artistic act, in the words of Samuel Taylor Coleridge, "shapes, as it develops itself, from within, and the fulness of its development is one and the same with the perfection of its outward form. Such as life is, such is the form." The entire body of American literary theory and expression after 1815 showed the impact of these beliefs.[30]

Third, the development of a native tradition of American letters was influenced by a particular set of contemporary circumstances affecting literary production. The United States had no tradition of literary patronage among the wealthy, and since very few American writers possessed sufficient resources to give their time wholly to letters, there were (until Charles Brockden Brown) no really professional authors in the United States. John Pickering, writing in 1816, explained that

. . . in this country we can hardly be said to have any *authors by profession.* The works we have produced have, for the most part, been written by men,

---

[30] R. E. Spiller, "Critical Standards in the American Romantic Movement," *College English,* VIII (1947), 344–352, is a useful brief article on this topic. See also Walter Fuller Taylor, *A History of American Letters* (Chicago, 1956), "The Romantic Impulse and The American Environment," pp. 69–86, and G. H. Orians, "The Rise of Romanticism," in Clark, *Transitions,* pp. 161–245.

who were obliged to depend upon other employments for their support, and who could devote to literary pursuits those few moments only, which their thirst for learning, stimulated them to snatch from their daily avocations.[31]

"It was positively inglorious to the commercial credit of a bookseller to undertake American works," publisher Samuel Goodrich remembered later. Henry Wadsworth Longfellow's father warned him that nobody could make a living from literature. "There is not wealth and munificence enough in this country," he wrote the young poet, "to afford sufficient encouragement and patronage to merely literary men."[32]

The reading public of the period lacked literary sophistication; its writers lacked self-confidence. Both were prone to accept the fashionable and the popular without discrimination, no doubt because both writers and readers were uncertain of their own critical judgments and reluctant to differ with British and European trends. Despite all the demands for a "fresh, new literature," the public and the artist felt more secure with the old and time-tested. It was safer to imitate Pope, on whose genius everyone agreed, than to hazard a judgment on an American poet.[33] It was far easier to admire Scott, who was generally assumed to be the greatest novelist of all time, than to offer an opinion about the unknown like J. F. Cooper—who, in order to get a hearing, was forced to foster the rumor that his first novel was really written by a "prominent Englishman."

There was also the very practical matter of the absence of an adequate copyright law in the United States. As late as 1830 only one book in three sold in the United States came from an American press. An American writer of the early nineteenth century, because of widespread pirating of English books, found himself forced to compete with cheap reprints of the great giants of English and European literature, making it a very thin market indeed.[34] Scott's novels, for example, sold

[31] John Pickering, *A Vocabulary or Collection of Words and Phrases* . . . (Boston, 1816), V.

[32] R. E. Spiller *et al.*, *Literary History of the United States* (New York, 1948), I, 240–241.

[33] Pope's *Essay on Man* went through 105 editions in the United States between 1790 and 1830. See Agnes Sibley, *Alexander Pope's Prestige in America, 1725–1835* (New York, 1949), for a complete study of Pope's influence.

[34] An anthology of Sterne's writings had five editions before 1795; Defoe's *Robinson Crusoe* nineteen prior to 1810, Fielding's *Tom Jones* nine, Goldsmith's *Vicar of Wakefield* nine, and Richardson's novels perhaps forty. On the matter of copyright problems, see Spiller, *Literary History*, I, 236–238. "Why should the Americans write books," sneered the critic Sydney Smith in *The*

in the United States for half what they did in England; a count of typical circulating library lists of 1804 showed over 2,000 English and French titles.[35]

Yet the prospects for American authors were not all gloomy. In America, as in England, the habit of reading was no longer restricted to the professionally educated. Americans, an observer remarked in 1772, had a "prevailing taste for books of every kind, that made almost every man a reader. . . ." A London bookseller, traveling in the United States in 1791, noted with surprise that "all ranks and degrees now READ." Boston in the 1770's had fifty bookstores, Philadelphia probably thirty or more, and peddlers hawked almanacs, chapbooks, broadsides, and standard books through every city street and backwoods hamlet. Between 1790 and 1820 the population of the United States doubled, which meant a doubled reading public, 90 per cent of it literate. Libraries multiplied. In 1825, it was calculated, New York, Boston, Philadelphia, and Baltimore libraries had twenty times as many books to lend as the entire nation had owned in 1800. Meanwhile, because of improvements in printing processes, the cost of book production dropped sharply. The Columbian Iron Press, cylinder and steam presses, printing from plates, better binding machines, and cheap cloth bindings all meant that more and less expensive books were available to the American public.[36]

Edinburgh Review (December, 1818), "when a six-weeks passage brings them in our own tongue, our sense, science, and genius, in bales and hogsheads?" Mott, *Golden Multitudes*, lists as best sellers the following: 1770–1779, Goldsmith's *Vicar of Wakefield*, Sterne's *Tristram Shandy*, Defoe's *Robinson Crusoe*, John Gregory's *A Father's Legacy to His Daughters*, Chesterfield's *Letters to His Son*, Paine's *Common Sense*, Milton's *Paradise Lost*, Thomson's *The Seasons*, Young's *Night Thoughts*; 1780–99, Trumbull's *M'Fingal*, Richardson's *Clarissa*, Cowper's *The Task*, Burns's *Poems*, *The Federalist*, Fox's *Book of Martyrs*, Swift's *Gulliver's Travels*, Franklin's *Autobiography*, Paine's *Age of Reason*, Hume's *History of Great Britain*, Susannah Rowson's *Charlotte Temple*, Hannah Foster's *The Coquette*, Volney's *Ruins*, Shakespeare's *Plays*, Regina Roche's *Children of the Abbey*; 1800–1820, Weem's *Life of Washington*, Addison and Steele's *The Spectator*, Byron's *Poems*, Irving's *History of New York* and *The Sketch Book*, Jane Porter's *Thaddeus of Warsaw* and *Scottish Chiefs*, Tom Moore's *Lalla Rookh*, Scott's *Poems*, *Waverley*, and *Rob Roy*. The decade 1820–1830 was dominated by Scott and Cooper.

[35] Too many American readers, complained John Adams, were "disposed to encourage a thousand foolish republications from Europe rather than one useful work of their own growth." *Ibid.*, p. 125; and P. L. Ford (ed.), *Statesman and Friend: Correspondence of John Adams with Benjamin Waterhouse 1784–1822* (Boston, 1927), p. 41.

[36] James D. Hart, *The Popular Book* (New York, 1950), pp. 39, 53.

The literature produced in America between 1776 and 1830 is not easily classifiable. It is usually lumped together as "pre-Romantic," or "late neoclassic," or "transitional," and treated in most literary histories as a sort of blank space between the Revolution and the mature work of Irving, Bryant, and Cooper. The fact is, of course, that these were years of intense and energetic (if not always distinguished) literary activity, and that out of them emerged a strong, native, belletristic tradition. In the last two decades of the eighteenth century and the first decade of the nineteenth, there emerged an American profession of letters, and with it a dim recognition of the function of literature as art rather than utility.

The United States no doubt possessed as large a percentage of men of talent as any other nation, but the effort needed to construct a new state channeled much of America's best talents into other than literary pursuits. There was far too much to know and to say about the rights of man, the nature of government, and the structure of society for men to deal exhaustively with the artistic aspect of life, too much to do to build a state to expend effort in making a poem. Politics, Samuel Miller explained quite truthfully in his *Retrospect of the Eighteenth Century* (1802), stifled American literature by making it a vehicle for partisanship rather than art. As Emerson remarked in the 1830's, fifty years of demands for a great American literature produced none at all.

A distinguishing trait of the literature produced during the period 1776–1830 was the growing popularity of those forms in which the ideas of the writer were shaped within a loosely knit artistic pattern (the novel, poem, drama, and essay), and the decreasing importance of such once-popular forms as the sermon, the journal, the travel narrative, and the autobiography.

The development of the essay depended, as it had in England, on the growth of the newspaper and periodical magazine. American essayists naturally copied the great British models—Addison, Steele, Swift, Goldsmith, Johnson, Butler—throughout the eighteenth century. After 1780, the political struggles of Federalist and Republican, the manners of a self-consciously sophisticated society, and the fads and follies of a gawky young republic all fitted the requirements of the eighteenth-century essay form.

By 1800 there were more than 150 newspapers in the United States and by 1810 double that number, few of them without a "Lounger," a

"Scriblerus," or a "Hermit" pretending to be latter-day Addisons or Swifts. Like their English models, American essayists posed as "Jonathan Oldstyle" (Irving), "Oliver Oldschool" (Joseph Dennie), "Tomo-Cheeki" (Philip Freneau), or "Salamagundi" (James Paulding and the Irvings), in an attempt to domesticate the British essay tradition. Noah Webster's *Prompter* (1791) and his *Essays and Fugitive Writings* (1790), Mrs. Judith Murray's *Gleaner* essays (1798), William Wirt's *Letters of a British Spy* (1803), and others like them were recognizable (though not especially successful) attempts to create an American essay in the orthodox neoclassic style. Dennie's *Lay Preacher* pieces, most of them published in *The Portfolio* after 1800, were probably the finest done in the traditional Addison manner. Washington Irving, who served his apprenticeship with the *Jonathan Oldstyle* (1802) and *Salamagundi* series (1807–8), became, with the appearance of *The Sketchbook* (1819–20), the first truly American essayist—in style, spirit, subject matter, and mood. With Irving the essay came of age in the United States.[37]

The American novel still faced lingering public and ecclesiastical hostility. Timothy Dwight and Noah Webster, who were barely willing to tolerate fiction, probably represented the majority point of view in their conviction that the novel was not really a valuable form of literary art, worthy of serious effort. Ministers cautioned that novels "lead onto a path of vice . . . inflame the passions and corrupt the heart . . . pollute the imaginations of young women and likewise give them false ideas of life." Nevertheless, the demand for fiction increased rapidly, magazine editors printed more and more novels, and circulating libraries stocked greater numbers of them each year. Despite the warnings, there was a profitable market for fiction which American authors hoped to supply. In response to accusations of "immorality" and "falseness to life," novelists claimed that their tales were really "moral lessons," usually appending a subtitle or preface to point out that their plots were "founded on fact" and were "truthful representations of human passions."

There were four major strains in the early American novel: the sentimental-didactic, the satiric, the Gothic, and the historical romance.[38] All were closely imitative of the eighteenth- and early-nine-

---

[37] Spiller, *Literary History,* pp. 174–177.
[38] See A. H. Quinn, *American Fiction* (New York, 1936), pp. 1–39; Lily M. Loshe, *The Early American Novel* (New York, 1907); Herbert Brown,

teenth-century British novel. The first of these, derived from Samuel Richardson and the British sentimentalists, was by far the most popular variety until it was displaced by the historical romances of Scott. After 1750 Richardsonian sentimentalism covered America and England with a rainstorm of tears, deluging the public with sad tales of seduction, suicide, and sentiment told in the form of letters in the "epistolary" style. Women read Richardson's *Pamela* or *Clarissa* or *Sir Richard Grandison* voraciously and slept with the books under their pillows. Goethe's *Sorrows of Werther* (1794), soaked in an even more excessive sentimentalism, made such a strong appeal in combination with Richardson that at least five novels were written against it; *The Slave of Passion* (1802), for example, has as its explanatory subtitle. "The Fruits of Werther." Though a widely reprinted article of 1791 argued "Novel Reading as a Cause of Depravity," Richardson's defenders claimed that such novels really "cultivated the Principles of Virtue and Religion in Minds of Youth of Both Sexes" by truthfully presenting the wages of sin—albeit titillatingly.[39]

Scores of Richardsonian imitations appeared in America in the 1780's and 1790's, built to the master's formula of sighs, seduction (successful and unsuccessful), duels or suicides, perhaps a marriage and always with a moral, decorated with alluring subtitles such as "Female Frailty," "Delicate Embarrassments," or "Venial Trespasses." There was even a journal, *The American Moral and Sentimental Magazine*, founded in 1797. Very few novels published in England or America during these years were free from Richardson's influence. Two characteristic American products may be noted. William Hill Brown's novel *The Power of Sympathy* (1789) (long atttributed to Sarah Morton) was "founded in truth" and, according to its preface, intended "to expose the dangerous consequences of Seduction and to set forth the advantages of Female Education," which it did with a spectacular plot compounded of seduction, near-incest, kidnaping, attempted rape, and suicide. Susannah Rowson's *Charlotte Temple* (1791), which eventually ran through nearly 200 editions, had a similar plot and a

---

The Sentimental Novel in America (Durham, N.C., 1940); and Alexander Cowie, *The Rise of the American Novel* (New York, 1948), for discussion of the early novel.

[39] Spiller, *Literary History*, I, 177–179. A detailed study is G. Harrison Orians, "Censure of Fiction in American Romances and Magazines 1789–1810," *PMLA*, LII (1937), 195–224.

sequel, *Lucy Temple,* the story of Charlotte's illegitimate daughter, which went through thirty-one editions itself.[40]

The satiric novel, never so popular as the sentimental, stemmed from Swift, Cervantes, Defoe, and Smollett. Royall Tyler's *Algerine Captive* (1797) poked jabs at New England, contemporary politics, sentimentalism, slavery, and kindred targets. More important, however, was Hugh Henry Brackenridge's *Modern Chivalry* (1792–97), a massive work published in sections which recited the adventures of an American Quixote, Captain Farrago, and his comic Irish servant Teague. Brackenridge left few contemporary attitudes, men, and institutions unscathed by his slashing wit, and although the book is as much polemic as fiction, it marked the beginning of an authentic American satiric tradition.[41]

The Gothic novel of terror, suspense, and mystery which, in the hands of Walpole, "Monk" Lewis, Mrs. Radcliffe, and William Godwin, swept over England found a gifted American practitioner in Charles Brockden Brown of Philadelphia. Brown, the most talented American novelist before Cooper, published *Wieland* (1798), *Ormond* (1799), *Arthur Mervyn* (1799), and *Edgar Huntly* (1799), all of them containing passages of real power, though uneven in quality. *Wieland,* his best novel, brought praise from such men as Keats, Godwin, and Hazlitt, who found it something more than simply another Gothic imitation. Brown hoped, he said, to create a truly native fiction by avoiding "the puerile superstitions and exploded manners, Gothic castles, and chimeras" of British novels and by using "only the American environment of the present." Never able to discipline his considerable talent, he scattered his energies in magazine editing, reviewing, hasty hack work, and philosophizing, and published no novels at all after 1804. Nevertheless, by virtue of his skill in adapting the Gothic tradition to American uses, Brown deserves to be called the first major American novelist.[42]

The fourth strand of American fiction, the historical romance, emerged directly from the work of Sir Walter Scott, whose novels of

[40] See Hart, *Popular Book,* Chap. IV.

[41] The best study of *Modern Chivalry* is C. M. Newlin's Introduction to his edition (New York, 1937), pp. ix–xi.

[42] There is as yet no satisfactory modern study of Brown. Martin Vilas, *Charles Brockden Brown* (Burlington, Vt., 1904); Lily D. Loshe, *The Early American Novel* (New York, 1902), pp. 29–58; and Ernest Marchand's Introduction to his edition of *Ormond* (New York, 1937), are useful sources.

history, legend, adventure, folklore, scenery, love, and patriotism took the early nineteenth century by storm. His popularity in the United States was immense. His verse was memorized by thousands of school-children and read aloud in countless family circles; Dickens in 1842 even discovered a Choctaw Indian who could recite whole sections of *The Lady of the Lake.* Announcement of a new Scott novel, according to bookseller Samuel Goodrich, caused "a greater sensation in the United States than some of the battles of Napoleon," while Fitz-Greene Halleck believed that Scott's American popularity was "probably never equalled in the history of literature."

Americans bought Scott novels by the thousands (a half-million volumes before 1823), adapted, summarized, dramatized, and imitated them. Though a stubborn minority of critics maintained that his cele-brations of feudalism and ceremony encouraged "a diseased and perverted taste for the luxurious and aristocratic" inconsistent with democracy, few of his admirers cared. In the South, where Scott's chivalric apparatus found an especially responsive audience, there were thirty-five towns named Waverley, hundreds of little girls named Rowena, and sidewheel steamers named *Rob Roy* and *Marmion.*[43]

Scott's fervent Scottish nationalism and his skillful use of historical materials were exactly what American authors hoped to emulate; why could not they, using their own past as Scott used his, create an art of equal value? Rufus Choate's oration at Salem in 1810, titled *The Im-portance of Illustrating New England History by a Series of Romances Like the Waverley Novels,* summarized popular opinion exactly; every week, John Neal grumbled, seemed to see a new novel "after the Scot-tish fashion" with "native Rodericks and Rob Roys" by dozens. James Kirke Paulding, Catherine Sedgwick, John Pendleton Kennedy, Wil-liam Gilmore Simms, Daniel Thompson, and Neal himself tried to fit the Scott formula to American materials without marked success.[44] But James Fenimore Cooper, after trying his hand at a Jane Austen-like novel of manners, wrote *The Spy* in 1821, *The Pioneers* in 1823, *The Last of the Mohicans* in 1826, and thirty more. When Natty Bumppo walked into American fiction and leaned on his long rifle, the American novel came of age.

[43] On the vogue of Scott in America, see *Golden Multitudes,* "The Wizard of the North," pp. 47–70, and Hart, *Popular Book,* pp. 69–78.
[44] E. E. Leisy, *The American Historical Novel* (Norman, Okla., 1950), has a good discussion of the post-Scott novels of history.

Before Cooper, however, the work of another writer provided evidence to show that American literature was slowly emerging from its colonial dependency. Washington Irving was not a novelist and did not intend to be. Born and reared in a well-to-do New York City family, Irving grew up into a somewhat dilettantish young man about town, casually studied law, traveled in Europe, and patronized the fashionable coffeehouses and theaters. With a group of other bright young New Yorkers he turned out *The Salamagundi Papers* (1807–8), the cleverest of all the Addisonian-style essays so widely popular at the time, and then by himself the burlesque *Knickerbocker's History of New York* (1809), which brought him immediate fame. After drifting in and out of the family hardware business, magazine editing, and travel, he returned to writing. *The Sketchbook* (1819–20), recognized at once as a major work and received with critical acclaim on both sides of the Atlantic, was followed by eleven years in Europe, *Bracebridge Hall* (1822), *Tales of a Traveller* (1824), *Columbus* (1828), *The Conquest of Granada* (1829), and *The Alhambra* (1832). In 1831 Irving returned to the United States to spend the rest of his years at his estate, Sunnyside on the Hudson, except for four years as American ambassador to Spain and a tour of the West, recounted in *Tour on the Prairies* (1835) and *Astoria* (1836).

Irving's work was a happy illustration of the late eighteenth century's blend of neoclassicism and Romanticism, compounded of humor, urbanity, sentiment, interest in nature, human nature, and manners, restrained by rationality and good sense. His greatest asset was an easy, pliable, charming style which placed him among the major prose writers of his (or any) age. Irving's art depended little on plot or action; a cursory analysis of an Irving story such as *Rip Van Winkle* or *The Legend of Sleepy Hollow* reveals how little actually happens, and how much of the tale's effectiveness depends on his skill in language, mood, color, description, and characterization. Plot, Irving wrote in 1824, was to him "merely a frame on which to stretch my materials." He was much more concerned with "the play of thought and sentiment and language, the weaving of characters . . . the familiar and faithful exhibition of scenes in common life; and the half-concealed vein of humor that is often playing through the whole." There was little intellectual or emotional depth in his work, and one may read through him without ever stumbling against an idea—though certainly no reader of Irving ever cared, as Irving himself did not. "I have always been of the opinion," he said in *Bracebridge Hall,* "that much good might be done by keeping mankind in good humor with one another," which is probably the best summary ever made of his art.

Washington Irving became the first American classic. He was the first to compel Europe to recognize an American author as a major literary figure—not as an imitator of a British author or style, but as an American artist with a mind and an art of his own. *The Sketchbook* was a swift, decisive answer to Sidney Smith's famous sneer of 1820, "Who reads an American book?" In addition, Irving served his generation as a sort of literary ambassador at large to Europe from America and to America from Europe. In the midst of a rancorous war between American and British critics, which often degenerated into name-calling, Irving had much to do restoring good manners and common sense to the argument. He was thoroughly American; yet he knew Europe well, revered its past and its traditions, and at the same time felt deep pride in his own native land and its potentialities. Eventually, by his pen and his example, he helped bring about a critical truce.

Poetry found hard going in the period 1776–1830. The desire for creative poetic art was strong, no doubt, but scattered and misdirected. There were a number of young men who believed that there had been too much politics and not enough poetry, such as John Trumbull, who in his master's oration at Yale chose not to deal with the customary topics of theology or politics, but titled his "An Essay on the Use and Advantage of the Fine Arts." Other men, such as Timothy Dwight, Joel Barlow, Francis Hopkinson, Hugh Brackenridge, and Philip Freneau, agreed with Trumbull that the time was right for the creation of an American poetic tradition equal to any that the world had to offer. But all of them found that the way of the poet was narrow and hard in a nation which within two generations suffered two wars with England, a near war with France, and bitter political rivalries that split society apart. Trumbull abandoned literature and turned to law, Barlow to politics, Dwight to theology and education. Freneau neglected his great lyric gifts for satire and journalism. "Barbers cannot exist as such among a people who have neither hair or beards," he once wrote despairingly. "How then can a poet hope for success in a city where there are not three persons possessed of elegant ideas?"[45]

American poetry, for the most part, was caught in the trap of imitation. Before 1800 the worship of neoclassicism hemmed in American

[45] Taylor, *American Letters,* pp. 56–57.

versifiers and vitiated what freshness and energy they had. If an American wished to write poetry, he could choose either the mock heroic, iambic pentameter style already exhausted by Pope and his followers, or the limited blank verse style of Thompson and Young. A little later he could write, if he wished, like Ossian, Leigh Hunt, Scott, Byron, Moore, Montgomery, or Gray, which gave him merely a wider choice of imitations.[46] What was popular in England was eagerly copied in the United States—it was easier, and much safer, for American poets to follow the accepted British masters and current British tastes than to attempt an original style. Dozens of promising young men thus chose to submit to the tyranny of imitation, despite loud demands from critics and public for a "native" American verse.

These demands for nationalism in literature created other problems. Convinced that they had to be "native" above all else, poets tended to protest too much that they were *American*, clouding their artistic judgments with patriotism. Talented poets therefore expended their energy on "national epics" such as Barlow's *Columbiad* (1807) and Dwight's *Greenfield Hill* (1794). The flood of imitative satiric verse inundated nearly everything else. Satire lent itself admirably to wartime anti-British feeling and postwar political partisanship; lampoons, mock heroics, Hudibrastics, burlesques, "Rolliads" and "Anarchiads," tirades, and retorts crowded the newspaper columns for forty years after 1770. *The Echo,* for example, a journal which ran for fourteen years, published very little else. Pope, Dryden, Butler, Swift, and Churchill gave Americans models to copy, the combative atmosphere of the times gave the impetus, and contemporary events provided ample materials. There was very little room for any other kind of poetry until the small voices of the Romantics began to be heard after 1800.

The obstacles faced by American poets during the Revolutionary and Federalist decades are aptly illustrated by the group known as the Connecticut (or Hartford) Wits.[47] All New Englanders, most of them loosely associated with Yale and Connecticut, the group is usually con-

---

[46] Joseph Hutton's collection, *Leisure Hours* (1812), provides an excellent example of what was wrong with most contemporary American verse. Hutton managed in separate poems to copy Goldsmith, Pope, Cunningham, Montgomery, Young, Gray, and Akenside, without an original line or thought of his own in the entire volume.

[47] The best study is Leon Howard, *The Connecticut Wits* (Chicago, 1943). V. L. Parrington's Introduction to *The Connecticut Wits* (New York, 1926) is old, but interesting and provocative.

sidered to include John Trumbull, Timothy Dwight, Joel Barlow (its three most prominent members), David Humphreys, Lemuel Hopkins, Richard Alsop, Theodore Dwight, and a few others. Trumbull, Dwight, and Barlow, at least, were men of real poetic gifts, yet none produced more than a few lines of memorable verse, nor broke away in the slightest from the rigid confines of eighteenth-century poetic tradition. All knew English satire thoroughly, acknowledged the rules of classicism, and followed Pope, Prior, Churchill, Thomson, and the rest so carefully that there is hardly an original line to be found among them. All of them abandoned poetry fairly early in life to plunge into the three most active fields of contemporary endeavor—law, theology, and politics.

John Trumbull first gained an audience with *The Progress of Dulness* (1773), a youthful, impish attack on fashionable education, and followed with *M'Fingal* (1776), a slashing wartime burlesque of Toryism. After these Trumbull busied himself with law. Timothy Dwight began his poetic career in 1785 with a 10,000-line New England epic called *The Conquest of Canaan*. His *Triumph of Infidelity* (1788) was a powerful satiric diatribe against deism and evangelism, while *Greenfield Hill* (1794), a close imitation of British models, was a loving Yankee portrait of New England. In 1795, however, Dwight became president of Yale, where he remained to earn the title of "Protestant Pope of New England" for his stout defense of Congregational orthodoxy. Joel Barlow, the youngest of the three, first planned a tremendous national epic, *The Vision of Columbus* (1787), which he later reworked into *The Columbiad* (1807), one of the most complete failures in American poetic hsitory. Inventor, politician, lawyer, revolutionary, minister to Algeria, and ambassador to France, Barlow had neither time nor opportunity to develop his talents. None of the Wits, despite their collective potential, made any lasting contributions to the development of an American poetic tradition.[48]

The case of Philip Freneau, the first real poetic voice to be heard in the United States, was somewhat different. Like Paine, Jefferson, and Barlow, Freneau was a child of the American Enlightenment, and like them he threw himself into a variety of contemporary causes. A Princeton graduate in the same class with Madison, Burr, and Bracken-

[48] Full-length studies are Alexander Cowie, *John Trumbull, Connecticut Wit* (Chapel Hill, N.C., 1936); Charles E. Cuningham, *Timothy Dwight* (New York, 1942); and James Woodress, *A Yankee's Odyssey: The Life of Joel Barlow* (Philadelphia, 1958).

ridge, Freneau collaborated with Brackenridge on a long, aggressively patriotic commencement poem in 1771, "The Rising Glory of America." Though determined to be a poet (for, as he said, "To write was my sad destiny/The worst of trades, we all agree"), Freneau first served a sentence on a British prison ship, enlisted in the Revolutionary army, sailed as a sea captain, and spent several years in political journalism. His poetry, issued in collected editions in 1786, 1788, 1809, and 1815, falls in four fairly clear divisions. His political verse, written in the usual neoclassic vein, was of uneven quality. Freneau hated British and Federalists with almost equal fury, and his anti-Federalist verse was so virulent that Washington himself called him "that rascal Freneau." He was proud of his service to the cause of liberalism, and of his determination to be

> Hostile to garter, ribbon, crown, and star;
> Still on the people's, still on Freedom's side,
> With full-determined aim, to baffle every claim,
> Of well-born wights, that aim to mount and ride.

Freneau's political satire is less important to the American poetic tradition than his other verse. His lyric poetry, dealing with nature, beauty, transience, the past, and personal experience, shows him to have been a man of genuine poetic imagination. The delicacy and skill of his lyric verse is unmatched by any American poet of his day—and by few British. At times reminiscent of Gray, Collins, and Akenside, there is in Freneau a strong strain of freshness and originality, anticipatory of Wordsworth, Coleridge, and the young Keats. Poems such as "The Wild Honeysuckle," "To the Brave Americans," "The Power of Fancy," "The Hurricane," and sections of "The House of Night" have a haunting beauty equal to the best poetry produced anywhere during the period.

Third, Freneau after 1812 produced an unusual kind of rough, realistic, local color verse, somewhat parallel to that of Robert Burns—"The Jug of Rum," "The Drunken Soldier," "The Virtue of Tobacco," and so on—which, had he continued it, might have initiated a new American style. Fourth, Freneau, in spite of the contradiction in terms, was a deist poet, who in a small body of excellent work put into verse such central deist-Unitarian doctrines as "The Uniformity and Perfection of Nature" and "The Religion of Nature." Most of all, Freneau's importance lies in the fact that he alone broke out of the constrictions of neoclassical imitation to look at life directly, read it imaginatively, and record it sensitively. He was, despite his restlessness and lack of artistic discipline, the first major American poet.[49]

Except for Freneau, American poetry was feeble and undistinguished until the appearance of Bryant, Poe, Emerson, and Longfellow. Poetry before 1820 generally lacked direction, status, and energy; furthermore, in an era dominated by Wordsworth, Coleridge, Scott, Byron, Shelley, and Keats, it was understandably difficult for lesser bards, American or English, to attract much notice. Except for the lyric voice of Freneau, American poetry was largely given over to minor imitators of little importance. In New York City a group of bright young men, known as "Knickerbockers," tried their hands at verse of some vigor, though hardly above mediocrity.[50] James Kirke Paulding, who also wrote novels, essays, and plays, wrote a frontier epic, *The Backwoodsman* (1818), of commendable freshness. Fitz-Greene Halleck, steeped in Scott, Byron, and Campbell, wrote of nature, Indians, and American history, leaving in "Marco Bozzaris" (1828), a poem on Greek independence, a schoolboy declamation piece that remained popular for fifty years. Joseph Rodman Drake, heralded as the best of the group, died young in 1820; Nathaniel P. Willis was a better essayist and critic than poet, but no more than mediocre as either. There were dozens of Scott imitators (E. C. Holland, James Fennell, and others), Byronists like John Neal and James Gates Percival, or moral sentimentalists such as Richard Dabney, whose *Poems* (1814) illustrated "simple moral emotions," and Mrs. Lydia Sigourney, the undisputed queen of sentimental verse, whose output totaled 67 volumes. No period in American literary history produced less distinguished poetry than the two decades from 1800 to 1820.

American literature from 1776 to 1830 was in large part derivative, imitative, dependent upon Britain for its standards and inspiration. It was, however, increasingly nationalistic in spirit, and consciously committed to the use of native materials and the expression of native

[49] The best brief estimates of Freneau are still Harry H. Clark's Introduction to *The Poems of Freneau* (New York, 1929), and Clark's "What Made Freneau the Father of American Poetry?" *Studies in Philology*, XXVI (1929), 1–22. Nelson Adkins, *Philip Freneau and the Cosmic Enigma* (New York, 1949), is a good study of his life, ideas, and influences, and Lewis Leary's *That Rascal Freneau* (New Brunswick, 1941) is the best biography.

[50] See Kendall Taft, *The Minor Knickerbockers* (New York, 1947), for estimates of this group and samples of its work.

attitudes. It was still ridden by a colonial complex, lacking in confidence of its own literary taste and ideas, fearful of not conforming to presumably superior British literary norms. It was also primarily moralistic. Americans still believed that novels should instruct, dramas draw moral lessons, satires discover and castigate error, essays debate and argue, poetry please and teach. Few American artists attempted to create a literature for its own values. In effect, they were trying to create a new, native, independent literature within the framework of an older colonial, British, basically neoclassic tradition. What Americans wanted, no matter how loudly they protested against "foreign domination," was their own Augustan age, built out of American materials and attitudes comfortably couched in the approved, time-tested literary forms that could be accepted with confidence and safety. The real attainment of American literary independence was yet to come.

Though the American colonies were settled at the height of England's Golden Age of drama, there was no colonial American theater for nearly a hundred years after the settlement.[51] Drama, a peculiarly social art, required a fairly sophisticated, cohesive urban life to support it, something that seventeenth-century America did not have. Actors and plays were viewed with suspicion and distaste by the early rulers of both Northern and Southern colonies. New England Calvinists, the Dutch of New York, and the Quakers of Pennsylvania all held strong religious objections to theatrical performances, which were believed to encourage shiftlessness, idleness, and immorality. In the eighteenth century, however, with the growth of cities and the establishment of a wealthy leisure class—and in the South the planter group—life became richer in social, intellectual, and artistic activities. New York, Philadelphia, Baltimore, Charleston, Williamsburg, and other cities contained a self-consciously cultivated society which could not only support a theater, but hoped to emulate the fashions of British aristocracy by encouraging the production of plays.

[51] Oral S. Coad and Edwin Mims, Jr., *The American Stage* (New Haven, 1929), is the most useful study of American theatrical history. However, one should also consult Crawford, Hornblow, Moody, and Quinn, listed in the Bibliography. A good brief treatment is A. H. Quinn, "The Early Drama, 1756–1860," in *The Cambridge History of American Literature* (New York, 1917), II, 185–215. Allan Gates Halline, *American Plays* (New York, 1935), reprints a number of representative early plays, with notes and introductions. Spiller *et al.*, *Literary History*, I, 184–192, has a brief discussion of early drama, and brief notes on early playwrights.

In the opening years of the eighteenth century itinerant English actors and companies made fairly regular tours of the Southern and Middle colonies, avoiding Puritan New England. Tony Aston, a comedian who advertised himself as "Gentleman, Lawyer, Poet, Actor, Soldier, Sailor, Exciseman, and Publican," made such a tour of the Carolinas in 1702–4, certainly one of the very first to do so. Williamsburg built a theater in 1716, New York in 1732, Charleston in 1735 (or 1736), though plays were more often presented in ballrooms, taverns, barns, and assembly halls. There are records of performances by college students at William and Mary and Yale, where one observer grumbled that they had "turn'd College into Drury Lane" to the detriment of "the more solid parts of learning."[52]

Murray and Kean's company had great success in New York and Philadelphia in 1750, but the first professional company to play regularly to American audiences was Lewis Hallam's London company, which opened at Williamsburg in 1752 and moved later to New York and Philadelphia. When Hallam died, his widow married David Douglass, who kept the troupe together until the Revolution drove the company to Jamaica for the duration. To accommodate the Hallams and other companies, new theaters sprang up in the 1760's, such as the Chapel Street and the John Street in New York City, and the Southwark in Philadelphia. Except for the accident of location, these companies were no different from British companies in England, drawing their talent from the London stage and playing Shakespeare, Gay, Otway, Addison, Colley Cibber, Farquhar, Sheridan, and others from the standard English repertoire. The single play written by an Americon be presented by a professional company before the Revolution, Thomas Godfrey's *Prince of Parthia* (1767), was an imitation (albeit a good one) of Jacobean tragedy.[53]

In 1774 the Continental Congress asked for the suspension of "horseracing, gambling, cockfighting, exhibitions of shows, plays, and other expensive diversions and entertainments." In the cities, most of which were occupied by the British, there were a few theatricals for the amusement of resident British and local society, but most actors retired either to London or the West Indies during the war. Immediately afterward they flocked back. A hastily organized company played the 1782–83 season in Baltimore and New York. Lewis Hallam, Jr., arrived with

[52] Spiller *et al.*, *Literary History,* I, 128, 184–191.
[53] Coad and Mims, *American Stage,* "Our Infant Stage," pp. 9–29.

another group in Philadelphia in 1784 and moved to New York in 1785. John Henry, a talented Irish actor, came to the United States at almost the same time to join Hallam and form the Old American Company, which dominated the American theater for another decade. In 1794 Thomas Wignell withdrew from it to form a company of his own in Philadelphia, leaving the Old American players, now owned by Hallam and William Dunlap, in control of the New York stage.[54]

Theological opposition to the theater gradually disappeared after the Revolution, though some prejudice remained. In 1788 it was still necessary to advertise plays as "moral lectures"; managers therefore billed *Richard III* as "The Fate of Tyranny," *Hamlet* as "Filial Piety," and *She Stoops to Conquer* as "Improper Education." Since the actors were almost unanimously British, they too faced hostility as "foreign minions, lately the enemy." During the great epidemics of the 1790's many citizens preferred to avoid crowds, and many too disliked the rowdiness of theatergoers, who sometimes shouted profanities and threw garbage. Theaters were also expensive; New York's Park Street Theater in 1798 charged $2 for a box and $1 for the gallery.[55]

On the other hand, George Washington's well-known love of the theater gave it a new kind of respectability. The President often attended plays, and during the war (the rumor was) he once approved a performance of Addison's *Cato* as beneficial to troop morale. Wealthy gentlemen in Boston, New York, Philadelphia, and Charleston, anxious to imitate London and Paris, campaigned against restrictive legislation and succeeded in repealing most of it by 1795. A Boston group built the Federal Street Theater (designed by the great Charles Bulfinch) and opened it in 1794, at almost the same time as Philadelphia's new Chestnut Street Theater. Charleston built its Church Street Theater in 1786, and New York's famous Park Theater was completed in 1798.[56] Ten years after Yorktown the American theater was in a rather sound state of health. At least two permanent companies, the Old American and Wignell's Philadelphia group, gave highly skilled professional performances probably equal to those of the better British troupes.

London still provided both plays and players for the American stage, with two notable exceptions, Royall Tyler (1757–1826) and William Dunlap (1766–1839). Tyler, a Boston lawyer who later became Chief

---

[54] *Ibid.*, pp. 31–44.
[55] *Ibid.*, pp. 21 ff.
[56] *Ibid.*, pp. 40, 47, 51–71, 82, 87–88.

Justice of the Vermont Supreme Court, wrote a delightful Sheridan-like comedy of manners, *The Contrast,* first performed in 1787. Built about the theme of native American worth versus foreign affectations, the play contrasted Colonel Manly, an upstanding, true-blue American, with Billy Dimple, an Anglicized fop, much to the former's advantage. The character of Jonathan, a Yankee farmer, played to the hilt by Thomas Wignell, was a major theatrical creation and the first of a long line of comic rustics.[57] More important in the history of American drama, however, was William Dunlap, who helped to organize and stabilize the theater during its most chaotic period. Dunlap, a talented painter who studied with the great Benjamin West in London, returned to New York with a play of his own, modeled on Tyler's success. It failed, but his second play, *The Father* (1788), started him on a long theatrical career that did not end until forty years later.[58]

Dunlap wrote at least sixty-five plays and adapted a large number of French and German plays for American production. His best play, *André* (1798), which dealt with the capture and execution of the British spy, was also his most successful one. He purchased a share of Hallam and Hodgkinson's Old American Company in 1796, managed it until its bankruptcy in 1805, and also managed New York's Park Theater for some years after 1798. In addition, Dunlap helped to found the National Academy of Design, taught painting, and wrote *The History of the American Theater* (1832) which, despite errors and personal bias, is still a landmark in American theatrical history. He wrote and produced many bad and mediocre plays, yet he was not afraid to experiment, encouraged originality, and was himself a serious student of producing, acting, staging, and management.[59]

Dunlap's collapse into bankruptcy illustrated the difficulties faced by the American theater in the decade before the War of 1812. Little hostility against the stage remained anywhere in the United States, but American drama needed a playgoing public accustomed to regular attendance, better playhouses, and good plays, none of which it pos-

[57] Halline, *American Plays,* Introduction to *The Contrast;* Spiller *et al., Literary History,* I, 184–192.

[58] Dunlap's prologue offered his drama as ". . . a frugal, plain repast, Fruit of our country's growth, food for the mind, Where moral truth and sentiment are joined."

[59] *Ibid.,* Introduction to *André;* Coad and Mims, *American Stage,* pp. 34, 52–59, 102, *passim;* Van Wyck Brooks, *The World of Washington Irving* (New York, 1944), Chap. VII, "William Dunlap and His Circle," is excellent reading.

sessed. Troubles with England and France, embargo, depression, and bitter political factionalism all contributed to problems of managers and actors. For one thing, the American stage lacked distinguished American playwrights. Of the dozens of authors who wrote for the stage before 1830, only James Nelson Barker (1784–1855) and John Howard Payne (1791–1852) gained noticeable reputations, and those small ones. Barker, a Philadelphian, wrote *Tears and Smiles* (1807), a successful comedy patterned on Tyler's hit, and followed with *The Indian Princess, or La Belle Sauvage* (1808), a very popular operatic drama centered on the Pocahontas-John Smith legend, a theme due to appear again and again in the American theater. Barker continued to use American materials and themes for his subsequent plays, the best of which was *Superstition* (1824), a powerful treatment of the Salem witchcraft delusions which A. H. Quinn called with some justice "The best play written so far in America."[60] Payne, who was a popular actor at London's Drury Lane, wrote more than sixty plays, nearly all of them adaptations of English, French, and German plays; his chief fame, however, came from his song, "Home, Sweet Home," which he inserted in his opera, *Clari,* in 1823.[61]

Though most of the plays written and produced by Americans during the years from 1800 to 1830 were undistinguished, an amazing number *were* written, and written with a deliberate emphasis on American materials for American audiences. Arthur Hobson Quinn counted 700 plays by Americans actually produced before 1860, perhaps one-third of them before 1832.[62] In them appeared a number of themes and characters destined to become familiar in American drama, poetry, and fiction—Pocahontas, Rip Van Winkle, the Indian-white conflict, the raw frontiersman, the Plymouth settlers, the stage Yankee, the city dude, the blustering soldier, the Revolutionary soldier-hero, and many others.[63] If a mature and artistic native drama had not yet appeared by

[60] Quinn, *American Drama*, p. 51.

[61] Spiller *et al., Literary History,* I, 238–239, 281–283. Quinn, "Early Drama," pp. 215–217.

[62] *Ibid.,* pp. 231–233.

[63] There were also large numbers of mediocre plays written about current events, such as Samuel Low's *Politicians Outwitted* (1789), concerning Constitutional ratification; Susannah Rowson's *Slaves in Algiers* (1794); John Murdock's *Triumphs of Love* (1795), inspired by the Whisky Rebellion; and William Dunlap's *Yankee Chronology* (1812), celebrating the *Constitution-Guerrière* battle. Charles Breck's *Fox Chase* (1806) and *The Trust* (1809) and A. B. Lindsley's *Love and Friendship* (1809) were popular imitations of

1830, it was not for lack of effort by American playwrights.

Between 1776 and 1830, then, the American stage showed encouraging signs of strength and independence. After 1812 traveling companies carried plays inland, down the Ohio and Mississippi and into the hinterlands to remote hamlets; amateur "Thespian" or "Aeolian" societies proliferated in colleges and cities. The increasing popularity of the theater is illustrated by the boom in building between 1820 and 1830—the Bowery, the Chatham, the Lafayette, and the New Park Street in New York, Boston's Tremont, the New Chestnut Street and Arch Street in Philadelphia, among others. The American stage supported several skilled groups of professional actors (some imported but a growing percentage native-trained), a corps of experienced managers, and a number of knowledgeable producers.

Still, few theaters or companies could be called prosperous. Actors were badly paid and managers were forced to hold "third nights" and "farewell tours" to augment stars' pay. Pay for playwrights was equally small; $500 for an original play was unusual, $100 for an adaptation generous.[64] The most serious defect of the American stage was the paucity of good plays. No dramatist appeared before the Civil War to equal the achievements of American poets, novelists, or essayists—though in justice it should be pointed out that contemporary British dramatic writing was similarly undistinguished. The American stage had not yet outgrown its dependence on England and Europe. Americans were no better than "mental colonists" insofar as the drama was concerned, wrote James Nelson Barker, who found it advisable himself to spread the rumor in 1808 that his play *Marmion* really came from London. The American state was still overawed by the powerful British dramatic tradition, and hesitant to compete with it.

Tyler's *Contrast*, though James Nelson Barker's *Tears and Smiles* (1807) was by far the best.

[64] Spiller *et al., Literary History,* I, 186 ff.

CHAPTER 12

The American Style in Architecture and Art

DEVELOPMENTS in American architecture between 1776 and 1830 were influenced by several important factors. Americans were always building for a shifting, expanding, highly mobile population; in a sense, few structures in the country were considered permanent. The early settlers built for necessity, adapting British and European styles and methods to local conditions. American climate, for example, produced extremes of heat and cold unknown to England or Continental Europe, requiring quite different kinds of living and working structures. Wood, already scarce in England, was the most plentiful American building material. Its wide use in place of stone and brick in Europe necessitated architectural alterations when foreign plans were transferred to American soil, where wood allowed a lightness, roominess, and delicacy of detail impossible in masonry construction. American building therefore from the beginning possessed a distinctively American appearance.

There were no professional architects in the United States until late in the eighteenth century, though there was always a large supply of skilled carpenters and building craftsmen. The majority of American builders followed British guidebooks, such as James Gibbs's *Book of Architecture* (1728), Kent's *Designs of Inigo Jones* (1722), Swan's *British Architect* (1745), and others. Though the main stream of architectural influence was naturally British, colonial builders were also familiar with a wide variety of non-English traditions—French, Swedish, Dutch, and German especially—which helped to give American architecture a definitely cosmopolitan air. There was never (at least until well into the nineteenth century) an identifiable American style of building from North to South to East to West. Even the frame cottage, the closest approach to a distinctively American type, was a composite of English, Dutch, and Swedish influences.[1]

The typical eighteenth-century American architectural style was Georgian, long popular in England through the work of Jones, Gibbs, Wren, and others. Georgian buildings, with their air of quiet opulence, fitted very well the needs of the wealthy American merchants and shippers who wanted dignified, fashionable homes. Georgian influence appeared in every part of the colonies, in public buildings, churches, city homes, and country houses. Working from British books and drawings, amateur architects produced a number of structures worthy of comparison with the better British buildings, among them Andrew Hamilton's Independence Hall and John Kearsley's Christ Church in Philadelphia, or Peter Harrison's Newport synagogue and Boston's King's Chapel.[2]

The Revolution virtually stopped American building. After the war, there was an immediate demand for public buildings to serve the new federal and state governments, and a corresponding demand for the services of expert professional architects. A number of these architects wanted to avoid British models in building, as in other things, and hoped somehow to produce an "American order" fitted to the spirit and ideals of the new nation. Other American builders, however, found much to admire in British architecture and could see no reason to abandon it, preferring to retain British patterns with American adaptations. By 1800 there were two distinct architectural traditions in the United States—a modified British style popular in New England and parts of the Middle States, and a classic style characteristic of the Middle Colonies and the South.[3] The two greatest practitioners of these contrasting architectural styles were Charles Bulfinch of Boston and Thomas Jefferson of Virginia.

Bulfinch, a Harvard graduate of 1781, spent two years touring

[1] For accounts of American architecture, 1776–1830, see Oliver Larkin, *Art and Life in America* (New York, 1949), pp. 34–44, 79–85, 88–96; T. E. Tallmage, *The Story of Architecture in America* (New York, 1936), chaps. II and III; Fiske Kimball, *American Architecture* (Indianapolis, 1928), chaps. VII and VIII; James Fitch, *American Building* (Boston, 1948), Chap. II; and Talbot F. Hamlin, *The American Spirit in Architecture* (New Haven, 1926), chaps. IX and X.

[2] Suzanne LaFollette, *Art in America* (New York, 1929), pp. 25–26; Larkin, *Art in America,* pp. 34–44.

[3] Hamlin, *American Spirit in Architecture,* pp. 6–9.

Britain and the Continent before returning to Boston to accept architectural commissions. Impressed by the work of the brothers Adam, John Soane, and John Wood in England, Bullfinch believed that the Adamesque blend of elegance and restraint suited his native New England exactly. He developed an American version of the Adam style from his London notebooks and sketches, modeling his Colonnade Row in Boston after the Adelphi terrace in London, and continuing with the graceful attached houses he built on Boston's Tontine (or Franklin) Crescent. Bulfinch also enlarged Faneuil Hall; designed capitols at Boston, Hartford, and Augusta; and built Boston's New South Church, India Wharf, and Massachusetts General Hospital. Later he served as architect in charge of the National Capitol in Washington, combining his early manner with modified classic.[4]

Bulfinch's Boston or "Federal" style left a permanent stamp on New England building, augmented by the work of men such as Samuel McIntire and Asher Benjamin. McIntire, who also studied Wren and Inigo Jones, rebuilt Salem into a veritable museum of Federal architecture. Benjamin, whose Charles Street Church in Boston could stand comparison with any of Bulfinch's, spread the Federal style through New England hamlets by his books *The Country Builder's Assistant* (1797, 1798), *The American Builder's Companion* (1806, 1811, etc.), *The Rudiments of Architecture* (1814), and *The Practical Home Carpenter* (1830). New England carpenters, when they moved westward, took Benjamin's books with them, scattering the Adam-Bulfinch style through the Northwest Territory and beyond the Mississippi.[5] Still today, in the small towns of Ohio, Michigan, Illinois, or Iowa, one may see dozens of examples of the Federal style built more than a century ago by frontier carpenters after Benjamin drawings.

Running parallel to the British-styled architecture of New England was the classic style, reflected in the majority of federal buildings constructed after 1790 and in the Southern architecture of Jefferson and his followers. Refusing to copy Britain, some Americans turned to Rome and Greece for inspiration, fancying an analogy between the

[4] Charles A. Place, *Charles Bulfinch, Architect and Citizen* (Boston, 1925), is a full-length biography. Ellen S. Bulfinch, *Life and Letters of Charles Bulfinch* (Boston, 1896), reprints much of the correspondence. Bulfinch's "Federal" style is illustrated and discussed in Walter H. Kilham, *Boston after Bulfinch* (Cambridge, Mass., 1946). See also Hamlin, *Spirit in Architecture*, pp. 93–124; Larkin, *Art and Life in America*, pp. 79–85.

[5] Larkin, *Art and Life in America*, pp. 87–89.

grandeur of the classic past and the bright future of the new republic. They were not at all averse to comparing themselves to noble Romans or Athenians; after all, they had already adopted a native version of the Roman eagle, various Greco-Roman slogans, and classical designs as national emblems.

If a nation's public buildings reflected its spirit, they believed, nothing was better fitted to the American scene than the shapes and forms of classic antiquity. The classic style presumably followed nature itself, embodying its pervasive harmony and proportion. Classic buildings gave an impression of logic, order, and stability, and as the Italian Palladio and the French classicists had shown, a building could be mathematically beautiful and architecture a scientific, rational art. All these things held great appeal for contemporary intellectuals and philosophers, steeped as they were in eighteenth-century axioms of natural law, cosmic order, and science.[6]

Furthermore, America, like Europe, was infected with the contemporary interest in the ancient world. Recent excavations at Pompeii and Herculaneum, the transfer of the Elgin marbles to London, and France's collection of classic antiquities for the Louvre all helped to focus attention on Greece. Napoleon, copying Alexander, was rebuilding Paris in imperial style, and well-publicized volunteers like Byron flocked to Greece to assist its war for independence. The same impulse that scattered names such as Troy, Rome, and Syracuse across New York State, or Ypsilanti, Ionia, Scio, and Pompeii across Michigan, or built wooden copies of the Parthenon beside log cabins in frontier towns, also built Philadelphia banks to look like Greek temples and created triumphal Roman arches for Washington's and Lafayette's tours. The United States hoped to draw a unique American style out of the pure sources of classicism, a style suited to its own greatness—not necessarily a new architecture, but a judiciously planned, dignified, eclectic tradition founded on those models which, Thomas Jefferson said, had "the approbation of thousands of years."

Jefferson did not particularly like Georgian architecture and thought British public buildings neither useful nor distinguished. The United States, he believed, needed buildings which—he fervently hoped—might not only be swiftly constructed but built in a style worthy of a big, vital, free nation. In traveling through Europe Jefferson was much

[6] Talbot Hamlin, *Greek Revival Architecture in America* (New York, 1944), is a thorough study. See also LaFollette, *Art in America*, pp. 97–107.

impressed by the Roman ruins of southern France, writing home that he gazed at the Maison Carrée in Nîmes for "whole hours, like a lover at his mistress." Contemporary French adaptations of Roman style, which Jefferson saw in the Place de la Concorde and Pantheon in Paris, interested him too. He also knew the work of Andrea Palladio, the sixteenth-century Italian who had reduced classic architecture to mathematical rules, as well as such books as Clerisseau's *Antiquities of France*.[7] In 1779 Jefferson drew plans for a governor's mansion at Williamsburg, which to his disappointment was never built. When in 1785 he was asked to design the new Virginia state capitol at Richmond, he saw "a favorable opportunity," he said, "of introducing into the State an example of architecture in the classic style of antiquity." The result was a beautifully adapted copy of the Maison Carrée, the first major example of American Classical architecture. Monticello, on which Jefferson worked for almost forty years, and the University of Virginia, together represented his crowning achievements in combining the Roman and Palladian styles.[8]

Though Jefferson believed that in Gallo-Roman architecture he had found a primary source for an American classic tradition, Benjamin Latrobe (1764–1820), after Jefferson the most distinguished architect of the early nineteenth century, was much less certain. Latrobe, born in England, came to the United States in 1796. Jefferson appointed him surveyor of public buildings in Washington in 1803, but Latrobe's outside commissions gained him more notice. His Bank of Philadelphia building, completed in 1801 and the first of the Greek Revival public buildings in America, was so widely copied that a dozen years later Latrobe could truthfully say, "I have changed the taste of a whole city." Latrobe was an engineer, and while serving as engineer for the Philadelphia water system he designed a Greek Revival waterworks building—the first important American structure to combine classical style with technological function. In addition, as engineer for the Chesapeake and Delaware Canal, he designed the first drydocks in the United States.

Latrobe was a restless man who moved about a good deal, leaving his buildings scattered through several states, among them the Baltimore Cathedral (the first real attempt to break out of the Wren tradi-

---

[7] Larkin, *Art and Life in America*, pp. 78–79, 80–81.

[8] Fiske Kimball, *Thomas Jefferson: Architect* (Boston, 1916), is a thorough study. See also Hamlin, *American Spirit in Architecture*, pp. 111–117.

tion), Christ Church in Washington, and the Louisiana Bank in New Orleans. In 1815 he was called to Washington to supervise rebuilding of the National Capital, where he drew plans for the House chambers, the rotunda, and the west and east fronts. A year before his death, he designed the Bank of the United States in Philadelphia, his last important work.[9]

Latrobe's inspiration was Greek, not Roman. "I am a bigoted Greek," he wrote Jefferson. "My *principles* of good taste are rigid in Grecian architecture." Roman architecture, in his opinion, was much too overblown and grandiose to fit the United States, and as the product of an empire hardly democratic in character, it was quite out of key with the spirit of American institutions. Greek art and Greek democracy, and American art and American democracy, he felt, both grew from the same roots. "The days of Greece," he told the Philadelphia Society of Artists, "may be revived in the woods of America, and Philadelphia may become the Athens of the Western world."[10] Latrobe and his followers, especially Robert Mills and William Strickland, made a deep impression on American architecture. After them came the Greek Revival that dominated American building for more than fifty years, and which left Greek post offices, banks, railroad stations, and homes in every corner of the nation.[11]

Nevertheless, the great Greek craze did not satisfy those who still searched for an American architectural style to match American poetry, music, or art. Robert Mills, though a Greek Revivalist, told his contemporaries to "study your country's tastes and requirements and make classic ground here for your art!" Thomas Walter, though a strong admirer of Latrobe, warned his fellow builders that American structures must "conform to the local circumstances of the country, and the republican spirit of its institutions." In the meantime, the Romantic concept of art as organic growth—of a building or a poem as externalizations of their own internal laws—began to find architectural converts.[12]

[9] Hamlin, *American Spirit,* pp. 109–110, 132, 141, 151; Larkin, *Art and Life in America,* pp. 92–94; Tallmage, *Story of Architecture,* pp. 110–112.

[10] Larkin, *Art and Life in America,* p. 93.

[11] The best source concerning Latrobe is his own journal, J. H. B. Latrobe (ed.), *The Journal of Latrobe* (New York, 1905), but see also Talbot Hamlin, *Benjamin Latrobe* (New York, 1955).

[12] Fitch, *American Building,* p. 59. For a discussion of the new Romanticism in architecture after 1830, see R. P. Adams, "Architecture and the Romantic Tradition," *American Quarterly,* IX (1957), 46–63.

From Bulfinch and Jefferson to Latrobe and the Greek Revival, American architects strove for an American style, never quite finding it in Yankee Adamesque, Gallo-Roman imperialism, or Greek revivalism. The scramble for individuality, set off by the American Romantic movement in the thirties and forties, led architecture instead into Italian villas, Old English cottages, Swiss chalets, Tudor castles, Norman keeps, and a variety of pseudo-Gothic horrors. The architecture of the United States, even by 1850, could not yet really be called American.

The eighteenth-century colonists were as ardent music lovers as their contemporaries in Britain, singing the same songs and hymns, playing the same instruments to the same music. Southern society maintained an especially strong musical tradition; ladies and gentlemen played as a matter of course (and often very well) flute, violin, spinet, harpsichord, guitar, or harp. Jefferson played the violin, Washington the flute (he also paid $1,000 for a spinet for Nelly Custis), and Franklin (who once composed a string quartet) the harp, guitar, and violin.[13] The Charleston St. Cecilia Society, organized in 1737, sponsored concerts and supported an excellent orchestra. In the larger cities, the gradual growth of a sophisticated, wealthy leisure class made music a much more important part of colonial cultural life.

In the North, music also flourished. The German Moravians at Bethlehem, Pennsylvania, founded a college of music in 1745, while their choir was undoubtedly one of the world's finest. New York's Trinity Choir, established in the fifties, was equally renowned. After 1790, immigration from Europe brought scores of talented musicians to the United States. The flood of French refugees exerted a strong new influence on American tastes. Cities such as New York and Philadelphia supported good concert orchestras, staffed almost wholly by foreign musicians who played Domenico Scarlatti, Haydn, Vivaldi, Mozart, Corelli, Gluck, and Purcell, much like orchestras in London.

Nearly all serious music composed and played in the United States before 1820 was done by foreign-born, and nearly all musical perform-

[13] Max Savelle, *Seeds of Liberty* (New York, 1948), pp. 532–534. Jefferson, though he sometimes rose at five in the morning to practice, was reputed to be the worst violinist in Virginia, with Patrick Henry a close second. Philip Fithian, the young Princetonian who went to Virginia to tutor the children of Robert Carter, found that the home possessed a guitar, harpsichord, piano, violins, flutes, musical glasses, and an organ.

ers and teachers were either born or trained abroad. English-born James Hewitt became an important musical figure in New York, Raynor Taylor in Philadelphia, and William Selby in Boston, as did Dutch Peter Van Hagen in Charleston, German Gottlieb Graupner in Boston, and Italian Lorenzo Da Ponte in New York.[14] An influx of French and Italian artists came during the 1790's, coincident with the popularity of opera and ballad-opera. In the cities, where the foreign-born population was largest, musical societies and academies sponsored dozens of public and private concerts—New York's Concordia Society, Euterpean Society, Sacred Music Society, and later its Philharmonic Society; Boston's Handel and Hayden Society, Academy of Music, and Philharmonic Society; Philadelphia's Musical Fund Society, "City Concerts," and so on.

Though almost inundated by waves of European and British musical talent, a small stream of native American music nevertheless continued to flow. Francis Hopkinson of Philadelphia, a charming dilettante who could do many things well, directed a chamber music group, served as organist at Christ Church, and composed a large number of songs and instrumental pieces beginning in 1759. Hopkinson composed only for his friends, however, and distributed his music privately, so that nearly all of his skillful but not brilliant work remained unpublished until the twentieth century. The first native American composer of any importance was probably William Billings (1746–1800), a New England tanner who quit his vats to open a music shop in Boston. An unsophisticated, humorous, and self-taught musician, Billings published the first significant volume of music by an American, his *New England Psalm Singer* (1770), and founded the oldest musical society in America at Stoughton, Massachusetts. Billings popularized the "fuguing style," in contrast to the psalmic plain song or the polyphonic complexities of Bach and Haydn, a style which he defined as "notes flying after each other, altho' not always with the same sound. . . . Music

[14] Da Ponte, one of the most unusual characters in musical history, was banished from Italy for extreme profligacy and went to Vienna, where he was Mozart's librettist until banished from Austria for the same reasons. In London he worked as librettist in various Drury Lane productions, until scandal and bankruptcy forced him to emigrate to the United States in 1805, where he opened a grocery store in New Jersey. However, his teaching of music and Italian so impressed his clients that he was finally appointed as professor of Italian literature at Columbia College in 1825, where he did much to introduce New York to the finest Italian music. For a biography, see J. L. Russo, *Lorenzo Da Ponte* (New York, 1922).

is said to be fuguing when one part comes after another." Blind in one eye, with a withered arm and a deformed leg, Billings had a virility and energy which he expressed in his music and which appealed particularly to Americans. Though his music was often crude and his style soon out of fashion after his death, it had an authentically native sound and strength that made him, during his lifetime at least, an important figure in American music.[15]

But American composers of secular music could hardly hope to compete with Gluck, Haydn, Mozart, Beethoven, and other musical giants of Europe.[16] Only in church music could American composers hold their own. Lowell Mason's hymns, especially "Nearer, My God, to Thee" and "From Greenland's Icy Mountains" became integral parts of American church music; Mason too was partially responsible for introducing musical instruction into the public schools, thereby giving tremendous impetus to a native musical tradition. By 1850 a thousand music teachers a year attended his annual music conventions. A year later "The Old Folks at Home," the first of more than two hundred Stephen Foster songs, introduced the greatest ballad writer of them all to American musical history.

Seventeenth-century American colonists had little time for or interest in painting. Some of them—notably the French Huguenots and the Dutch—brought paintings with them to the new land, but the English Puritans suspected pictorial art and most certainly carried little of it to New England. Since New Englanders had no prejudice against portraits, the "limner" of family likenesses was in great demand throughout the century. The first known American painting, in fact, was a portrait of Governor Bellingham of Massachusetts, done by William Read of Boston in 1641. Wealthy merchants and planters during the eighteenth century provided employment for dozens of portrait paint-

---

[15] Raymond Morin, "William Billings, Pioneer in American Music," *New England Quarterly*, XIV (1941), 25–34. See also J. Murray Barbour, "The Texts of Billings' Church Music," *Criticism*, I (1959), 49–61.

[16] Americans found it difficult to produce even their own patriotic songs. Francis Scott Key wrote the words to "The Star-Spangled Banner" under well-known circumstances during the War of 1812 to the tune of an old British song, "Anacreon in Heaven." Samuel Smith's "America," written in 1831, used the melody of "God Save the King," to the confusion of countless Americans and Englishmen since.

ers, of whom at least two, Robert Feke and John Smibert, were probably as good as their average English contemporaries.[17]

The American environment was not particularly conducive to art, even at the close of the eighteenth century, and not many Americans expressed great interest in it. Painting, wrote John Trumbull, who was himself an artist and knew whereof he spoke, was generally regarded in the United States as "frivolous, little useful to society, and unworthy of a man who had talents for more serious pursuits." Even such a well-educated man as John Adams once remarked, "I would not give sixpence for a picture of Raphael or a statue of Phidias."

Those Americans who liked paintings and could afford to patronize artists preferred the foreign product; it was difficult for native American painters to compete with such giants as Reynolds, Romney, or Gainsborough, whose influence on contemporary painting was all pervasive. The United States possessed very few private collections or galleries, no art schools, no native artistic tradition, and no court or aristocracy to provide encouragement or patronage. Busy with the opening of the West and the organization of the new nation, Americans poured their efforts into practical affairs, rather than creative aesthetic effort.[18] The United States had produced very little of notice in art, Samuel Miller concluded apologetically in his *Retrospect* in 1803, nor were prospects much brighter in the future, since "pursuits of more immediate utility and profit have generally occupied the attention of our citizens." Nevertheless, Miller could point with some pleasure to five first-class painters, all born before the Revolution, who showed more than mediocre talents. These were Benjamin West (1738–1820), John Singleton Copley (1737–1815), Charles Willson Peale (1741–1827), Gilbert Stuart (1755–1828), and John Trumbull (1756–1843).[19]

These painters, like their contemporaries the poets, were born into

---

[17] The most complete study of pré-Revolutionary painting is James T. Flexner, *American Painting; First Flowers of Our Wilderness* (Boston, 1957). Chapter XI, "The Early American Tradition," summarizes trends in American painting to 1776. The most useful general histories of American painting are Larkin, *Art and Life in America;* LaFollette, *Art in America;* and Virgil Barker, *American Painting* (New York, 1950).

[18] LaFollette, *Art in America,* pp. 66–69; J. C. T. Flexner, "The Scope of Painting in the 1790's," *Pennsylvania Magazine of History,* LXXIV (1950), 74–89.

[19] *Retrospect of the Eighteenth Century* (New York, 1803), I, 428.

an artistic era rapidly moving from neoclassicism to Romanticism. They were, perhaps even more than poets and architects, part of an international movement in art, powerfully influenced by European theory and practice, drawing its inspiration directly from London, Paris, and Rome. All of these men had reached artistic maturity by the time of American independence; their art was rooted in a colonial youth and a British artistic tradition. No native tradition of painting existed in 1776; no American aesthetic theory emerged in their time.

Benjamin West and his American contemporaries learned their art during the great flowering of neoclassicism. Painters discovered, about the middle of the eighteenth century, the ideal of classic antiquity. Excavations at Pompeii and Herculaneum, among others, and the development of the new science of archaeology, caught and fired the imaginations of poets, historians, philosophers, sculptors, and painters alike. Here, in the remains of the classic past, artists found body and reality for Rome and Greece of which they had read; they could reconstruct a living civilization, clear to the eye and hand, in the galleries of the Vatican, the Louvre, the British Museum, and elsewhere. Rome, the new capital of art, was virtually a huge exhibition gallery to which all painters and sculptors (and poets too) were expected to make pilgrimages—to the Apollo Belvedere, the Laocoön, the Farnese Hercules, and so on—before they touched brush or chisel. No man, or so many felt, was properly an artist until he saw these things and reacted to them.[20]

Greek and Roman art, eighteenth-century critics assumed, represented a double perfection: as form and design, and as expression of a culture. After 1750 a body of artistic theory took shape, inspired by Greek and Roman models and motivated by the desire of artists to remake their own world on classical lines. And as soon as they formulated a set of abstract theories about art, critics gained importance as arbiters or judges, until, by the close of the eighteenth century, art seemed to be an expression not of the way painters saw things, but of what critics said art should be. The German critic Winckelmann (whose *History of Ancient Art* was tremendously influential) evolved a theory in which he defined "serenity, nobility, and sublimity" (the hallmarks of classic art as he saw them) as the primary characteristics

[20] Just as young Benjamin West from Pennsylvania charmed Rome by exclaiming, when he saw the Apollo, "How like a Mohawk savage!"

of ideal beauty.[21] Art teachers such as Anton Raphael Mengs of Rome and J. L. David of France codified the "laws" of painting into a coherent whole which could be practiced and learned, a method which could (and usually did) reduce painting to a matter of pictorial quotations or rulebook exercises.[22]

Benjamin West, a poor Quaker boy, was sent to Europe in 1759 by a group of wealthy Pennsylvanians who felt it "a pity that such genius should be cramped for the want of a little cash." His visit to Italy, at twenty, precluded any possibility that he might become an *American* painter, since he immediately and eagerly absorbed the current minutiae of the neoclassic style then in vogue. West had a tremendous memory, and was apparently influenced by everything he heard, read, and saw. When he went to England to settle down as a painter (where Sir Joshua Reynolds was lecturing over an eleven-year span on the "grand style"), West's career was fixed as a painter of what the critics and theorists agreed that painting should be.

West showed great skill at historical painting, became court painter to George III, and for almost sixty years received the majority of all court commissions. After the death of Sir Joshua Reynolds, West succeeded him as president of the Royal Academy. Although he used American history as subject matter for classical-historical paintings (as in his two most famous canvases, *Penn's Treaty with the Indians,* 1771, and *The Death of Wolfe,* 1771), he could hardly be called an American painter except for the accident of his birthplace. His carefully composed, bombastic "ten-acre canvases," as Gilbert Stuart called them, were really British-neoclassic in spirit and set a British style. West had facility and talent, if not genius, and his skill at satisfying critical as well as popular taste brought him great fame. All his life he followed the academic rules of composition, color, and drawing, in an excellent but basically synthetic art.[23]

[21] Beauty, said Winckelmann, derived from an imitation of concepts of the mind, not nature. The important, stable elements of painting were drawing and form (representing intellect) and not color (representing emotion or passion), and the use of classical subject matter. Edgar P. Richardson, *The Way of Western Art, 1776–1914* (Cambridge, Mass., 1939), Chaps. I, II.

[22] Students learned from Mengs, for example, that all groupings *must* form a pyramid, the basic form of a picture, and that if the outer side of one hand were shown, it must be balanced by showing the inner side of the other.

[23] Lloyd Goodrich, "The Painting of American History 1775–1900," *American Quarterly,* III (1951), 283–294, contains a good treatment of West,

West's importance to American painting lay chiefly in the example he set for ambitious young Americans and the encouragement he gave them. He opened his home and his studio to dozens of struggling artists—among them Copley, Stuart, Peale, Trumbull, Allston, Dunlap, Samuel Morse, and Robert Fulton—and helped them to obtain commissions. "I have been zealous in promoting merit," he once wrote. "Ingenious artists have received my ready aid, and my galleries and my purse have been opened to their studies and their distresses."

John Singleton Copley, a Boston boy, was the busiest portrait painter in America by the late 1750's, having developed a restrained, realistic style that made him also the best in the colonies. In 1774, caught in the middle of Tory-patriot conflicts in Boston, Copley went to Rome and thence to London, from which he never returned. He was, like West (with whom he studied for a time), powerfully affected by the "grand style." But Copley was much more artistically modest than West. His grandiosity of subject and style was often balanced by a sincerity that came through the academic rules, and by a humanity that survived the robes, drapes, and togas of the heroic style.[24]

Charles Willson Peale, before taking up painting, was a saddler, coachmaker, clockmaker, and silversmith. He was a talented jack-of-all-trades, with an insatiable curiosity, tremendous energy, and a strong sense of humor and public relations.[25] He too studied with West but returned to America to enlist in the Revolution; he commanded troops at White Plains and Trenton and found time to do forty portraits at Valley Forge. A vigorous patriot, Peale hoped to raise the level of American taste, popularize American painting, and encourage the beginnings of an American tradition. He propagandized tirelessly for American art, founded the first museum in the United States (1786), organized the first public art exhibition in the United States (Philadelphia, 1794), and in 1805 helped to establish the Pennsylvania Academy of Fine Arts in Philadelphia.

Peale was not a great artist, but a good one. His best work was done

---

Copley, and others. See also Flexner, *American Painting,* pp. 176–194; La-Follette, *Art in America,* pp. 52–55; and Barker, *American Painting,* pp. 199–211.

[24] LaFollette, *Art in America,* pp. 46–52; Larkin, *Art and Life in America,* pp. 60–63, *passim;* Barker, *American Painting,* pp. 212–214.

[25] Peale's Philadelphia museum, a forerunner of Barnum's, contained a wax figure of himself so perfectly made that it fooled many of his friends, who often attempted to shake hands with it.

in portraiture, where he showed a talent for catching the personality of his sitters with a charming honesty of style, best illustrated in his portrait of Franklin at eighty-one. His energy in behalf of art constituted Peale's real contribution to the American tradition. His museum, in which paintings, stuffed animals, gadgets, and mastodon bones vied for public attention, at least helped to make his patrons art conscious. Of his children (whom he named resoundingly Raphaelle, Rembrandt, Titian, Franklin, Linnaeus, Angelica Kauffmann—and James) at least four became good painters themselves.[26]

Gilbert Stuart's talent so impressed Benjamin West that when the young man visited him in London he gave him free room, board, and lessons. Stuart, however, though he learned the proper formulae in West's workshop, had too much independence to follow them blindly. "I will not follow any master," he wrote rebelliously. "I wish to find out what nature is for myself, and see her *with my own eyes*. This appears to me to be the road to excellence."[27] Since his interest was in people, Stuart specialized in portraiture, rapidly excelling West himself and (though assimilating much of Reynolds and Gainsborough) developing a bold, distinctive style of his own. In 1782 he opened a London studio which was an immediate success. High living soon depleted his fortunes and in 1792 he returned to the United States, where he was equally successful.

Stuart dominated American portrait painting for the next thirty years. He had, said Washington Allston, a genius for "distinguishing between the accidental and the permanent" in his subjects' characters and an uncanny ability "to catch the more subtle indication of the individual mind." His "Athenaeum" portrait of Washington (reproduced on postage stamps) is a good example of his work, which he refused usually to sign, saying bluntly, "My mark is all over them." Stuart became increasingly interested in faces—in many of his portraits he simply stylized the pattern, not caring to bother with a new arrangement for each picture. What Stuart wanted was directness, immediacy, spontaneity, freshness of impression. Because of this he made color and texture, not line, the dominant factor in his portraiture, breaking for

[26] Charles C. Sellers, *Charles Willson Peale* (Philadelphia, 1947), is the standard biography. See also Larkin, *Art and Life in America,* pp. 66–68, 114–117; LaFollette, *Art in America,* pp. 55–59; and Barker, *American Painting,* pp. 315–323. As further proof of his versatility, Peale made Washington's false teeth.

[27] Barker, *American Painting,* p. 244.

the first time with contemporary neoclassical practice and producing a kind of impressionism that lay closer to Velázquez and the Spaniards than to his old teacher, West.[28]

After the removal of the federal government to Washington, Stuart moved there and remained for five years, painting portraits of prominent figures. The rest of his life he spent in Boston, where his love for social life and his salty wit made him as popular as his paintings. Stuart executed the amazing total of 1,150 portraits during his career, including those of the first five Presidents of the United States. He was the first genuinely American portrait artist and the best of his time.[29]

John Trumbull, a Revolutionary soldier of distinction, studied with West after the war. Powerfully affected by West's "grand style," Trumbull first attracted attention for his historical paintings, such as *The Death of General Montgomery* and *Bunker's Hill*. It was his aim, Trumbull determined, to become the "graphic historiographer" of the "great events" of his time. Since Trumbull was a strong nationalist, he naturally centered his attention on the American Revolution, painting a series of portraits of Revolutionary leaders (forty-eight in all) and of Revolutionary scenes, including his famous *Surrender of Cornwallis*. In 1804 Trumbull settled in New York to become a portrait painter; but as time passed, competition from younger men and his own fading talents forced him to turn once more to historical painting. In 1817 he became head of the American Academy of the Arts, a post in which he could have become a dominant force in American painting. Instead, he ruined the Academy's treasury by selling it his own works at high prices, and got into so many arguments with his fellow painters that a rebellion among the younger members led to the founding of the National Academy of the Arts and Design. After some astute political maneuverings Trumbull received a commission in 1817 for four war scenes to be done in the National Capitol at $8,000 each. The paintings themselves, which did not wholly satisfy Congress, were among his last works. Trumbull's place in the American painting tradition derives less from his own talents than from his fervent nationalism and his consistent use of native subject matter. He found a usable American

[28] Stuart's various Washingtons are good representatives of his style, but better are such canvases as *Mrs. Richard Yates* (c. 1793) or *Admiral Coffin* (1810).

[29] LaFollette, *Art in America*, pp. 82–86; Larkin, *Art and Life in America*, pp. 120–122.

past, and encouraged many other painters to search there, as he did, for materials and inspiration.[30]

John Vanderlyn (1775–1852), though too young to be mentioned by Miller in his list of American artists, was the first of the major American painters to study in Paris. Aaron Burr, who befriended the twenty-year-old youth, financed five years of Paris study for him (1796–1801) and was rewarded by Vanderlyn's success. After visiting the United States briefly, Vanderlyn returned to Europe for twelve years, enjoying great popularity in France. Napoleon gave him a gold medal, and his nude, *Ariadne,* created a furor when it was exhibited in 1814. After his return to the United States Vanderlyn took portrait commissions from wealthy merchants and politicians and tried to make money by exhibiting huge painted panoramas. His panoramic painting of Versailles, which covered 3,000 square feet of canvas, was not a commercial or artistic success. In 1837 he was one of four men commissioned by Congress to paint scenes in the Capitol rotunda, which he executed without especial distinction. Though Vanderlyn's subject matter was often American, his style, as the American editor John Neal observed, was more "Frenchified" than native.[31]

The painting of the first generation after the Revolution reflected the peculiarly divided character of contemporary American art. Born as British subjects, trained in a European tradition, these painters quite naturally considered themselves directly within the main stream of European art. At the same time they were, in varying degrees, American—products of an American past and an American experience, keenly conscious of their Americanism.

The American branch of neoclassical painting which they represented, while derivative and imitative of European trends, was yet different from the European and British, though hardly "native" in any real sense. The American painters showed an interest, at least, in the factual and concrete, in a "direct vision" less common in Europe. West, conventional as his work was, nevertheless put his generals into authentic uniforms instead of togas and drew his Indians as Indians, not Greeks in war paint. American painters seemed less smitten with Greece and Rome, less absorbed in reconstructing Herculaneum, than

[30] LaFollette, *Art in America,* pp. 75–76; Larkin, *Art and Life in America,* pp. 128, 130–133.

[31] Larkin, *Art and Life in America,* pp. 118, 131–134; LaFollette, *Art in America,* pp. 75–77; Barker, *American Painting,* pp. 300–304, 329–330.

their European teachers. They painted their heroes in the grand style approved by Winckelmann and Mengs and David, but with the feeling that it was *their* antiquity, worthy of dignified and respectful treatment. Their painting had its overblown rhetoric and its artificialities, but it also now and then had the flavor of an American achievement.

American painters (like the poets and the critics) of the Revolutionary era groped for an "American style" in painting equivalent to that in literature or politics or architecture. Lacking a clear concept of what this Americanism was (as well as a set of symbols to express it), they were unable to voice it clearly, no matter how strongly they felt it. They believed that an American art, as the critics and philosophers of the age endlessly repeated, must have its roots in American society, that it keep a close relationship to the life of the nation, and that it have a necessary function in the development of a national character. A great nation must have great art (or, conversely, great art is the mark of great nations) and neither artist nor layman doubted that the United States would fail to produce it. "I have no notion," Tom Paine said confidently, "of yielding the palm of the United States to any Grecians or Romans that were ever born."[32]

The next generation of painters, men born during or shortly after the Revolution, came to artistic maturity with no memories of life under British rule. They were Americans, and not at all embarrassed by it; there was no reason, they believed, why an American could not be a great painter. After 1800 more and more of these confident young men traveled in Europe, not simply as provincials copying the masters, but as independent American artists inspecting the Old World.[33] These globe-trotting young cosmopolitans, wandering the ruins and galleries of Europe, were likely to meet in Paris or Rome or Florence, lunch with Irving or Cooper or Coleridge, and turn up again in Boston or New York or Philadelphia with ease and assurance. They had not yet discovered how to catch in their painting the configurations of American life, but theirs was an American art, without the Europeanized-colonial feel of their predecessors.

Though West, Trumbull, and Stuart were still alive and active, the historical-classical school of painting which they represented was losing popularity. The classical world was still a major source of inspiration, as the younger painters were quick to admit, but by 1800 a revolt was brewing against the ironclad rules of the neoclassical theorists. Nature,

[32] Larkin, *Art and Life in America*, p. 80.
[33] James T. Flexner, *The Light of Distant Skies* (New York, 1954).

the second generation of painters claimed, was a far better source than Mengs; so too was the Middle Ages, the exotic, the faraway, the common, melancholy, and sentimental. In other words, the Romantic movement was flooding art as it was literature. Painters, like poets, were finding powerful creative energy in the intuitive, the emotional, and the sentimental instead of only the rational and orderly. They were discovering what Lord Byron aptly called "excited passions" as a source of art.

To express excitement, emotion, passion, or feeling, the formulations of Winckelmann and Mengs were simply inadequate. Color and light, the emotional elements of painting, began to displace line and form. Subjectivity (what the artist felt) became more important than objectivity (what the observer saw, or what the critic believed he should see). Young Washington Allston, visiting the Louvre for the first time, was moved not by the Greek statuary but by Titian and Veronese and by "the gorgeous concert of *colors,* or rather of indefinite forms (I cannot call them sensations) of pleasure with which they filled the imagination. It was the poetry of color I felt."[34] What Allston felt was typical of the younger American painters, among them Rembrandt Peale, Thomas Sully, John Izard Middleton, and Samuel Morse, who preceded the great flowering of American Romantic painting that bloomed in the Hudson River School.

Rembrandt Peale (1778–1860), the most talented of the "painting Peales," also studied with West, and was good enough to exhibit with the Royal Academy at the age of twenty-five. Returning to Philadelphia in 1804, Peale began a career that spanned more than half a century. His great skill lay in portraits, which he did in a variety of styles at a rate of thirty to fifty per year. His finest portrait, perhaps, was that of Jefferson, done in 1805, in which he caught the quality of the great Virginian as no one else ever did. Peale was a talented but unstable man; in fact, angered by criticisms, he once quit painting completely for eight years. Somehow his talent never quite came to fruition, though he undeniably possessed it. Like his father, he encouraged young artists and taught drawing; he also helped to establish the Pennsylvania Academy, and in 1825 replaced Trumbull as president of the American Academy of Fine Arts.[35]

Thomas Sully (1783–1832), who like Peale excelled in portraiture,

[34] Richardson, *Painting in America,* p. 144.
[35] *Ibid.,* pp. 111–114, 116–117; LaFollette, *Art in America,* pp. 58, 64, 71; Barker, *American Painting,* pp. 334–336.

was born in England but settled in Charleston, where he began work as a painter of miniatures. He studied in West's London studios and with Stuart, and after Stuart's death became unquestionably the finest portrait painter in America. He averaged 37 portraits a year, leaving more than 2,600 canvasses behind at his death. One of Sully's best, and certainly his best-known portrait, is his sensitive study of Edgar Allan Poe.[36]

The most representative painter of the second generation of American artists was Washington Allston (1779–1843), who tried in his life and his art to synthesize the earlier neoclassical modes and techniques with the newer Romantic attitudes. Born in South Carolina into a well-to-do family, Allston attended Harvard and graduated in 1800 "determined," he wrote, "if resolution and perseverence will effect it, to be the first painter, at least, from America." He sold his share of the family properties to finance his studies abroad, arriving in London in 1801 to become a Royal Academy student of West's. However, three years later he went to Paris and then to Italy. Rome, the current mecca of artists, captured Allston so completely that he remained in Italy for four years. There he met Samuel Taylor Coleridge, the English poet, who influenced his thinking profoundly ("To no other man do I owe so much") and whose friendship continued for twenty-five years. In 1808 Allston returned to Boston, married William Ellery Channing's sister, painted some portraits, and left for London, where he stayed for seven years, painting and writing poetry. Here his wife died.[37]

Ill and lonely after the death of his wife, Allston came back to Boston in 1818 to be greeted as "America's greatest artist" and accepted eagerly into the influential Boston-Cambridge circle of poets, critics, philosophers, and preachers. Allston, however, after two decades of painting, had found no style of his own and though he had by no means painted a "great" picture, everyone expected that he soon would. His grand project, *Belshazzar's Feast,* was never quite finished after twenty years of work, and though he painted a good deal, the awaited masterpiece never came. His admirers were still expecting it when he died in 1843.

As Allston came to grips with issues of artistic theory in the eighteen-

[36] Larkin, *Art and Life in America,* pp. 124–126; Barker, *American Painting,* pp. 275–277.
[37] The definitive biography is Edgar P. Richardson, *Washington Allston* (Chicago, 1948).

twenties and thirties, he turned more and more to philosophy, seeking answers to internal problems of art and the artist. Partially, perhaps, through his admiration for Coleridge, and certainly by reason of his exposure to the New England climate of ideas which surrounded him, he evolved a theory of art which strongly resembled the Emersonian system.[38]

Because Allston never became the great master that New England expected him to be, it is easy in retrospect to label him as a failure.[39] But Allston was an important figure in the history of American painting for reasons other than his production of canvases.[40] He was, for one thing, the first American painter to explore the whole range of art (portraits, landscapes, history, sculpture, still lifes, poetry, fiction, philosophy) in an attempt to unify artistic theory and practice. He was to American painting what Emerson was to American philosophy, or Hawthorne to the American novel—an authentic American eclectic, probing into fundamental areas of contemporary American culture. Allston was trying to find answers to such problems as the American lack of a strong technical tradition, the proper relationship of an artist to his society, the persistence of American "colonialism," the adjustments of imaginative to practical life, and so on. He was the only American painter of his era who really tried to evolve a set of new artistic concepts, instead of imitating the old or the European.

Allston's direct influence on American painting was small. He accepted a few pupils and had little interest in teaching. After 1825, young painters tended to concentrate in New York, where there were a large number of studios and schools and where the National Academy of the Arts and Design, under the energetic presidency of Samuel F. B. Morse, had created a lively art colony. Allston's great impact on American painting was by example, by the quality and aspiration of his life. Allston, painters everywhere in the United States understood, had succeeded in living the life of an artist to his fingertips—the fact that he was *there,* respected and admired, dedicated to serious painting, work-

[38] Allston summarized his thinking in *Lectures on Art and Poems,* a book published after his death by his friend Richard Henry Dana, Jr. The function of the artist, he explained, is to perceive and present the organic relationships between art and nature.

[39] See, for example, Van Wyck Brooks, *The Flowering of New England* (New York, 1936), pp. 159–165; and, for another view, Richardson's *Allston.*

[40] *Belshazzar's Feast,* had it been finished, would probably have been less successful than such paintings as his *Moonlit Landscape,* in which he caught beautifully that "poetical treatment of pigment" for which he strove.

ing and speaking as a painter and nothing else, meant much to the painters of the raucous age of Jackson and gave encouragement of a very real sort to the next generation.[41]

Young American artists of Sully's or Allston's time found few schools or academies at home in which they might learn the rudiments of their art, and few galleries or museums in the United States where they might view the work of the masters of it. Those who could afford it, before 1800, usually went to England to study, chiefly because of Benjamin West. British portrait painting was presumed to be the world's best, and since the American market was interested chiefly in portraits, it was natural for Americans at first to gravitate toward London. John Vanderlyn was the first prominent American to study in Paris, and after 1805 Italy and France outdrew London as the painter's haven.

At least forty-five American painters studied abroad between 1790 and 1830, with probably many more unaccounted for. The less fortunate studied at home in minor art schools, or, if they were lucky, with men such as Stuart or Allston, who were willing now and then to take a few pupils. The Robertson brothers opened studios for instruction in New York in 1792, and Philadelphia had several competent art schools by 1800. The organization of professional academies marked the next stage in art education. The energetic Charles Willson Peale, after several attempts, helped to found the Pennsylvania Academy of Fine Arts in 1805, the first effort, as Peale wrote, "to promote the cultivation of the Fine Arts in the U.S.A. by introducing correct and elegant copies from the first masters in Sculpture and Painting . . . by occasionally conferring moderate but honorable premiums, and otherwise assisting the studies and exciting the efforts of the Artists, gradually to unfold, enlighten, and invigorate the talents of our countrymen."[42]

Peale's venture was followed by others, such as the Society of the Artists of the United States (1810), Cincinnati's Academy of Drawing and Painting (1812), and New York's Academy of the Fine Arts (1816). The National Academy of the Arts of Design (1826) was the first such academy controlled by professional artists. Samuel F. B. Morse, its president, believed like Peale that it was the Academy's patriotic duty to encourage a native artistic tradition worthy of a democratic culture, and felt that while Americans might lean on their

---

[41] Richardson, *Allston*, pp. 22–24.

[42] Larkin, *Art in America*, pp. 114–115; John A. Krout and D. R. Fox, *The Completion of Independence* (New York, 1944), p. 340.

techniques abroad, "our own soil must warm into life the seeds of native talent."[43]

American painting, well into the nineteenth century, was almost wholly concerned with portraits or historical scenes, for the good reason that if a painter hoped to find commissions, he must paint what could be sold. A public conscious of its recent heroic past, and government officials anxious to commemorate it, created demands for historical art. Wealthy families—and even those in modest circumstances—could usually afford to commission family likenesses. The fashionable portraitists (Stuart, Sully, and Vanderlyn) built their clienteles in the large cities; others sought out commissions by traveling to the cities where they were, to Richmond, Albany, St. Louis, Cincinnati, or New Orleans. Even better painters, such as Rembrandt Peale, John Wesley Jarvis, Samuel Waldo, or William Dunlap, were not ashamed to make yearly tours through the states after jobs. Lesser men toured the small towns and frontier settlements, like Benjamin Trott, who rode horseback with his colors and brushes into the most remote hamlets. "By and by," grumbled old Gilbert Stuart, "you will not by chance kick your foot against a dog-kennel but out will start a portrait painter," a situation that continued until the popularity of the daguerreotype drove out portraits.[44]

Landscape painting came late to American art. First of all, there were very few private collectors or galleries in the United States willing to buy landscapes. Engravers, of course, etched and sold thousands of them, and a few colonial artists did "landskips," but there was little interest in painting the native scene until after 1800. The formalized, "picturesque" painting of Poussin, Claude Lorrain, and Salvator Rosa dominated landscape style well into the nineteenth century. The first noteworthy landscapists in the United States, William Winstanley, William Groombridge, Thomas Beck, and Francis Guy—all of whom arrived from England between 1790 and 1795—were strongly influenced by the French. Gradually, as they continued to work in an American environment, they saw less and less with academic, European eyes and more of what was actually so. Guy's *Tontine Coffee House*

[43] Morse was an excellent portraitist and teacher, but his interest in electricity led him to stop painting at the very point at which his talent was just developing. For a biography of this interesting man, see Carlton Mabee, *American Leonardo: A Life of Samuel F. B. Morse* (New York, 1943).

[44] Van Wyck Brooks, *The World of Washington Irving* (New York, 1944), p. 159.

was a direct report on New York City, while Beck's *Niagara Falls* was most certainly non-European.

Though Allston, Vanderlyn, Morse, and others occasionally did landscapes, it took some time for Americans to discover that the face of the United States was well worth painting—as Cooper, Freneau, Irving, and Bryant had long known. The Romantic interest in nature, reinforced by a natural American pride in one's own land, finally brought painters to a recognition of the fact that the American landscape at least equaled the ruins of Rome or the brooks of England as artistic material.[45] Joshua Shaw, who visited almost every state of the Union to collect prints for his *Picturesque Views of American Scenery*, concluded that the United States held "all the varieties of the sublime, the beautiful, and the picturesque in scenery." In the Susquehanna, the White Mountains, the Catskills, the Hudson Valley, and other "scenes of wild grandeur peculiar to our country," as William Cullen Bryant called them, Americans of the next generation found much to paint.

Sculpture, though never popular as an art form in England and doubly suspect by the Puritans as "graven images," began to attract the interest of American artists in the 1790's.[46] There was an obvious connection between sculpture and politics, of course. Classical liberty was a treasured heritage in the new United States; comparisons of the American Republic with Greece and Rome were so commonplace as to be almost automatic. If Greece and Rome had produced great sculpture, why not the United States?

The Revolution and the War of 1812 gave the United States a set of symbolic heroes to be immortalized in stone as the Greeks and Romans had immortalized theirs; the desire for statuary was a normal concomitant of hero worship. Thus Charles Sumner could say quite seriously, and with popular approval, that a statue of Washington was "the highest work with which an American artist can occupy himself." Then too there were hundreds of new public buildings to be adorned— state capitols, banks, business buildings, government offices, and of course the National Capitol itself—which offered hitherto-undreamed-of opportunities for sculptors and stoneworkers.[47]

[45] Larkin, *Art and Life in America*, pp. 135–137.

[46] As late as 1810, copies of nude sculpture from the Louvre, displayed at the Pennsylvania Academy of Fine Arts, were kept covered by sheets if ladies were present in the gallery. Krout and Fox, *Completion of Independence*, p. 345.

[47] Albert T. Gardner, *Yankee Stonecutters* (New York, 1945), pp. 4–9.

The demand for sculptors was far greater than the United States could supply. Most of the work in stone done before 1820 was executed by German, Italian, and French artists; for example, the first sculptors to work in the National Capitol, Giuseppe Franzoni and Giovanni Andrei, were both imported.[48] The first major work in marble done by an American was probably that of John Frazee in 1824, but by the 1820's a stream of young Americans were pouring into Italy to learn the art.[49] The sculpture they learned was based on the reigning pseudo-classical style of Antonio Canova and Bertel Thorvaldsen of Rome, whose work, patterned on the Greek and Roman statuary recently excavated in the great archaeological revival, dominated the sculptural style of all Europe.[50] Horatio Greenough and Hiram Powers, the two most famous American sculptors of the eighteen-forties and fifties, were both powerfully influenced by Canova's style. Greenough's Washington, carved in Roman robes (or "without a shirt," the irreverent said), created great controversy, while Powers' nude *Greek Slave* was probably the most talked-about and reproduced piece of art of the early nineteenth century. Both Greenough and Powers spent most of their creative years abroad, isolated from the American scene, and contributed little directly to a native American sculpture tradition.[51]

A few years later, the development of cemeteries in American cities provided a tremendous impetus to sculpture. New York's Greenwood Cemetery, Boston's Mount Auburn, and Philadelphia's Laurel Hill were tourist showplaces which attracted thousands of visitors, many of whom

---

To "keep bright the fires of patriotism," sculptor Hiram Powers believed that the nation must "surround the Capitol with the statues and monuments of illustrious men, who have devoted themselves to the glory of the country." For a brief account of sculpture in America to 1840, see Larkin, *Art and Life in America*, pp. 101–106, and his "Early American Sculpture," *Antiques*, LVI (1949), 176–179.

[48] Gardner, *Stonecutters*, p. 59, lists fifty-four stonecutters in the United States before 1800, twenty-one foreign-born.

[49] Van Wyck Brooks, *The Dream of Arcadia* (New York, 1958), Chap. IV, counts at least one hundred American sculptors in Italy from 1825 to 1861.

[50] Canova's nude statue of Napoleon (1807–10), a copy of Roman statues of emperors, set a popular pattern. His statue of Washington as a seminude emperor, commissioned for the North Carolina state house, was destroyed (perhaps fortunately for American art) in a fire in 1831. Thorvaldsen, a Dane, had studios in Rome from 1797 to 1838.

[51] Greenough, however, deserves attention for his writings on art and sculpture. His *Travels of a Yankee Stonecutter*, ed. Nathalia Wright (Gainesville, Fla., 1952), and his *Form and Function*, ed. H. E. Small (Berkeley, Calif., 1947), are worth reading.

bought detailed guidebooks to explain the profusion of statuary and stonework. At the same time, the popularity of the bust (usually machine-made) put sculpture in thousands of American homes. By no means, however, could American sculpture be called a native art, or an aesthetically mature one.

American artistic life, during the early years of the Republic, was influenced by two powerful forces, nationalism and Romanticism.[52] It seemed disarmingly simple after the Revolution for American artists to be "native" and thus to create a "national" art; yet the attempt to do so led artists of the period into a perplexing dilemma.. The need for self-expression and the compulsion of a youthful culture to break with the past, clashed with the need of the artist to give his art shape, relevance, and continuity in relation to what had been done before him. In creating an "original" or "native" art, for example, by what standards might an American be measured, except by British and European? To what other set of standards could he possibly be related? The drive for nationalism, which provided vigorous motivation in so many areas of American life during these decades, created a steady tension in literature and art between the necessity for tradition and the necessity for self-delineation and self-exposition.

The American artist after 1776 was caught between a need to break away from foreign culture and a need to imitate, to build upon it, and to use its instruments to express an *American* art. A common reaction was merely to try to put the new wine into old bottles—to write an American epic in Augustan couplets, stage an American comedy copied from Sheridan, build an American bank that looked like a Roman temple. Some tried to avoid both the form and spirit of "foreign" art; others tried conscientiously to copy it; still others tried to do both, hoping to find an agreeable compromise by which they might escape the dilemma of nationalism and imitation.

No American artists were foolish enough to believe that anything could be gained by deliberately breaking their bond with the great artistic tradition of western civilization. Many were equally aware that nothing American could be created by sterile imitation of foreign

[52] There are many forces which combine to affect art, and what developed in America cannot be wholly ascribed to these two general influences alone, nor to a particular combination of influences. Writers write and painters paint for their own inner reasons as well as in relation and response to outer artistic and social stimuli. Still, nationalism and Romanticism are distinguishable as rubric threads in the pattern of American artistic accomplishment at this time.

models. The criteria of art were transported from Britain and Europe; the problem was to produce an American art within their boundaries, neither imitating nor rejecting too much. This was a difficult balance to strike. Only a few, notably Freneau and Irving, managed to accomplish it successfully. What made it more difficult was the fact that the artistic standards of Britain and Europe were being used to evaluate the products of a new civilization which was all the time consciously moving away from Britain and Europe, fashioning a quite different kind of political, social, and intellectual milieu.[53]

Meanwhile, American artists were groping for their own way of making their own statements, without losing the thread of the western artistic tradition. Emerson's attack on "the timid, imitative, and tame" in American creative life, made in his address to the young men of Harvard in *The American Scholar* in 1837, wrote an end to the years of trial and doubt. Emerson's ringing assertion that henceforth "We will walk on our own feet; we will work with our own hands; we will speak our own minds" marked the close of the transitional years, 1776–1830, in which the distinctive configurations of a recognizably American art took shape.

A consideration of Romanticism as a factor in the development of American art in the period 1776–1830 involves a similar problem. American cultural life during these years obviously owed much to the influence of that powerful, elusive force, transmitted from British and European artistic and philosophical theory and practice, yet to ascribe to it the major share of responsibility for the creation of an American art is to oversimplify the case. At least some of the trends later labeled "romantic" were already implicit in the American environment, the American past, and the American form of society and government. It is neither feasible nor necessary to attempt to disentangle that which was root and that which was branch, that which was cause and that which was effect. But it is safe to say that American art was by no means a simple recapitulation of England and Europe; it might well have developed somewhat as it did had no British or Continental Romantic movement taken place.

The two major traits which may be located at the center of that

[53] As John A. Kouwenhoven pointed out in *Made in America* (New York, 1948), p. 6, the United States is "the only major world power to have taken form as a cultural unit in the period when technological civilization was spreading throughout the world." The implications of this fact remain largely unexplored.

indefinable attitude called Romanticism—diversity as opposed to uniformity, and an emphasis on art as an expression of subjective experience—could conceivably have emerged from the American experience without external help, or at most might have developed as they did with no more than strong reinforcement from foreign sources.[54] Yet it is most clear from the example and testimony of American painters, poets, sculptors, architects, novelists, and playwrights that they did respect British and Continental models and theories of art, and that they did receive both form and inspiration from their overseas contemporaries. It is equally clear that they did not accept all of English and European romanticism.[55] They chose rather that which was most closely congruent with American cultural needs and aspirations, that which complemented their strong nationalistic urge for self-expression. The result, as observed in the culture of the times, was the beginnings of an American point of view and an American style in art.

[54] For a general discussion of Romanticism, see A. O. Lovejoy, *The Great Chain of Being* (Cambridge, Mass., 1942), and for a discussion of some of the difficulties involved in the use of the term, Howard Mumford Jones, *Ideas in America* (Cambridge, Mass., 1945), pp. 107–110, *passim*. A useful earlier discussion is Norman Foerster (ed.), *A Reinterpretation of American Literature* (New York, 1928), pp. 32–34.

[55] American critics, for example, did not accept Wordsworth's theories of diction for many years, ignored Keats before 1840, and gave Shelley only belated recognition; see Annabel Newton, *Wordsworth in American Criticism* (Chicago, 1928), and the discussion in G. H. Orians, "The Rise of Romanticism," in H. H. Clark (ed.), *Transitions in American Literary History* (Durham, N.C., 1953), pp. 168–169. Byron was popular and widely imitated in America (by even so staid a young Quaker as Whittier), but his personal life and moral ideas were widely censured; so too with Schiller. American Romanticism could not accept the rebelliousness and "immorality" of the British and European variety.

Bibliography

The Foundations of American Thought

Excellent general histories of colonial America are Clinton Rossiter, *Seedtime of the Republic* (New York, 1953), and Max Savelle, *Seeds of Liberty: The Genesis of the American Mind* (New York, 1948), both of which contain information on the intellectual backgrounds of the colonies and good bibliographies. A recent excellent study of the colonial period is Daniel Boorstin, *The Americans: The Colonial Experience* (New York, 1958). Other discussions occur in Carl Degler, *Out of Our Past* (New York, 1959). Useful background books are George Kitson Clark, *The English Inheritance* (New York, 1950); Edward M. Burns, *The American Sense of Mission* (New Brunswick, N.J., 1957); and Lawrence Gipson, *The Coming of the Revolution, 1763-1776* (New York, 1954). Albert Weinberg, *Manifest Destiny* (Baltimore, 1935), has an interesting discussion in its early chapters of nationalism, natural rights, and the westward movement. More specific treatments of the late eighteenth and early nineteenth centuries in America are John C. Miller, *Origins of the American Revolution* (Boston, 1943), and *The Triumph of Freedom* (Boston, 1948); Merrill Jensen, *The New Nation: A History of the United States During the Confederation* (New York, 1950); George Dangerfield, *The Era of Good Feelings* (New York, 1952); and of course Henry Adams' monumental *History of the United States during the Administrations of Jefferson and Madison* (New York, 9 vols., 1888–91).

Valuable studies of the backgrounds of eighteenth-century thought in America and Europe are Ernst Cassirer, *The Philosophy of the Enlightenment* (Princeton, 1951); Crane Brinton, *The Political Ideas of the English Romanticists* (Oxford, 1926); Basil Willey, *The Eighteenth Century Background* (London, 1929); and portions of R. G. Collingwood, *The Idea of History* (London, 1946), and H. J. Muller, *The Uses of the Past* (New York, 1952). Pertinent articles include F. E. L. Priestley, "Newton and the Romantic Concept of Nature," *University of Toronto Quarterly*, XVII (1948), 323–336;

Peter Gay, "The Enlightenment in the History of Political Theory," *Political Science Quarterly*, LXIX (1954), 374–389; A. O. Lovejoy, "The Meaning of Romanticism for the Historian of Ideas," *Journal of the History of Ideas*, II (1941), 257–278.

Key essays on the American mind during its formative years are Leon Howard, "The Late Eighteenth Century: An Age of Contradictions," and Merrill Heiser, "The Decline of Neoclassicism," in Harry Hayden Clark (ed.), *Transitions in American Literary History* (Durham, N.C., 1954). Excellent extended treatments of the intellectual milieu of the period are Daniel Boorstin, *The Lost World of Thomas Jefferson* (New York, 1948), and Macklin Thomas, "The Idea of Progress in Franklin, Freneau, Barlow, and Rush" (unpublished doctoral dissertation, Wisconsin, 1938). Other useful studies are Merle Curti, Chaps. IV to X in *The Growth of American Thought* (New York, 1943), and his essay, "The Great Mr. Locke," in *Probing Our Past* (New York, 1955); Howard M. Jones, "The Drift to Liberalism in the American Eighteenth Century," in *Ideas in America* (Cambridge, Mass., 1944); R. E. Delmage, "American Ideas of Progress, 1750–1860," *American Philosophical Society Proceedings*, XCI (1947), 309–318; Ralph H. Gabriel, "The Enlightenment Tradition," in F. E. Johnson, *Wellsprings of the American Spirit* (New York, 1948); and the relevant portions of Charles and Mary Beard, *The American Spirit* (New York, 1930). Arthur Ekirch, *The Idea of Progress in America 1815–1860* (New York, 1944), is an excellent study. No student of the American eighteenth century, of course, should miss Carl Becker's *Heavenly City of the Eighteenth Century Philosophers* (New Haven, 1932) or his *Declaration of Independence* (New York, 1942); J. B. Bury's *The Idea of Progress: An Inquiry into Its Origin* (London, 1932); or the first two volumes of Vernon L. Parrington's provocative *Main Currents of American Thought* (New York, 1927, 1930). An interesting re-evaluation of Becker's work is Peter Gay's "Carl Becker's Heavenly City," in Raymond O. Rockwood (ed.), *Carl Becker's Heavenly City Revisited* (Ithaca, 1958). Henry Guerlac, "Newton's Changing Reputation in the Eighteenth Century," in the same volume is an informative essay as well.

The Roots of an American Faith

For European views of the United States, see Werner Stark, *America: Ideal and Reality* (London, 1947); William Sachse, *The Colonial American in Britain* (Madison, Wis., 1956); Michael Kraus, "America and the Utopian Ideal," *Mississippi Valley Historical Review*, XXII (1936), 487–505; and Gilbert Chinard, "The American Dream," in Robert E. Spiller *et al.* (eds.), *The Literary History of the United States* (New York, 1948), I, 192–219. The rise of nationalism is treated by Hans Kohn, *American Nationalism* (New York, 1957); Merle Curti, *The Roots of Loyalty* (New York, 1946); and Benjamin Spencer, *The Quest for Nationality* (Syracuse, 1957). For the development of nationalism in historical writing, see Michael Kraus, *The Writing of American History* (Norman, Okla., 1953), and a useful study by Ralph N. Miller, "The Historians Discover America" (unpublished doctoral dissertation, Northwestern, 1946). The best general history of American philosophy is Herbert W. Schneider, *A History of American Philosophy* (New York, 1946), though I. Woodbridge Riley, *American Thought from Puritanism to Pragmatism* (rev. ed., New York, 1925), is still valuable. Joseph N. Blau, *Men and Movements in American Philosophy* (New York, 1952), is excellent, while A. A. Roback, *History of American Psychology* (New York, 1952), and Jay W. Fay, *American Psychology before William James* (New Brunswick, N.J., 1939), contribute much useful information toward an understanding of the period's ideas. Samuel Miller's charming and informative *Retrospect of the Eighteenth Century* (2 vols., New York, 1803) is still an interesting introduction to the intellectual and cultural patterns of the times. The emergence of the American mind can best be studied, however, by a more thorough reading of the works of such men as Franklin, Jefferson, Paine, Freneau, John Adams, Barlow, Rush, Hamilton, Timothy Dwight, and Noah Webster.

Science and Scientific Knowledge

For an understanding of the backgrounds of eighteenth-century scientific thought, see Herbert Butterfield, *Origins of Modern Science* (London, 1949); A. R. Hall, *Scientific Revolution 1500–1800* (London, 1954); and J. B. Bernal, *Science in History* (London, 1957), pp. 352–479. General studies of American science in the late eighteenth and early nineteenth centuries include William and Mabel Smallwood, *Natural Science and the American Mind* (New York, 1941); Dirk Struik, *Yankee Science in the Making* (Boston, 1948); Frederick E. Brasch, *The Royal Society of London and Its Influence upon Scientific Thought in America* (Washington, D.C., 1931); Abraham Wolf, *A History of Science, Technology, and Philosophy in the Eighteenth Century* (London, 1952); and Ralph S. Bates, *Scientific Societies in the United States* (New York, 1945). Preserved Smith's "Newtonian Science," Chap. II of his *History of Modern Culture* (New York, 1934), is a superb essay. Winthrop Tilley, "The Literature of Natural and Physical Science in the American Colonies from the Beginnings to 1765" (unpublished dissertation, Brown, 1933), is a useful guide.

Valuable general studies are the relevant portions of Daniel Boorstin, *The Lost World of Thomas Jefferson* (New York, 1948), and Brooke Hindle, *The Pursuit of Science in Revolutionary America* (Chapel Hill, 1956). Key articles include H. H. Clark, "The Influence of Science on American Ideas," *Transactions of the Wisconsin Academy*, XXXV (1944), 305–349; Herbert Drennon, "Newtonianism: Its Methods, Theology, and Metaphysics," *Englische Studien*, LXVIII (1933–34), 297–409; J. W. Oliver, "Science and the Founding Fathers," *Scientific Monthly,* XLVIII (1939), 256–260; F. E. Brasch, "The Newtonian Epoch in the American Colonies," *American Antiquarian Society Proceedings,* LIX (n.s., 1939), 314–332; and Michael Kraus, "Scientific Relations between America and Europe in the Eighteenth Century," *Scientific Monthly,* LV (1942), 259–272.

Biographical studies of American scientists, of course, are an important source of information about the science of the period. Among these are Edwin T. Martin, *Thomas Jefferson: Scientist* (New York, 1952); I. Bernard Cohen, *Benjamin Franklin: His Contribution to the American Tradition* (Indianapolis, 1953), and *Benjamin Franklin's Experiments* (Philadelphia, 1941); Courtney R. Hall, *Samuel Latham Mitchill: A Scientist in the Early Republic* (New York, 1934); Ernest Earnest, *John and William Bartram, Botanists and Explorers* (Philadelphia, 1940); John F. Fulton and Elizabeth Thompson, *Benjamin Silliman* (New York, 1947); Edgar F. Smith, *The Life of Robert Hare* (Philadelphia, 1917); Edward Ford, *David Rittenhouse, Astronomer Patriot, 1732–1796* (Philadelphia, 1936); Maurice Babb, "David Rittenhouse," *Pennsylvania Magazine of History and Biography,* LV (1932), 193–224; Nathan Goodman, *Benjamin Rush, Physician and Citizen* (Philadelphia, 1934); and Carleton Mabee, *The American Leonardo: A Life of Samuel F. B. Morse* (New York, 1943). Briefer sketches of scientists may be found in Bernard Jaffe, *American Men of Science* (New York, 1944); James Crowther, *Famous American Men of Science* (New York, 1937); David Starr Jordan (ed.), *Leading American Men of Science* (New York, 1910); J. McKeen Cattell, *American Men of Science* (New York, 1938); and Clarence J. Hylander, *American Scientists* (New York, 1935).

Information relating to the status and progress of particular branches of science during the period may be found in George P. Merrill, *The First Hundred Years of American Geology* (New Haven, 1924), and "Contributions to the History of American Geology," *Annual Report of the United States National Museum . . . for 1904* (Washington, 1906); A. S. Packard, "A Century's Progress in American Zoology," *American Naturalist,* X (1876), 591–599; Theodore Hornberger, *Scientific Thought in American Colleges 1638–1800* (Austin, Tex., 1945); Louis W. McKeehan, *Yale Science: The First Hundred Years 1701–1801* (New York, 1947); E. S. Dana (ed.), *A Century of Science in America* (New York, 1918); Edgar F. Smith, *Chemistry in America* (New York, 1914); David E. Smith and Jekuthiel Ginsberg, *A History of Mathematics in the United States before 1900* (Chicago, 1934); Florian Cajori, *The Early Mathematical Sciences in North and South America* (Boston, 1928); S. W. Geiser, *Naturalists of the Frontier* (Dallas, 1937); R. T. Young, *Biology in America* (Boston, 1922); and William A. Lacy, *Biology and Its Makers* (New York, 1928). Other sources are Howard A. Kelly, *Some American Medical Botanists* (Troy, N.Y., 1914); Alphonso Murrill, *Historic Foundations of Botany in Florida and North America*

(Gainesville, Fla., 1945); Andrew P. Rogers, *John Torrey—A Story of North American Botany* (Princeton, 1942). Among articles, consult Courtney R. Hall, "A Chemist of a Century Ago," *Journal of Chemical Education,* V (1928), 253–256; Lyman C. Newell, "Chemical Education in America from the Earliest Days to 1820," *ibid.,* IX (1932), 677–696; Charles A. Browne, "The History of Chemical Education between 1820 and 1870," *ibid.,* IX (1932), 696–728; Whitfield Bell, "The Scientific Environment of Philadelphia, 1775–1790," *Proceedings of the American Philosophical Society,* XCII (1948), 6–14; Margaret Denny, "The Royal Society and American Scholars," *Scientific Monthly,* LXV (1947), 415–427; I. Bernard Cohen, "Science and The Revolution," *Technology Review,* XXVII (1945), 76–85; and Austin H. Clark, "Background and Origin of the American Association for the Advancement of Science," *Summarized Proceedings of the American Association for the Advancement of Science* (June, 1929—January, 1934), pp. 15–25. An informative picture history is Mitchell A. Wilson, *American Science and Invention* (New York, 1954), while Charles D. Walcott, *Source Book in the History of the Sciences* (New York, 1929–39), affords bibliographical information.

Materials for a history of American agriculture as a branch of science are readily available in the periodical *Agricultural History* and the Columbia University series of *Studies in the History of American Agriculture.* Good and accessible general sources are Joseph Schafer, *The Social History of American Agriculture* (New York, 1936); Lyman Carrier, *The Beginnings of Agriculture in America* (New York, 1923); Everett Edwards, *Jefferson and Agriculture* (Washington, 1943); William H. Clark, *Farms and Farmers: The Story of American Agriculture* (Boston, 1945); and Harry J. Carman's edition of the famous eighteenth-century farmers' guide, *American Husbandry* (New York, 1939). Everett Edwards, *A Bibliography of the History of Agriculture in the United States* (Washington, 1930), is a definitive earlier source.

Medicine is by far the most comprehensively studied branch of American science. Maurice Bear Gordon, *Aesculapius Comes to the Colonies* (Ventnor, N.J., 1949), is a mine of information. Richard Shryock's *The Development of American Medicine* (Philadelphia, 1936) and his *Eighteenth Century Medicine in America* (Worcester, Mass., 1950) are the best general studies, though Henry B. Shafer, *The American Medical Profession 1733–1850* (New York, 1936), is also useful. Other studies include Wyndham Blanton, *Medicine in Virginia* (Richmond, 1930); Henry Viets, *A Brief History of Medicine in Massachusetts* (Boston and New York, 1930); John Duffy, *Epidemics in Colonial America* (Baton Rouge, 1953); Joseph Carson, *History of the Medical Department of the University of Pennsylvania* (Philadelphia, 1869); William Norwood, *Medical Education in the United States Before the Civil War* (Philadelphia, 1944); James J. Walsh, *A History of Medicine in New*

York (5 vols., New York, 1919); and Thomas F. Harrington, *The Harvard Medical School: A History* (3 vols., Cambridge, Mass., 1905). A valuable contemporary account is Daniel Drake's *Practical Essays on Medical Education and the Medical Profession in the United States,* reprinted in the Johns Hopkins University's *Bibliotheca Medica Americana* (Baltimore, 1952).

The New Society and Social Life

There are a number of excellent studies of the social history of the late eighteenth and early nineteenth centuries in the United States. Among the most useful are Harvey Wish, *Society and Thought in Early America* (New York, 1950), and John A. Krout and Dixon R. Fox, *The Completion of Independence* (New York, 1944), the most satisfactory modern social history of the period. No student of social history should, however, neglect the first six chapters of Henry Adams' *History of the United States During the Administrations of Jefferson and Madison,* cited earlier, which have been edited by Herbert Agar under the title *The Formative Years* (2 vols., London, 1948); nine chapters are reprinted by Dexter Perkins as *The United States in 1800* (Ithaca, 1957). See also the early chapters of John Bach McMaster's *History of the People of the United States* (New York, 1884–94). Other valuable sources are Thomas J. Wertenbaker, *The Golden Age of American Culture* (New York, 1942); Dixon Wecter, *The Saga of American Society* (New York, 1937); Van Wyck Brooks, *The World of Washington Irving* (Boston, 1944); Edmund Morgan, *Virginians at Home* (Williamsburg, 1952); and Marshall Davidson, *Life in America* (2 vols., Boston, 1951). See also Carl Bridenbaugh, *Cities in Revolt* (New York, 1938), and his *Rebels and Gentlemen* (New York, 1942); Louis Wright, *Culture on the Moving Frontier* (Bloomington, Ind., 1955); Michael Kraus, *Intercolonial Aspects of American Culture on the Eve of the Revolution* (New York, 1928); Mary S. Benson, *Women in Eighteenth Century America* (New York, 1935); and Julia Spruill, *Women's Life and Work in the Southern Colonies* (Chapel Hill, 1938).

The reports of foreign observers are often especially illuminating. See J. P. Brissot de Warville, *New Travels in the United States* (2 vols., London, 1794); Francois Jean de Chastellux, *Travels in North America* (2 vols., Dublin, 1787); Andrew Burnaby, *Travels Through the Middle Settlements in North America* (3rd ed., 1798); Johann Schoepf, *Travels in the Confederation,* ed. Alfred Morrison (2 vols., Philadelphia, 1911); and particularly Kenneth and Anna Roberts, *Moreau de St. Méry's American Journey* (Garden City, N.Y., 1947). Timothy Dwight's *Travels in New England and New York* (New Haven, 1821–22) is a mine of information on early-nineteenth-century society, written by a shrewd commentator, while James Fenimore Cooper's *American Democrat* (1838) is one of the best commentaries on the period's social aims and patterns. See also the relevant chapters in Henry Steele Commager, *America in Perspective* (New York, 1947); Jane Mesick, *The English Traveller in America 1785–1835* (New York, 1922); and Allan Nevins, *American Social History as Recorded by British Travellers* (New York, 1923). No student of American life should fail to read Alexis de Tocqueville's masterful *Democracy in America* (4 vols., Paris, 1835–40); the most recent edition is that of Phillips Bradley (2 vols., New York, 1945).

Some of the details of American life in the years 1776–1830 are treated in such sources as Anne Wharton, *Social Life in the Early Republic* (Philadelphia, 1902); Nancy V. McClement, *Furnishing the Colonial and Federal Houses* (New York, 1947); W. E. Woodward, *The Way Our People Lived* (New York, 1944); Arthur Train, *The Story of Everyday Things* (New York, 1941); W. C. Langdon, *Everyday Things in American Life, 1606–1876* (2 vols., New York, 1941); George R. Stewart, *American Ways of Life* (Garden City, N.Y., 1954); and Arthur W. Calhoun, *The Social History of the American Family* (3 vols., Philadelphia, 1917–19). Other informative specialized studies are William Goodsell, *A History of Marriage and the Family* (New York, 1935); Alice M. Earle, *Two Centuries of Costume in America* (2 vols., New York, 1903); Foster R. Dulles, *America Learns to Play* (New York, 1940); Jennie Holliman, *American Sports 1785–1835* (Durham, 1931); and Richard O. Cummings, *The American and His Food* (Chicago, 1940). The development of manners and codes is explained in Arthur M. Schlesinger, *Learning How to Behave* (New York, 1946), and Edwin H. Cady, *The Gentleman in America* (Syracuse, 1949).

Any study of regionalism in the United States might well begin with Frederick Jackson Turner's *The Significance of Sections in American History* (New York, 1932). Other excellent studies are W. J. Cash, *The Mind of the South* (New York, 1941); C. S. Sydnor, *The Development of Southern Sectionalism* (Durham, 1948); B. W. Bond, *Civilization of the Old Northwest* (New York, 1934); R. A. Billington, *Westward Expansion* (New York, 1949); Albert Weinberg, *Manifest Destiny* (Baltimore, 1935); J. N. Miller, *The Genesis of Western Culture* (New York, 1938); Henry Nash Smith, *Virgin Land* (Cambridge, Mass., 1950); and Van Wyck Brooks, *The Flowering of New England* (Boston, 1936). An excellent essay is Fulmer Mood, "The Origin, Evolution, and Application of the Sectional Concept 1750–1900," in Merrill Jensen (ed.), *Regionalism in America* (Madison, Wis., 1951). Franklin Jameson's pioneer work, *The American Revolution Considered as a Social Movement* (Princeton, 1926), is still a useful primary source; see also Frederick B. Tolles, "The American Revolution Considered as a Social Movement: A Reconsideration," *American Historical Review,* LX (1954), 1–12, and Robert E. Brown, "Economic Democracy Before the Constitution," *American Quarterly,* VII (1955), 257–275.

The Training of Free Minds

There are a number of general histories of education in the United States. Among the most useful volumes for general reference are E. P. Cubberley, *A History of Education* (New York, 1920); Edgar W. Knight, *Twenty Centuries of Education* (Boston, 1940), and *Education in the United States* (Boston, 1951); H. G. Good, *A History of American Education* (New York, 1956); James Mulhern, *A History of Education* (New York, 1946); Adolph E. Meyer, *An Educational History of the American People* (New York, 1957); Stuart G. Noble, *A History of American Education* (New York, 1951); or John T. Wahlquist, *Introduction to American Education* (New York, 1950). Especially relevant to this chapter are R. Freeman Butts and L. A. Cremin, *A History of Education in American Culture* (New York, 1953); R. Freeman Butts, *A Cultural History of Western Education* (New York, 1955); Allen O. Hansen, *Liberalism and Education in the Eighteenth Century* (New York, 1926); Merle Curti, *The Social Ideals of American Educators* (New York, 1935); Samuel Brown, *The Secularization of American Education* (New York, 1912); and Chaps. II–V of William E. Drake, *The American School in Transition* (New York, 1955).

Useful specialized studies include Vera M. Butler, *Education as Revealed by New England Newspapers Prior to 1850* (Philadelphia, 1935); A. A. Holtz, *A Study of Moral and Religious Elements in American Education up to 1800* (Menasha, Wis., 1917); and three articles, C. H. Judd, "Changing Conceptions of Secondary and Higher Education in America," *The School Review,* XLX (1937), 93–105; B. A. Hinsdale, "Notes on the History of Foreign Influences upon Education in the United States," *Report of the Commissioner of Education,* I (1897–98), 591–629; W. H. Cowley, "European Influences on American Higher Education," *Educational Record,* XX (1939), 165–190. Josiah Quincy's *Figures of the Past* (Boston, 1926), ed., M. A. DeWolfe Howe, contains three charming essays on early-nineteenth-century schools, while Harry R. Warfel, *Noah Webster, Schoolmaster to America* (New York, 1936), is the best biography of the great schoolman.

An excellent history of American higher education is Richard Hofstadter and C. DeWitt Hardy, *The Development and Scope of Higher Education in the United States* (New York, 1952). Charles Thwing, *A History of Higher Education in America* (New York, 1906), is still useful. Three especially valuable studies are George P. Schmidt, *The Old Time College President* (New York, 1930); his *Liberal Arts College* (New Brunswick, 1957); and Donald G. Tewkesbury, *The Founding of American Colleges and Universities Before the Civil War* (New York, 1932). Beverly McAnear, "College Founding in the American Colonies, 1745–1775," *Mississippi Valley Historical Review,* XLII (1955), 24–44, is a helpful article. Among the numerous histories of individual colleges and universities are Samuel Eliot Morison, *Three Centuries of Harvard, 1636–1936* (Cambridge, Mass., 1936); Thomas J.

Wertenbaker, *Princeton 1746–1896* (Princeton, 1946); E. P. Cheyney, *The History of the University of Pennsylvania* (Philadelphia, 1940); Herbert B. Adams, *The College of William and Mary* (Washington, 1887); Walter Bronson, *The History of Brown University* (Providence, 1914); Leon Richardson, *A History of Dartmouth College* (2 vols., Hanover, N.H., 1932); *A History of Columbia University 1745–1904* (New York, 1904); Milton Thomas (ed.), *Clement C. Moore, The Early History of Columbia College* (New York, 1940); Anson P. Stokes, *Memorials of Eminent Yale Men* (New Haven, 1914); William L. Kingsley, *Yale College: A Sketch of Its History* (New York, 1879); and Leverett W. Spring, *A History of Williams College* (Boston, 1917). Higher education for women is treated in Thomas Woody, *A History of Women's Education in the United States* (2 vols., Lancaster, Pa., 1929). For the history of academic organization, see E. C. Elliot and N. M. Chambers, *Charters and Basic Laws of Selected Universities and Colleges* (New York, 1934), and J. E. Kirkpatrick, *Academic Organization and Control* (Yellow Springs, Ohio, 1931). The history of entrance and curricular requirements is well treated in Edwin C. Broome, *A Historical and Critical Discussion of College Entrance Requirements* (New York, 1902); Louis F. Snow, *The College Curriculum in the United States* (New York, 1907); and R. Freeman Butts, *The College Charts Its Course* (New York, 1939).

The history of American elementary and secondary education is treated in I. L. Kandel, *History of Secondary Education* (Boston, 1938); William A. Smith, *Secondary Education in the United States* (New York, 1932); Leonard V. Koos, *The American Secondary School* (New York, 1922); Walter Monroe and Oscar Weber, *The High School* (New York, 1928); E. D. Grizzell, *Origin and Development of the High School in New England Before 1865* (Philadelphia, 1922); Elmer E. Brown, *The Making of Our Middle Schools* (New York, 1903); and W. S. Monroe, *A History of the Pestalozzian Movement in The United States* (Syracuse, 1907). The development of secondary-school curricula is handled by J. M. Gwynn, *Curriculum Principles and Social Trends* (New York, 1943), and Calvin O. Davis, *Our Evolving High School Curriculum* (Yonkers, 1927). Readable and informative studies are Monica Kiefer, *American Children Through Their Books 1700–1835* (Philadelphia, 1948), and Clifton Johnson, *Old Time Schools and Schoolbooks* (New York, 1904).

The history of relations between school and church is considered in R. Freeman Butts, *The American Tradition in Religion and Education* (Boston, 1950). Carter G. Woodson, *The Education of the Negro Prior to 1861* (Rev. ed., New York, 1928), and Horace M. Bond, *The Education of the Negro in the American Social Order* (New York, 1934), are specialized studies of value. W. J. McGucken, *The Jesuits and Education* (Milwaukee, 1932), is useful, though a history of Catholic education in the United States is needed.

Jefferson's impact on American education may be studied in R. J. Honeywell, *The Educational Work of Thomas Jefferson* (Cambridge, Mass., 1931); some source material is collected in C. F. Arrowood, *Thomas Jefferson and Education in a Republic* (New York, 1930). The development of the teaching profession is treated in W. S. Elsbree, *The American Teacher* (New York, 1939); and the tradition of academic freedom in H. K. Beale, *A History of the Freedom of Teaching in American Schools* (New York, 1941), and Richard Hofstadter and W. F. Metzer, *The Development of Academic Freedom in the United States* (New York, 1955).

The Church and Revivalism

The best general sources for the study of American religious history are the volumes of William Walter Sweet, *Religion in the Development of American Culture, 1765–1840* (New York, 1952); *The Story of Religion in America* (3rd ed., New York, 1950); *American Culture and Religion* (Dallas, 1951); and *Religion on the Frontier* (New York, 1931–39). Other useful studies of a general nature are Thomas C. Hall, *The Religious Background of American Culture* (Boston, 1930); Willard Sperry, *Religion in America* (New York, 1946); Jerald C. Brauer, *Protestantism in America* (Philadelphia, 1953); Ernest S. Bates, *American Faith* (New York, 1940); and A. L. Drummond, *The Story of American Protestantism* (Boston, 1950). Still a standard source is the thirteen-volume *American Church History Series* (New York, 1893–98), ed. Philip Schaff, H. C. Potter, and S. M. Jackson. Informative short articles include Sidney Mead, "American Protestantism during the Revolutionary Epoch," *Church History,* XXII (1953), 279–297; J. L. Diman, "Religion in America 1776–1876," *North American Review,* CXXII (1876), 1–47; and H. S. Commager, "The American Religious Scene," *Nineteenth Century,* CLXIII (1948), 13–21. An excellent specialized study is H. Shelton Smith, *Changing Conceptions of Original Sin: A Study in American Theology since 1750* (New York, 1955).

There are a number of histories of the major American religious denominations. N. M. Armstrong, L. A. Loetscher, and C. M. Anderson (eds.), *The Presbyterian Enterprise* (Philadelphia, 1956); Andrew Zenos, *Presbyterianism in America* (New York, 1937); and Leonard J. Trinterud, *The Forming of an American Tradition: Colonial Presbyterianism* (Philadelphia, 1949), provide information on the Presbyterian Church. For Congregationalism, see G. G. Atkins and F. L. Fagley, *The History of American Congregationalism* (Boston, 1942); F. H. Foster, *A Genetic History of the New England Theology* (Boston, 1907); Ralph Barton Perry, *Puritanism and Democracy* (New York, 1944); Chard P. Smith, *Yankees and God* (New York, 1954). Unitarian history may be traced in George W. Cooke, *Unitarianism in America* (Boston, 1902), and Conrad Wright, *The Beginnings of Unitarianism in America* (Boston, 1955). The histories of other churches are traced in such works as Abel Stevens, *A History of American Methodism* (New York, 1867); William W. Manners, *A History of The American Episcopal Church* (Milwaukee, 1935); William S. Perry, *A History of The American Episcopal Church 1587–1883* (2 vols., Boston, 1885); James Bowdoin, *The History of the Society of Friends in America* (2 vols., Philadelphia, 1850–54); and Rufus M. Jones, *The Quakers in the American Colonies* (Philadelphia, 1911). Venerable but still useful are the *Annals of the American Pulpit* (4 vols, New York, 1857–1858), ed. William Sprague. Two interesting studies in New England church history are Mary Gambrell, *Ministerial Training in Eighteenth Century New England* (New York, 1937), and Ola Winslow, *Meetinghouse Hill, 1630–1783* (New York, 1952). Joseph Harotunian, *Piety versus Moralism: The Passing of the New England Theology* (New York, 1932), is a good study of the decline of Puritanism, while C. H. Faust, "The Decline of Puritanism," in H. H. Clark (ed.), *Transitions in American Literary History* (Durham, 1954), is excellent.

Deism is treated in G. H. Koch, *Republican Religion* (New York, 1933), and Herbert Morais, *Deism in Eighteenth Century America* (New York, 1934). Albert Post, *Popular Freethought in America* (New York, 1943), treats some of the less orthodox sects.

Western revivalism has attracted a good deal of interest among religious historians: two excellent studies are W. W. Sweet, *The Rise of Methodism in the West* (New York, 1920), and his *Revivalism: Its Origin, Growth, and Decline* (New York, 1945); in addition, consult Elizabeth Nottingham, *Methodism and the Frontier* (New York, 1941), and Whitney R. Cross, *The Burned-Over District: The Social and Intellectual History of Enthusiastic Religion in Western New York, 1800–1850* (Ithaca, N.Y., 1950). Also valuable are Peter G. Mode, *The Frontier Spirit in American Christianity* (New York, 1923); Oliver Elsbree, *The Rise of the Missionary Spirit in America 1790–1815* (Williamsport, Pa., 1928); Wesley M. Gewehr, *The Great Awakening in Virginia 1740–1790* (New York, 1930); and Catherine C. Cleaveland, *The Great Revival in the West* (Chicago, 1916); but few books can match for interest Peter Cartwright's own *Autobiography* (New York, 1856). Charles A. Johnson, "The Frontier Camp-meeting," *Mississippi Valley Historical Review*, XXXVII (1950), 91–110, and R. H. Gabriel, "Evangelical Religion and Popular Romanticism in the Early Nineteenth Century," *Church History*, XIX (1950), 34–47, are good articles. An exhaustive source is W. W. Sweet (ed.), *Religion on the American Frontier 1783–1850* (New York and Chicago, 1931–46), Vol. I, *The Baptists;* Vol. II, *The Presbyterians;* Vol. III, *The Congregationalists;* Vol. IV, *The Methodists.*

Sources for the history of Jewry in America are Jacob R. Marcus, *Memoirs of American Jews, 1775–1865* (Philadelphia, 1956); L. M. Friedman, *Early American Jews* (Cambridge, Mass., 1934); Morris U. Schappes, *A Documentary History of the Jews in the United States, 1654–1875* (New York,

1950); and Rufus Learsi, *The Jews in America* (Cleveland, 1954). The development of organized religion among Negroes is treated by Carter G. Woodson, *The History of the Negro Church* (Washington, D.C., 1921); Ruby F. Johnston, *The Development of Negro Religion* (New York, 1954); and Harry V. Richardson, *Dark Glory* (New York, 1947). The history of American Catholicism may be traced in Theodore Roemer, *The Catholic Church in the United States* (St. Louis, 1954); Theodore Maynard, *The Story of American Catholicism* (New York, 1954); and Sister Mary Augustana (Ray), *American Opinion of Roman Catholicism in the Eighteenth Century* (New York, 1936). Gustavus Myers, *The History of Bigotry in the United States* (New York, 1943), and R. A. Billington, *The Protestant Crusade, 1800–1860* (New York, 1938), deal with problems of religious toleration.

Problems of church-state relations in the United States are discussed in Sanford H. Cobb, *The Rise of Religious Liberty in America* (New York, 1902); E. F. Humphrey, *Nationalism and Religion in America* (Boston, 1924); William G. Torpey, *Judicial Doctrines of Religious Rights in America* (Chapel Hill, 1948); E. B. Greene, *Religion and the State* (New York, 1941); Hamilton J. Edwards, *Separation of Church and State in Virginia* (Richmond, 1910); Leo Pfeffer, *Church, State, and Freedom* (Boston, 1953); Reba C. Strickland, *Religion and State in Georgia in the Eighteenth Century* (New York, 1939); Herbert Wright, "Religious Liberty Under the Constitution," *Virginia Law Review,* XXVII (1940), 75–87; and A. P. Stokes, *Church and State in the United States* (3 vols., New York, 1950). The role of the clergy in the Revolutionary controversy is interestingly handled by Alice M. Baldwin, "Sowers of Sedition," *William and Mary Quarterly,* V (1948), 52–76, and her *New England Clergy and the American Revolution* (Durham, N.C., 1928); see also the sermons reprinted in J. W. Thornton, *The Pulpit in the American Revolution* (Boston, 1876).

Literature, Architecture, and Art

The most thorough study of American literary nationalism is Benjamin T. Spencer, *The Quest for Nationality* (Syracuse, 1957). Other excellent sources are H. H. Clark, "Nationalism in American Literature," *University of Toronto Quarterly,* II (1933), 491–515; W. E. Sedgwick, "The Materials for an American Literature: A Critical Problem of the Early Nineteenth Century," *Harvard Studies and Notes in Philology and Literature* (1935); E. K. Brown, "The National Idea in American Criticism," *Dalhousie Review,* XIV (1934), 133–147; H. H. Clark, "Literary Criticism in the *North American Review,*" *Transactions of the American Academy,* XXXII (1940), 299–350; Earl Bradsher, "The Rise of Nationalism in American Literature," in N. M. Caffee and Thomas Kirby (eds.), *Studies for William A. Reed* (Baton Rouge, 1940); J. C. McCloskey, "The Campaign of Periodicals after the War of 1812 for a National Literature," *PMLA,* L (1935), 262–273; and Howard M. Jones, "A National Spirit in Literature," in his *Theory of American Literature* (Ithaca, 1948).

Two key essays in the study of American literature 1800–1850 are M. F. Heiser, "The Decline of Neo-Classicism," and G. H. Orians, "The Rise of Romanticism," in H. H. Clark (ed.), *Transitions in American Literary History* (Durham, N.C., 1953). For a general history of American letters during the eighteenth and early nineteenth centuries, no source is more useful than vol. I of R. E. Spiller *et al.* (eds.), *The Literary History of the United States,* cited earlier. Excellent briefer histories are Walter F. Taylor, *A History of American Letters* (Chicago, 1956); Fred Lewis Pattee, *The First Century of American Literature 1770–1870* (New York, 1935); and Moses Coit Tyler's pioneer work, *The Literary History of the American Revolution* (2 vols., New York, 1897). Critical backgrounds of American literature during the period are treated by William Charvat, *The Origins of American Critical Thought 1810–1835* (Philadelphia, 1936). Frank Luther Mott, *Golden Multitudes* (New York, 1947), and James D. Hart, *The Popular Book* (New York, 1950), are entertaining and informative studies of popular literary taste. Van Wyck Brooks, *The World of Washington Irving* (New York, 1944), evokes the atmosphere of the age more expertly than anyone else, and makes both interesting and profitable reading. Excellent general histories of the American novel are Arthur H. Quinn, *American Fiction* (New York, 1936); Alexander Cowie, *The Rise of the American Novel* (New York, 1948); and Edward Wagenknecht, *The Cavalcade of the American Novel* (New York, 1952). Herbert Brown, *The Sentimental Novel in America 1798–1860* (Durham, N.C., 1940), and E. E. Leisy, *The American Historical Novel* (Norman, Okla., 1950), are useful treatments of particular types of American fiction, while Lily Loshe, *The Early American Novel* (New York, 1907), is still a good source of information.

Problems of foreign influences on American artistic endeavor are posed in Donald Drew Egbert, "Foreign Influences in American Art," in David F. Bowers, *Foreign Influences in American Life* (Princeton, 1941). No thorough study of the impact of Italy on American culture has been made; however, Van Wyck Brooks, *The Dream of Arcadia: American Writers and Artists in Italy* (New York, 1958), is a graceful beginning. Howard Mumford Jones, *America and French Culture* (Chapel Hill, 1927), is a pioneer work of its kind and still eminent. Stanley T. Williams, *The Spanish Background of American Literature* (2 vols., New Haven, 1955), is exhaustive. Henry A. Pochmann, *German Culture in America* (Madison, Wis., 1957), is a monumental work of scholarship. For an account of Europe's impact on an early group of American artists, no reader should miss Henry James, *William Wetmore Story and His Friends* (Boston, 1903).

Studies of Philip Freneau are Lewis Leary, *That Rascal Freneau* (New

Brunswick, 1941), and Nelson Adkins, *Philip Freneau and the Cosmic Enigma* (New York, 1949). H. H. Clark's introduction to his *Poems of Freneau* (New York, 1929) and his "What Made Freneau the Father of American Poetry?" *Studies in Philology,* XXVI (1925), are still important studies of Freneau's art and ideas. No thorough study of Charles Brockden Brown has yet appeared, but Ernest Marchand's introduction to Brown's *Ormond* (New York, 1937) is a good estimate. The authoritative study of Brackenridge is Claude M. Newlin, *Life and Writings of Hugh Henry Brackenridge* (Princeton, 1932), and a good critical study is Newlin's introduction to *Modern Chivalry* (New York, 1937). The definitive biography of Washington Irving is Stanley T. Williams, *The Life of Washington Irving* (2 vols., New York, 1935); Henry A. Pochmann's introduction to *Washington Irving: Representative Selections* (New York, 1934) is a good brief treatment. Leon Howard, *The Connecticut Wits* (Chicago, 1943), is a valuable study of the Hartford group. Alexander Cowie, *John Trumbull, Connecticut Wit* (Chapel Hill, 1936); Charles E. Cuningham, *Timothy Dwight, 1752–1817* (New York, 1942); and James Woodress, *A Yankee's Odyssey: The Life of Joel Barlow* (Philadelphia, 1958), are good studies of individual Wits. Others are Amos L. Herold, *James Kirke Paulding: Versatile American* (New York, 1926); Robert E. Spiller, *Fenimore Cooper: Critic of His Times* (New York, 1931); and H. Milton Ellis, *Joseph Dennie and His Circle* (Austin, Tex., 1915). Fred L. Pattee's edition of the essays of John Neal, *John Neal's American Writers* (Durham, N.C., 1937), contains interesting estimates of early American literary figures by a contemporary editor and critic.

The most satisfactory history of American painting is perhaps Edgar P. Richardson, *Painting in America* (New York, 1956), though Virgil Barker, *American Painting* (New York, 1950), is equally good in other ways. Excellent general treatments of painting from colonial times to the nineteenth century are found in the relevant chapters of Oliver Larkin, *Art and Life in America* (New York, 1949), and James T. Flexner, *American Painting: First Flowers of the Wilderness* (Boston, 1957). Flexner's *America's Old Masters* (New York, 1939) concentrates on West, Copley, Peale, and Stuart; and his *Light of Distant Skies* (New York, 1954) on the painters of the next generation. Other useful sources are F. J. Mather, C. R. Morey, and W. J. Henderson, *The American Spirit in Art* (New Haven, 1927); the early chapters of Edgar P. Richardson, *The Way of Western Art 1776–1914* (Cambridge, Mass., 1939); Suzanne LaFollette, *Art in America* (New York, 1929); Oskar Hagen, *The Birth of an American Tradition in Art* (New York, 1940); Eugen Neuhaus, *The History and Ideals of American Art* (Palo Alto, Calif., 1931); and Alan Burroughs, *Limners and Likenesses* (Cambridge, Mass., 1936). Individual studies of value are W. T. Whiteley, *Gilbert Stuart* (Cambridge, Mass., 1932); Charles C. Sellers, *Charles Willson Peale* (Philadelphia,

1947); and Edgar P. Richardson, *Washington Allston* (Chicago, 1948). Lorado Taft, *A History of American Sculpture* (New York, 1930), and Albert T. Gardner, *Yankee Stonecutters* (New York, 1945), provide information on early American sculpture. However, those interested in the artistic theory of the times should read also Nathalia Wright's edition of Horatio Greenough's *Travels of a Yankee Stonecutter* (Gainesville, Fla., 1952); H. E. Small's edition of Greenough's *Form and Function* (Berkeley, Calif., 1947); and R. H. Dana's edition of Washington Allston's *Lectures on Art* (New York, 1850).

John Tasker Howard, *Our American Music* (New York, 1939), and Sigmund Spaeth, *A History of Popular Music in America* (New York, 1948), are readable accounts of American musical tastes. An interesting collection is Olin Downes and Elie Siegmeister, *A Treasury of American Song* (New York, 1943). O. G. T. Sonneck, *Early Concert Life in America* (New York, 1949); his *Early Opera in America* (New York, 1915); and his biography, *Francis Hopkinson* (Washington, D.C., 1905); and Henry Wilder Foote, *Three Centuries of American Hymnody* (Cambridge, Mass., 1940), add information. Older but still useful are F. L. Ritter, *Music in America* (New York, 1883), and L. C. Elson, *A History of American Music* (New York, 1904).

Good general histories of the American stage are M. C. Crawford, *The Romance of the American Theater* (New York, 1940); Arthur Hornblow, *A History of the Theater in America* (Philadelphia, 1919); and Richard Moody, *America Takes the Stage* (Bloomington, Ind., 1955). Oral S. Coad and Edwin Mims, Jr., *The American Stage* (New Haven, 1929), and Arthur H. Quinn, *The History of the American Drama from the Beginnings to the Civil War* (rev. ed., New York, 1943), are much more complete. Oral Coad's *William Dunlap* (New York, 1917) is an excellent biography; Paul H. Musser, *James Nelson Barker* (Philadelphia, 1929), and Clement E. Foust, *Life and Dramatic Works of Robert Montgomery Bird* (New York, 1919), are helpful individual studies. William Dunlap's own *History of the American Theater* (2 vols., London, 1833) is still a readable and indispensable book.

The development of American architecture until the Civil War may be studied in Talbot F. Hamlin, *The American Spirit in Architecture* (New Haven, 1926); T. E. Tallmage, *The Story of Architecture in America* (rev. ed., New York, 1936); James M. Fitch, *American Building* (Boston, 1948); and Fiske Kimball, *American Architecture* (Indianapolis, 1928). Harold Shurtleff, *The Log Cabin Myth* (New York, 1939), and Hugh S. Morrison, *American Architecture from the First Colonial Settlements to the National Period* (New York, 1952), are helpful. Special studies include Talbot F. Hamlin, *Greek Revival Architecture in America* (New York, 1944); his monumental *Benjamin Henry Latrobe* (New York, 1955); and Fiske Kimball,

Domestic Architecture of the American Colonies and Early Republic (New York, 1922). Other sources are Thomas Waterman, *The Dwellings of Colonial America* (Chapel Hill, 1950); Charles A. Place, *Charles Bulfinch, Architect and Citizen* (Boston, 1925); Walter H. Kilham, *Boston After Bulfinch* (Cambridge, Mass., 1946); Fiske Kimball, *Thomas Jefferson: Architect* (Boston, 1916); and J. B. H. Latrobe (ed.), *The Journals of Latrobe* (New York, 1905).

Index

academies, 161–163, 168–169
Academy of Natural Sciences, 72
achievement, sense of, 4
Adams, Abigail, 135
Adams, Charles Francis, 30, 138
Adams, Daniel, 159
Adams, Henry, 99, 110, 111, 113, 114, 124, 127, 128–129, 184
Adams, James Truslow, 105
Adams, John, 5, 18–19, 25–26, 30, 47, 51, 57, 59, 63, 72–73, 100, 102–105, 107, 130, 131, 155, 196, 205, 231, 250, 277
Adams, John Quincy, 61, 123, 133–134, 144, 242
Adams, Nehemiah, 224
Adams, R. P., 273
Adams, Samuel, 160
Addison, Joseph, 58, 111, 251, 264
Adkins, Nelson F., 261
Agar, Herbert, 99
Agassiz, Louis, 65, 94
Age of Reason, 3, 6, 14, 20–21, 24, 50
Age of Reason, The, 13, 63–64, 211–212, 214
Age of Romanticism. *See* Romanticism
agriculture, science of, 82–84
Ahlstrom, S. E., 34
Akenside, Mark, 260
Alcott, Bronson, 163, 167, 233
Alexander, Archibald, 35
Allen, Ethan, 63, 210–211
Allen, Mary, 135
Allston, Washington, 28, 285–290
Alsop, Richard, 259
"American," meaning of, 37–40
American Antiquarian Society, 43, 228

American civilization, mission of, 48
American culture, "progress" and, 32
American Educational Society, 178
American educational system, 150–170; *see also* education
American faith, revival of, 216–234; roots of, 29–53
American Journal of Medical Sciences, 80
American Journal of Science, 55
American literature. *See* national literature
American Medical Society, 72, 80
American Mineralogical Journal, 91
American Patriotic Songbook, 45
American Philosophical Society, 21, 57, 67, 71, 84, 96, 156
American point of view, 99 ff.
American Quarterly Review, 241
American Revolution. *See* Revolutionary War
Americas, British and European attitude toward, 40–41
American society, classes in, 105–106; structure of, 99–123
American Society for Promoting and Propagating Useful Knowledge, 71
American Spelling Book, 158, 243
American thought, foundations of, 3–28
American Unitarian Association, 225
American university, idea of, 171–194
American way of life, 48, 146–149; *see also* American society
Ames, Fisher, 18–19, 102, 106, 111, 120
Andrei, Giovanni, 291
Andrews, J. D., 22, 26, 30 n.
Anglican Church, 197